AFFORDABLE FOREIGN ERRORS

ON POSTAGE STAMPS OF THE WORLD

PAUL S. GREENLAW, Ph. D.
IN COLLABORATION WITH MARTIN SELLINGER

Published by

krause
publications

700 East State Street, Iola, WI 54990-0001

Please call or write for our free catalog. Our toll-free number to place an order or obtain a free catalog is 800-258-0929 or please use our regular business telephone 715-445-2214 for editorial comment and further information.

Library of Congress Catalog Number: 98-84093
ISBN: 0-87341-614-7

Printed in the United States of America

DEDICATION

TO MY WIFE
Shirley M. Greenlaw

She typed
She scanned
She chose colors
She planned.

Affordable Foreign
Errors

400

PREFACE

Martin Sellinger has authorized the
Sellinger's INVERTED CENTER, Stam
augmented the value of our work
appreciation to Mr. Sellinger for his

EHJ

FOREWORD

In 1997 I saw an advertisement for a foreign error stamp priced at slightly under two-hundred dollars. I bought it because it was different and I wanted to be creative and then I ate nothing but bread and water for five weeks. But I enjoyed it and later bought a second foreign error—this time for a more modest twenty-five dollars, and my diet regained its form. From these experiences I learned the value of inexpensive foreign errors. Through my own foreign error collecting, I quickly learned that there was no book on affordable foreign errors, so I wrote one. What I have written follows. I do hope you will enjoy it.

Paul S. Greenlaw Ph. D.
State College, Pennsylvania

About the Author

Paul S. Greenlaw received his doctorate in Political Science and Public Administration from Syracuse University. He taught Political Science at Duke University, and did management development work at both the Kroger Co., and Dayco Corp.

The author was Professor of Management at Pennsylvania State University from 1960 to 1997. Over the years he has collected stamps of the United States, Germany, France, Luxembourg and other Western European nations. After a recent foray into French Independent Africa, he found his true love—foreign errors. The collection of errors is the focus of this book.

Dr. Greenlaw's wife, Shirley, is an accomplished computer scientist who helped him considerably with this book. The Greenlaws have four children and eight grandchildren. Dr. Greenlaw is the author of 13 books and 75 articles—mostly in the fields of management and law.

CHAPTER I: INTRODUCTION

"To err is human, to forgive divine." These words spoken by Alexander Pope[1] are extremely applicable to philately today. Stamp errors are often held in high esteem and are expensive and glamorous. You might say: "But why discuss errors with me?—I'm no John D. Rockefeller, I can't afford them." You can! Many errors are quite affordable even to the ordinary person. For example, Cambodia 76a and 77a would be valued together at $3.50 (Scott 1998 Catalogue)[2] Of course it's not all that easy—the Canadian invert (387a) catalogs at $8000 for a mint specimen.

United States errors have been studied extensively[3]; however, foreign errors have been neglected, and the focus of this book will be affordable foreign errors. By foreign we mean outside the continental United States, its outlying possessions (and the United Nations). We will consider foreign errors priced[4] affordably if valued at $200 or less (an admittedly arbitrary figure), and give full attention to them. We will also touch on stamps that are not affordable (NA's) such as the Mauritius "penoe" errors. In the first draft of this book we provided full information on all NA's. This had to be eliminated, however, to meet the size requirements for the book. We believed that this was the best way to reduce size in light of the thrust of the book—"affordable" foreign errors. The number of errors for each country are still indicated.

When is an Error not an Error

Before proceeding further, the question must be raised: "What is an error?" Some stamp errors are sincerely repented mistakes, while others are purposely flawed to be sold to stamp collectors. We often call these "suspects" since suspicion exists that they were designed on purpose, though often we are not completely sure. Many of the independent African nations have been especially suspect of this practice and the beautiful rare Chad souvenir sheet shown in this volume (reputedly only nine copies exist)[5] may or may not be a purposeful error.

Fakes

When is a fake not an error? There is no error if someone attempts to deceive others to believe a purposely created error is a real one. Some fakes are enormously cleverly done while others are poorly executed.

Although we know of no research evidence to shed light on the subject, we think that making suspect errors is probably a greater problem with foreign stamps than turning out fakes. Still, some "exquisite" foreign fakes have been crafted. This is because Americans are more familiar with their country's stamps and faking rather than creating false errors is probably the safest route.

Regardless, faking is a problem, but there is a way of coping with it—"expertizing." You might be thinking that hiring an expert to examine your stamp will cost a fortune. Not so. The current expertizing fee of the broadest-based expertizer, the American Philatelic Society, headquartered in State College, Pa., is only a minimum of $15. When we have stamps priced at only $10 or $15 expertizing each will, of course, not pay. But for your higher priced $175 or $200 stamps, the opposite is true, especially since the dealer may bear the cost of the expertizing. In early 1997, for example, I bought a Chad error for $120 and the dealer picked up the fee.

Types of Errors

Different philatelists will have different ways of classifying errors. In his classic book *Errors on U.S. Postage Stamps*, Stephen R. Datz focuses on the relatively simple schema of imperforates, inverts and colors omitted[6]. With a broader scope of (foreign) stamps covered, we have chosen a somewhat more elaborate taxonomy:

1. Repositioned
2. Transmuted
3. Augmented
4. Omitted

Datz's inverts fall under our class "repositioned," his "omitted's" are somewhat similar to ours, and because their meaning and value vary so much from country to country, as will be explained below, we will all but ignore imperforates. Let us now explain the meaning of our four classifications.

Repositioned

President Kennedy is upside down—his hair is where his collar should be. This change of position—the invert—is one of the most famous and highly regarded of philatelic errors. Not only have famous personages been shaken upside down on stamps—among them Charles Lindbergh[7] and the British Royalty[8]—buildings, flags[9] and other objects have known the wrath of the inverter.

A not-so-distant relative of the pure invert is the inverted overprint, which comes in various colors with black the most common. Many such overprints are non-distinctive, but they can be most beautiful as in the very rare Chad Christmas sheet referred to earlier.

Sometimes an inverted overprint will be found along with a regular one, such as in the Central Africa Elvis Presley[10] collection. In spite of no listing, the collection has been expertized by the distinguished Alex Rendon. Some of the collection are quite scarce (e.g. 8-9 copies exist). Even lesser-known (but not necessarily rarer) is the "backwards" invert. Here, part of the stamp (or all) is printed on the back of the stamp with the rest of the design on the front. For aesthetic purposes, one backward invert and one normal stamp should be available for mounting purposes—so that the viewer can see both sides of the stamp simultaneously.

Much less beautiful but potentially scarce is another type of invert—the inverted watermark. The least visually pleasing of errors, watermarks will not be treated in this book. Rather, for more information on watermark errors, refer to my article "The Unique Error Collection" in *The American Philatelist*.

Transmuted

Some stamps, instead of having the position of something changed have something in themselves changed—color, watermark, perforation or paper. With respect to color, for example, the Peru #335 "Waterlow and Sons" specimen is dark violet instead of green. Or, I have Haiti in light blue and black rather than green and black.

Overprints too may be in the wrong color (e.g. Portugal 1S60 var. as intended). Watermarks may also be misplaced in error. Although watermarks will generally not be treated in this text, it is interesting that Great Britain 79b is watermarked in error 29 instead of 30, a clear transmutation rather than repositioning. For perfs, wrong perfs often appear on stamps and sometimes their scarcity leaves little doubt that they should be considered errors (e.g. New South Wales 41b). Many perf variations, however, are only worth a few cents or nothing at all. Further, too much attention to such variations would do nothing but "clutter" this volume, and hence will not be treated. Paper is again a transmutation that will not be treated—paper transmutations are primarily a product of the 19th century.

Omitted

Quite frequently (but often in scarce supply) a color is omitted from a stamp. Common practice is to display the error along with the regular stamp so the viewer will see just what is missing in case it is not apparent. It also happens sometimes that "paperfolds" occur that blot out the color in places only on the stamp. Here we have partial missing colors.

Everyone has seen stamps where perforations have repositioned themselves wildly. Frequently, perforations are missing and we have an imperforate or semi-imperforate stamp. As an example: take a pair of stamps and perforate around them but leave imperf between them. These are usually errors and may be quite expensive. For example, Datz's 1M287 (Scott 160qb) is priced at $1750[11]. Datz places considerable emphasis on these United States stamps since a large proportion of U.S. errors are of this type. (Only 13 invert stamps are shown in Datz's volume by way of comparison.)

For foreign stamps there is a much greater variation in the relationship between imperforates and errors. Some imperforates are errors—many are not. For this reason, we exclude imperforate errors from this volume:

1. As we have seen, U.S. imperforate errors are critical, but we are not considering the United States.
2. At the other extreme, some countries produce imperfs "by the carload." For example, Burkina Faso (formerly Upper Volta) has taken the following position: "Most Upper Volta stamps from 1959 onward exist imperforate in issued and trial colors and also in small presentation sheets in issued colors[12]." That such imperforates cannot be classified as errors is attested to by my purchase of eleven MNH imperforate Upper Volta complete sets each at only 50 percent of catalog prices

3. France also produces hundreds of imperforates. Many are scarce but could not be called errors. For example, drawing directly from the French Catalogues, Yvert[13], prices for the randomly chosen examples are:

1476 (1966) perforated 2 francs imperforate 500 francs (p.118)
1724 (1972) perforated 20 francs imperforate 425 francs (p.139)
1959,60 (197) perforated 10 francs imperforate 600 francs (p.160)[14]

Watermarks can be omitted (which we will not treat) but we will cover personages (President Kennedy on Guinea 325 and C56), and places, too (missing U.N. on Haiti 469).

Our northern neighbor, Canada, also turns out dozens of imperfs. They are more highly priced than the perforated variety, however, they are not errors. Further, we have encountered many error dealers who will not send foreign imperfs to us in the U.S. unless there is another error on the stamp (C168 and C 169) or objects—a missing flag on Liberia 368.

Augmented

Stamps may get something extra—incrementation or augmentation. Three types of this phenomena exist: overprints, double impressions and a stamp being printed on both sides.

Multiple Errors

A number of stamps are flawed in more than one way—for example, the stamp just referred to or a double inverted overprint. Often the "multiple" is achieved by counting imperforacy as one error.

The Remainder of this Volume

Two parts are left remaining in this volume: (1) Chapter 2-7, the voluminous CATALOGUE OF ERRORS; and (2) a concluding chapter: "Epilogue," where some of the following will be answered: (1) What foreign errors are the most common? Least common? (2) What nation has produced the most inverted centers per stamp issued?

The Catalogue of Errors

Since it is so predominant in this volume we will give special attention to all the terms and symbols contained in the Catalogue of Errors. This will enable the reader to move right ahead into Chapter 2 with full understanding.

Code

Each stamp has been coded so it is more readily identifiable. The codes are alpha-numerical—e.g. the first three Gabon errors are GAB1, GAB2, and GAB3.

Usage and Value

The value of each unused error is the first of the two given (assuming two are available and given with the used value last. Nuances are dispensed with;

terms such as MNH (mint, never hinged), OG (original gum) and CTO (canceled to order) are ignored. Of course, in the actual purchase or sale of errors these conditions may be highly relevant.

Source of Valuation

Many errors listed in this catalog have been valued based on prices to be found in a standard catalog. Others have been based on actual retail, wholesale, or mail sale bids to (and by) me. For convenience, we will list no symbol next to any catalogue-based valuation and an R (retail) for all others.

Denomination and Color

The denomination and color of each error is given (e.g. 1 p blue).

No Errors; No Affordable Errors

When a nation has produced no errors (Abu Dhabi) such will be indicated.

Analysis

A brief summary analysis of each country's errors will be provided where appropriate[15].

Organization of the Catalogue

The catalogue is organized alphabetically by nation with Abu Dhabi leading the parade. Within each country regular issues will be ordered chronologically with the same for semi-postals, airmails and so on. You will also find a color section, where we showcase some of our favorite errors. If the stamps on those pages don't have a corresponding listing, it means we were unable to locate them in any of the catalogs.

Quantities Issued and Existing Expertization

Quantities of an error issued or existent is probably more difficult for foreign stamps than United States issues. This is because of the broad scope and diversity of our phenomenon. When we do have quantity figures, however, they will be indicated along with the error with the symbol "Q." We have expertization certificates for only a small number of our total catalogue population. Whenever we possess an expert certificate we will designate the error by an "X."

TYPE OF ERROR

Last but not least is the TYPE OF ERROR we encounter. Here we bypass the generic type (reposition, etc.) and indicate the specific type of error—inverted overprint, double surcharge, color omitted, and so on.

SUMMARY

In this chapter we have shown the importance of and defined errors and fakes. We have provided a fourfold classification of errors and defined the scope of errors covered in this volume. Finally we have defined the basic terms in the six-chapter catalogue.

SUMMARY OF SYMBOLS

1. CYL, for example, is the abbreviation symbol for Ceylon errors; CLT for Central Lithuania, etc.
2. NA means not affordable (>$200).
3. (vc) means very common <u>type</u> of error but not necessarily inexpensive. The basic two vc's are the inverted (invtd) overprint and double (dbl) overprint (ovpt).
4. (u) means unique or uncommon—e.g. printed on both sides, double impression, color omitted. No symbols will be placed where there is neither a vc or u.
5. With respect to pricing:
    a. No symbol will be used if the price is based on current market prices.
    b. An R will be used if we use a retail price.
    c. A __ will be used if the error is not priced.
    d. Prices for mint condition are listed first, used second.
    e. Prices in italics are usually high and not 100% known.
    f. If known the quantity issued will be designated by Q.

NOTES

1. In "An Essay on Criticism," 1711, Bartlett's Familiar Quotations, 16th ed. 1992, Little Brown, p. 299.
2. Volume 2, p.1
3. Datz, Stephen R., 1998 Catalogue of Errors on U.S. Postage Stamps, 8th ed., Iola, WI: Krause Publications.
4. We will use Scott Catalogue (1998) prices or retail or wholesale prices when able.
5. Personal correspondence from Martin Sellinger to author.
6. See Datz, op.cit. passim.
7. Spain, C56.
8. St. Vincent inverts 1017-1020.
9. Liberia, #368 var. For example.
10. See CAF in Chap. 3
11. Datz, op.cit. p. 37.
12. Scott, 1998, volume 1.
13. Catalague Yvert et Tellier, 1997, Tome, Timbres de France, 1997.
14. Ibid.
15. In many cases short poems will be substituted for the summaries.

CHAPTER II: A-B

ABU DHABI

ABU	M 17		20f on 20np blue	invtd ovpt	60.00	—
ABU	M 18		30f on 30np orange	Arabic "2" for "3"	NA	

Abu Dhabi has not even produced three

ADEN

ADN1	38a	(1951)	15¢ on 2-1/2 a	dbl surch (vc)	NA	

Kathiri State of Seiyun

ADK1	13a	(1946)	2-1/2 a deep blue (R)	invtd ovpt (vc)	NA	
ADK1A	19a	(1949)	1r on 1sh blue	surch omitted	NA	
ADK2 M		(1966)	44a 10f on 15c dk blue grn (R)	invtd ovpt	NA	
ADK3 M		(1966)	44b 10f on 15c dk bl green	shifted ovpt "ADEN" not covered by bar of the ovpt	200.00	—
ADK4 M	49a		50f on 1/-red orange	shifted ovpt "ADEN" not covered by bar of the ovpt	200.00	—
ADK5 M	50a		65f on 1.25 sh bl grn	shifted ovpt "ADEN" not covered by bar of the ovpt		
ADK6-8					all NA	
ADK9	M 64a		50f on 1/-red orange (G)	stop after "fils"	105.00	—
ADK10-22				all NA		
ADK23	M 123b		50f on 1/-(red ovpt)	"World Peace" type ovpt shifted	200.00	—
ADK24-25					NA	—
ADK26-28					all NA	
ADK29	M 141a		10f on 15c (dk bl green)		150.00	—
ADK30	M 145a		250f on 5/-(bl vio & bl)		150.00	—
ADK31-36					all NA	

Quaiti State

ADQ1-3					all NA	
ADQ4	M 270		(on #268) 500f Wright Brother 1903	inscribed "1909 England" instead of "1903-USA"	12.75	7.00
ADQ5	M 274		550f multicolor!	Rare error on impf s/s: 1909 Eng. instead of 1903 USA.	165.00R	(CAT. M 7500.00)

See Photo in Color Section

ADQ6	M 148		25f light blue	printed in only one color Q=1 sheet of 20	NA	

Aden's mostly nothing but a big NA
It's a shame to start THIS book that way —The Bard

AFARS AND ISSAS has produced no errors

AFGHANISTAN

AFG1	10a	(1873)	1sh black	corner ornament missing	NA	
AFG2	10b			corner ornament retouched (u)	30.00	25.00
AFG3	15a	(1875)	1sa black	wide outer circle	NA	
AFG4	17a		1sa brown violet	wide outer circle (u)	110.00	—
AFG5	236c	(1928)	15p pink semi-perf block	imperf	20.00R	
AFG6	329a	(1949)	80p chocolate	80p dull red violet (error)	—	—
AFG7	368a	(1950)	1.25af deep blue	1.25af black (error)	6.00	—
AFG8	396a	(1951)	125p ultra	cliche of 35p in plate of 125p (u)	80.00	80.00
AFG9	473a	(1960)	50p bluish green	cliche of 25p in plate of 50p (u)	20.00	20.00

Afghanistan, a Republic in Central Asia, has produced relatively few errors. Of these, the two cliches (AFG8, AFG9) seem most appealing and for the beginning error collector, AFG9 seems an inexpensive start.

AEGEAN ISL. has produced no errors

AITUTAKI

AIT1	32a*	6p slate & red br	invtd Q=major rarity, 100 or less		NA

* Not found in The Minkus Catalogue-from Martin Sellinger's <u>Inverted Center Stamps of the World Catalogue</u> 1994-5, p.7

AJMAN

AJM1	Mi,BL12B (1967)	2R Kennedy	imp s/s of 4 Q=Major rarity 100 or less	70.00	130.00R
AJM2	Mi,BL177 (1970)	20R gold s/s Napolean	Q=Major rarity 100 or less	70.00	130.00R
AJM3	Mi,BL186	20R Gold s/s Apollo11	Q=Major rarity 100 or less	70.00	130.00R
AJM4	Mi,BL	20R Gold s/s Apollo 13	Q=Major rarity 100 or less	70.00	130.00R
AJM5	Mi,BL219	20R gold s/s Olympics	Q=Major rarity 100 or less	70.00	130.00R
AJM6	Mi,BL220	20R gold s/s Eisenhower	Q=Major rarity 100 or less	70.00	130.00R
AJM7	Mi,BL292 (1971)	20R Gold s/s Olympics	Q=Major rarity 100 or less	70.00	130.00R
AJM8	Mi,BL295	5R Nixon Meeting s/s	Q=Major rarity 100 or less	30.00	70.00R

*Michel Catalog reported by Sellinger, op. cit., p.7

AJM9		unlisted 16 stamp sheet	dbl impression	—	_ R

See Photo in Color Section

AJM10		unlisted presidents	invtd ovpt	—	_ R
AJM11		Michel Block 187	gold invtd space R	100.00	—

*AJM 2-7 have marginal inscriptions inverted in respect to the gold stamp.

Ajman has produced some scarce stamps, yet the prices of them do not seem astronomical—especially AJM8. One reason for this is the obscurity of the country. Also, none of the errors are listed in Minkus. You can find them in foreign catalogues.

ALAOUITES

ALA1	25a	(1925)	10¢ dk violet	dbl ovpt (vc)	15.00	15.00
ALA2	26a		25¢ olive black	invtd ovpt (vc)	10.00	10.00
ALA3	26b			blue ovpt (u)	20.00	20.00
ALA4	27a		50¢ yellow green	invtd ovpt (vc)	10.00	10.00
ALA5	27b			blue ovpt (u)	20.00	20.00
ALA6	27c			red ovpt	17.50	17.50
ALA7	28a		75c br or	invtd ovpt (vc)	9.00	9.00
ALA8	30a		1.25 deep grn	red ovpt	17.50	17.50
ALA9	31a		1.50p rose red (bl)	invtd ovpt (vc)	10.00	10.00
ALA10	31b			black ovpt	20.00	20.00
ALA11	32a		2p dk brown (u)	blue ovpt	25.00	25.00
ALA12	33a		2.50p pck blue	black ovpt	25.00	25.00
ALA13	34a		3p orange brown	invtd ovpt (vc)	6.50	6.50
ALA14	34b			blue ovpt (u)	25.00	25.00
ALA15	35a		5p violet	red ovpt	25.00	25.00
ALA16	38a	(1926)	38a 3.50p on 75c brn orange	surcharged on face & back (u)	5.00	4.50
ALA17	41a		12p on 1.25p dp grn	invtd surch (vc)	10.00	10.00
ALA18	43a		4.50p on 75c brn org	invtd surch (vc)	25.00	—
ALA19	46a	(1928)	5c on 10c dk violet	dbl surch (vc)	13.00	—
ALA20	49a		4p on 25¢ olive black	dbl impression (u)	—	—
ALA21	C1a	(1925)	2p on 40¢	ovpt reversed (u)	60.00	—
ALA22	C2a		3p on 60¢	ovpt reversed (u)	60.00	60.00
ALA23	C10		3p orange brown	invtd airplane		
ALA24	C17a	(1929)	50¢ yellow green (R)	plane ovpt dbl (u)	15.00	15.00
ALA25	C17b			plane ovpt on face & back	11.00	—
ALA26	C17c			pair with plane ovpt tete beche	35.00	—
ALA27	C19a		25p ultra (R)	plane ovpt invtd (u)	60.00	60.00
ALA28	C20a	(1929-30)	2p on 1.25p	surch invtd (vc)	4.00	—
ALA29	C20b			dbl surch (vc)	3.50	—
ALA30	C21a		15p on 25p (b + R)	plane ovpt invtd (u)	35.00	35.00

Alaouites also provides a good starting point for the error collector. There are a number of errors available and many are relatively inexpensive. Also—and we have not made this point before— Alaouites, with their plane overprints, make a good addition to an air (and space) topical error collection, which are becoming more and more common.

ALBANIA

ALB1   21(Sel)   (1913)   10pa violet

ALB 21-33 have the double-headed eagle or the value inverted, and are priced up to 30.00 according to Sel.

ALB2	22(Sel)		20pa red & black	Q=over 200	up to 30.00	
ALB3	23(Sel)		1gr black	Q=over 200	up to 30.00	
ALB4	24(Sel)		2gr blue & violet	Q=over 200	up to 30.00	
ALB5	25(Sel)		5gr violet & blue	Q=over 200	up to 30.00	
ALB6	26(Sel)		10gr blue	Q=over 200	up to 30.00	
ALB9	27b10		pa green	eagle & value in green	25.00	—
ALB10	27(Sel)		10pa green	Q=over 200	up to 30.00	
ALB11	27c		10pa red (error) (u)		20.00	20.00
ALB12	27d		10 pa violet (error) (u)		20.00	20.00
ALB13	29b		20pa red	20 pa green (error) (u)	20.00	20.00
ALB14	29(Sel)		20pa red	Q=over 200	up to 30.00	
ALB15	30		30pa violet	30pa ultramarine (error) (u)	20.00	20.00
ALB16	30b			30pa red (error) (u)	20.00	20.00
ALB17	30(Sel)		30 pa violet	Q=over 200	up to 30.00	
ALB18	31a		1 gr ultramarine	1gr green (error) (u)	20.00	20.00
ALB19	31(Sel)		1 gr ultramarine	Q=over 200	up to 30.00	
ALB20	31b			1 gr black (error) (u)	20.00	20.00
ALB21	31c			1 gr violet (error) (u)	20.00	20.00
ALB22	31(Sel)		1gr ultramarine	Q=over 200	up to 30.00	
ALB23	33(Sel)		2gr black	Q=over 200	up to 30.00	
ALB23A	33b		2gr blue (error) (u)		20.00	20.00
ALB24	47a		5pa on		5.00	5.00
ALB24A	48a		10pa on 5q		5.00	5.00
ALB24B	49a		20pa on 10q		5.00	5.00
ALB24C	50a		1gr on 25q		6.50	6.50
ALB24D	51a		2gr on 50q		7.50	7.50
ALB24E	52b		5gr on 1fr		21.00	21.00
ALB25	52a		10pa black & red		90.00	90.00
ALB26	52A(Sel) (Yv,37a)		10pa violet & red		30.00	70.00
ALB27	53(Sel) (Yv,37Aa)		25pa violet & red		30.00	70.00
ALB28	53a (Yv.37Aa)		25pa violet & red	25 pa black & red (error) (u)	150.00	150.00
ALB29	63a	(1917-18)	2¢ red brown & grn	CTM for CTS	30.00	30.00
ALB30	64a		3 ¢ black & grn	CTM for CTS	30.00	30.00
ALB31	121a	(1920)	10 q rose (bk)	dbl ovpt (vc)	21.00	24.00
ALB32	178a	(1925)	1q on 2q orange	invtd ovpt (vc)	7.00	7.00
ALB33	180a		5q yellow green	invt ovpt (vc)	7.00	7.00
ALB34a	108		unlisted	ovpt incomplete R	10.00	—
ALB35	Sel-14 J32	(1926)	20q green without ovpt	dbl impression	30.00	70.00
ALB36	Sel-15 J34		50q dark brown without ovpt Imp.	dbl impression	30.00	70.00
ALB37	208a	(1928)	1q on rose red	invtd surch (vc)	3.75	3.75
ALB38	209a		5q on 25q dk blue (R)	invtd surcharge	3.75	3.75

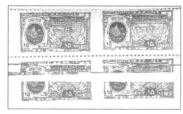

AFG5

AJM10

ALA24

ALB39	C8a	(1927)	5q green	dbl ovpt, one invtd	35.00	35.00
ALB40	C9a		10q rose red	invtd ovpt (vc)	30.00	30.00
ALB41	C9b			dbl ovpt, one invtd	35.00	35.00
ALB42	C11a		50q dark green	invtd ovpt (vc)	30.00	30.00
ALB43	C12a		1 fr dk violet & black	invtd ovpt (vc)	30.00	30.00
ALB44	C12b			dbl ovpt (vc)	30.00	30.00
ALB45	C15a	(1928)	5q green	invtd ovpt (vc)	20.00	—
ALB46	C36a	(1931)	5q yellow green ·	dbl ovpt (vc)	65.00	—
ALB47	C42a		3fr purple	invtd ovpt (vc)	*175.00*	—
ALB48	C45a		20q on 50q dr grn	invtd ovpt (vc)	—	—

Sel =Inverts listed by Martin Sellinger in op. Cit., p.7 (Sel) These are varieties.
*ALB35 and36 are dbl impressions, one inverted.

Albania would be an excellent starting place for the error collector from two vantage points (1) diversity and (2) expense. Albania has produced errors of various types such as color errors more than most countries, inverted centers more than most countries, inverted surcharges etc.

ALEXANDRETTA has produced no errors

ALGERIA

ALG1	23a	(1924-6)	60c lt violet	invtd ovpt (vc)	—	NA
ALG2	25a		75c blue(R)	dbl ovpt (vc)	65.00	—
ALG2a	B26a Sel	(1930)	5 fr + 5fr green & car.	Q=major rarity, 100 or less exist		NA
ALG3	122a	(1938)	25c on 50c red	dbl surch (vc)	35.00	30.00
ALG4	122b			invtd surch (vc)	20.00	18.00
ALG5	131b	(1939-40)	1fr on 90c crimson(I)	dbl surch I (vc) (bars 6mm)	35.00	—
ALG6	131c			invtd surch I (bars 6mm)	22.50	—
ALG7	131d			pair, one without surch (I)	NA	—
ALG8	131f			invtd surch (vc) II(bars 7mm)	27.50	—
ALG9	131g			pair one without surch (II)	NA	—
ALG10	136b	(1941)	50c on 65c ultramarine	invtd surch (vc)	21.00	—
ALG11	136c			pair, one without surch	52.50	—
ALG12	166a	(1943)	2fr on 5fr red orange	surch omitted	140.00	—
ALG13	179a	(1944-5)	1.50fr dark blue	dbl impression	20.00	—
ALG14	180a		2fr red	dbl impression	22.50	—
ALG15	187a	(1944)	30c on 15c org br	invtd surch (vc)	10.00	4.00
ALG16	190a	(1945)	50c in 1.50 fr bright rose	invtd surch (vc)	15.00	—
ALG17	207a	(1946)	2fr on 1.50 fr. henna brn	without 2F	110.00	—
ALG18	288a	(1962)	45c bright violet & olive gray	handstamped ovpt	*15.00*	*10.00*
ALG19	289a		50c sl green & lt claret	handstamped ovpt (u)	15.00	12.00
ALG20	290a		1fr dark bl, slate & bistro	handstamped ovpt (u)	4.00	1.50
ALG21	B9a	(1927)	50c + 50c dp bl (R)	dbl surch (vc)	200.00	200.00
ALG22	B26a	(1930)	5 fr + 5 fr grn & carmine	center invtd	NA	—
ALG23	B38a	(1942)	90c + 60c henna brown	dbl surch (vc)	55.00	—
ALG24	J27a	(1944)	50c on 20c yellow green	invtd surch (vc)	3.50	—
ALG25	J27b			dbl surch (vc)	9.50	—
ALG26	P1a	(1924-26)	1/2 c on 1c dk gray	triple surch	87.50	—

ALLENSTEIN

Allenstein, a district of East Prussia, was involved in a plebiscite in 1920. All of its seven errors are NA.

ANDORRA

AND1	22ab	(1938)	1p	control number omitted	NA	

ANGOLA

ANG1	63a	(1902)	115r on 10r green	invtd surch (vc)	—	—
ANG2	69a		400r on 5r black (R)	dbl surch (vc)	—	—
ANG3	117a	(1912)	25r on 75r red violet	REPUBLICA	27.50	25.00
ANG4	117b			"25" omitted	27.50	25.00
ANG5	117c			REPUBLICA omitted	27.50	25.00
ANG6	118a Sel	(1914)	var	inscriptions invtd Q>200	up to 30.00	
ANG7	133 (Sel) var.		7-1/2 ¢ yellow brown	inscriptions invtd, R Q>200	up to 30.00	

ANG8	135 (Sel) var.	10¢ orange brown	inscriptions invtd P Q>200	up to 30.00	
ANG9	159 var	10r yellow green (R)	"R" of REPUBLICA reversed & invtd	10.00	
ANG10	163 var	75 red violet (G)	Republica ovpt dbl & in red	12.00	R__
ANG11	183 var Sel.	50r on 65r dull blue	(R) Republica ovpt dbl	15.00	R__
ANG12	220 var (1919)	1/2 on 75¢ bis brown	surch dbl (vc)		
ANG13	220 var		surch invtd (vc)	8.00	__
ANG14	RA 25var		dbl perfs vertically right side	3.00	R S__

Two comments are in order concerning Angola. First, as part of the Portuguese group, many stamps and errors are similar to those of other countries. Second, with some countries, errors are simply unlisted in any major catalogue. Somewhat related errors are listed as varieties (var.) of regular issues. Errors of Portuguese nations are often sold as var. by the largest Portuguese dealer in the western hemisphere. They explain that some of these error var. are extremely minor and hence skipped by the major catalogues, other issues dropped from earlier catalogue issues, and still others simply are missed by the major catalogues (e.g. Mozambique #511 value omitted, still others are unlisted because they were supposedly produced for collectors).

ANGRA has produced no errors

ANGUILLA has produced no errors

ANJOUAN has produced no errors

ANNAM AND TONKIN

AAT1	1a	(1888)	1c on 2c brn, *buff*	invtd surch (vc)	100.00	100.00
AAT2	1b			sideways surcharge	100.00	100.00
AAT3	2a		1c on 4c claret, *lav*	invtd surch (vc)	100.00	100.00
AAT4	2b			dbl surch (vc)	125.00	125.00
AAT5	2c			sideways surch	100.00	100.00
AAT6	3a		5c on 10c blk, *lav*	invtd surch (vc)	100.00	100.00
AAT7	3b			dbl surch (vc)	125.00	125.00
AAT8	7a		1c on 2c brn, *buff*	invtd surch (vc)	NA	

ARGENTINA

ARG1	7a	(1862)	15c blue	without accent on "u" (u)	NA	
ARG2	30a	(1877)	1c on 5c vermillion	invtd surch (vc)	NA	200.00
ARG3	31a		2c on 5c verm	invtd surch (vc)	NA	
ARG4	32b		8c on 10c green	invtd surch (vc)	NA	
ARG5	41a	(1882)	1/2c¢ on 5c ver	dbl surch (vc)	80.00	*80.00*
ARG6	41b			invtd surch (vc)	20.00	*20.00*
ARG7	41c			"PROVISORIO" omitted (u)	80.00	80.00
ARG8	41d			fraction omitted (u)	50.00	__
ARG9	41e			"PROVISORIO" (u)	30.00	30.00
ARG10	41f			pair, one without surch (u)	200.00	NA
ARG11	41g			small "p" in "PROVISORIO" (u)	NA	
ARG12	41h			dbl surch with small "p" in "PROVISORIO" (u)	32.50	32.00
ARG13	41i			invtd surch with small "p"in "PROVISORIO" (u)	40.00	40.00

ANG14

ANG3

ANG12

ANG13

ANG10

ARG14	4li			Fraction omitted with small "p" in "PROVISORIO" (u)	15.00	15.00
ARG15	42a		1/2c on 5c verm	perf. across middle of stamp: "PROVISORIO" (u)	40.00	40.00
ARG16	42b			same as 42a but large "p" in "PROVISORIO" (u)	30.00	22.50
ARG17	47a	(1884)	1/2 c on 15c blue	Groundwork of horiz. lines (u)	100.00	80.00
ARG18	47b			invtd surch (vc)	27.50	20.00
ARG19	48a		1c on 15c blue	groundwork of horiz. lines (u)	10.00	6.00
ARG20	48b			invtd. surch (vc)	80.00	55.00
ARG21	48c			dbl surch (vc)	40.00	32.50
ARG22	48d			triple surch (u)	NA	
ARG23	49a		1/2c on 5c ver	invtd surch (vc)	150.00	110.00
ARG24	49b			date omitted (u)	150.00	—
ARG25	49c			pair, one without surch (u)	NA	
ARG26	49d			dbl surch (vc)	NA	
ARG27	50a		1/2c on 15c blue	groundwork of horiz. lines (u)	30.00	25.00
ARG28	50b			invtd surch (vc)	70.00	55.00
ARG29	50c			pair, one without surch (u)	NA	
ARG30	51a		4c on 5c ver	invtd surch (vc)	25.00	25.00
ARG31	51b			dbl surch (vc)	NA	
ARG32	51c			pair, one without surch but with "4" in manuscript (u)	NA	
ARG33	51d			pair, one without surch (u)	NA	—
ARG34	83b		1/4c on 12c blue	dbl surch (vc)	75.00	35.00
ARG35	83c			invtd surch (vc)	80.00	—
ARG36	84a		1/4c 12c blue (R)	dbl surch (vc)	52.50	52.50
ARG37	90a		2c lt blue	dbl impression (u)	190.00	
ARG38-53	All are inverted centers & NA except ARG48, 53.					
ARG38	139a	(1899)	1p blue & black	Q<100	NA	
ARG39	140a		5p orange & black	Q<100	NA	
ARG40	140a		5p red & black	(die proof)		
ARG41	141a		10p green & black			
ARG42	142a		20 p red & black	punch cancel only way invert known	NA	47.35
ARG43	160a	(1910)	1/2c bl & gray blue	Q<50		
ARG44	161a		1c bl grn & black	Q<50		
ARG45	162a		2c olive & gray	Q<50		
ARG46	164a		4c dark blue & green	Q<50		
ARG47	167a		12c bright blue	Q<50		
ARG48	167pa		12c proof on card		200.00	NA
ARG49	171a		50c carmine & black	Q<50	NA	
ARG50	173a		5p orange & violet	Q<50	NA	
ARG51	246a	(1917)	20 p blue & claret	Q=known-12 mint, 10 used	NA	
ARG52	338a	(1923)	20 p slate & brn lake			
ARG53	582d	(1948)	s/s one of 4 stamps invtd	85c ship is the invert	70.00	130.00R
ARG54	361a	(1926)	25c chocolate	"1326" for "1826" (u)	6.00	.75
ARG55	365a	(1927)	5c red	period after value (u)	3.50	1.90
ARG56	397a	(1931)	5c red	plane omitted, top left corner (u)	3.00	1.65
ARG57	B43a	(1963)	12p + 6p horsemanship	dark carmine (jacket) omitted omitted (u)	—	—

ARG45a

ARM10

AFFORDABLE FOREIGN ERRORS

ARG58-61					all NA	
ARG62	O3b	(1884-7)	1c red	dbl ovpt (vc)	35.00	35.00
ARG63	O4b		2c green	dbl ovpt (vc)	35.00	
ARG64	O14b		90c blue	dbl ovpt (vc)	50.00	45.00
ALL INVERTED OVERPRINTS (vc) O1a-O14a						
ARG65	O1a		1/2		16.00	12.50
ARG66	O2a		1c perf 14		50.00	40.00
ARG67	O2ac		1c perf 12		32.50	30.00
ARG68	O3a		1c		1.50	1.00
ARG69	O4a		2c		65.00	40.00
ARG70	O5a		4c		40.00	32.50
ARG71	O6a		8c		60.00	60.00
ARG72	O8b		12c perf 12		12.50	—
ARG73	O9a		12c		125.00	65.00
ARG74	O10a		24c		2.75	1.65
ARG75	O13a		60c		90.00	50.00
ARG76	O14a		90c		50.00	40.00
ARG77	O15a	(1884)	16c green	dbl ovpt (vc)	15.00	—
ARG78	O15b			invtd. ovpt (vc)	125.00	—
ARG79	O17a		24c blue	invtd ovpt (vc)	4.00	2.50
ARG80	O17b			dbl ovpt one inverted	NA	
ARG81	O18a	(1885)	2c green	invtd ovpt (vc)	40.00	32.50
ARG82	O19a		4c brown	invtd ovpt (vc)	40.00	30.00
ARG83	O19b			dbl ovpt (vc)	50.00	—
ARG84	O24a	(1884)	2c green diagonal ovpt	horiz ovpt (u)	150.00	125.00
ARG85	O58a	(1945-6)	10c brown	dbl ovpt (vc)	—	—
Buenos Aires						
ARG86	7b	(1859)	I in pesos blue	impression on reverse in blue (u)	NA	
ARG87	7c			dbl impression (u)	NA	

ARMENIA

ARM1	244a	(1920)	10r on 35K red brn & green	with additional surch "5r"	1.50	1.50
ARM2	355a	(1922)	20(K) on 500r	with "K" written in red	10.00	10.00*
*a lesser value than 355 itself (u)						
ARM3	368a		35(K) on 20000r, imperf	with "K" written in violet (u)		
ARM4	368			as a, perf	65.00	65.00
ARM5	368d			with "Kop" written in violet, imperf		
ARM6			50K on 25,000 61	surcharged 50 only.	50.00	50.00
ARM7	Yv97(Sel)	(1920)		25r grn + brn, Mt Ararat	Q>200	30.00
70.00						
ARM8	Yv98(Sel)			orange & brn	Spinner Q>200	30.00
70.00						
ARM9	Yv99(Sel)			blue & brn, Mt Ararat	Q>200	30.00
70.00						
ARM10	Yv100		70r violet & brn,	Spinner Q>200	30.00	70.00
ARM11	Yv101(Sel)		100r red & brn, Mt Ararat	Q>200	70.00	130.00

*The 5 Yvert items, although none found in Minkus, are all contained in Sellinger, op.cit., p9.

The Armenian errors are distinct in four ways. First, the Scott subscripts for almost all stamps produced up to 1920 indicate simply imperf or perf. Sometimes, the value of the subscripted is higher than the non-subscripted and vice versa. Further, all of the "other errors" listed in Scott's are "nit-pickers" (ARM1—additional surch "5r"). The five Yvert-Sellinger items, on the other hand, all cover the most prized of all errors—inverted centers. These inverted centers (see ARM) are attractive, relatively inexpensive and represent a good buy for novice invert hunters.

ASCENSION has produced no errors

AUSTRALIA

AST2, 4-9, 11-18, 20, 22, 23 are NA

AST1	19a	(1921-4)	1/2 p emerald	"thin" 1/2 at right (u)	NA	
AST3	60a	(1918-23)	1/2 p emerald. Thin	1/2 at right (u)	110.00	*45.00*

AST10	391a		5p multicolored	purple (5d) omitted (u)	190.00	—
AST19	430f		7c black, red & green	green omitted (u)	50.00	—
AST21	M2a	(1946-7)	sp brown vio	blue overprint	100.00	67.50

AUSTRALIAN STATES (1)
New South Wales

The early stamps of New South Wales are all error-laden and NA. Rather than elaborate on them all we will list a sample of errors to give the reader a flavor of "early" New South Wales errors: Zg no clouds, Zh no trees, 5d pick and shovel omitted, 5e, no whip, 10d "WALE", 15a "WAEES", 17b "WACES", 18b "WALLS". After 20b, errors become affordable and we cover all errors as usual.

NSW1	23a	(1854-5)	1p orange	no leaves to right of "SOUTH" (U)	NA	60.00
NSW2	23b			two leaves to right of "SOUTH" (u)	NA	100.00
NSW3	23c			"WALE"	NA	125.00
NSW4	25a		3p green	"WACES"	—	80.00
NSW5	32b		1p red	printed on both sides (u)	—	—
NSW6	59a	(1871-84)	9p on red brown	dbl surch, blk & bl (u)	195.00	—
NSW7			3p Green	dbl impression	—	—
NSW8	76a	(1894)	10sh rose & violet	dbl ovpt (vc)	NA	—
NSW9	90a	(1891)	3p green	dbl impression	—	—
NSW10	92b		1/2 p on 1 p gray	surch omitted	—	—
NSW11	92c			dbl surch (vc)	—	—
NSW12	96b	(1897)	9 p on 10 p red brn (bk)	surch omitted	125.00	—
NSW13	96c			dbl surch (vc)	125.00	100.00
NSW14	F2a		(6p) red & blue	frame printed on back (NA)	—	—
NSW15	O4b*	(1879-80)	3p green	dbl ovpt (vc)	—	—
NSW16	O11a	(1880)	5 sh lilac	dbl ovpt (vc)	—	—
NSW17	O14a	(1881)	3p green	dbl ovpt (vc)	—	—
NSW18	O18a		8p yellow	dbl ovpt (vc)	NA	50.00
NSW19	O19a		lsh black (R)	dbl ovpt (vc)	—	—
NSW20	O29a	(1888-9)	lsh viol brown	dbl ovpt (vc)	—	—
NSW21	O34a		1/2 on l p gray & black	dbl ovpt.	—	—

The early stamps of New South Wales represent engravings and are prone to error.

South Australia
| SOA1-15 | | | | | all NA | |
| SOA16 | 58a | (1868-75) | 2p orange red | printed on both sides (u) | — | 200.00 |

South Australian errors have a very interesting characteristic. The OS stamps are dominated by expensive (vc) overprint errors while the country's regular issues are dominated by the (u) printed on other side error.

Tasmania
TAS1	11c	(1857)	1p carmin	dbl impression (u)	—	165.00
TAS2	13b		4p blue	dbl impression (u)	—	—
TAS3	14b	(1858)	6 p gray lilac	dbl impression (u)	—	200.00
TAS4	25a	(1864-9)	4 p blue	dbl impression (u)	—	125.00
TAS5	29c		1p carmine	dbl impression (u)	—	82.50
TAS6	32e		6p red lilac	dbl impression (u)	—	100.00
TAS7	34a		lsh vermillion	dbl impression (u)	—	120.00
TAS8	48c	(1870-71)	2p green	dbl impression (u)	—	—
TAS9	54e	(1871-6)	2p deep green	dbl impression	—	—
TAS10		(1880-3)	4 p lem	printed on both sides (u)	NA	—
TAS11	65a		1/2 p on l p carmine	"a" sideways on surch (u)	NA	—
TAS12			2-1/2 p on 9 p lt blue	dbl surch, one invtd (u)	NA	—
TAS13			2-1/2 p on 9 p lt blue	surcharged in blue	—	—

Tasmania is dominated by double impressions, which are expensive but often affordable.

Queensland
QUE1	57c	(1879-81)	l p rose red	"OOENSLAND" (u)	110.00	32.50
QUE2	58c		2 p gray blue	"PENGE" (u)	—	70.00
QUE3	62a	(1878-9)	1 p brown org	"OOEENSLAND"	NA	—

QUE4	63a		2 p deep ultra	"PENGE"	NA	
QUE5	65a	(1881)	1/2 p on l p br orange	"OOEENSLAND" (u)	NA	
QUE6	68a	(1882-3)	4 p yellow	"PENGE" (u)	125.	45.00
QUE7		(1890-2)	4 p orange	"PENGE" (u)	65.00	27.50
QUE8	101a	(1895)	1/2 p green	without moire on back (u)	55.00	—
QUE9	102a		l p orange	"PE" missing (u)	—	—
QUE10	103b		1/2 p green	printed on both sides (u)	60.00	—
QUE11	F3		(6p) golden yellow	dbl impression (u)	NA	

Queensland does not have as many errors as New South Wales. What it does have an abundance of, however, is spelling errors. OOEENSLAND 3 times, PENGE 4 times

AUSTRIA
Occupation Stamps
Issued Under Italian Occupation
Issued in Trieste
There is such a plethora of these errors (over 70) and we will not list them here (for full descriptions, see the Scott Catalogue (vol.1, 1998, p. 457) Most of the errors are of the (vc) inverted ovpt or dbl surcharge. These are generally inexpensive with some prices as low as $5. Although "off the beaten track," these errors may provide fertile ground for the novice error collector—too many double surcharges and inverted overprints

AUS1	1a	(1850)	1 kr yellow	printed on both sides (u)	NA	
AUS2	3c		3kr red	printed on both sides (u)	NA	
AUS3	5d		9kr blue type II	printed on both sides (u)	NA	
AUS4	29c	(1867-72)		cliché of 3 kr in plate of 5 kr (u)	NA	
AUS5	70a	(1899)	1 kr lilac	numerals invtd (u)	NA	
AUS6	72b			"3" in lower right corner sideways (u)	NA	
AUS7	81b		50h gray blue	all 4 50's parallel (u)	NA	
AUS8	193a	(1918-19)	80h orange br	invtd ovpt (vc)	175.00	175.00

*AUS9 - AUS17 inverts from Sellinger as well as Scott.

AUS9	219a	(1919)	2k verm + black, Parlmt. (u)	Q=major rarity, fewer than 100	NA	
AUS10	222a		4k carmine + black, Parliament (u)	Q=major rarity, fewer than 100	NA	
AUS11	226a	(1920)	20k lilac & red, Parliament			
AUS12		(1854)	2 Fl. Revenue Erler 10			
AUS13		(1858)	1/2 kr Revenue	typo E Erler 22		
AUS14			3 fl Revenue E Erler 44			
AUS15			4fl Revenue E Erler 45			
AUS16			5fl Revenue E Erler 46			
AUS17			10k Revenue Cat in Folder			
AUS18	C2a	(1918)	250 k on 35 ocher (vc)		NA	
AUS19	O4		5h rose red	invtd ovpt (vc)	200.00	NA
AUS20	J48a	(1916)	1h gray	pair, one without ovpt	125.00	
AUS21	J102a	(1921)	7-1/2 k on 15h bister	invtd ovcharge (vc)	185.00	185.00
AUS22	P9b	(1874-6)	(l kr) violet	dbl impression (u)	—	175.00
AUS23	PR2b	(1858-9)	1 kr blue	printed on both sides (u)	—	—
AUS24	OE5a	(1919)	2h claret, yellow	invtd ovpt (vc)	175.00	

AUSTRIA
Offices in the Turkish Empire

AUS25	14b	(1886)	10 pa on 3 sld green	invtd surch (vc)	NA	
AUS26	15a	(1888)	10 pa on 3 kr green	01 para 10 (u)	NA	
AUS27	17b		lp1 on 10 kr blue	dbl surch NA		
AUS28	29a		20 p1 on 2 gold carmin	dbl surch (vc)	—	

Lombardy Venetia

AUS29	1a	(1850)	5¢ buff	printed on both sides (u)	NA	
AUS30	10b	(1858-62)		printed on both sides (u)	—	NA
AUS31	12b		15s blue	printed on both sides (u)	—	NA

Except for the occupation errors, Austria has not produced too many.

AZERBAIJAN

AZE1	68a	(1922-3)	200,000 r on 25r (vc)	* black surcharge	26.00	27.50
AZE2	70a		500,000 r on 2000r (vc)	black surcharge	27.50	29.00
AZE3	72A		1g 500,000r on 5000r (vc)	black surcharge	16.00	15.00

AZE1-3 may be considered more varieties than errors. The price of AZE3 for example is identical to that "unerred" in one of the major catalogues.

AZE4	Unlisted		50,000 r ovpt on blue and gray-bister	ovpt invtd (vc)	—	15.00R

There is really little to say about Azerbaijan—the only specimen of the "true" error, AZE4, that we have seen is heavily canceled and poor in appearance.

AZORES

AZR1	8a	(1968-70)	10r yellow	invtd ovpt (vc)	NA	150.00
AZR2	10a		25r rose	invtd ovpt (vc)	—	—
AZR3	21a	(1871-75)	5r black (c)	invtd ovpt (vc)	47.50	30.00
AZR4	23a		10r yellow	invtd ovpt (vc)	—	—
AZR5	25a		25r rose	invtd ovpt (vc)	—	—
AZR6	25b			dbl ovpt (vc)	35.00	25.00
AZR7	25d			dbl impression of stamp (u)	—	—
AZR8	29a		120r blue	invtd ovpt (vc)	—	—
AZR9	33a	(1875-80)	15r lilac brown	invtd ovpt (vc)	125.00	—
AZR10	39b	(1880)		dbl ovpt (vc)	—	—
AZR11	41a	(1882)	25r brown	dbl ovpt (vc)	—	—
AZR12	44a	(1882-85)	5r slate	dbl ovpt (vc)	—	—
AZR13	44c			invtd ovpt (vc)	—	—
AZR14	45a		10r green	invtd ovpt (vc)	—	—
AZR15	46a		10r green	dbl ovpt (vc)	—	—
AZR16	47b		15r lilac brn	invtd ovpt (vc)	—	—
AZR17	48a		20r bister	invtd ovpt (vc)	—	—
AZR18	49a		20r carmine	dbl ovpt (vc)	165.00	100.00
AZR19	52a		50r blue	dbl ovpt (vc)	—	—
AZR20	53b		80r yellow	dbl ovpt (vc)	—	—
AZR21	61a	(1887)	20r pink	invtd ovpt (vc)	—	—
AZR2	61b			dbl ovpt (vc)	—	—
AZR23	62a		25r lilac rose	invtd ovpt (vc)	—	—
AZR24	62b			dbl ovpt, one invtd (u)	—	—
AZR25	63a		25r red violet	dbl ovpt (vc)	—	—
AZR26	65a	(1894)	5r orange yel	invtd ovpt (vc)	45.00	45.00
AZR27	66a		10r violet rose	dbl ovpt (vc)	—	—
AZR28	66b			invtd ovpt (vc)	—	—
AZR29	68a		20r violet	dbl ovpt (vc)	—	—
AZR30	69a		25r green	dbl ovpt (vc)	50.00	50.00
AZR31	69b			invtd ovpt (vc)	50.00	50.00
AZR32	73a		100r lt br, pale buff	dbl ovpt (vc)	—	—
AZR33	77a		1000r gray blk, yelsh	dbl ovpt (vc)	—	—
AZR34	101a	(1910)	2-1/2 r gray	invtd ovpt (vc)	25.00	25.00
AZR35	102a		5r orange yel	invtd ovpt (vc)	25.00	25.00
AZR36	126a		2-1/2 r violet	invtd ovpt (vc)	9.00	9.00
AZR37	127a		5r black	invtd ovpt (vc)	9.00	9.00
AZR38	128a		10r dk green	invtd ovpt (vc)	9.00	9.00
AZR39	129a		15r lilac brown	invtd ovpt (vc)	9.00	9.00
AZR40	130a		20r carmine(G)	invtd ovpt (vc)	16.00	16.00
AZR41	130b			dbl ovpt (vc)	16.00	16.00
AZR42	133a		75r bister brn	dbl ovpt (vc)	9.00	9.00
AZR43	147a	(1911)	100r yellow brown	dbl surch (vc)	35.00	35.00
AZR44	150a		10r magenta	"Acores" dbl (u)	20.00	20.00
AZR45	152a		200r brown buff	"Acores" invtd (u)	—	—
AZR46	155a	(1912-31)	1/4c olive brown	invtd ovpt	9.00	—
AZR47	157a		1c deep green	invtd ovpt (vc)	9.00	—
AZR48	158a	(1918)	1c deep brown	invtd ovpt	—	—

AZR49	159a	(1913)	1-1/2 c choc	invtd ovpt	9.00 _	
AZR50	160a	(1918)	1-1/2 c deep green	invtd ovpt (vc)	—	—
AZR51	161a		2c carmine	invtd ovpt (vc)	14.00	—
AZR52	162a		2c orange (1918)	invtd ovpt (vc)	14.00	—
AZR53	192a	(1923)	20c deep green	dbl ovpt (vc)	—	—
AZR54	J4a	(1904)	30r gray green	dbl ovpt (vc)	—	—
AZR55	J15a	(1918)	1/2 c brown	invtd ovpt (vc)	4.00	4.00
AZR56	J15b			dbl ovpt (vc)	4.00	4.00
AZR57	J16a		1c orange	invtd ovpt (vc)	4.00	4.00
AZR58	J16b			dbl ovpt (vc)	4.00	4.00
AZR59	J17a		2c red lilac	invtd ovpt (vc)	4.00	4.00
AZR60	J17b			dbl ovpt (vc)	4.00	4.00
AZR61	J18a		3c green	invtd ovpt (vc)	4.00	4.00
AZR62	J18b			dbl ovpt (vc)	4.00	4.00
AZR63	J19a		4c gray	invtd ovpt (vc)	4.00	4.00
AZR64	J19b			dbl ovpt (vc)	4.00	4.00
AZR65	J20b		5c rose	dbl ovpt (vc)	4.00	4.00
AZR66	P1a	(1876-88)	2-1/2 r (a) olive	invtd ovpt (vc)	—	—
AZR67	P2a	(1882)	2-1/2 r (b) olive	invtd ovpt (vc)	—	—
AZR68	P2b			dbl ovpt (vc)	—	—
AZR69	P3a	(1885)	2r black kk	invtd ovpt	—	—
AZR70	P3b			dbl ovpt, one invtd	—	—
AZR71	P4a	(1882)	2-1/2 r (b) bister	dbl ovpt	—	—
AZR72	Q1a	(1921-22)	1c lilac brown	invtd ovpt (vc)	4.00	4.00
AZR73	Q2a		2c orange	invtd ovpt (vc)	4.00	4.00
AZR74	Q3a		5c light brown	invtd ovpt (vc)	5.00	5.00
AZR75	Q3b			dbl ovpt (vc)	5.00	5.00
AZR76	Q4a		10c red brown	invtd ovpt (vc)	5.00	5.00
AZR77	Q4b			dbl ovpt (vc)	5.00	5.00
AZR78	Q5a		20c gray blue	invtd ovpt (vc)	5.00	5.00
AZR79	Q5b			dbl ovpt (vc)	5.00	5.00
AZR80	Q6a		40c carmine	dbl ovpt (vc)	6.50	6.50
AZR81	Q9a		70c gray brown	dbl ovpt (vc)	—	—

Azores stamps were taken over by Portugal in 1931. Before that time it could be called the "land of the overprint"—"Acores" and "Republica," for most or all of its stamps were overprints.

B

BAHAMAS
BAH1-18 are all NA

BAHRAIN

BHR1	64a	(1948)	2-1/2 on 2-1/2 brt ultra	dbl surch (vc)	NA	
BHR2	811a	(1953)	1/2 a on-1/2 p red org	" 1/2" omitted (u)	200.00	NA

BANGKOK

BNK1	2a	(1882)	4c rose	invtd ovpt (vc)	—	—
BNK2	12a		2c rose (1883)	invtd ovpt (vc)	NA	
BNK3	12b			dbl ovpt (vc)	NA	
BNK4	12c			triple ovpt (u)	NA	
BNK5	14a		4c brown	dbl ovpt (vc)	—	—
BNK6	16a	(1883)	6c violet	dbl ovpt (vc)	—	—
BNK7	17a		8c yel orange	invtd ovpt (vc)	NA	
BNK8	18a		10c slate	dbl ovpt (vc)	—	—

Bankok is a bore. As a country it is no more. All of its errors are NA..All of its errors are (vc) double or inverted overprints except for one—a rare triple overprint valued by some at $10,000. Need I say more. Let's move on to the next country.

BANGLADESH

BNG1	371	(1990)	10t UN Conference	UN & inscriptions	up to 30.00R	
	unlisted			invtd (u)		

(Q=major rarity, 100 or fewer probably exist). See Sellinger, op.cit., p.9)

If this invert is such a scarce one, why is it not priced higher? Probably because the country is not popular. If you really love errors and inverts here you may have a bargain. If you are just satisfied with errors, try:

BNG2	161		40p multicolored	triple ovpt	—	—
BNG3	163		5t multicolored	dbl ovpt (vc)	—	—

BARBADOS

BRB1	69a	(1892)	1/2 p on 4 p brown	without hyphen (u)	6.00	*10.00*
BRB2	69b			dbl surch (vc)	—	—
BRB3	69c			dbl surcharge, red & black (u)	NA	
BRB4	69d			as "c" without hyphen (u)	NA	
BRB5	209a	(1947)	1 p on 2p brt red rose	dbl surch (vc)	—	—
BRB6	391a		4c on 25 c multi	"4c" omitted (u)	20.00	—
Semi-postals						
BRB7	B1a	(1907)	1p on 2 p sl & org	no period after 1 d (u)	15.00	17.50
BRB8	B1b			invtd surch (vc)	1.75	2.50
BRB9	B1c			invtd surch, no period after 1 d (u)	15.00	17.50
BRB10	B1d			dbl surch (vc)	NA	
BRB11	B1e			dbl surch, both invtd	NA	

Barbados has produced several (vc) double surcharges (some very expensive).

BARBUDA has produced no errors

BASUTOLAND

BTO1	46	(1954)	1/2 p dk. brown & gray	invtd (u) Q=60 exist		NA
BTO2	61a	(1961)	1/2 c on 1/2 p dk brown & gray blk (vc)		NA	
BTO3	63a		2c on 2 p org & dp bl	invtd surch (vc)	125.00	—
BTO4	64b		2-1/2 c on 3p (II)	invtd surch	NA	
BTO5	67a		10c on 1sh (I)	type II	40.00	40.00
BTO6	J8a	(1961)	5c on 2p dark pur ("5" 3-1/2 mm high)		17.50	25.00

With the exception of the one NA invert, the other Basutoland errors are all surcharge errors. The errors vary in price with BTO6 being quite reasonable. There is no single trait that stands out among them.

BATUM

BTM1	19a	(1919)	5r brown	"CCUPATION" (u)	190.00	190.00

BECHUANALAND

BCH1-6					all NA	
BCH7	23a	(1888)	1p on 1p lilac	dbl surch (vc)	—	—
BCH8	25a		red surch 2p on 2p lilac	"2" with curved tail (u)	200.00	150.00
BCH9	31a	(1891)	1p rose	horiz pair, one without ovpt(u)	NA	—
BCH10	31b			"British" omitted (u)	—	NA
BCH11	31c			"Bechuanaland" omitted	NA	—
BCH12	32a		2p bister	without period (u)	200.00	—

BNG2

BNG3

BCO20a

BCH13	38a	(1893-95) 1p rose	no dots over the "i's" of	75.00	75.00
	q		"British" (u)		
BCH24	38b		"British" omitted (u)	NA	—
BCH25	38c		as "a" reading up (u)	—	750.00
BCH26	38d		pair, one without ovpt (u)	—	—
BCH27	39a	2p bister	dbl ovpt (vc)	NA	
BCH28	39b		no dots over the "i's"	125.00	125.00
			of British" (u)		
BCH29	39c		"British" omitted (u)	NA	
BCH30	39d		as "b" reading up (u)	NA	

Bechuanaland has produced two major types of errors: (1) gross overprint errors—the vc inverted overprint and double surcharge errors, and (2) minor typographical errors—i.e. "No dots over the ii's" of "British."

BECHUANALAND PROTECTORATE

BCP1	51a	(1888-90) 1/2 p vermillion	dbl ovpt (vc)	NA	
BCP2	52a	('89) 1/2 p vermillion	dbl ovpt (vc)	NA	
BCP3	53a		invtd ovpt (vc)	65.00	80.00
BCP4	53b		dbl ovpt (vc)	80.00	90.00
BCP5-17				all NA	
BCP18	17C	lr owen 10sh (ll, "Rl" at lower center)	type I (u)	NA	110.00
BCP19	17b	1c on 1p car rose (ll)	dbl surch (ll) (vc)	140.00	—

The Beches are a ritish bunch
But forgot their B's when coming to lunch
For us this omission
Was an expensive proposition
It made their errors cost much more
And made some philatelists quite sore. —The Bard

The BCP's are copycats
They bowed to the Beches and tipped their hats
But instead of ritish 'twas a simple "o."
But the price was the same of "no," "no," "no."
The Beches and BCP's are vowed to omission
Who will be their savior and provide commission? —-The Bard

BELARUS has produced no errors

BELGIAN CONGO

BCO1-3				all NA	
		perf 14			
BCO2	18a	perf 15 10¢ grn blue & blk, perf.15	invtd Q=1 unused copy exists	NA	
BCO3	30a	(1898) 10 fr yel grn & blk, (1898) steamer	center invtd (u)	NA	
BCO4	61d	(1915) 10¢ car & blk,	bklt pane found Q= blk of 4 & 6 sgls exist		
BCO5	70a	(1921) 1fr carmine & blk	dbl ovpt (vc)	20.00	—
BCP6	34c	25c lt blue & blk	dbl ovpt (#34) (vc)	185.00	—
BCO7	36b	50c olive & blk	invtd ovpt (#38) (vc)	NA	
BCO8	70a	(1921) 1fr carmine & blk	dbl ovpt (vc)	NA	
BCO9	77b	(1922) 30c on 10c (ll)	dbl surch (vc)	4.75	4.75
BCO10	80a	10c on 5c (R)	invtd surch (vc)	17.50	17.50
BCO11	80b		dbl surch (vc)	4.75	—
BCO12	80c		dbl surch one invtd	40.00	—
BCO13	80d		pair, one without surch (u)	42.50	—
BCO14	80e		on # 45 (u)	125.00	125.00
BCO15	81a	25c on 40c	invtd surch (vc)	17.50	17.50
BCO16	81b		dbl surch (vc)	5.50	—
BCO17	81c		"25c" dbl (vc)	—	—
BCO18	81d	25c on 5c, no. 60 (u)		100.00	100.00
BCO19	84a	10c on 1 fr (R)	dbl surch (vc)	14.00	—
BCO20	84b		invtd surch (vc)	17.50	17.50

BCO20a	87	(1922)	carmine & black	30c overprint, 0.25-invtd center, invtd handstamp, R	15.00	
BCO21	184a	(1941-42)	5c on 1.50fr (bl)	invtd surch (vc)	14.00	14.00
BCO22	185a		75¢ on 1.75fr ('42)	invtd surch (vc)	14.00	14.00
BCO23	186a		2.50(fr) on 2.40fr('42)	dbl surch (vc)	27.50	27.50
BCO24	186b			invtd surcharge	14.00	14.00
BCO25*	193	(1950)	50c deep green, palm tree			
BCO27	194		60c chestnut, palm tree			
BCO28	197		1.25fr rose red & blk, woman			
BCO29	200		2.50fr carmine, leopard			
BCO30	211		30c blue, palm tree			
BCO31	214		75c dull lilac & blk, woman			
BCO32	217		1.75fr dk gray brn, leopard			
BCO33	219		2.50fr carmin, leopard			

*BCO25-BCO33 are all invtd centers, retail price $30.00-$70.00 each.

Air Post Stamp

BCO34	C17	(1942)	50c on 1.50fr green	invtd surch (vc)	6.50	6.50
BCO35	Parcel post Q4	(1887-93)	3.50fr on 5fr	violet blk surch ('88)(u)		NA

The Belgian Congo has both interesting NA errors and vc ones. There are over ten double surcharges or inverted overprints, and many of them are inexpensive ($20 or under). The inverted centers are much more rare in most standard catalogues but not so in Sellinger's invert catalogue.

BELGIUM

BLG1	32	(1869-70)	10¢ w dbl impr	invtd proof on colored paper	30.00	70.00R
BLG2	36a	(1870)	1fr dull lilac	1fr rose lilac	NA	20.00
BLG3	68a	(1900)	25c ultra	no ball to "5" in upper left corner (u)	32.50	12.00
BLG4	139a	(1920)	65c claret & black	center invtd (u)	NA	
BLG5	140a	(1921)	20c on 5c	invtd surch (vc)	185.00	185.00
BLG6	141b		20c on 10c	invtd surch (vc)	185.00	185.00
BLG7	142a		20c on 15c (R)	invtd surch (vc)	185.00	185.00
BLG8	143a		red surch 55c on 65c claret & blk	pair, one without surch (u)	1.75	.85
BLG8a	365	(1946)	currency reform ovpt,	pair, color varies R		15.00
BLG9	B9a	(1911)	semi-postal 1c gray	invtd ovpt (vc)	—	—
BLG10	O26a	(1941-44)	10c olive bister	invtd ovpt (vc)	—	40.00
BLG11	O28a		50c dark blue	invtd ovpt (vc)	—	—
BLG12	P22a	(1921-31)	parcel post 40c olive green (vc)	invtd ovpt	—	—
BLG13-17					all NA	
BLG18	Q173a		2.30fr on 2.40fr violet	invtd surch (vc)	57.50	—

Belgium has not produced too many errors—5 or 6 vc's and then a number of u's.

BLV25

BLG8a

BLV1

BLV50a

BLV52a

BELIZE

BLZ1   834   (1986)   strip of 3 with invtd inscription   NA

We can't see rushing out to pay more than $200 for inverted inscriptions from a not-too-well-known country.

BENIN Neither Benin nor The People's Republic of Benin have produced any errors

BERMUDA
BRM1-11 are all NA

BHUTAN has produced no errors.

BOLIVIA

BLV1	79	(1909)	10¢ green black	invtd center (u) R	up to 30.00	
				Q=over 200 exist		
BLV2	80		20¢ orange & black	invtd R Q=over 200 exist	up to 30.00	
BLV3	81		2b red & black	invtd R Q=over 200 exist	up to 30.00	
BLV4	84		red & black	imperf		
BLV5	92	(1910)	5¢ green & black			
BLV6	93		10¢ claret & indigo			
BLV7	95a		5c on 2c green	invtd surch (vc)	5.00	5.00
BLV8	95b			dbl surch (vc)	15.00	—
BLV9	95c			period after "1911" (vc)	3.50	.80
BLV10	95d			blue surch (u)	75.00	60.00
BLV11	95e			dbl surch, one invtd	15.00	—
BLV12	96a		5c on 20c vio & blk	invtd surcharge	30.00	30.00
BLV13	98a	(1912)	2c green (bk)	invtd ovpt (vc)	5.00	—
BLV14	99a		10c ver (bl)	invtd ovpt (vc)	5.00	—
BLV15	100a		5c orange (R)	invtd ovpt (vc)	5.00	—
BLV16	100b			pair, one without ovpt (vc)	12.50	—
BLV17	100c			black ovpt (vc)	50.00	—
BLV18	101a		10c on 1c bl (R)	invtd surch (vc)	6.00	—
BLV19	101b			dbl surch (vc)	6.00	—
BLV20	101c			dbl surcharge, one invtd	7.50	—
BLV21	101d			black surcharge	100.00	100.00
BLV22	101e			as "d" invtd	—	—
BLV23	101f			as "d," dbl surcharge.	—	—
BLV24	101g			pair, one without black surch	NA	—
BLV25	113 c	(1916-17)	2c car & blk	center invtd (u) R		
BLV26	113d			imperf, center invtd (u) R	17.50	—
BLV27	116b		10c org & bl	no period after "Legislativo" (u)	1.00	.15
BLV28	116c			center invtd (u)	40.00	40.00
BLV29-32					all NA	
BLV33	138a		5c on 1c car (bl)	invtd surch (vc)	5.00	5.00
BLV34	138b			dbl surch (vc)	5.00	5.00
BLV35	139a		15c on 10c ver (bk)	invtd surch	6.00	6.00
BLV36	140a		15c on 22c lt bl (bk)	invtd surch	5.25	5.25
BLV37	140b			dbl surch, one invtd (u)	—	—
BLV38	142a		15c on 10c ver (bk)	invtd surch (vc)	6.00	6.00
BLV39	143a		15c on 10c ver (bk)	invtd surch (vc)	6.00	6.00
BLV40	143b			dbl surch (vc)	5.00	5.00
BLV41	160a	(1927)	5c on 1c car (bl)	invtd surch	6.00	6.00
BLV42	160b			black surch (vc)	22.50	22.50
BLV43	162a		10c on 24c pur (bk)	invtd surch (vc)	30.00	30.00
BLV44	162b			red surch (vc)	22.50	22.50
BLV45	182a	(1928)	15c on 20c #132	black surch (vc)	30.00	—
BLV46	184a		15c on 24c #124	invtd surch (vc)	5.00	5.00
BLV47	184b			blue surch (vc)	50.00	—
BLV48	193a	(1930)	1c on 2c (bl)	".10" for "0.01" (u)	12.50	12.50
BLV49	237a	(1937)	1b on 2b plum	"1" missing (u)	7.50	7.50
BLV50	239a		3b on 50c brt vio	"3" of value missing (u)	6.00	6.00
BLV50a	270	(1941)	10c rusty brown	misperforated R	10.00	
BLV51	271b		15c lt green	dbl impression (u)	6.00	—
BLV52	272a		45c carmine rose	dbl impression (u)	6.00	6.00

BLV 52a	326	(1948)	2B yellow green	misperforated R	(pair) 15.00	
BLV53	C1a	(1924)	10c ver & blk	invtd center (u)	NA	
BLV54	C24a	(1930)	1.50b on 15c	invtd surch (vc)	57.50	57.50
BLV55	C24b			comma instead of period after "1" (u)	35.00	35.00
BLV56	C25a		3b on 20c	invtd surch (vc)	62.50	62.50
BLV57	C25b			comma instead of period after "3" (u)	40.00	40.00
BLV58	C26a		6b on 35c	invtd surch (vc)	110.00	110.00
BLV59	C26b			comma instead of period after "6" (u)	62.50	62.50
BLV60	C52a	(1937)	5c on 35c yel grn	"Carreo" (u)	12.50	—
BLV61	C52b			invtd surch (vc)	—	—
BLV62	C53a		20c on 35c red brn	invtd surch (vc)	17.50	—
BLV63	C54a		50c on 35c red brn	invtd surch (vc)	17.50	—
BLV64	C55a		1b on 35c red brn	invtd surch (vc)	—	—
BLV65	C56a		2b on 50c org & blk	invtd surch (vc)	—	—
BLV66	C57a		12b on 10c ver & blk	invtd surch (vc)	22.50	—
BLV67	C58a		15b on 10c ver & blk	invtd surch (vc)	—	—
BLV68	C61a	(1925)	5b on 2b org (G)	dbl surch (vc)	90.00	—
BLV69	C62a		10b on 5b blk brn	dbl surch (vc)	35.00	—
BLV70	C89a		5b magenta	dbl impression (u)	—	—
BLV71	C128a	(1950)	4b on 10c red	invtd surch (vc)	17.50	17.50
BLV72	C129a		10b on 20b dp brn	invtd surch (vc)	17.50	17.50
BLV73	C261a	(1966)	10c on 27b	Agraria/Agraria (u)	10.00	—
BLV73a	Sanabria 264a	(1960)		10 B orange surch omitted R	45.00	
BLV74		(1939)	postal tax stamp RA1 5c dull violet	dbl impression (u)	—	—
BLV75	RA		1 printed on gummed side R		20.00	
BLV76	RA-22		3b yellow green	surch shifted to right R	40.00 (block of four)	

Bolivia looks like a fine spot to start an error collection—many types of errors—vc's, double impressions, blue and red surcharges, and inverted centers—some at reasonable prices (under $20). With almost forty errors, come, let's have a ball.

BOTSWANA has produced no errors

BOZNIA AND HERZEGOVNIA

BOZ1	P2	(1913)	purple,	dbl ovpt (vc)	—	—
BOZ1a	126b	(1918)	2h violet	invtd ovpt (vc)	15.00	—
BOZ2	126d			dbl ovpt (vc)	35.00	—
BOZ3	126f			dbl ovpt, one invtd	—	—
BOZ4	127a		2h bright blue	pair, one without ovpt	—	—
BOZ5	127b			invtd ovpt	15.00	—
BOZ6	127c			dbl ovpt	13.00	—

BLV75

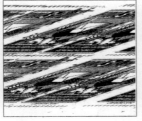

BLV76

BOZ1

BRZ28

BOZ7	127d			dbl ovpt, one invtd	—	—
BOZ8	B5a	(1915)	7h on 5h (R)	"1915" at top & bottom (u)	35.00	37.50
BOZ9	B6a		12h on 10h(bl)	surcharged "7 Heller" (u)	35.00	37.50

Boznia and Herzegovnia do not have much to offer the error collector—a handful of 1918 vc's and some misprinted surcharges. Although not extremely expensive, the country's now non-existence would help explain that.

BOTSWANA has produced no errors

BRAZIL

BRZ1	109a	(1891)	100r blue & red-head	invtd (u) Q=very scarce 100-200 exist	70.00	130.00R
BRZ2	109c		ultrmarine & red	Q=very scarce 100-200 exist.		
BRZ3	1a	(1843)	30r black	in pair with no. 2	—	NA
BRZ4	126a	(1898)	1000r on 700r yel	surcharged "700r" (u)	NA	
BRZ5	131a		300r on 200r blk	dbl surch (vc)	160.00	175.00
BRZ6	132a		200r on 100r violet	dbl surch (vc)	80.00	175.00
BRZ7	132b			invtd surch (vc)	80.00	175.00
BRZ8	135a		1000r on 700r ultra	invtd surch (vc)	200.00	200.00
BRZ9	137a		200r on 100r red lilac	dbl surch (vc)	NA	
BRZ10	139a		100r on 50r green	blue surch	12.50	
BRZ11			Revenue stamp printed by Waterlow	Q=12		—
BRZ12	151a	(1899)	50r on 20r gray grn	dbl surch (vc)	125.00	125.00
BRZ13	152b		100r on 50r gray grn	dbl surch (vc)	100.00	100.00
BRZ14	153a		300r on 200r pur	dbl surch (vc)	NA	
BRZ15	153b			pair, one without surch (u)	NA	
BRZ16	154b		500r on 300r sl vio	pair, one without surch (u)	NA	
BRZ17	155b		700r on 500r ol bis	pair, one without surch (u)	NA	
BRZ18	157a		1000r on 700r fawn	pair, one without surch (u)	NA	
BRZ19	158b		2000r on 1000r yel buff	pair, one without surch (u)	NA	
BRZ20	160a	(1900)	100r rose	frame around inner oval (u)	100.00	4.00
BRZ21	272a	(1924)	200r bl, blk, yel, & red	red omitted (u)	NA	
BRZ22	293a	(1928)	700r on 500r orange	invtd surch (vc)	175.00	175.00
BRZ23	SaE2a	(1929)	300r vio & red	semi-official air		
BRZ24	356b	(1931)	200r on 300r rose red	invtd surch (vc)	40.00	—
BRZ25	357a		200r on 300r rose red	invtd surch (vc)	60.00	60.00
BRZ26	377a	(1933)	200r on 300r rose red	invtd surch (vc)	35.00	—
BRZ27	377b			dbl surch (vc)	35.00	—
BRZ28	713	(1951)	60c orange +brown	left color shift R	6.00	

*air post stamps

BRZ29	C1a	(1927)	50r on 10r	invtd surch (vc)	NA	—
BRZ30	C1b			top ornaments missing (u)	75.00	—
BRZ31-41					all NA	
BRZ42	C28a	(1931)	2500r on 3000r vio	invtd surch (vc)	160.00	—
BRZ43	C28b			surch on front & back (u)	160.00	
BRZ44	C47b	(1942)	5.40cr on 5400r sl grn	surch invtd (vc)	60.00	75.00
BRZ45	C50a	(1943)	1cr blk & dull yel	dbl impression (u)	30.00	
BRZ46	C51a		2cr blk & pale grn	dbl impression (u	40.00	
BRZ47	E1a	(1930)	1000r on 200r dp blue	invtd surch (vc)	NA	
BRZ-Rio Grande do Norte (Sel)		(1912)	Revenue stamp, printed by Waterlow	Q=12 copies known		
BRZ-Semi-Official Airs SakKE2a (Sel)		(1929)	3004 vio & red, Empresa T.A., Airfee stamps			

One will get ill
If he's in Brazil
But an overprint
Will surely end that illness stint   —The Bard

BRITISH ANTARCTIC TERRITORY has produced no errors

BRITISH CENTRAL AFRICA

All nine BCA errors are NA.

All BCA errors are NA - stay away.
If you must trade your car, choose the invert by far. —The Bard

BRITISH EAST AFRICA

All 32 BEA errors but BEA25 are NA.

BEA25	59a		2-1/2 a on 1a 6p bis brown	"1/2" without fraction line	70.00	—

BRITISH GUIANA

BG1-9					all NA	
BG10	108a	(1882)	2c orange	"2 CENTS" double	—	—
BG11	148a	(1890)	1c on $1 grn & blk	dbl surch (vc)	80.00	80.00
BG12	149a		1c on $2 grn & blk	dbl surch (vc)	80.00	80.00
BG13	150a		1c on $3 grn & blk	dbl surch (vc)	80.00	—
BG14	151a		1c on $4 grn & blk, type 1	dbl surch (vc)	80.00	
BG15	151Bc		1c on $4 grn & blk, type II	dbl surch (vc)	—	—
BG16	157a	(1899)	2c on 5c brn & grn	without period	60.00	60.00
BG17	158a		2c on 10c red & bl black	"GENTS"	55.00	75.00
BG18	158b			invtd surch (vc)	NA	
BG19	158c			without period	22.50	45.00
BG20	159a		2c on 15c bl & red brown	without period	50.00	55.00
BG21	159b			dbl surch (vc)	NA	
BG22	159c			invtd surch (vc)	NA	

The early errors of British Guiana are very expensive. Not until the red double surcharges of the 1890's did we achieve affordability. Some of the 1899 "without Period" errors are also affordable. It seems appropriate to pick up a couple of these from this stately nation that has given us the world's rarest stamp, British Guiana No. 13.

BRITISH HONDURAS

BH1-10					all NA	
BH11	34b			"6" only invtd	—	NA
BH12	35a		5c on 3c on 3p brown	dbl surch of "five" & bar	200.00	NA
BH13	37a	(1891)	15c (R) on 6c on 3p blue	dbl surch (vc)	—	—
BH14	48a	(1899)	5c ultramarine	"BEVENUE"	70.00	80.00
BH15	49a		10c lilac & green	"BEVENUE"	190.00	NA
BH16	50a		25c red brn & grn	"BEVENUE"	135.00	135.00
BH17	51a		50c on 1sh gray (no. 32)	"BEVENUE"	NA	
BH18	168a	(1962)	2c gray	green omitted (u)	175.00	—
BH19	169a		3c lt yel green	dark grn (legs) omitted (u)	NA	
BH20	172a		10c beige	blue omitted	NA	
BH21	175b		50c pale blue	blue (beak & claw) omitted	—	—
BH22	182a	(1964)	1c multicolored	yellow omitted (u)	125.00	
BH23	MR1a	(1916-17)	1c green	"WAR" invtd	NA	
BH24	MR3a		3c orange '17	dbl ovpt	NA	

British Honduras produced some variety in its error production—several vc's, 4 "BEVENUE'S" several colors omitted, plus miscellaneous items. Many prices are NA, although a couple colors omitted are affordable to expensive, making this country favorable in comparison to Australia.

BRITISH INDIAN OCEAN TERRITORY has produced no errors

BRUNEI

All five BUN errors are NA.

Brunei has produced five errors, each priced in the thousands of dollars—hardly what you could consider "affordable foreign errors."

AFFORDABLE FOREIGN ERRORS

BULGARIA

BUL1	7a	(1881)	5s black & orange	background invtd (u)	—	NA
BUL2	12a	(1882)	3s orange & yel	background omitted	NA	
BUL3	38a	(1892)	15s on 30s brn	invtd surch (vc)	70.00	52.50
BUL4	40a	(1895)	1s on 2s	invtd surch (vc)	6.00	5.00
BUL5	40b			dbl surch (vc)	62.50	62.50
BUL6	40c			pair, one without surch	125.00	125.00
BUL7	55a	(1901)	5s on 3s bister brn	invtd surch (vc)	42.50	42.50
BUL8	55b			pair, one without surch (u)	70.00	70.00
BUL9	56a		10s on 50s green	invtd surch (vc)	50.00	50.00
BUL10	56b			pair, one without surch (u)	70.00	70.00
BUL11	73a	(1903)	10s on 15s	invtd surch (vc)	57.50	57.50
BUL12	73b			dbl surch (vc)	57.50	57.50
BUL13	73c			pair, one without surch (u)	100.00	100.00
BUL14	73d		10s on 10s rose &		NA	
			& black (u)			
BUL15	77a	(1909)	1s lilac	invtd ovpt (vc)	21.00	17.50
BUL16	77b			dbl ovpt, one invtd (u)	25.00	25.00
BUL17	78a		5s yellow green	invtd ovpt (vc)	25.00	25.00
BUL18	78b			dbl ovpt (vc)	25.00	25.00
BUL19	79a		5s on 30s brown (bk)	"5." dbl (u)	NA	
BUL20	79b			"1990." for "1909." (u)	NA	
BUL21	80a		10s on 15s org (bk)	invtd surch (vc)	17.50	17.50
BUL22	80b			"1909." omitted (u)	27.50	27.50
BUL23	81a		10s on 50s dr grn (R)	"1990." for "1909."(u)	100.00	100.00
BUL24	81b			black surch (u)	52.50	52.50
BUL25	83a		5s on 15s (bl)	invtd surch (vc)	21.00	21.00
BUL26	84a		10s on 15s (bl)	invtd surch (vc)	21.00	21.00
BUL27	85a		25s on 30s (R)	dbl surch (vc)	70.00	70.00
BUL28	85b			"2." of "25." omitted (u)	87.50	87.50
BUL29	85c			blue surch (u)	NA	175.00
BUL30	87a	(1910)	1s on 3s	"1910." omitted (u)	21.00	—
BUL31	97a	(1911)	50s ocher & blk	center inverted, cavalry (u)	NA	
				Q=30 used copies		
BUL32	1196a	(1962)	2s on 20s orange	"2CT." on two lines (u)	.15	.15
BUL33	1197a		3s on 25s brt bl (R)	black surch (u)	7.00	4.00
BUL34	1367	(1964)	2s val & olympic rings	invtd (perf & imperf) (u)		NA
BUL35	3085	(1985)	60s multicolor,		70.00	130.00
			swimming (u)			
BUL36	C4a	(1927-28)	Air Post Stamp 1 l on	invtd surch (vc)	NA	
			6 l dp bl & pale lem (C)			
BUL37	C4b			pair, one without surch (u)	NA	—

Bulgaria seems to have a little of everything although not everything is priced inexpensively. A number of vc's have been produced and the price of some of these is quite reasonable. Also we have inverted backgrounds, an inverted center, a "1909 omitted" and "1910 omitted." We suggest exploring Bulgaria by selecting items other than just vc.

BURKINA FASO

BKF1	8a	(1920-28)	10c claret & bl ('25)	ovpt omitted (u)	80.00	—
BKF2	12a		25c blk & bl grn ('22)	ovpt omitted (u)	65.00	
BKF3	29a	(1922)	0.01c on 15c (bk)	dbl surch (vc)	50.00	50.00

A double surcharge and two overprints omitted—all moderately affordable—represent this country's error story.

BURMA

BUR1	72a	(1947)	9p dull green	invtd ovpt (vc)	12.50	12.50
BUR2	2N9a	(1942)	4a on 4s dk green	4a on 4s + 2s dk green (#B5)	75.00	87.50
BUR3	2N10a		8a on 8s dk pur	red surch	140.00	150.00
			& pale vio			
BUR4	2N12a		2r on 20s ultra	red surch	37.50	37.50
BUR5	2N13a		5r on 30s pck bl	red surch	15.00	15.00
BUR6	2N16a		5c on 1a on 5s	"3C." in blue	75.00	100.00

BUR7	2N17a		5c on 1a on 5s	"3C." in blue	125.00 —
BUR8	2N20a		20c on 8a on 8s (#2N10)	on #2N10a	125.00 100.00
BUR9	2N 23a			"3c" in blue	75.00 87.50
BUR10	2N 24a			"5c" in violet	87.50 100.00
BUR11	2N59a	(Nov.1, 1944)	2c yel green	invtd surch (vc)	150.00 200.00

Burma has produced a few vc's, but its surcharges under Japanese occupation are more interesting. They're handstamped or resurcharges in black, but then resurcharged mostly in red. All of this group (although sometimes expensive) is affordable. For the error collector who has everything, here's something different.

BURUNDI

BRU1	34		3.50 fr on 3fr ultra & red dbl ovpt (vc)		set 85.00R
BRU2	35		6.50fr on 3fr ultra & red	dbl ovpt (vc)	
BRU3	45		2fr brown olive & dk br	invtd ovpt (vc)	(pair) 50.00R
BRU4	46		50fr bright pink & dk br	invtd ovpt R	15.00

See Photo in Color Section

BRU5	B28		4fr + 1fr multi

(28-30 contain Churchill dates, overprint error)

BRU6	B29	15 fr+2fr multi
BRU7	B30	20fr+3fr multi

The chief of Burundi
Bought errors on Sunday.
Most of these were vc's
And kept people displeased
But along came some dates
That were thrown by the fates
On Churchill that were wrong
And the chief sang a song. —The Bard

BUSHIRE

BSH1	N6a	(Aug. 15, 1915)	9c yel brn & vio	dbl ovpt (vc)	NA
BSH2	N9a		1k ultra & car	dbl ovpt (vc)	NA
BSH3	N27a	(Sept. 1915)	5k sil, brn & grn	invtd ovpt (vc)	— —

Three vc's if that's what makes us pleased
Two priced so high they hit the sky
The other is fairer than most any error —The Bard

BRU3

BRU4

BRU5

BRU6

BRU6

BRU7

CHAPTER III: C-F

CAMBODIA

CMB1	76a	(1960)	2r carmine & sepia	Cambodian 20r (u)	1.50	1.50
CMB2	77a		5r ultra & dp brown	Cambodian 20r (u)	2.00	2.00
CMB3	231a	(1970)	3r multicolored	Cambodian & Arabic 3's transposed (u)	3.00	—

CAMEROONS has produced no errors

CAMEROUN

CMR1	54a	(1915)	blue surch, 1/2 p on 5pf grn	dbl surch (vc)	NA	
CMR2	54b			black surch (vc)	12.50	15.00
CMR3	55a		1p on 10pf car	"1." with thin serifs (u)	15.00	17.50
CMR4	55b			dbl surch (vc)	175.00	175.00
CMR5	55c			black surch (vc)	175.00	175.00
CMR6	55d			as "c," "1," with thin serifs (u)	67.50	80.00
CMR7-12					all NA	

Corps Expeditionnaire, Franco-Anglais

CMR13	109a	(1915)	35c dk vio & grn	dbl ovpt (vc)	NA	

Occupation Francaise du Cameroun

CMR14	122a	(1916)	Wmk. Branch of thistle 15c dl vio & ol grm	invtd ovpt (vc)	90.00	90.00
CMR15	137a	(1916-17)	25c blue & grn	triple ovpt (u)	NA	
CMR16	138a		scar & grn	dbl ovpt (vc)	200.00	—
CMR17	150a	(1921)	5c dl red & org	dbl ovpt (vc)	NA	
CMR18	166a	(1924-25)	25c on 5fr red & gray	pair, one without new value & bars (u)	—	—
CMR19	209a		5 fr brn & blk, bluish	cliche of 2 fr in plate of 5 fr (u)	NA	
CMR20	261b	(1940)	25c blk brn	invtd ovpt (vc)	110.00	110.00
CMR21	264a		50c lt grn & cer	invtd ovpt (vc)	125.00	—
CMR22	298a	(1946)	60c on 5c (R)	invtd surch (vc)	60.00	—
CMR23	C61	(1966)	200 fr ultra & dk purple	missing period, R	20.00	

Cameroun has produced its share of vc's and three interesting other items; a triple overprint (u), a cliche (u) and reverse "S" overprints (u). We have not seen reverse "S"s before and are attracted to both triple overprints and cliches. Price, however, rules all three out (all NA).

There are a few vc's within the NA limit, but the country does not offer any affordable unique or unusual items. If this volume focused attention on "anything is affordable" we'd be strongly inclined to acquire the three items in question.

BRITISH COLUMBIA & VANCOUVER IS. have produced no errors

NEWFOUNDLAND

NWF1	127a	(1920)	127a 2c on 30c slate	invtd surch (vc)	NA	
NWF2	128a		3c on 15c scar (I)	invtd surch (vc)	NA	
NWF3	130a		3c on 35c red (II)	lower bar omitted (u)	110.00	110.00
NWF3	160a	(1929)	3c on 6c gray black (II)	invtd surch (II)(vc) (R)	NA	
NWF4	163a		1c green	dbl impression (u)	NA	
NWF5	163b			vert. Pair, imperf. btwn (u)	160.00	—
NWF6	211a	(1933)	15c brown	pair, one without ovpt (U)	NA	
NWF7	211b			ovpt reading up (u)	NA	
NWF8	237a	(1937)	10c olive gray	dbl impression (u)	—	—
NWF9	C2a	(1919)	$1 on 15c scarlet	without comma after "Post" (u)	175.00	200.00
NWF10	C3a	(1921)	35c red	with period after "1921" (vc)	125.00	140.00
NWF11-14					all NA	

**Newfoundland's high
It reaches the sky
It's not a good buy
Lest you're a rich guy. —The Bard**

NOVA SCOTIA has produced no errors

PRINCE EDWARD ISLAND

PED1	2b	(1861, Jan. 1)	3 p blue	dbl impression (u)	NA	
PED2	5f	(1862-65)	2p rose	"TWC" for "TWO" (u)	45.00	22.50

**Only 2 errors from old Prince Ed
The first one's nice, but high it's said
But if you'd take a TWC for TWO
It won't be very costly for you. —The Bard**

CANADA

CAN1	36f	(1870-89)	2c green ('72)	dbl impression (u)	—	—
CAN2	139a	(1926)	2c on 3c carmine	pair, one without surch (vc)	NA	
CAN3	139b			dbl surch (vc)	175.00	
CAN4	140b			triple surch (u)	175.00	
CAN5-18, 20-22 are all NA						
CAN18	1376b			engraved inscriptions invtd	—	
CAN19	C3a		6c on 5c brown olive	invtd surch (vc)	150.00	
CAN23-32 The same error, no period after "S"						
CAN24	CO1a	(1949)	7c deep blue		85.00	45.00
CAN25			Official Stamps	O1a 1c green	45.00	45.00
CAN26	O2a		2c brown		62.50	62.50
CAN27	O6a		10c olive		50.00	45.00
CAN28	O7a		14c black brown		67.50	62.50
CAN29	O8a		20c slate black		80.00	75.00
CAN30	O9a		50c dk blue-green		NA	
CAN31	O10a		$1 red violet		NA	
CAN32	O15a	(1950)	5c deep blue		47.50	45.00
CAN33	O26a	(1950-51)	10c black brown	pair, one without "G"	NA	
CAN34	O47a	(1963, May 15)	2c green	pair, one without "G"	NA	

Canada has four basic characteristics. First, most of its "errors" are imperfs, which in Chapter I we indicated were not "mistakes" but made for collectors as they are in France or Burkina Faso. Second, these are expensive although not always above the NA cutoff. Third, there are several "inscription" or "color" omitted errors. Fourth we are finding a number of Canadian errors in recent years whereas errors in many many countries end about 1970.

**Up there they sing "O Canada"
And of imperfs galore
And recent errors too, can it be true
Of stamps they want e'er more? —The Bard**

CAPE JUBY

CPJ1	8a	(1919)	2c dk brn (Bk)	dbl ovpt (vc)	17.50	7.50
CPJ2	8b			dbl ovpt (Bk + (R)	45.00	32.50
CPJ3	9a		5c green (R)	dbl ovpt (vc)	17.50	7.50

CMR6

CPV15a

CPV15b

CPV18

CPV4

AFFORDABLE FOREIGN ERRORS

CPJ4	9b			invtd ovpt (vc)	24.00	16.00
CPJ5	10a		10c car (Bk)	dbl ovpt (Bk + R) (vc)	45.00	32.50
CPJ6	11b		15c ocher (Bk)	dbl ovpt (vc)	17.50	7.50
CPJ7	13a		25c dp bl (R)	dbl ovpt (vc)	17.50	7.50
Special Delivery Stamps						
CPJ8	E1b	(1919)	20c red (Bk)	dbl ovpt (vc)	21.00	12.50

All Cape Juby are overprints—vc's with one exception—a double overprint, red and one black. ALL of the errors are fairly inexpensive, making this a good place to start for the error collector, if he doesn't mind the fact they're all vc's.

CAPE OF GOOD HOPE

CGH1-9, 11-14, 18-28 are all NA
Surcharged in Black

CGH10	32a	(1880)	3p on 3p lilac rose	invtd surch (vc)	NA	37.50
CGH15	55a	(1891)	2 -1/2 p on 3p vio rose	"1" of 1/2 has straight serif	50.00	32.50
CGH16	58a	(1893, Mar.)	1p on 2p bister	dbl surch (vc)	NA	
CGH17	58b			no period after "PENNY"	40.00	14.00

CAPE VERDE

CPV1	5a	(1877)	40r blue	cliche of Mozambique in Cape Verde plate, in pair with #5	NA	
CPV2	5b			as "a," perf 13 -1/2	NA	
CPV3	13b	(1881-85)	40r yellow buff	cliche of Mozambique in Cape Verde plate, in pair with #13	50.00	50.00
CPV4	13c			as "b," imperf., error circled in red ink, R	15.00	

See Photo in Color Section

CPV5	71a		On issue of 1894 115r on 5r orange	invtd surch (vc)	40.00	40.00
CPV6	77a		400r on 50r light blue	invtd surch (vc)	65.00	55.00
CPV7	79a		On Newspaper Stamp of 1893 400r on 2-1/2 r brown	invtd surch (vc)	30.00	20.00
CPV8	83a		75 rose ('03)	invtd ovpt (vc)	40.00	40.00
CPV9	43	(1903)	25r carmin & blk	inscription invtd, invtd center	—	—
CPV10	139a	(1914)	75r rose	"PROVISORIO" dbl (G & R)	45.00	40.00
CPV11	188a	(1915)	115r on 5r orange	invtd ovpt (vc)	30.00	—
CPV12	192a		130r on 80r yel grn	invtd ovpt (vc)	30.00	—
CPV13	195a	(1921)	1/2 c on 1c green	"1/2," instead of " -1/2," as shown	10.00	10.00
CPV14	198a		4c on 10c on 100r	on no. 118 (error)	150.00	150.00
CPV15	200a		6c on 100r dk bl, bl	no accent on "U" of surch	12.50	8.00
(No. 200 has an accent on the "U" of the surcharge.)						
CPV15a	215var		1cpa	"1 c," dbl R	15.00	
CPV15b	260var			purple p "crto" instead of "porto" R	4.00	
CPV16	276a	(1951, May 21)	2e on 10e	1e on 10e	225.00	175.00
CPV17	RA14a	(1971)	50c on 1c org (Bl)	black surch ('68?) (vc)	7.50	8.75
CPV18	RA15c	(1969)	50c on 2c org (Bk)	invtd surch (vc) R	85.00	
CPV19	RA20a	(1971)	1e on 2c org (G)	blue surch ('71)	1.10	.60
CPV20	RA20b			black surch	3.50	3.00

Like Angola and the Azores, Cape Verde is in the Portuguese group and has similar philatelic patterns, though not all are necessarily errors. One can categorize Cape Verde as a "generalist" with: (1) four cliches, 2 NA and 2 not NA; (2) a number of vc's at various (moderate) prices; and (3) low priced (u) scattered items. Most countries do not have low (medium) cliches if they have any at all— a real opportunity.

Cape Verde has four cliches.
Each one neatly kept in trays
Two are surely high NA's
While for the others we all can pay. —The Bard

CAROLINE ISLANDS

CAR1-2, 5-8 are all NA

CAR3	3a		10pf carmine	75.00	150.00
CAR4	4a		20pf ultra	75.00	150.00

CASTELLORIZO

Used values in italics are for postally used copies. Stamps with CTO or fake cancels sell for about the same as hinged, unused stamps. Stamps of French offices in Turkey overprinted:

CAS1	1a	(1920)	1c gray	invtd ovpt (vc)	65.00	65.00
CAS2	2b			dbl ovpt (vc)	80.00	80.00
CAS3	3a		3c red orange	invtd ovpt (vc)	65.00	65.00
CAS4	4a		5c green	invtd ovpt (vc)	65.00	65.00
CAS5	6a		15c pale red	invtd ovpt (vc)	110.00	110.00
CAS6-10				all NA		

On stamps of France:

CAS11	30a		10c red	invtd ovpt (vc)	—	100.00
CAS12	31a		25c blue (R)	invtd ovpt (vc)	—	100.00
CAS13	54a	(1922)	20c brn org	dbl ovpt (vc)	—	100.00
CAS14	72a	(1924)	60c carmine	dbl ovpt (vc)	60.00	—

Castellorizo's all vc
Not another error to see
But most vc's are <u>not</u> NA
So let's go get some—whad'ya say! —The Bard

CAYMAN ISLANDS

CAY1-6 are either NA or not priced

CAY7		(1967, Dec. 1)	4p multi & gold	gold omitted	100.00	—
CAY8		(1968, Nov. 18)	203a 1/4 brown & multi	gold omitted	190.00	—
CAY9	MR1	(1917, Feb. 26)	War Tax stamps 1-1/2 p on 2-1/2 p	fraction bar omitted	70.00	110.00

Errors skit across the Grand Cay
Where all philatelists come out to play,
An affordable here, an affordable there
Makes our collecting so just and so fair.

CENTRAL AFRICA

Elvis Presley Error Collection (X)
Overprint Scott 851A; 851B 1987
Unlisted in Minkus—All prices (w) and for mint (from Sellinger)

CAF1	70fr invtd Elvis Presley	perf Q=40	65.00
CAF2	70fr invtd Elvis Presley	imperf Q=40	85.00
CAF3	485fr invtd '485'	perf Q=60	60.00
See Photo in Color Section			
CAF4	485fr dlb ovpt '485'	perf. Q=40	75.00
CAF5	485fr invtd Elvis Presley	perf Q=60	60.00
CAF6	485fr invtd Elvis Presley	imperf Q=60	80.00
CAF7	485fr dbl ovpt "485F"	imperf Q=20	125.00
CAF8	s/s 70fr invtd Elvis Presley	perf Q=9	NA
CAF9	s/s 485fr invtd Elvis	perf Q=19	125.00
CAF10	s/s 485fr invtd Elvis Presley	imperf Q=15	135.00
CAF11	70fr invtd Elvis Presley	perf Q=80	100.00 red ovpt (R*)

* the "R" here is for "red" not "retail"

CAF12	70fr invtd Elvis Presley	perf Q=20	135.00 (R)
CAF13	485fr invtd Elvis Presley	perf Q=80	85.00 (R)
CAF14	485 invtd Elvis Presley	imperf Q=40	135.00 (R)
CAF15	485fr invtd Elvis Presley	485 perf Q=20	125.00 (R)
CAF16	485fr invtd Elvis Presley	485 fr Q=20	140.00 (R)
CAF17	485fr dbl "485" w/invtd Elvis	perf Q=20	125.00 (R)
CAF18	invtd "485f"	imperf Q=20	140.00 (R)

CAF19		485fr db "485" one invtd	imperf Q=20	140.00 (R)	
CAF20		s/s 70 Elvis invtd	Q=8 (R)		NA
CAF21		s/s 485 invtd	Q=9 (R)		NA
CAF22	C61	multicolor	dbl surch R	150.00	

See Photo in Color Section

Elvis presents a long series of errors like nothing we have seen before. These errors are not inexpensive, but the errors are not listed in major catalogues like Minkus. Nonetheless, all twenty-one errors have been expertized by the distinquished Alex Rendon, a member of the Association Internationale des Experts Philateliques.

CENTRAL LITHUANIA

CLI1	13a	(1920, Nov.23)	2m on 15sk lil	invtd surch (vc)	125.00	
CLI2	14a		4m on 10sk red	invtd surch (vc)	125.00	
CLI3	15a		4m on 20 sk dl bl (Bk)	invtd surch (vc)	125.00	
CLI4	16a		4m on 30 sk buff	invtd surch (vc)	125.00	
CLI5	17a		6m on 50sk lt grn	4m on 50 sk	125.00	
CLI6	17b		10m on 50sk (error)		125.00	—
CLI7	18a		6m on 60sk vio & red	4m on 60sk (error)	125.00	
CLI8	18b			10m on 60sk (error)	125.00	
CLI9	19a		6m on 75sk bis & red	4m on 75sk (error)	125.00	
CLI10	19b		10m on 75sk (error)		125.00	
CLI11	20a		10m on 1auk gray & red	invtd surch (vc)	190.00	

Central Lithuania has produced two distinct types of errors: (1) vc's and (2) wrong denomination overprint errors. Both are expensive but affordable. Nothing exciting—no errors other than overprint errors for this obscure country.

CEYLON

CEY1-5, 7-10				all NA	
CEY6	109a	30c on36c	invtd surch (vc)	200.00	100.00
CEY11	119a	5c on 16c vio	invtd surch (vc)	—	NA
CEY12	143a	(1888-90) 2c on 4c lilac rose (vc)		14.00	14.00
CEY13	143b		dbl surch, one invtd (vc)	—	110.00
CEY14	144a	2c on 4c rose	invtd surch (vc)	12.50	12.50
CEY15	144b		dbl surch (vc)	—	125.00

CAF1

CAF2

CAF3

CAF11

CAF12

CAF13

CAF17

CEY16	145a		2c on 4c lilac rose	invtd surch (vc)	27.50	27.50
CEY17	145b			dbl surch (vc)	35.00	35.00
CEY18	145c			dbl surch, one invtd	35.00	30.00
CEY19	146a		2c on 4c rose	dbl surch, one invtd	40.00	45.00
CEY20	146b			dbl surch (vc)	35.00	40.00
CEY21	146c			invtd surch (vc)	125.00	—
CEY22	147a		2c on 4c lilac rose	invtd surch (vc)	65.00	35.00
CEY23	147b			dbl surch, one invtd	85.00	—
CEY24	148a		2c on 4c rose	invtd surch (vc)	8.50	8.00
CEY25	148b			dbl surch, one invtd	8.00	8.00
CEY26	148c			dbl surch (vc)	—	—
CEY27	149a		2c on 4c lilac rose	invtd surch (vc)	70.00	30.00
CEY28	150a		2c on 4c rose	invtd surch (vc)	10.00	5.50
CEY29	150b			dbl surch (vc)	50.00	55.00
CEY30	150c			dbl surch, one invtd	10.00	5.50
CEY31	151a		2c on 4c rose	invtd surch (vc)	11.00	5.50
CEY32	151b			dbl surch (vc)	50.00	45.00
CEY33	151c			dbl surch, one invtd	13.00	8.00
CEY34	151i			"S" of "Cents" invtd	—	95.00
CEY35	151De		2c on 4c lilac rose	invtd surch (vc)	47.50	40.00
CEY36	151Df			dbl surch (vc)	—	125.00
CEY37	151Dg			dbl surch, one invtd	55.00	55.00
CEY38	151Dh			"S" of "Cents" invtd	—	—
CEY39	152a	(1890)	5c on 15c ol green	"fIve" instead of "five"	85.00	75.00
CEY40	152b			"REVENUE" omitted	85.00	75.00
CEY41	152c			invtd surch	25.00	27.50
CEY42	152d			dbl surch (vc)	90.00	90.00
CEY43	152e			as "a" invtd surch (vc)	—	NA
CEY44	152f			invtd "s" in "Cents"	30.00	35.00
CEY45	152g			as "f," invtd surch	NA	
CEY46	152h			as "b," invtd "s" in "Cents"	NA	
CEY47	156a	(1892)	3c on 4c rose	dbl surch, one invtd	—	—
CEY48	157a		3c on 28c slate	dbl surch (vc)	80.00	—
CEY49	248a	(1926)	2c on 3c slate	dbl surch (vc)	40.00	40.00
CEY50	248b			bar omitted (vc)	27.50	—
CEY51	249a		5c on 6c violet	dbl surch	—	—

CHD17

CHD19

CHD20

CEY52	338a	(1958, Jan.15)	4c dp blue & lt yel	invtd ovpt (vc)	12.50	—
CEY53	338b			dbl ovpt (vc)	12.50	—
CEY54	339a		10c dk gray, yel & brt pink	invtd ovpt (vc)	20.00	—
CEY55	368a	(1963, June 1)	2c on 4c brt red & choc	invtd surch (vc)	25.00	
CEY56	368b			dbl surch (vc)	17.50	—
CEY57	377a	(1964-69)	60c yel & multi	blue omitted	50.00	—
CEY58	377b			red omitted	50.00	—
CEY59	378b		75c ol, blk, org & brn	as "a" overprinted	1.00	—
CEY60	379c		1r brown & grn	brown omitted	125.00	—
CEY61	MR1a	(1918)	WAR TAX STAMPS 2c brn orange	dbl ovpt (vc)	40.00	35.00
CEY62	MR1b			invtd ovpt (vc)	40.00	35.00
CEY63	MR2b		3c dp grn (Die 1a, type)	dbl ovpt (Die 1) (vc)	80.00	80.00
CEY64	MR3a		5c red violet	dbl ovpt (vc)	30.00	30.00
CEY65	MR3b			invtd ovpt (vc)	40.00	40.00
CEY66	MR4a		1c on 5c red violet	dbl ovpt (vc)	—	—

VC is the name for thee—almost. An overwhelming number of Ceylon's earlier stamps are vc's and a number inexpensive (145a, b, and c for example). Later (1964-9) blue, red and brown are all omitted— and affordable too—joining Ceylon with its commonwealth counterparts: Canada, Cayman Islands and Malta.

Red, brown and blue
Ceylon misses all three of you.
It also has its vc's too
What a mix of errors too? —The Bard

CHAD

CHD1	1a	(1922)	1c red & violet	ovpt omitted	100.00	—
CHD2	2a		2c ol brn & salmon	ovpt omitted	140.00	—
CHD3	14a		60c on 75c vio, *pnksh*	"TCHAD," omitted	140.00	—
CHD4	14b			"60" omitted,	140.00	—
CHD5	19a	(1924-33)	1c red & vio	"TCHAD" omitted (vc)	75.00	—
CHD6	19b			dbl ovpt (vc)	110.00	—
CHD7	20a		2c ol brn & sal	"TCHAD" omitted (vc)	75.00	—
CHD8	21a		4c ind & vio	"TCHAD" omitted	NA	—
CHD9	22a		5c choc & grn (bl)	"TCHAD" omitted	75.00	—
CHD10	23a		5c choc & grn	"TCHAD" omitted	100.00	—
CHD11	32a		30c dk grn & grn ('27)	"Afrique Equatoriale Francaise" omitted	175.00	—
CHD12	35a		45c vio & grn	dbl ovpt (R + Bk)	125.00	—
CHD13	36a		50c dk bl & pale bl	invtd ovpt (vc)	72.50	—
CHD14	40a		75c dp bl & lt bl (R) ('25)	"TCHAD" omitted	125.00	—
CHD15	51a	(1924-27)	60c on 75c dk vio	pnksh "60." omitted	90.00	—

CHD21

CHD22

CHD16	55a		1.25fr on1fr dk bl & ultra (R) (´26)	"Afrique Equatoriale Francaise" omitted	80.00	
CHD17	231A, 231C	(1971)	multicolor, uncut gutter pair R			65.00
CHD18	231			B missing color (and normal) R	50.00	
CHD19	232	(1971-3)		missing color & (multicolor normal)		
CHD20	233			dbl impression		

See Photo in Color Section

CHD21	244AF		multicolor	invtd "Christmas 1971" in gold Q=9	175.00R	
CHD22	244A			F missing color		
CHD23	246A-C	(1972)	multicolor	imperf & invert-exp		120.00R
CHD24	251E			multicolor-gold dbl overprint+ missing part (vc) R	55.00	

See Photo in Color Section

Some philatelics, that's too bad
Grace the stamps of the Chad
But there are many beauties, too
That would win the hearts of me and you. —The Bard

CHILE

CHI1	9d	(1858)	5c rose red	printed both sides (u)	—	NA
CHI2	9e			dbl impression (u)	—	—
CHI3	11a	(1862)	1c lemon yellow	dbl impression (u)	—	NA
CHI4	14b	(1865)	5c rose red	printed on both sides (u)	NA	
CHI5	14d			dbl impression (u)	—	165.00
CHI6	48a	(1901)	5c dull blue	printed on both sides(u)	—	—
CHI7	50a	(1900)	5c on 30c rose car	invtd surch (vc)	27.50	14.00
CHI8	50b			dbl surch (vc)	90.00	57.50
CHI9	50c			dbl surch, both invtd	90.00	57.50
CHI10	50d			dbl ssurch, one invtd	90.00	57.50
CHI11	50e			surcharged on front & back	90.00	57.50
CHI12	57a	(1903)	10c on 30 c orange	invtd surch (vc)	17.50	10.50
CHI13	57b			dbl surch (vc)	21.00	10.50
CHI14	57c			dbl surch, one invtd	21.00	10.50
CHI15	57d			dbl surch, both invtd	21.00	10.50
CHI16	57e			stamp design printed on both sides	—	—
CHI17	58b	(1904)	1c on 20c ultra	invtd surch (vc)	42.50	42.50
CHI18	59a		2c yel brn,	invtd ovpt (vc)	17.50	17.50
CHI18a (block of 4)	59			misplaced surch R	12.00	
CHI19	59b			pair, one without ovpt	42.50	42.50
CHI20	60a		5c red,	invtd ovpt, (vc)	17.50	17.50

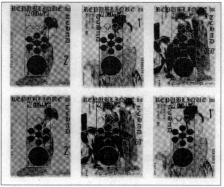

CHD23

CHI18a

AFFORDABLE FOREIGN ERRORS

CHI21	60c			pair, one without ovpt	42.50	42.50
CHI22	61a		10c ol grn,	invtd ovpt (vc)	42.50	42.50
CHI23	63a		3c on 5c brn red	invtd surch (vc)	—	—
CHI24	65a		5c red.	invtd surch (vc)	—	—
CHI25	67a		12c on 5c brn red	no star at left of "Centavos"	1.90	1.25
CHI26	67b			invtd surch (vc)	35.00	35.00
CHI27	67c			dbl surch (vc)	42.50	42.50
CHI28-30, 32-34 are all NA						
CHI31	105a		20c org & blk	center invtd (u)	60.00	60.00
CHI35	O9a	(1907)	1c green	invtd ovpt (vc)	17.50	
CHI36	O10a		3c on 1p brn	invtd ovpt (vc)	52.50	
CHI37	O11a		5c ultra	invtd ovpt (vc)	35.00	
CHI38	J48	(1924)	2c red & blue	Q>200	up to 30.00	
CHI38-48 are all invtd centers						
CHI39	J49		4c red & blue			
CHI40	J50		8c red & blue			
CHI41	J51		10c red & blue			
CHI42	J52		20c red & blue			
CHI43	J53		40c red & blue			
CHI44	J54		60c red & blue			
CHI45	J55		80c red & blue			
CHI46	J56		1P red & blue			
CHI47	J57		2P red & blue			
CHI48	J58		5P red & blue			
CHI49	Revenue		(1907)	(Sel.) 1p consular issue all invtd centers		
CHI50	2p		consular issue			
CHI51	5p		consular issue			
CHI52	10p		consular issue			
CHI53			consular issue			

Chile hot, Chile cold, what kinds of Chile sold
As usual vc's that never please
But then printed on front and back
That presents a dazzling attack
Then the center invert comes along—
What a beautiful song.
Finally comes the impression double
Which all errorists love to see.

CHINA

CHA1-2, 4-23 are all NA						
CHA3	28a	(1897)	1/2 c on 3c	"1," instead of "1/2" (vc)	190.00	
CHA24	78a		1c on 3c red	no period after "cent" (u)	125.00	100.00
CHA25	78b			central character with large "box" (u)	110.00	90.00
CHA26	79a		2c on 3c red	invtd surch (vc)	NA	
CHA27	79b			invtd "S" in "CENTS" (vc)	200.00	150.00
CHA28	79c			no period after "CENTS"	200.00	140.00
CHA29	79d			comma after "CENTS"	200.00	140.00
CHA30-35					all NA	
CHA36	146a	(1912)	1/2 c brn	invtd ovpt (vc)	25.00	25.00
CHA37	146b			dbl ovpt (vc)	60.00	—
CHA38	147b		1c ocher (R)	invtd ovpt (vc)	95.00	60.00
CHA39	147c			dbl ovpt (vc)	110.00	90.00
CHA40	149a		3c slate grn (R)	invtd ovpt (vc)	65.00	35.00
CHA41	153a		10c ultra (R)	dbl ovpt (vc)	110.00	—
CHA42	153b			pair, one without ovpt	NA	
CHA43	153d			invtd ovpt (vc)	150.00	150.00
CHA44	158a		$1 red & pale rose	invtd ovpt (u)	NA	
CHA45	159a		$2 brn red & yel	invtd ovpt (u)	175.00	175.00
CHA46	161a		1c ocher	invtd ovpt (vc)	90.00	90.00
CHA47	161c			dbl ovpt (vc)	95.00	—
CHA48	162 a		2c green	invtd ovpt (vc)	NA	

CHA49	166a		3c slate grn (C)	invtd ovpt (vc)	NA	
CHA50	237a	(1915)	$2 blue & blk	center invtd (u)	NA	
CHA51	274a	(1925)	3c on 4c gray	invtd surch (vc)	NA	
CHA52	289a	(1930)	1c on 3c blue green	no period after "Ct"	17.50	17.50
CHA53	325a	(1933)	1c on 4c olive green	no period after "Ct"	17.50	17.50
CHA54	461a	(1941)	$2 blue & blk	center invtd (u)	NA	
CHA55	484r	(1941)	7c on 8c (#383) (h7)	without (star) in uniform button (u)	65.00	
CHA56	489r	(1942)	40c on 50c dk bl (#386)	invtd surch (Yunnan) (vc)	90.00	—
CHA57	525s		16c (Bk)	invtd ovpt (Shensi) (vc)	175.00	—
CHA58	527r		50c on 16c (Bk) (c,f)	invtd surch (W. Szech.) (vc)	110.00	—
CHA59	527s			"k" surch on #493) (u)	110.00	—
CHA60	528r		50c on 16c (R)	invtd surch (Kweichow) (u)	90.00	—
CHA61	528s			"p" surch on #526(f) (u)	110.00	110.00
CHA62	530r	(1943)	50c on 16c (C)	invtd surch (Hunan) (vc)	40.00	—
CHA63	530s			"05," instead of "50," (Kweichow) (u)	NA	
CHA64	623a	(1945)	$20 on 40c orange	green surch invtd	60.00	—
CHA65	672a	(1946-47)	$100 on 1c (#422)	without secret mark (#422a) (u)	65.00	65.00
CHA66	676a		$100 on 8c (#383)	without "star" in uniform button (#383a)	25.00	16.00
CHA67	703a	(1946-48)	$20 on 8c (#383)	without "star" in uniform button (no. 383a)	4.50	4.50
CHA68	703b			invtd surch (vc)	20.00	—
CHA69	703c			dbl surch, one on back (u)	32.50	32.50
CHA70	703d			dbl surch (vc)	32.50	—
CHA71	706a		$20 on 8c (#454)	invtd surch (vc)	13.00	—
CHA72	706b			dbl surch (vc)	13.00	—
CHA73	708a		$50 on 5c (#352)	invtd surch	27.50	—
CHA74	711a		$50 on 5c (#427)	invtd surch (vc)	27.50	—
CHA75	712a		$50 on 5c (#452)	dbl surch (vc)	16.00	—
CHA76	715a	(1946)	$10 on 1c org (#422)	without secret mark (#422a) (u)	10.00	12.00
CHA77	715b			invtd surch (vc)	8.00	10.00
CHA78	716a		$10 on 1c org (#450)	dbl surch (vc)	27.50	—
CHA79	718a		$20 on 2c brt ultra (R) (#451)	invtd surch (vc)	20.00	—
CHA80	718b			dbl surch (vc)	16.00	—
CHA81	719a		$20 on 3c dl cl (#350)	dbl surch (vc)	22.50	—
CHA82	721a		$30 on 4c pale vio (R)(#426)	invtd surch (vc)	9.00	—
CHA83	829a	(1948-49)	5c on $30 (C) (#626)	dbl surch (vc)	16.00	—
CHA84	839a		10c on $70 (#573)	dbl surch (vc)	13.00	—
CHA85	845a		20c on $100 (#640)	invtd surch (vc)	19.00	—
CHA86	845b			dbl surch (vc)	14.00	—
CHA87	847a		50c on 1/2 c (#421)	invtd surch (vc)	27.50	—
CHA88	919b	(1949)	$10 on $30 dk vio, III (Bl)	dbl surch, (vc)	—	—
CHA89	967a		10c on $1000 car	invtd surch (vc)	60.00	—
CHA90	968b		20c on $1000 red (V)	invtd surch (vc)	27.50	—
CHA91	993a		2-1/2 c on $500 rose III (892)	invtd surch (vc)	35.00	—
CHA92	995a		15c on $10 grn (887)	invtd surch (vc)	40.00	—
CHA93	1058a	(1952)	3c on 10c dp lil	invtd surch (vc)	—	—
CHA94	1258a	(1960, June 18)	$2 grn	invtd ovpt (vc)	200.00	200.00
CHA95	B13a		$15,000 & $2000 gray	cross omitted, without gum	—	—
CHA96	C48a	(1946)	$23 on 30c lt red	invtd surch (vc)	100.00	—
CHA97	C48b			"2300." omitted	100.00	—
CHA98	C48c			last character (kuo) of surch omitted	65.00	—
CHA99	C50a		$73 on 25c lt orange	invtd surch (vc)	NA	
CHA100	C52a		$200 on $5 lake	invtd surch (vc)	80.00	—

CHA101	J26b	(1912)	1c brown	invtd ovpt (vc)	175.00	—
CHA102	J30a		5c brown	invtd ovpt (vc)	150.00	125.00
CHA103	J36a		1c brown	invtd ovpt (vc)	175.00	150.00
CHA104	M11a	(1944)	8c olive green	right character invtd	165.00	—

China has turned out a mass of stamps and the recent ones (as with most countries) are relatively error-free.

Taiwan (Republic of China)

CHN1	3a	(1945)	10s pale blue	invtd ovpt (vc)	85.00	—
CHN2	3b			dbl ovpt (vc)	95.00	—
CHN3	9a		10y brown vio	invtd ovpt (vc)	150.00	—
CHN4	10a	(1946)	70s on $20 green (vc)		150.00	—
CHN5	20a	(1946-47)	1y on 20c lt bl	invtd surch (vc)	70.00	—
CHN6	92a	(1949-50)	5c on $44 (RV) ('50)	violet surch	40.00	6.50
CHN7	94a		20c on $44 (Bk)	dbl surch (vc)	65.00	—
CHN8	1N1a	(1942)	2c olive green	invtd ovpt (vc)	65.00	—
CHN9	1N14a		1c orange	invtd ovpt (vc)	65.00	65.00
CHN10	1NJ1a	(1945)	$100 on $2 yel org	nvtd surch (vc)	NA	—
CHN11	2N62a	(1942)	4c on 8c (#353)	invtd surch (vc)	55.00	55.00
CHN12	2N66a		50c on k$1 (#359)	on no. 347,	45.00	45.00
CHN13	2N66b			on no. 344	NA	
CHN14	2N69a		15c on 30c (#385)	invtd surch (vc)	55.00	55.00
CHN15	2N115a	(1945)	10c on 1c org (#2N43a)(R)	without secret mark (China #313)	32.50	32.50
CHN16	2N116b		50c on 2c ol grn (#2N1a) (Bk)	on #2n1	20.00	20.00
CHN17	2N122a	(1945)	10c on 1c orange (R)	on #2N33	16.00	22.50
CHN18	7N15a	(1941)	$1 #359. II	on no. 347, I	140.00	140.00
CHN19	8N19a	(1942)	15c on 30c scar	invtd surch (vc)	65.00	65.00
CHN20	8N43		2c on 4c dl grn	invtd surch (vc)	35.00	—
CHN21	8N49a		20c on 40c orange	invtd surch (vc)	45.00	—
CHN22	8N78a		40c brt orange	invtd ovpt (vc)	35.00	35.00
CHN23	8N90a	(1944)	$1 org brn & sepia	red ovpt invtd (vc)	30.00	30.00
CHN24	C2a				NA	

Sinkiang

CHN25	16a		$1 ocher & blk (R)	second & third characters of ovpt transposed	NA	

Tibet

CHN26	1a	(1911)	3p on 1c ocher	invtd surch (vc)	NA	
CHN27	6a		3a on 16c ol grn	large "S" in "Annas"	NA	

China, People's Republic Of

CHN28	3L65a	(1949, Apr.)	$50 on $109 dk grn, surch 15mm wide (R)	surch 13mm wide	27.50	8.00
CHN29	3LQ 15a		$30 on $2 dk grn	red surch	20.00	7.00
CHN30	4L7a	(1946, Nov.)	$30 on $1 grn	rectangular lower left character	NA	
CHN31	4L65a	(1949, Oct. 15)	$50 rose	$200 cliche in $50 plate (u)	*175.00*	—
CHN32	5L13a		$5 pale brn (ovpt 4 x 4mm)	without ovpt	60.00	60.00
CHN33	5L44c	(1949, May 4)	$3 on $20 vio brn	surch invtd (vc)	200.00	—
CHN34	5L51a		$5 on 50c on $20 brn II (B)	grn surch	100.00	*50.00*

CHRISTMAS ISLAND has produced no errors

CILICIA

CIL1	76		30pa on rose	dbl ovpt (vc) R	20.00	
CIL1a	100a	(1920)	20pa on 10c rose red	"PARAS" omitted	9.00	9.00
CIL2	100b			surcharged on back	1.65	1.65
CIL2a			5pa orange	invtd ovpt R	20.00	
CIL2B				5pa dbl ovpt, one invtd R	20.00	

CIL3	117a		5pa on 2c vio brn	invtd surch (vc)	5.00	4.75
CIL4	117 b			dbl surch	6.00	—
CIL5	117c			"Cililie"	4.75	4.75
CIL6	117d			surch 5pi (error)	10.00	10.00
CIL7	119a		10pa on 5c grn	invtd surch (vc)	5.00	4.50
CIL8	119b			surch 10pa (error) invtd	11.00	11.00
CIL9	121a		20pa on 10c red	invtd surch (vc)	5.00	4.50
CIL10	121b			surch 10pa (error) invtd	11.00	11.00
CIL11	122a		1pi on 25c blue	dbl surch (vc)	8.00	—
CIL12	122b			invtd surch (vc)	5.00	4.50
CIL13	123a		2pi on 15c gray grn	dbl surch (vc)	8.00	—
CIL14	123b			invtd surch (vc)	5.00	4.50
CIL15	124a		5pi on 40c red & gray bl	dbl surch (vc)	12.00	—
CIL16	124b			invtd surch (vc)	7.00	6.50
CIL17	124c			"PIASTRES"	10.00	10.00
CIL18	125a		10pi on 50c bis brn & lavender	"PIASTRES"	10.00	10.00
CIL19	126a		50pi on 1fr claret & ol grn	"PIASTRES"	12.50	12.50
CIL20	126b			invtd surch (vc)	14.00	12.00
CIL21	127a		100 pi on 5fr dk bl & buff	"PIASTRES"	25.00	25.00
CIL22	C2		5pi on 40c red & gray bl	"PIASTRES"	—	—

C-I-L-I-C-I-A
Means a bargain basement day
Vc's and misspellings too
Cilicia is the land for you. —The Bard

COCHIN CHINA

All three errors are NA or unpriced

Only three errors, all NA
that really does spoil my day —-The Bard

COCOS ISLANDS has produced no errors

COLOMBIA

COL1	3b	(1859)	5c violet	"50." instead of "5,"	—	—
COL2	24a	(1863)	5c orange	star after "Cent"	87.50	57.50
COL3	25a		10c blue	period after "10,"	175.00	22.50
COL4	26a		20c red	star after "Cent"	190.00	67.50
COL5	28a		10c blue	period after "10,"	140.00	29.00
COL6	29a		50c green	star after "Cent"	165.00	67.50
COL7	31a		10c blue	period after 10	42.50	12.00
COL8	42b	(1865)	1p vermillion	period after "PESO"	110.00	16.00
COL9	54d	(1868)	10c lilac (l)	printed on both sides	6.25	2.00
COL10	106a	(1881)	5c blue	printed on both sides	—	—
COL11	117d	(1883)	1c gray grn, grn	"DE LOS" in very small caps	11.00	11.00
COL12	119a		10c org, yel	"DE LOS" in large caps	45.00	20.00
COL13	170a	(1899)	1c brn, buff	altered from 10c	25.00	25.00
COL14	171a		2c blk, buff	altered from 10c	25.00	25.00
COL15	172b		5c mar, grnsh bl	without ovpt	8.75	8.75
COL16	175a		1c (ctvo) blk, bl grn	"cvo"	90.00	12.00
COL17	175b			"cvos."	35.00	6.00

CIL1

CIL2a

CIL2B

COL63a

COL18	175c			"centavo"	42.50	6.00
COL19	177a		5c blk, pink	name at side (V)	50.00	7.50
COL20	179a		20c blk, *yellow*	name at side (G)	70.00	10.00
COL21	180a		1c (ctvo.) Blk, *bl grn*	"centavo"	100.00	15.00
COL22	182a		5c blk (G)	"ctvos" smaller	40.00	6.00
COL23	185a	(1901)	1c black	without ovpt (vc)	1.90	1.90
COL24	185b		dbl ovpt (VC)	2.00	2.00
COL25	185d		invtd ovpt (vc)	1.00	1.00
COL26	186b		2c blk, rose	without ovpt	1.90	1.90
COL27	186c		dbl ovpt (vc)	2.00	2.00
COL28	188b		2c brown	without ovpt	.85	.85
COL29	189a	(1902)	5c violet	without ovpt (u)	1.75	1.75
COL30	189b		dbl ovpt (vc)	1.75	1.75
COL31	190a		10c yel brn	dbl ovpt (vc)	1.75	1.75
COL32	190c		without ovpt	1.75	1.75
COL33	190d		printed on both sides	2.50	2.50
COL34	191a	(1902)	5c yel brn	without ovpt	1.65	1.65
COL35	192a		10c black	without ovpt	1.00	1.00
COL36	325c	(1908)	1/2 c orange	without imprint	4.00	4.00
COL37	326a		1c yel grn	without imprint	.60	.15
COL38	331b	(1910)	1/2 c violet & blk	center invtd	NA	
COL39	369a	(1921)	3c on 4c violet	dbl surch (vc)	13.00	—
COL40	377a	(1924)	3c on 4c vio	dbl surch (vc)	12.00	—
COL41	377b		dbl surch, one invtd	112.00	—
COL42	377c		with added surch "3cs" in red	—	—
COL43	383a	(1925)	4c violet (R)	invtd surch (vc)	7.00	7.00
COL44	384a		1c on 3c bis brn	invtd surch (vc)	15.00	15.00
COL45	385a		4c violet (G)	invtd ovpt (vc)	7.50	7.50
COL46	409a	(1932)	1c on 4c dp bl (R)	invtd surch (vc)	5.25	5.25
COL47	410a		20c on 30c ol bis	invtd surch (vc)	17.50	—
COL48	410b		dbl surch (vc)	17.50	—
COL49	452a	(1937-38)	1c on 3c lt grn	invtd surch (vc)	1.75	1.75
COL50	453a		5c on 8c dk bl	invtd surch (vc)	1.75	1.75
COL51	455a		5c on 8c bl blk	invtd surch (vc)	1.50	1.50
COL52	456a		10c on 12c dp bl ('38)	invtd surch (vc)	8.50	8.50
COL53	495a	(19420	10c dull orange	"2.XI.1902," instead of "21.XI. 1902,"	14.00	15.00
COL54	527a	(1946)	1c on 5c brown	invtd surch	.90	—
COL55	543a		50c red (Bk)	dbl ovpt (vc)	25.00	—
COL56	544a		50c red (G)	dbl ovpt (vc)	25.00	—
COL57	C117a	(1939)	5c on 20c (Bk)	dbl surch (vc)	12.00	—
COL58	C117b		pair, one with dbl surch	14.00	—
COL59	C117c		invtd surch (vc)	12.00	12.00
COL60	C119	(1940)	15c on 30c	invtd surch (vc)	12.00	—
COL61	C120a		15c on 40c (R)	dbl surch (vc)	12.00	—
COL62	F23a	(1917)	4c grn & ultra	center invtd - Registration Issue, Q<100 (u)	NA	
COL63	RA14a	(1943)	1/2 c on 1c violet	invtd surch (vc)	1.50	—
COL63a	RA36		1c on 5c brown	dbl surch (vc) R	
COL63b			1c on 50c ultramarine	dbl surch (vc) R	

COL63B

CMR1+2

CMR5

COL64	RA46a	(1950)	5c on 2c gray, red, blk & yel	"195," instead of "1950,"	1.40	1.40
COL65	RA46b			top bar & "19," of "1950," omitted	1.40	1.40
COL66	RA47a		5c blue	invtd ovpt (vc)	.90	—

If Cilicia is a bargain barn
Colombia is even better, by darn. —The Bard

Bolivar (originally a State, now a Department of the Republic of Colombia)

BOL1	1a	(1863-66)	10c green	five stars below shield	NA	
BOL2	2b		10c red ('66)	stars used below shield	75.00	67.50
BOL3	13a	(1879)	20c red	20c green (error)	10.00	10.00
BOL4	32a	(1884)	2p violet	value omitted	27.50	27.50

COMORO ISLANDS

CMR1+2	209	(1976)	35f multicolor	1 orange, 1 red R (for both)	75.00	
CMR3+4	34		21e 400f	one missing yellow R (for both)	95.00	
CMR5			200f multicolored	dbl gold ovpt; black ovpt misplaced R		75.00
CMR6	433	(1979)	200F	overprinted incorrectly	—	_R

CONGO DEMOCRATIC REPUBLIC

CON1	593a	(1967)	1k on 2fr	invtd ovpt (vc)	6.00	—
CON2	596a		6.60k on 1fr (R)	invtd ovpt (vc)	4.75	—
CON3	597a		9.60k on 50c	invtd ovpt (vc)	4.75	—

CONGO PEOPLE'S REPUBLIC

CPR1	C29a	(1965)	25fr on 50fr dk brn & red	surch omitted	15.00	15.00

One little error sneaked in,
It made the Congo full of sin —The Bard

COOK ISLANDS

All 10 errors are NA or unpriced

Some center inverts
And vc's
But only NA's
That's not to please. —The Bard

CORFU

CRF1	NC10a	(1941)	50d violet	dbl ovpt	—	175.00

COSTA RICA

CTR1	58a	(1905)	1c on 20c lake & blk	invtd surch (u)	10.00	10.00
CTR2a	58b			diagonal surch (u)	.60	.55
CTR2b	59 Sel.	(1907)	1c red brn & Indigo,	invtd center (u) Q>200	up to 30.00	
CTR2c-2f					all NA	
CTR2g	67					
CTR3	77a	(1911)	2c yel grn & blk	invtd ovpt (vc)	5.00	5.00
CTR4	77b			dbl ovpt, both invtd (u)	42.50	—
CTR5	78a		1c grn & blk (R)	blk ovpt (vc)	32.50	18.00
CTR6	78b			invtd ovpt (vc)	—	—
CTR7	79a		1c red brn & indigo (bk)	invtd ovpt (vc)	4.25	3.50

CMR6

CTR26

CTR48a

CTR8	79b			dbl ovpt (vc)	5.00	5.00
CTR9	80a		2c yel grn & blk (bk)	invtd ovpt (vc)	3.50	3.50
CTR10	80b			dbl ovpt, one as on no. 77,	40.00	25.00
CTR11	80c			dbl ovpt, one invtd (u)	13.00	13.00
CTR12	82a		5c yel & bl (Bl)	"Habilitada"	3.25	2.50
CTR13	82b			"2911,"	5.50	3.25
CTR14	82c			Roman "I" in "1911,"	3.00	2.00
CTR15	82d			dbl ovpt (vc)	5.00	5.00
CTR16	82e			invtd ovpt (vc)	5.50	3.75
CTR17	82f			black ovpt (vc)	—	2.00
CTR18	82g			triple ovpt (u)	5.50	—
CTR19	83a		10c bk & blk (Bk)	as #83, Roman "I" in "1911,"	7.00	5.00
CTR20	83c			as #83, dbl ovpt (vc)	19.00	11.50
CTR21	84a		10c bl & blk (R)	Roman "I" in "1911,"	17.50	16.00
CTR22	86a		1c on 10c bl (R)	"Coereos"	7.75	5.50
CTR23	86b			invtd ovpt (vc)	—	—
CTR24	88a		1c on 25c vio (Bk)	"Coereos"	7.75	5.50
CTR25	88b			pair, one without surch	19.00	—
CTR26	88c			dbl surch (vc)	7.75	—
CTR27	88e			dbl surch one invtd	11.50	—
CTR28	89a		1c on 50c red brn (Bl)	invtd surch (vc)	5.00	5.00
CTR29	89b			dbl surch (vc)	4.25	—
CTR30	93a		2c on 5c brn org (Bk)	invtd surch (vc)	7.75	3.75
CTR31	93b			"Correos" invtd (vc)	7.75	—
CTR32	93c			dbl surch (vc)	7.75	—
CTR33	94b		2c on 10c bl (R)	"Correos" invtd	—	—
CTR34	95a		2c on 50c cl (Bk)	invtd surch (vc)	3.75	3.25
CTR35	95b			dbl surch (vc)	11.50	—
CTR36	96a		2c on 1 col brn (Bk)	invtd surch (vc)	11.50	—
CTR37	96b			dbl surch (vc)	15.00	—
CTR38	97a		2c on 2col car (Bk)	invtd surch (vc)	7.00	5.00
CTR39	97b			"Correos" invtd	—	—
CTR40	97c			dbl surch (vc)	25.00	15.00
CTR41	98a		2c on 5col grn (Bk)	invtd surch (vc)	9.00	7.00
CTR42	98b			"Correos" invtd	15.00	4.25
CTR43	99a		2c on 10col mar (Bk)	"Correos" invtd	—	—
CTR44	100a		5c on 5c org (bl)	dbl surch (vc)	25.00	15.00
CTR45	100b			invtd surch (vc)	25.00	8.50
CTR46	100c			pair, one without surch	16.00	—
CTR47	111a	(1922)	5c violet	invtd ovpt (vc)	10.00	—
CTR48	111b			dbl ovpt (vc)	15.00	—
CTR48a	111c		brown 1c	red invtd ovpt	—	— R
CTR48b	111c			blue invtd ovpt	—	— R
CTR49	111Jk	(1923)	5c orange	"VD" for "UD"	60.00	60.00
CTR50	139a	(1925)	45c on 1col ol grn	dbl surch (vc)	—	—
CTR51	148a	(1928)	5(c) on 15c dp violet	invtd surch (vc)	25.00	—
CTR52	150a	(1929)	13c on 40c deep grn	invtd surch (vc)	.85	.70
CTR53	201a	(1941)	5c green	flags omitted	60.00	—
CTR53b	C3 Sel.		5 on 10 brown & C4,	both invtd ovpt R	55.00	
			20 on 50 ultramarine		for both	

CTR48b

CTR53a

CTR53b

CTR53c	C156	(1947)	San. 75c blue green	invtd surch R	28.00	
See Photo in Color Section						
CTR54	O21c	(1887)	10c orange	dbl ovpt (vc)	30.00	—
CTR55	O23c		10c orange	dbl ovpt (vc)	25.00	—
CTR56	O44b		2c ver & blk	"PROVISIORO"	6.00	6.00
CTR57	O44d			invtd ovpt (vc)	6.00	4.00
CTR58	O44f			as "b" invtd	10.00	8.00
CTR59	O59a	(1921)	10c on 5c orange	"10 CTS" invtd	16.00	—
CTR60	RA2a	(1954)	5c on 10c dk bl & blk	invtd surch (vc)	7.50	—

Lot of inverts and vc's
Best of all the prices please
GO MAN, GO! A GOOD STARTER! —The Bard

GUANACASTE - A province of Costa Rica

GUC1	2a	(1885)	2c carmine	"Gnanacaste"	*150.00*	—
GUC2	4a		1c green	"Gnanacaste"	*150.00*	—
GUC3	4b			ovpt in blk & red	NA	
GUC4	5a		5c blue violet	"Gnanacaste	NA	
GUC5	16a		1c green	dbl ovpt, one in blk	125.00	—

CRETE

CRE1	61a		1d gray violet	(vc)	NA	
CRE2	72a	(1901)	25 1 blue	first letter of ovpt invtd	300.00	200.00
CRE3	73a	(1904)	73a 5 1 on 20 1 orange	without "5," at right	100.00	50.00
CRE3A	85		1 1 pale maroon	invtd ovpt		
CRE3B	88					
See Photo in Color Section						
CRE4	96b	(1908)	10 1 brn red	invtd ovpt (vc)	20.00	—
CRE5	96c			dbl ovpt (vc)	30.00	—
CRE6	98a	(1909)	5 1 on 20 1 orange	invtd surch	—	—
CRE7	101b		2 1 on 20 1 red	invtd surch (vc)	70.00	—
CRE8	101c			2nd letter of surch "D," instead of "P,"	50.00	50.00
CRE9	103a		10 1 brn red	invtd ovpt (vc)	80.00	—
CRE9B	J1					
See Photo in Color Section						
CRE10	O3a	(1908)	10 1 dull claret	invtd ovpt (vc)	75.00	—
CRE11	O4a		30 1 blue	invtd ovpt (vc)	60.00	—

Many vc's although not all
But nothing for an exciting call.
This land of Crete has long been dead
Enough about it has been said. —The Bard

There were two inverts issued by the <u>insurgent</u> government in 1905 as reported by Yvert - Sellinger op. cit (p. 13).

CROATIA has produced no errors

CUBA

CUB1	15a	(1860)	1/4r p on 2r p dl rose	1 of 1/4 invtd	NA	125.00
CUB2	106a	(1883)	5 on 5c (R)	triple surch (u)	—	—
CUB3	106b			dbl surch (vc)	17.50	17.50
CUB4	106c			invtd surch (vc)	22.50	22.50
CUB5	106d			without "5," in surch,	12.50	12.50
CUB6	106e			dbl surch, types "a" & "d"	—	—
CUB7	107a		10 on 10c (bl)	invtd surch, (vc)	—	—
CUB8	107b			dbl surch, (vc)	20.00	20.00
CUB9	108a		20 on 20c	"10," instead of "20,"	60.00	60.00
CUB10	108b			dbl surch(vc)	—	—
CUB11	109a		5 on 5c (R)	invtd surch (vc)	20.00	20.00
CUB12	109b			dbl surch (vc)	17.50	17.50
CUB13	110a		10 on 10c (bl)	invtd surch (vc)	25.00	25.00
CUB14	110b			dbl surch(vc)	—	—
CUB15	111a		20 on 20c	dbl surch (vc)	50.00	25.00

CUB16	111b			dbl surch, types "b," & "c"	—	—
CUB17	112a		5 on 5c (R)	invtd surch (vc)	25.00	25.00
CUB18	112b			dbl surch, types "c" & "d" (vc)	—	
CUB19	113a		10 on 10c (Bl)	invtd surch, (vc)	30.00	30.00
CUB20	113b			dbl surch (vc)	30.00	30.00
CUB21	114a		20 on 20c	"10," instead of "20,"	75.00	60.00
CUB22	114b			dbl surch, (vc)	75.00	75.00
CUB23	114c			dbl surch, types "a" & "c"	—	—
CUB24	115a		5 on 5c (R)	invtd surch, (vc)	25.00	25.00
CUB25	115b			dbl surch, (vc)	20.00	20.00
CUB26	116a		10 on 10c (bl)	invtd surch,	25.00	25.00
CUB27	116b			dbl surch, (vc)	22.50	22.50
CUB28	117a		20 on 20c	dbl surch, types "a" & "d"	—	—
CUB29	118a		5c gray blue (R)	dbl ovpt (vc)	27.50	27.50
CUB30	119a		10c olive bis (bl)	dbl ovpt (vc)	30.00	30.00
CUB31	120a		20c red brn	dbl ovpt (vc)	100.00	100.00
CUB32	177a	(1898-99) 1c on 1m org brn		broken figure "1"	75.00	65.00
CUB33	177b			invtd surch,(vc)	200.00	
CUB34	177d			as "a" invtd,	NA	
CUB35	178a		2c on 2m org brn	invtd surch, (vc)	NA	50.00
CUB36	179a		2c on 2m org brn	invtd surch, (vc)	NA	100.00
CUB37	179Ba		3c on 1m org brn	dbl surch	NA	
CUB38	179De		3c on 1m org brn	dbl surch	NA	
CUB39	180Ea		3c on 3m org brn	invtd surch (vc)	—	*100.00*
CUB40	181a		3c on 3m org brn	invtd surch(vc)	—	*200.00*
CUB41-44					all NA	
CUB45	188a		5c on 3m org brn	invtd surch (vc)	NA	200.00
CUB46	188b			dbl surch (vc)	—	
CUB47	189a		5c on 5m org brn	invtd surch(vc)	—	NA
CUB48	189b			dbl surch(vc)	—	—
CUB49	190a		5c on 1/2 m bl grn	invtd surch (vc)	NA	150.00
CUB50	190b			pair, right stamp without surch	—	NA
CUB51	191a		5c on 1/2 m bl grn	invtd surch(vc)	NA	200.00
CUB52	192a		5c on 1/2 m bl grn	dbl surch, one diagonal	NA	
CUB53	196a		3c on 1c blk vio	invtd surch (vc)	—	NA
CUB54	197a		3c on 1c blk vio	invtd surch (vc)	—	NA
CUB55	198a		5c on 1c blk vio	invtd surch (vc)	—	125.00
CUB56	198b			surch vert up,	NA	
CUB57	198c			dbl surch (vc)	NA	
CUB58	198d			dbl invtd surch	—	—
CUB59	199a		5c on 1c blk vio	invtd surch (vc)	—	NA
CUB60	199b			vertical surch	—	NA
CUB61	199c			dbl surch (vc)	NA	
CUB62	200a		10c on 1c blk vio	broken figure "1" (vc)	40.00	100.00
CUB63-86 are all NA or unpriced						
CUB87	224a		3c on 3c purple	period btwn "B" & "A"	35.00	35.00
CUB88	226b		10c on 10c brn, type I	"CUBA" omitted	NA	
CUB89	232a	(1902)	1c on 3c purple	invtd surch (vc)	150.00	150.00
CUB90	232b			surch sideways (numeral horizontal)	—	—
CUB91	232c			dbl surch (vc)	200.00	200.00
CUB92	239a	(1910)	1c grn & vio	center invtd.(u)	150.00	150.00
CUB93	240a		2c car & grn	center invtd (u)	NA	
CUB94	244a		10c brn & bl	center invtd (u)	NA	—
CUB95	E1a	(1899)	10c on 10c blue	no peeeriod after "CUBA"	NA	
CUB96	E4a	(1910)	10c orange & blue	center invtd	NA	—
CUB97	J2a	(1899)	2c on 2c dp claret	invtd surch (vc)	—	NA
CUB98	RA7a	(1942)	1c salmon	invtd ovpt (vc)	60.00	50.00

Typos, inverts and vc's
The invert's price is not to please
The number of vc's is so high
That there's always those to buy —The Bard

CYPRUS

CYP1-13 are all NA

CYR14	815a	(1993)	20c multicolored	inscribed "MUFFLON"	35.00	—

Overprints are the story,
Doubles, triples and by my lori
One that's been struck still another T. —The Bard

CYRENAICA

CYA1	15a	(1924)	1 l bl & blk	dbl ovpt (vc)	NA

Cyrenaica has one error
Why don't you guess and see
Is it an inverted center?
Or a mostly common vc?

CZECHOSLOVAKIA

CZE1	1038a	(1961)	60h dk blue	"ORSZACH" instead of "ORSZAGH"	85.00	75.00
CZE2	1908a	(1973)	1k multi, vio bl inscript.	1k multi, black inscript	15.00	14.00
CZE3	B119a	(1915-18)	10f grn & red	pair, one without ovpt	—	—
CZE4	B142a	(1926)	200h blue 9 (R)	dbl ovpt (vc)	—	—
CZE5	C1a	(1920)	14k on 200h (R)	invtd surch (vc)	125.00	—
CZE6	C2a		24k on 500h (Bl)	invtd surch (vc)	175.00	—
CZE7	C3a		28k on 1000h (G)	invtd surch (vc)	175.00	—
CZE8	C3b			dbl surch (vc)	175.00	—
CZE9	C6a		28k on 1000h (G)	invtd surch (vc)	110.00	110.00
CZE10	C7a	(1922)	50h on 100h dl grn	invtd surch (vc)	175.00	—
CZE11	C7b			dbl surch (vc)	200.00	—
CZE12	C8a		100h on 200h vio	invtd surch (vc)	175.00	—
CZE13	C9a		250h on 400h brn (V)	invtd surch (vc)	175.00	—
CZE14	J52a		50h on 20h car	50h on 50h carmine (error) (vc)	—	NA

Don't look at regular issues
For errors they are rare
Rather scan the skies
And look into the air. —The Bard

BOHEMIA AND MORAVIA - Czech German Protectorate

BOH1	13a	(1939)	1.60 ol grn	'Mähnen"	16.00	27.50

D

DAHOMEY

DAH1	33a	(1912)	5c on 4c claret, lav C	dbl surch (vc)	190.00	—
DAH2	36a		5c on 25c blue C	invtd surch	165.00	
DAH3	38a		10c on 40c red, straw	invtd surch (vc)	250.00	
DAH4	87a		60c on 75c vio, pnksh	dbl surch (vc)	100.00	100.00
DAH4A	C199	(1974)	100f brown & green	invtd ovpt (vc) R	30.00	
DAH4B	C217		15f multicolored	invtd ovpt (vc) R	—	
DAH5	232a	(1967)	30fr on 65fr	dbl surch (vc)	15.00	—
DAH6	233a		30fr on 85fr	dbl surch (vc)	22.50	—
DAH7	233a			invtd surch (vc)	22.50	

DALMATIA

DAL1	E1	(1921)	25c on 25c rose red	dbl surch (vc)	25.00

DANISH WEST INDIES

DWI1	6e	(1874-79)	3c blue & carmine	invtd frame	17.50	—
DWI2	7d		4c brn & dull blue	invtd frame	NA	
DWI3	8b		5c grn & gray	invtd frame	20.00	15.00
DWI4	9b		7c lilac & orange	invtd frame	30.00	60.00
DWI5	10b		10c blue & brn	"cent.s"	25.00	17.50
DWI6	10c			invtd frame	20.00	10.00

DWI7	12a		14c lilac & grn	invtd frame	NA	
DWI8	14b	(1887-95)	1c on 7c lilac & org	dbl surch (vc)	200.00	NA
DWI9	14c			invtd frame	65.00	90.00
DWI10	16a	(1896-1901)	1c grn & red vio '98	normal frame	200.00	NA
DWI11	17a		3c blue & lake	normal frame	NA	
DWI12	18b		4c bister & dull blue	invtd frame	35.00	30.00
DWI13	20a		10c blue & brn	invtd frame	NA	
DWI14	20b			"cent.s"	60.00	95.00
DWI15	23a	(1902)	2c on 3c blue & car	"2," in date with straight tail	NA	
DWI16	23b			normal frame	NA	—
DWI17	24a		2c on 3c blue & lake	"2," in date with straight tail	15.00	20.00
DWI18	24b			dated "1901,"	NA	
DWI19	24c			normal frame,	150.00	175.00
DWI20	25a		8c on 10c blue & brn	"2," with straight tail	15.00	22.50
DWI21	25b			on no. 20b	15.00	25.00
DWI22	25c			invtd frame	NA	
DWI23	27a		2c on 3c blue & lake	normal frame	200.00	NA
DWI24	28b		8c on 10c blue & brn	invtd frame	200.00	NA
DWI25	40a	(1905)	5b on 4c bis & dull blue	invtd frame	30.00	45.00

It's a shame that an inverted frame
Could so dominate a land.
Just like a bride to be
Getting her wedding band. —The Bard

DANZIG

DZG1	11a	(1920)	2m blue	dbl ovpt (vc)	NA	—
DZG2	15a		5m slate & car	center & "Danzig," invtd	NA	—
DZG3	15b			invtd ovpt	—	NA
DZG4	20a		10pf on 20pf (R)	dbl surch (vc)	125.00	175.00
DZG5	21a		25pf on 30pf (G)	invtd surch (vc)	125.00	175.00
DZG6	22a		60pf on 30pf (br)	dbl surch (vc)	125.00	175.00
DZG7	25a		1m on 30pf org & blk, buff (bk)	pair, one without surch	—	—
DZG8	27d		2m on 35pf red brn (bl)	surch omitted	55.00	75.00
DZG9	33a		3pf brn	dbl ovpt (vc)	55.00	55.00
DZG10	34a		5pf grn	dbl ovpt (vc)	27.50	—
DZG11	37b		15pf dk violet	dbl ovpt (vc)	27.50	—
DZG12-22 are all NA or unpriced						
DZG23	62a		60pf on 75pf	dbl surch (vc)	80.00	80.00
DZG24	68a		30pf blue & car	center invtd	24.00	—
DZG25	69a		40pf grn & car	center invtd	24.00	—
DZG26	73a		1m org & car	center invtd	24.00	—
DZG27	96a	(1922)	6m on 3m car lake	dbl surch (vc)	—	—
DZG28	97a		8m on 4m dk blue	dbl surch (vc)	47.50	47.50
DZG29	137a	(1923)	40th m on 200m	dbl surch	60.00	—
DZG30	147b		5mil m on 10,000m	dbl surch (vc)	60.00	—
DZG31	151a		40mil m on 10,000m	dbl surch (vc)	50.00	—
DZG32	C1a	(1920)	40pf on 40pf	dbl surch (vc)	NA	
DZG33	C2a		60pf on 40pf C	dbl surch (vc)	NA	
DZG34	C11a		60pf dk vio	dbl impression	50.00	—

DAH4A

DAH4B

DZG35	C25b		5mil m on 50,000m scar	cliche of 10,000m in sheet of 50,000m	30.00	40.00
DZG36	O2a	(1921-22)	10pf dk brn	invtd ovpt	50.00	—
DZG37	O18a		2m gray & car	invtd ovpt (vc)	20.00	15.00
DZG38	O28a		6m on 3m	invtd ovpt (vc)	25.00	—
DZG39	O36a		50m pale blue	invtd ovpt (vc)	20.00	—
DZG40	O38a		200m orange	invtd ovpt (vc)	20.00	—

Danzig has lots of vc's
They surely do serve to please
But inexpensive inverts and a DI, *(double impression)*
Are sure to bring pleasure to any stamp guy. —The Bard

I was also in the mood
To pick Sellinger's brood. Sellinger op.cit (p.14) from Yvert.

DENMARK

DEN1-2, 4-6, 10-13, are all NA

DEN3	18b		4s	invtd frame	NA	130.00
DEN7	25a	(1875-79)	3o gray blue & gray	1st "A" of "DANMARK" missing	60.00	125.00
DEN8	25c			invtd frame	18.00	10.00
DEN9	34b		100o gray & org	invtd frame	140.00	55.00
DEN14	41b		3o	invtd frame	15.00	2.75
DEN15	42a		4o	invtd frame	7.00	.15
DEN16	44a		8o	invtd frame	6.00	.15
DEN17	46a		12o	invtd frame	7.00	2.25
DEN18	47a		16o	invtd frame	25.00	3.00
DEN19	50a		25o	invtd frame	75.00	12.00
DEN20	51a		50o	invtd frame	75.00	21.00
DEN21	52a		100o	invtd frame	NA	57.30
DEN22	41d		3o	invtd frame	75.00	50.00
DEN23	42c		4o	invtd frame	110.00	95.00
DEN24	50c		25o	invtd frame	135.00	55.00
DEN25	51c		50o	invtd frame	200.00	95.00
DEN26	52c		100o	invtd frame	NA	
DEN27	56a	(1904-12)	15o on 24o brn	short "15," at right	35.00	50.00
DEN28	79a	(1912)	35o on 16o	invtd frame	200.00	NA
DEN29	80a		35o on 20o	invtd frame	60.00	125.00
DEN30	136a		80o on 12o	invtd frame	NA	
DEN31	137a		80o on 8o	"POSTERIM"	45.00	165.00
DEN32	144a	(1902)	1c dk grn & blk	Q=>200	<30.00	
DEN33	145a		2c scarlet & blk	Q=>200	<30.00	
DEN34	146a		5c blue & blk	Q=>200	<30.00	
DEN35	148a		12c purple & blk	Q=>200	<30.00	
DEN36	149a		20c rose & blk	Q=>200	<30.00	
DEN37	150a		50c brn & blk	Q=>200	<30.00	
DEN38	191a		7o on 20o indigo	dbl surch (vc)	NA	
DEN38A	Yv267A	(1938)	50 yellow green	1938 deleted R	12.00	

DEN38A

DUB7

DUB8

AFFORDABLE FOREIGN ERRORS

DEN39	263 a	(1923)	1oo grn	dbl ovpt	NA	
DEN40	J8	(1921)	1oo red	"S" invtd	125.00	150.00
DEN41	J17		2oo grnsh blue	dbl impress	NA	—
DEN42	M1a		5o grn	"S" invtd	NA	
DEN43	M2a		1oo red	"S" invtd	175.00	200.00
DEN44	Q3a	(1919-41)	1oo red	"POSFFAERGE" (u)	165.00	NA
DEN45	Q4a		15o violet	"POSFFAERGE" (u)	165.00	—
DEN46	Q11a		1k yel brn	"POSFFAERGE" (u)	NA	
DEN47	C236	(1975)	10c yel & multi, dove, Christmas		—	—

An error here and an error there
A different error everywhere —The Bard

DIEGO-SUAREZ

DIE1	11a	(1892)	5c on 10c blk, lav (R)	invtd surch (vc)	NA	190.00
DIE2	12a		5c on 20c red, grn	invtd surch (vc)	NA	—
DIE3	24a	(1892)	1fr brnz grn, straw (R)	dbl ovpt	150.00	125.00
DIE4	J4a		2c blk	invtd ovpt (vc)	NA	175.00
DIE5	J8a		10c blk	invtd ovpt (vc)	NA	160.00
DIE6	J9a		15c blk	dbl ovpt (vc)	NA	
DIE7	J11a		30c blk	invtd ovpt (vc)	NA	160.00

Diego-Suarez has a few vc's
That's not enough for us to please —The Bard

DJIBOUTI has produced no errors

DOMINICA

DOM1 and five other errors are NA

DOM3	11a		1/2 p on half of 1p	surch reading downward (u)	40.00	32.50

The Bard has become tired
So now's the time to see
What this famous author
Can come and do for thee. —The Bard

With presumably better technology, Dominica has not produced an error since 1886. These are few in number and all overprints. They were all NA and very expensive except DOM3, which is an unusual surch and could become a good buy.

DOMINICAN REPUBLIC

DMR1, 4-9 are all NA

DMR2	11b		1r blk, bl	no space btwn "Un" & "real"	NA	200.00
DMR3	11c			without inscription at top & bottom	NA	200.00
DMR10	44b	(1880)	1p gold	dbl impression (u)	42.50	42.50
DMR11	54b	(1883)	5c on 1c grn	invtd surch (vc)	21.00	21.00
DMR12	54c			surcharged "25 centimos" (u)	50.00	50.00
DMR13	54d			surcharged "10 centimos" (u)	27.50	27.50
DMR14	55b		5c on 1c grn	dbl surch (vc)	100.00	—
DMR15	55c			invtd surch (vc)	65.00	65.00
DMR16	56b		5c on 1c grn	surcharged "10 centimos" (u)	35.00	35.00
DMR17	56c			surcharged "25 centimos" (u)	37.50	37.50
DMR18	57a		10c on 2c red	invtd surch (vc)	27.50	27.50
DMR19	57d			surcharged "5 centimos" (u)	52.50	52.50
DMR20	57e			surcharged "25 centimos" (u)	75.00	75.00
DMR21	58a		10c on 2c red	"Centimso"	—	—
DMR22	58b			invtd surch (vc)	37.50	37.50
DMR23	58c			surcharged "25 centimos" (u)	60.00	60.00
DMR24	58d			"10," omitted (u)	60.00	—
DMR25	59a		25c on 5c blue	surch "5 centimos" (u)	52.50	—
DMR26	59b			surch "10 centimos" (u)	52.50	52.50
DMR27	59c			surch "50 centimos" (u)	75.00	75.00
DMR28	59d			invtd surch (vc)	50.00	50.00
DMR29	60a		25c on 5c bl	invtd surch (vc)	45.00	37.50

DMR30	60b		surch "10 centimos" (u)	45.00	37.50
DMR31	60e		"25," omitted	75.00	
DMR32	60f		surcharged on back (u)	—	75.00
DMR33	61a	50c on 10c rose	invtd surch (vc)	50.00	45.00
DMR34	62a	50c on 10c rose	invtd surch (vc)	52.50	52.50
DMR35	64a	1fr on 20c brb	comma after "Franco"	27.50	27.50
DMR36	65a	1fr on 20c brn	invtd surch (vc)	—	75.00
DMR37	66a	1fr25c on 25c vio	invtd surch (vc)	65.00	65.00
DMR38	67a	2fr50c on 50c orange	invtd surch	35.00	27.50
DMR39	68b	3fr75c on 75c ultra	invtd surch (vc)	60.00	60.00
DMR40	71b	5c on 1c grn	invtd surch (vc)	22.50	22.50
DMR41	71c		dbl surch	22.50	22.50
DMR42	71d		surch "25 centimos"(u)	42.50	42.50
DMR43	72a	5c on 1c grn	invtd surch (vc)	60.00	60.00
DMR44	73b	5c on 1c grn	surch "10 centimos" (u)	50.00	42.50
DMR45	73c		surch "25 centimos" (u)	60.00	
DMR46	74a	10c on 2c red	surch "5 centimos"	52.50	45.00
DMR47	74b		surch "25 centimos" (u)	67.50	67.50
DMR48	74c		"10," omitted (u)	57.50	—
DMR49	75a	10c on 2c red	invtd surch (vc)	30.00	17.00
DMR50	76a	25c on 5c blue	surch "10 centimos" (u)	75.00	—
DMR51	76b		surch "5 centimos" (u)	60.00	—
DMR52	76c		surch "50 centimos"(u)	67.50	—
DMR53	77a	25c on 5c blue	invtd surch (vc)	—	—
DMR54	77b		surch on back (u)	—	—
DMR55	78a	50c on 10c rose	invtd surch (vc)	50.00	30.00
DMR56	78b		surch "25 centimos" (u)	60.00	—
DMR57	79a	50c on 10c rose	invtd surch (vc)	60.00	—
DMR58	81a	1fr on 20c brn	comma after "Franco"	35.00	35.00
DMR59	81b		invtd surch (vc)	75.00	—
DMR60	83a	1fr25c on 25c vio	invtd surch (vc)	75.00	—
DMR61	84a	2fr50c on 50c orange	invtd surch (vc)	35.00	27.50
DMR62	86a	5fr on 1p gold	invtd surch (vc)	—	—
DMR63	117a	20c lilac	20c rose (error) (u)	5.75	5.75
DMR64-69	144a - 150a	1c	Center invtd, all (u)	3.25	
DMR65	145a	2c		3.25	—
DMR66	146a	5c		3.25	—
DMR67	148a	12c		3.25	—
DMR68	149a	20c		3.25	—
DMR69	150a	50c		3.25	—
DMR70	152b	2c on 1p	"2," omitted	50.00	50.00
DMR71	152a	c 2c on 1p	as "a" "2," omitted	80.00	80.00
DMR72	157a (1904)	5c dk blue & blk	invtd ovpt (vc)	6.50	5.50
DMR73	158a	2c scarlet & blk	invtd ovpt (vc)	15.00	5.00
DMR74	160a	10c yel grn & blk	invtd ovpt (vc)	12.50	12.50
DMR75	161a	1c on 20c yellow & blk	invtd surch (vc)	6.50	6.50
DMR76	162a	1c on 2c olive gray	"entavos" (u)	—	—
DMR77	162b		"Dominican" (u)	200.00	200.00
DMR78	162c		"Centavo" (u)	200.00	200.00
DMR79	163a	1c on 2c olive gray	invtd surch (vc)	3.50	2.50
DMR80	163b		"Domihicana" (u)	15.00	15.00
DMR81	163c		as "b" invtd (u)	40.00	40.00
DMR82	163d		"Dominican" (u)	10.50	10.50
DMR83	163g		"entavos" (u)	30.00	
DMR84	164a	2c olive gray	"Domihicana" (u)	11.00	11.00
DMR85	164b		invtd ovpt (vc)	1.90	1.90
DMR86	164c		as "a" invtd (u)	25.00	25.00
DMR87	164d		"Dominican" (u)	5.75	5.75
DMR88	164e		"Centavo omitted (u)	12.50	10.00
DMR89	164f		"entavos" (u)	12.50	12.50
DMR90	164h		as "d" invtd (u)	40.00	40.00
DMR91	165a	1c on 4c olive gray	"Domihicana" (u)	10.00	10.00

DMR92	165c			invtd surch (vc)	1.75	1.75
DMR93	165d			"1," omitted (u)	3.50	3.50
DMR94	165e			as "a" invtd (u)	32.50	32.50
DMR95	165f			as "d" invtd (u)	40.00	40.00
DMR96	165g			dbl surch (vc)	30.00	30.00
DMR97		(1905)	166a 2c on 20c dk brn	invtd surch (vc)	15.00	15.00
DMR98	167a			invtd surch (vc)	16.00	16.00
DMR99	167b			dbl surch (vc)	25.00	25.00
DMR100	169a	(1906)	1c on 4c olive gray	invtd surch (vc)	10.50	10.50
DMR101	169b			dbl surch (vc)	25.00	—
DMR102	170a		1c on 10c olive gray	invtd surch (vc)	10.50	10.50
DMR103	170b			dbl surch (vc)	14.00	14.00
DMR104	170c			"OMINICANA" (u)	20.00	20.00
DMR105	170d			as "c" invtd (u)	150.00	—
DMR106	171a		2c on 5c olive gray	invtd surch (vc)	10.50	10.50
DMR107	171b			dbl surch (vc)	35.00	
DMR108	177a	(1911)	2c scarlet & blk	"HABILITAOO" (u)	8.75	6.00
DMR109	177b			invtd ovpt (vc)	21.00	—
DMR110	177c			dbl ovpt (vc)	21.00	—
DMR111	194a	(1915)	1/2 c on 20c orange & blk	invtd surch (vc)	6.00	6.00
DMR112	194b			dbl surch (vc)	8.75	8.75
DMR113	194c			"Habilitado" omitted (u)	5.25	5.25
DMR114	195a		1c blue grn & blk	invtd ovpt (vc)	6.00	6.00
DMR115	195b			dbl ovpt (vc)	7.00	—
DMR116	195c			overprinted "1915," only (u)	12.50	—
DMR117	196a		2c scarlet & blk	invtd ovpt (vc)	5.25	5.25
DMR118	196b			dbl ovpt (vc)	7.75	7.75
DMR119	196c			ovpt "1915," only (u)	8.75	
DMR120	197a		5c dk blue & blk	invtd ovpt (vc)	7.00	7.00
DMR121	197b			dbl ovpt (vc)	8.75	8.75
DMR122	197c			dbl ovpt one invtd (u)	27.50	—
DMR123	197d			ovpt "1915," only (u)	8.50	—
DMR124	198a		10c yellow grn & blk	invtd ovpt (vc)	15.00	—
DMR125	199a		20c orange & blk	"Habilitado," omitted (u)	—	—
DMR126	203a		2c ol grn & blk (II)	center omitted (u)	87.50	—
DMR127	203b			frame omitted (u)	87.50	—
DMR128	204a		5c magenta & blk	pair, one without ovpt	65.00	—
DMR129	220b		1/2 c lilac rose & blk	invt ovpt (vc)	—	—
DMR130	220c			dbl ovpt (vc)	—	—
DMR131	220d			dbl ovpt, one invtd	—	—
DMR132	221a		1c yellow grn & blk	ovpt omitted (u)	70.00	—
DMR133	537a	(1960-61)	9c on 4c lilac & rose	invtd surch (vc)	21.00	—
DMR134	539a		36c on 1/2 c brn	invtd surch (vc)	18.00	—
DMR135	C14a	(1931-33)	20c dk blue	numerals reading up at left & down at right (u)	5.00	2.00
DMR136	CO1a	(1930)	10c light blue	pair, one without ovpt	NA	
DRM137	E3a	(1927)	10c red brn	"E EXPRESO" at top (u)	55.00	55.00
DMR138	G1	(1935)	8c on 7c ultra	invtd surch (vc)	18.00	—
DMR139	G2		15c on 10c org yellow	invtd surch (vc)	18.00	—
DMR140	RA22a	(1954)	1c blue & red	red (cross) omitted	55.00	—
DMR141	RAC1b	(1930)	5c + 5c blk & rose (R)	"Habilitado Para" missing (u)	52.50	—
DMR142	RAC2b		10c + 10c blk & rose	"Habilitado Para" missing (u)	52.50	—
DMR143	RAC2c			gold surch (u)	80.00	80.00
DMR144	RAC4b		5c + 5c ultra & rose	invtd surch (vc)	42.50	—
DMR145	RAC4d			pair, one without surch	190.00	—
DMR146	RAC4e			"Habilitado Para" missing (u)	15.00	—
DMR147	RAC5b		10c + 10c yel & rose	"Habilitado Para" missing (u)	18.00	—
DMR148	RAC6b		5c + 5c ultra & rose (R)	"Habilitado Para" missing (u)	18.00	—
DMR149	RAC7b			"Habilitado Para" missing (u)	18.00	—
DMR150	RAC8a	(1933)	2c scarlet	dbl ovpt (vc)	9.00	—
DMR151	RAC8b			pair, one without ovpt	NA	

DUBAI

DUB1	18	(1963)	1np ultra, yel & red,	imperf, invtd Cresc. & inscrip. Q=<100	130.00	200.00
DUB2	C11		40NP S/S imper	inv. Cresc. & inscrip. Q=<100		NA
DUB3	C25	(1964)	75np 3-5 Kennedy	US seal & colors different	130.00	200.00
DUB4	C26		1R Kennedy essay		70.00	130.00
DUB5	C27		1.25 R Kennedy essay		130.00	200.00
DUB6	C27a		S/S 1.25R Kennedy	(unique) Q=1 known		NA
DUB7	C34	(1964)	1-1/2 R multi	invtd ovpt R	36.00	
See Photo in Color Section						
DUB8	C35		multi	dbl ovpt (vc) R	25.00	
DUB9	J1	(1963)		1np clam invtd, imperf	70.00	130.00
DUB10	J3			3np oyster invtd	70.00	130.00
DUB11	J5			5np mussel invtd, imperf	70.00	130.00

DUB1-9 from Sellinger

E

EAST AFRICA AND UGANDA PROTECTORATES

EAF1	62a	(1919)	4c on 6c carmine	dbl surch (vc)	125.00	150.00
EAF2	62b			without squares over old value	25.00	25.00R?
See Photo in Color Section						
EAF3	62c			pair, one without surch	NA	
EAF4	62d			invtd surch (vc)	150.00	175.00

Four errors on one stamp, none upon the others
I'd rather not discuss this land if I had my druthers. —The Speechless Bard

EASTERN RUMELIA has produced no errors

EASTERN SILESIA

EAS1	20a	(1920)	500h red brn (bl)	blk ovpt	8.75	7.00
EAS2	21a		1000h violet (bl)	blk ovpt	140.00	80.00
EAS3	E1a		2h red violet, yel	blk ovpt	1.00	.80
EAS4	E2a		5h yel grn, yel	blk ovpt	6.00	5.00
EAS5	J1a		5h deep bis (bl)	blk ovpt	37.50	30.00

Some overprints in black—that's that! —The Bard

ECUADOR

ECU1	6b	(1866)	4r red	arms in circle (u)	200.00	100.00
ECU2-6 all NA or not priced						
ECU7	35a		5c on 50c maroon	invtd surch (vc)	1.75	—
ECU8	70a	(1896)	1c on 1c ver, "1893-1894,"	invtd surch (vc)	1.25	1.00
ECU9	70b			dbl surch (vc)	4.00	3.50
ECU10	71a		2c on 2c bl, "1893-1894,"	dbl surch (vc)	2.00	1.75
ECU11	72a		5c on 10c org "1887-1888,"	invtd surch (vc)	2.00	.85
ECU12	72c			surch "2cts" (u)	.50	.40
ECU13	72d			"1893-1894," (u)	2.75	2.50
ECU14	73a		10c on 4c brn, "1887-1888,"	invtd surch (vc)	2.00	.85
ECU15	73b			dbl surch (vc)	3.00	1.75
ECU16	73c			dbl surch, one invtd	—	—
ECU17	73d			surch "1 cto," (u)	1.00	1.40
ECU18	73e			"1891-92,"(u)	8.50	6.75
ECU19	76a		10c on 50c dk bl (R)	dbl surch (vc)	—	—
ECU19A	115		1c pink	dates in surch incomplete R?		
ECU20	125a	(1897)	10c ocher	dbl ovpt (vc)	5.25	4.75
ECU21	122a		1c	ovpt invtd (vc)	3.00	2.75
ECU22	123a		2c	ovpt invtd (vc)	3.00	2.75
ECU23	124a		5c	ovpt invtd (vc)	3.00	2.75
ECU24	125b		10c	ovpt invtd (vc)	2.75	2.75

ECU25	136a	(1899)	5c on 10c brn	dbl surch (vc)	—	—
ECU26	155a	(1903-06)	1c on 25c yellow	dbl surch (vc)	—	—
ECU27	219a	(1912)	2c on 10s yellow	invtd surch (vc)	7.50	6.00
ECU28	266a	(1927)	1c olive green	"POSTAI"(u)	1.40	.85
ECU29	266b			dbl ovpt (vc)	2.00	.85
ECU30	266c			invtd ovpt (vc)	2.00	.85
ECU31	267a		2c deep grn	"POSTAI" (u)	1.40	.85
ECU32	267b			dbl ovpt (vc)	2.00	.85
ECU33	268a		20c bister brn	"POSTAI" (u)	8.50	5.00
ECU33A	273a	(1928)	20c brown	dbl ovpt, one invtd R?		
ECU34	279a	(1928)	2c on 3c yel brn	dbl surch, one reading up (u)	7.25	7.25
ECU35	281a		2c on 5c lt blue	dbl surch, one reading up (u)	5.00	5.00
ECU36	283a		5c on 6c red org	"5 ctvos" omitted (u)	14.00	14.00
ECU37	285a		20c on 8c apple green	dbl surch (vc)	2.25	2.00
ECU38	292a		10c on 2c on 7c brn	red surch dbl (vc)	5.00	5.00
ECU39	303a	(1929)	1c dk blue	ovpt reading down	.15	.15
ECU40	318a	(1933)	10c olive brn	invtd ovpt (vc)	5.00	5.00
ECU41	320a		10c on 16c red & yel grn	invtd ovpt (vc)	4.00	4.00
ECU42	346a		1c rose red	dbl surc (vc)		
ECU43	416a	(1943)	30c on 50c red brn	without bars	.35	.15
ECU44-47					all unpriced	
ECU48	804(Sel.)	(1970)	1s multicolor, butterfly		up to 30.00	
ECU49	C1a	(1929)	50c on 10c grn	("Provisional" at 41degree angle, ECU49-51)	125.00	110.00
ECU50	C2a		75c on 15c carmine		150.00	140.00
ECU51	C3a		1s on 20c gray		125.00	140.00
ECU52	C32a	(1930)	1s car lake (bk)	dbl ovpt (vc) (R br + bk)	70.00	—
ECU53	C37a		1s on 5s ol grn (bk)	dbl surch (vc)	87.50	—
ECU54	C108a	(1943)	50c dp red violet	dbl ovpt (vc)	30.00	—
ECU55	C135a	(1945)	40c on 5c blue	dbl surch (vc)	7.00	—
ECU56	C136a		3s orange	invtd ovpt (vc)	21.00	—
ECU57	C136b			dbl ovpt (vc)	21.00	—
ECU58	C210a	(1949)	60c on 3s orange	dbl surch (vc)	15.00	—
ECU59	C214a	(1950)	60c on 50c gray	dbl surch (vc)	15.00	—
ECU60	C226a	(1951)	1s on 1.90s	invtd surch(vc)	12.00	—
ECU61	C389a		1s dp bl (1961)	"de Galapagos" on top line (u)	2.00	2.00
ECU62	C390a		1.80s rose violet	UNESCO emblem omitted (u)	1.25	1.25
ECU62A	C399	(1963)	3s multicolor	dbl perf at bottom R	20.00	
ECU63	CF1	(1928-29)	1s on 20c (#C3)	1s on 20c (#C3a) ('29)	140.00	110.00

ECU19A

ECU45

ECU33A

ECU62A

ECU80A

ECU115

ECU64	CO6a	(1929)	1s dark blue	invtd ovpt (vc)	NA	—
ECU65	E3a		10c on 2c blue	"10 CTVOS" invtd	10.50	13.00
ECU66	O92a		5c on 50c lilac	invtd surch (vc)	1.00	1.00
ECU67	O93a		10c on 20s orange	dbl surch (vc)	1.50	1.50
ECU68	O97a		5c on 50c lilac	dbl surch (vc)	1.40	—
ECU69	O97b			dbl surch, blk & grn	4.50	—
ECU70	O97c			same as "b," blk surch Invtd	1.40	—
ECU71	O98a	(1899)	5c on 50c lilac	dbl surch (vc)	1.40	—
ECU72	O98b			dbl surch, blk & red	1.75	—
ECU73	O99a		20c on 50s grn	invtd surch (vc)	3.50	—
ECU74	O99b			dbl surch, red & blk	5.50	—
ECU75	O116a	(1916-17)	2c blue & blk	invtd ovpt (vc)	1.00	1.00
ECU76	O123a		4c red & blk	invtd ovpt (vc)	5.00	—
ECU77	O130a		3c blk (R)	invtd ovpt (vc)	—	—
ECU78	O136a	(1920)	1c green	invtd ovpt (vc)	4.25	4.25
ECU79	O139a		4c dk green	invtd ovpt (vc)	6.00	10.00
ECU80	O160a	(1924)	1c orange	invtd ovpt (vc)	5.00	—
ECU80A	O161	(1924)	2c green	invtd ovpt (vc) R?		
ECU81	O169a	(1925)	1c scarlet & blk	invtd ovpt (vc)	5.00	—
ECU82	O170a		1c orange	invtd ovpt (vc)	1.25	—
ECU83	O171a		2c green	invtd ovpt (vc)	1.25	—
ECU84	O186a	(1928)	3c yellow brn	invtd ovpt (vc)	2.00	—
ECU85	O190a		20c violet	ovpt reading up	1.50	1.00
ECU86	RA2a	(1920)	1c red & blue	"de" invtd	4.00	4.00
ECU87	RA2b			dbl ovpt (vc)	4.00	.45
ECU88	RA2c			invtd ovpt (vc)	4.00	.45
ECU89	RA3a		1c deep blue	invtd ovpt (vc)	2.50	.70
ECU90	RA3b			dbl ovpt (vc)	2.50	.70
ECU91	RA6a	(1917-18)	20c olive green (R)	dated 1919-20	12.50	
ECU92	RA8a		1c on 5c green	dbl surch(vc)	—	—
ECU93	RA9a		1c on 5c green	dbl surch (vc)	5.00	3.50
ECU94	RA17a	(1924)	2c on 20c bis brn	invtd surch (vc)	3.50	3.50
ECU95	RA17b			dbl surch (vc)	2.00	2.00
ECU96	RA18a		1c rose red	invtd ovpt (vc)	1.50	—
ECU97	RA19a		2c blue	invtd ovpt (vc)	1.50	1.50
ECU98	RA24a	(1934)	2c green	blue ovpt invtd	1.40	1.50
ECU99	RA24b			blue ovpt, dbl, one invtd	1.75	1.00
ECU100	RA26a		2c on 10c olive brn	dbl surch (vc)	2.50	—
ECU101	RA28a	(1936)	2c green	both ovpts in red	.25	.15
ECU102	RA31a	(1935)	3c on 2c yel grn	dbl surch (vc)	—	—
ECU103	RA32a	(1936)	3c on 1c rose red	lines of words reversed	1.00	.15
ECU104	RA33a		20c ultra & yel	dbl ovpt (vc)	—	—
ECU105	RA37a		10c on 1c rose	dbl surch (vc)	—	—

ECU116

ECU117

ECU120

ECU121

AFFORDABLE FOREIGN ERRORS

ECU106	RA39d	(1937)	5c lt brn & red	invtd ovpt (vc)	10.00	—
ECU107	RA44a	(1939)	5c on 1c rose	dbl surch (vc)	—	—
ECU108	RA44b			triple surch (u)	—	—
ECU109	RA45a	(1940)	5c on 1c rose red	dbl surch (vc)	3.50	3.50
ECU110	RA46a		20c on 50c blk & multi	dbl surch, one invtd	—	—
ECU111	RA52a		20c on 50c blk & multi	dbl surch (vc)	5.00	—
ECU112	RA57a	(1943)	20c on 10c orange	dbl surch (vc)	—	—
ECU113	RA59a	(1944)	30c on 20c org red	dbl surch (vc)	—	—
ECU114	AC1a	(1945)	20c on 10c dk grn	pair, one without surch	45.00	—
ECU115	San.207C			30c light blue Aereo omitted R	20.00	
ECU116	San 207f		30c blue	invtd planes R	50.00 pair	
ECU117-9	San.209-11		all 30c violet, brown blue Aereo in red R		15.00	
See Photos in Color Section						
ECU120	San.210a		30c blue	red ovpt "Aereo" invtd R	20.00	
ECU121	San277		30c	FDR portrait shifted R	50.00	

Who's the biggest bargain store
For every error? Ecuador! —The Bard

Pick up a double overprint for a couple of bucks, or, the overprint misspelling— "POSTAI" costs even less. These are among the Ecuadorian goodies. Even more unusual is the double surcharge, one reading up. Some date back to 1896, so we know that they were not concocted for collectors in 1996. This is a good place to start collecting since not all are vc's. Beware, however, ECU1 AND ECU2, though not both NA's, are quite expensive.

EGYPT

EGT1	5d	(1866)	5pi rose	inscription of 10 pi, imperf,	NA	—
EGT2	27c	(1879)	5pa on 2 -1/2 pi dull vio	invtd surch (vc)	40.00	40.00
EGT3	28c		10pa on 2 -1/2 pi dull vio	invtd surch (vc)	45.00	35.00
EGT4	42a	(1884)	20pa on 5pi green	invtd surch (vc)	27.50	22.50
EGT5	60a	(1915)	2m on 3m orange	invtd surch (vc)	80.00	80.00
EGT6	78a	(1922)	1m olive brn	invtd ovpt (vc)	40.00	40.00
EGT7	78b			dbl ovpt (vc)	50.00	50.00
EGT8	79a		2m red	dbl ovpt (vc)	40.00	40.00
EGT9	81a		4m grn	invtd ovpt (vc)	—	—
EGT10	86a		20m olive grn	invtd ovpt (vc)	140.00	140.00
EGT11	86b			dbl ovpt (vc)	80.00	80.00
EGT12	87a		50m maroon	invtd ovpt (vc)	NA	
EGT13	88a		100m blk	invtd ovpt (vc)	150.00	150.00
EGT14	88b			dbl ovpt (vc)	150.00	150.00
EGT15	117a	(1926)	15m on 200m brt violet	dbl surch (vc)	160.00	
EGT16	148a	(1932)	500m choc & Prus bl	entirely photogravure (u)	40.00	5.75
EGT17	149a	(1937)	£1 dk grn & org brn	entirely photogravure (u)	42.50	3.50
EGT18	B2a	(1943)	5m + 5m	Arabic date "1493,"	175.00	150.00
EGT19	C38a		30m grn	dbl ovpt (vc)	90.00	62.50
EGT20	C38b			invtd ovpt (vc)	125.00	100.00
EGT21	C52a	(1948)	22m on 200m	date omitted	—	—
EGT22	J14a	(1888)	5pi gray	period after "PIASTRES"	65.00	37.50
EGT23	J19a	(1898)	3m on 2pi orange	invtd surch (vc)	20.00	15.00
EGT24	J19b			dbl surch (vc)	65.00	50.00
EGT25	J26a	(1922)	2pi orange	ovpt right side up	5.50	2.50
EGT26	O8a	(1913)	5m carmine rose	invtd ovpt (vc)	—	25.00
EGT27	O8b			no period after "S"	4.25	1.75
EGT28	O9a	(1914-15)	2m green	invtd ovpt (vc)	14.00	10.00
EGT29	O9b			dbl ovpt (vc)	160.00	
EGT30	O9c			no period after "S"	4.00	3.00
EGT31	O10a		4m brn red	invtd ovpt (vc)	90.00	55.00
EGT32	O11a	(1914)	1m olive brown	no period after "S"	1.60	1.25
EGT33	O12a		3m orange	no period after "S"	3.50	2.50
EGT34	O13a		5m lake	no period after "S"	2.50	2.00
EGT35	O13b			two periods after "S"	2.50	2.00
EGT36	O14a	(1915)	2m green	invtd ovpt (vc)	6.50	5.00
EGT37	O14b			dbl ovpt (vc)	10.00	—
EGT38	O16a		5m lake	pair, one without ovpt (u)	140.00	—

EGT39	O24a		4m green	2 periods after "H" none after "S"	65.00	65.00
EGT40	O25a		5m pink	two periods after "H" none after "S"	35.00	35.00
EGT41	O27a	(1923)	10m lake	two periods as above	50.00	37.50
EGT42	O29a		15m indigo	two periods as above	200.00	200.00

Egypt produced mostly vc's. Many are expensive. Beginning error collectors especially should shy away from Egypt.

ELOBEY, ANNOBON AND CORISCO

EAC1	35a	(1906)	10c on 1c rose (bk)	invtd surch (vc)	6.50	4.75
EAC2	35b			value omitted	22.00	12.50
EAC3	35c			frame omitted	11.50	5.75
EAC4	35d			dbl surch (vc)	6.50	4.75
EAC5	35e			surcharged "15 cents"	22.50	12.50
EAC6	35f			surcharged "25 cents"	35.00	17.50
EAC7	35g			surcharged "50 cents"	35.00	17.50
EAC8	35h			"1906," omitted	12.50	5.75
EAC9	36a		15c on 2c dp vio (R)	frame omitted	8.50	4.25
EAC10	36b			surcharged "25 cents"	11.50	7.00
EAC11	36c			invtd surch (vc)	6.50	4.75
EAC12	36d			dbl surch (vc)	6.50	4.75
EAC13	37a		25c on 3c blk (R)	invtd surch (vc)	6.50	4.75
EAC14	37b			dbl surch (vc)	6.50	4.75
EAC15	37C			surch "15 cents"	11.50	7.00
EAC16	37d			surch "50 cents"	17.50	8.50
EAC17	38a		50c on 4c red (bk)	invtd surch (vc)	6.50	4.75
EAC18	38b			value omitted	27.50	14.00
EAC19	38c			frame omitted	12.50	6.25
EAC20	38e			dbl surch (vc)	6.50	4.75
EAC21	38f			"1906," omitted	12.50	6.25
EAC22	38g			surch "10 cents"	25.00	12.50
EAC23	38h			surch "25 cents"	25.00	12.50

The 1906 issue of EAC contains 23 overprint errors. Vc's, dates omitted, frames omitted, erroneous surch values, etc., and none of the prices are exorbitant. But who has ever heard of EAC? Therefore each individual must ask: is EAC a land for me?

EPIRUS
EPI1-8 are all NA or not priced

EQUATORIAL GUINEA

EQG1	R25		yellow, green, blue	value missing R	25.00

See Photo in Color Section

ERITREA

ERT1	1a	(1892)	1c bronze grn	invtd ovpt (vc)	NA	200.00
ERT2	1b			dbl ovpt (vc)	NA	—
ERT3	2a		2c org brn	invtd ovpt (vc)	NA	200.00
ERT4	2b			dbl ovpt (vc)	NA	—
ERT5	3a		5c green	invtd ovpt (vc)	NA	
ERT5A	12		1c on brown R		15.00	
ERT6	14a	(1895-99)	5c green	invtd ovpt (vc)	NA	
ERT7	19a	(1903-28)	1c brown	invtd ovpt (vc)	100.00	30.00
ERT8	24a		25c blue	dbl ovpt (vc)	NA	70.00
ERT9	52a	(1916)	20c on 15c slate	"CEN," for "CENT"	20.00	14.00
ERT10	52b			"CENT" omitted	75.00	60.00
ERT11	52c			"ENT"	10.00	20.00
ERT12	63a	(1922)	50c on 5a yellow	"ERITREA" dbl	—	NA
ERT13	64a		1 1 on 10a lilac	"ERITREA" dbl	NA	
ERT14	85a	(1924)	25c on 2-1/2 a bl (R)	dbl surch (vc)	165.00	—
ERT15	88a		1c brown	invtd ovpt (vc)	140.00	—
ERT16	99a	(1926)	75c dk red & rose	dbl ovpt (vc)	125.00	—

ERT17	103a		50c deep orange	dbl ovpt (vc)	12.50	
ERT18	B1a	(1929)	10c + 5c rose	"EPITREA"	15.00	8.50
ERT19	B1b			invtd ovpt (vc)	85.00	160.00
ERT20	B3a	(1915-16)	20c + 5c orange	"EPITREA"	15.00	14.00
ERT21	B3b			invtd ovpt (vc)	55.00	70.00
ERT22	B3c			pair, one without ovpt	—	NA
ERT23	B6a	(1925)	B6a 30c + 15c dk brn & brn	dbl ovpt (vc)	—	—
ERT24	B8a		60c + 30c dp rose & brn	invtd ovpt (vc)	—	—
ERT25	E1a	(1907)	25c rose red	dbl ovpt (vc)	—	—
ERT26	J1a	(1903)	5c buff & magenta	dbl ovpt (vc)	175.00	—
ERT27A	J1ba	(1920)	5c buff & mag., post.	Due—Q=<200	30.00	70.00
ERT27	J1bc		5c bluff & magenta	numeral & ovpt invtd	150.00	—
ERT28	J17a	(1934)	20c rose red	invtd ovpt (vc)	42.50	—

A state of Italian East Africa, Eritrea has produced a number of vc's, some priced at less than a dollar, others above NA levels, and several containing the error "EPITREA." We do not find the errors of Eritrea attractive since basically they are overprint errors. The most desirable issues are error-free.

ESTONIA

EST1	3a	(1919)	35p brown	printed on both sides	75.00	—
EST2	93a	(1929)	5s red (grn)	5 feet on lowest lion	16.00	12.50
EST3	35	(1919)	5m yellow & blk	invtd center (u) Sel. Q=<200,	70.00	130.00
EST4	B1	(1920)	35p + 10p red & olive grn	invtd center, (u) Sel. R	130.00	200.00

Estonia has produced very few errors—two inverted centers and the other two errors listed above. EST3 is NA, as may be noted, so this leaves relatively little to choose from for this country. Those who want a five-footed lion will find this rarity relatively low-priced.

ETHIOPIA

ETH1	64a	(1906)	5c on 1/4 g green	surcharged "20,"	45.00	45.00
ETH2	74a	(1907)	2 on 2g dk brn	surcharged "40,"	50.00	—
ETH3	75a		4 on 4g lil brn	surcharged "40,"	50.00	—
ETH4	113a	(1907)	4g green & car (bl)	black ovpt	8.75	8.75
ETH5	142a	(1926)	1/2 g on lt rose & gray blk	without colon ('28)	12.50	12.50
ETH5A	153	(1927)	purple & black	invtd ovpt (vc) R	16.00	
ETH6	227a	(1931)	1/2 m on 4m, type II	1/2 m on 4m, type I	9.00	9.00
ETH6A	269	(1945)	10c orange	dbl ovpt R	25.00	
ETH7	C19a	(1947)	50c on 25c	"26-12-46,"	100.00	—
ETH8	C20a		$2 on 60c "26-12-46,"	"26-12-46,"	170.00	—

The following are reprints from Sellinger, all priced 30.00 to 70.00, all invtd centers (u) R all 30.00 to 70.00

ETH9	120	(1919)	1/8g violet & brn, Gazelle			
ETH10	121		1/4g blue grn & db, giraffes			
ETH11	122		1/2 g scarlet & ol grn, leopard			
ETH12	123		1g rose lilac & grn, prince			
ETH13	124		2g dp ultra & fawn, Prince T.			
ETH14	125		4g turq, blue & org, Prince T.			

EQG1

ERT5A

ETH5A

ETH6A

ETHIOPIA

ETH15	126	6g lt blue & org, cathedral
ETH16	127	8g ol grn & blk brn, rhino
ETH17	128	12g red vio & gray, ostriches
ETH18	129	1T roise & gr blk, elephant
ETH19	130	2T blk & brn, water buffalo
ETH20	131	3T grn & dp org, lions
ETH21	132	4T brn & lilac rose, empress
ETH22	133	5T carmin & gray, empress
ETH23	134	10T gray grn & bistre, empress

Most of the Ethiopian excitement centers around Eth4-Eth18. These are attractive stamps often reprinted with inverted centers. None of these are as costly as indicated above if one is willing to bring reprints into the error collection.

F

FALKLAND ISLANDS
FLK1-3 are all NA or not priced

FAR EASTERN REPUBLIC

FER1	8a	(1920)	7k on 15k red brn & bl	invtd surch (vc)	25.00	—
FER2	8b			pair, one ovptd. "DBP" only	—	—
FER3	14a		20k on 14k bl & rose	surch on back	30.00	—
FER4	25a	(1917)	7k on 15k red brn & dp bl	pair, one without surch	—	—
FER5	26b			pair, one ovptd "DBP" only	—	—
FER6	30a		35k on 2k green	"DBP" on back	20.00	40.00
FER7	62a	(1922)	2k gray green	invtd ovpt (vc)	32.50	—
FER8	63a		4k rose	invtd ovpt (vc)	32.50	—
FER9	63b			dbl ovpt (vc)	30.00	—
FER10	64a		5k claret	invtd ovpt (vc)	32.50	—
FER11	64b			dbl ovpt (vc)	30.00	—
FER12	65a		10k blue	invtd ovpt (vc)	75.00	—
FER13	66a	(1923)	1k on 100r red	invtd surch (vc)	27.50	—
FER14	69a		10k on 50r brown	invtd surch (vc)	19.00	—
FER15	N3a	(1920)	5r on 5k claret	dbl surch (vc)	27.50	—

This short-lived republic in Siberia produced a number of overprint errors. The stamps themselves are not elegant but the price of most errors is reasonable. But why would one collect this short-lived country from the early 1920's that has no social or cultural ties to the west?

FAROE ISLANDS has produced no errors

FERNANDO PO

FPO1	25a	(1896-98)	5c on 12 -1/2 c brn (bl)	black surch	13.00	3.00
FPO2	27a		5c on 2c rose (bl)	black surch	11.00	3.00
FPO3	29a		5c on 6c dk vio (R)	violet surch	8.75	8.00
FPO4	33a		5c on 25c claret (bk)	blue surch	16.00	5.00
FPO5	43Ab	(1899)	15c on 25c green (R)	black surch	NA	
FPO6	88a	(1900)	50c on 4c orange (V)	green surch	22.50	12.00

Most exciting as we shall see
What color surch will it be? —The Bard

FIJI

All 34 Fiji errors are NA or not priced except for one

FIJ30	52a	(1892)	5p on 6p	"FIVE" & "PENCE" 3mm apart	60.00	65.00

FINLAND

FIN1	9a		20p bl, *bl*, III	printed on both sides (40p blue on back)	—	NA
FIN2	57a		3 -1/2 r black & gray	3-1/2 r black & yellow (error)	NA	

FIN2a	72b		10p carmine, Russian eagle	background invtd (u) Sel. R Q=>200	30.00	70.00
FIN3	126a		1 -1/2 m on 50p blue	thin "2," in "1/2,"	9.00	2.75
FIN4	C1a	(1930)	10m gray lilac	1830 for 1930	NA	

One Semi-postal, one Airmail—both NA. Plus one low-priced typographical (1921) and two earlier NA's. There aren't many Finnish errors to talk about so we won't.

FIUME

FIU1	B1a	(1918)	10f + 2f rose	invtd ovpt (vc)	18.00	5.75
FIU2	B2a		15f + 2f dl vio	invtd ovpt (vc)	18.00	4.50
FIU3	B3a		40f + 2f brn carmine	invtd ovpt (vc)	18.00	4.50

FRANCE

FRA1	60a	(1875)	10c bis, rose	cliche of 15c in plate of 10c	NA	
FRA1a		(1939)	light orange- common design, Caillie Issue	Colony name omitted R	50.00	
See Photo in Color Section						
FRA1b	111	(1900-24)	orange imperf	dbl impression R	(pair) 125.00	
See Photo in Color Section						
FRA2	116a	(1929)	10c carmine	numerals printed separately	19.00	6.25
FRA3	228a	(1926-27)	25c on 35c violet	dbl surch (vc)	200.00	
FRA4	243a	(1927)	90c dull red	value omitted	NA	—
FRA5	244a		1.50fr deep blue	value omitted	NA	—
FRA6	401a	(1941)	50c on 55c dl vio	invtd surch (vc)	NA	—
FRA7	406a		50c on 90c ultra	invtd surch (vc)	200.00	—
FRA8	406b			"05," instead of "50,"	NA	—
FRA9	408a		1fr on 1.40fr brt red vio (R)	dbl surch (vc)	NA	—
FRA10	411A		2.50 fr on 5fr dp ultra	dbl surch (vc)	140.00	57.50
FRA11	C3a	(1928)	10fr on 90c	invtd surch (vc)	NA	
FRA12	C3b			space between 10 & bars 6-1/2 mm	NA	
FRA13	C4a		10fr on 1.50fr	space between 10 & bars, 6-1/2 mm	NA	
FRA14	C6b	(1931)	1.50 fr dk bl	with perf initial, E.I.P.A.30,"	NA	
FRA15	J53a		40c on 50c red	dbl surch(vc)	130.00	—
FRA16	M1a	(1901)	15c orange	invtd ovpt (vc)	140.00	60.00
FRA17	M3a	(1904)	15c slate grn	no period after "M"	100.00	40.00
FRA18	M4a	(1906)	10c rose	no period after "M"	85.00	40.00
FRA19	M5a	(1907)	10c red	invtd ovpt (vc)	65.00	37.50
FRA20	M6a	(1929)	50c vermillion	no period after "M"	40.00	15.00
FRA21	M6b			period in front of F	40.00	15.00
FRA22	M7a	(1934)	50c rose red	no period after "M"	*20.00*	*12.50*
FRA23	M7b			invtd ovpt (vc)	95.00	45.00
FRA24	M8a	(1938)	65c brt ultra (R)	no period after "M"	27.50	22.50

FRA1B

FRA30

FRA32

FRA31

FRA33

FRA25	P7a	(1919)	1/2 c on 1c gray	invtd surch (vc)	NA	
FRA26	S1a		90c ultramarine	period after "F"	22.50	18.00
FRA27	N25a		1fr25c on 1m carmine	dbl surch (vc)	125.00	—
FRA28	N26a		2fr50c on 2m gray bl	dbl surch (vc)	125.00	—
FRA29	N50a		15pf maroon	invtd surch (vc)	125.00	—
FRA30	San.554,		grayish black	semi-official denomination missing, R	15.00	
FRA31	San 556c			violet semi denomination invtd R	15.00	
FRA32	San 557c			green invtd surch R	50.00	
FRA33	San 559b			dark gray, semi officialsurch black vs red R20.00		

FRENCH OFFICES ABROAD

FOA1	6a	(1894-1900)	25c blk, *rose* (R)	dbl ovpt (vc)	70.00	35.00
FOA2	9a		50c car, *rose* l	red ovpt	40.00	—
FOA3	11a		1fr brnz grn, *straw*	dbl ovpt (vc)	250.00	
FOA4	12Ab		5fr red lilac, *lav*	red ovpt	NA	
FOA5	17a	(1901)	16c on 25c blk, *rose*	blk surch	—	NA
FOA6	45a	(1903)	5c on 15c pale red	invtd surch (vc)	55.00	55.00
FOA7	58a	(1907)	4c on 10c rose red	pair, one without surch	*30.00*	—
FOA8	60a		8c on 20c brn vio	"8," invtd	30.00	30.00
FOA9-14 are all NA or not priced						
FOA15	J10a		30c brn, *bister*	purple handstamp	NA	60.00
FOA16	J14a		5c green	purple handstamp	NA	
FOA17	J15a		10c rose red	purple handstamp	NA	90.00
FOA18	J16a		15c pale red	purple handstamp	NA	95.00
FOA19	J20a		5c yel grn	purple handstamp	NA	200.00
FOA20	J21a		10c blk, *lavender*	purple handstamp		NA
FOA21	J22a		15c blue	purple handstamp	NA	65.00
FOA22	J23a		30c brn, *bister*	purple handstamp	NA	55.00
FOA23	J27a		5c green (C)	purple handstamp	NA	
FOA24	J28a		10c rose red (C)	purple handstamp	NA	30.00
FOA25	J29a		15c pale red (C)	NA	30.00	
FOA26	J33a		2c on 5c blue	dbl surch (vc)	75.00	75.00
FOA27	J34a		4c on 10c chocolate	dbl surch (vc)	75.00	75.00
FOA28	J35a		8c on 20c ol grn	dbl surch (vc)	75.00	75.00
Canton						
FOA29	6a	(1901)	15c gray	dbl ovpt (vc)	14.00	—
FOA30	29a		75c deep violet on *org*	"INDO-CHINE" invtd, Sel	NA	
FOA31	69a		4c on 10c (Bl)	Chinese "2," instead of "4,"	19.00	19.00
FOA32	74a		14c on 35c	closed "4,"	6.00	6.00
FOA33	28a		75c dp vio, org	"INDO-CHINE" invtd Sel.	NA	—
FOA34	69a		4c on 10c (Bl)	Chinese "2," instead of "4,"	19.00	19.00
FOA35	73a		12c on 30c	dbl surch (vc)	80.00	80.00
FOA36	74a		14c on 35c	closed "4,"	6.00	6.00
Hoi Hao						
FOA37a	71a	(1919)	4c on 10c (Bl)	Chinese "2," instead of "4,"	5.00	5.00
FOA38	73a		8c on 20c	"S" of "CENTS" omitted	67.50	67.50
FOA39	76a		14c on 35c	closed "4,"	8.00	8.00
FOA40	83a		2pi on 5fr (R)	triple surch of new value (u)	NA	—
Kwangchowan						
FOA41	35a	(1908)	10fr pur & blk	dbl surch (vc)	NA	
FOA42	35b			triple surch (u)	NA	
FOA43	39a	(1919)	2c on 5c	"2 CENTS" invtd	50.00	—
FOA44	45a		14c on 35c	closed "4,"	18.00	16.00
FOA45	50a		40c on 1fr (Bl)	"40 CENTS" invtd	—	—
FOA46	55a		1/5c dp bl & blk (R)	blk ovpt	65.00	
FOA47	98a		2pi red, dp bl & org (R)	dbl ovpt (vc)	75.00	
FOA48	116D	(1941)	9c blk, *Yel* (R)	blk ovpt	5.00	5.00
Mongtseu						
FOA49-51, 53-55 are all NA						
FOA52	60a	(1919)	14c on 35c	closed "4,"	7.50	7.50

AFFORDABLE FOREIGN ERRORS

Pakhoi

FOA56	14a	(1903)	75c dp vio, *org*	"INDO-CHINE" invtd, Sel.	NA	—
FOA57	52a	(1919)	2/5c on 1c	"PAK-HOI" and Chinese dbl	95.00	95.00
FOA58	60a		12c on 30c	"12 CENTS" dbl	100.00	100.00
FOA59	61a		14c on 35c	closed "4,"	5.50	5.50

Tchongking

FOA60	60a	(1919)	14c on 35c	closed "4,"	8.25	8.25
FOA61	61a		6c on 40c	"16 CENTS" dbl	67.50	67.50

Yunnan Fou

FOA62	13a	(1903)	75c dp vio org	"INDO-CHINE" invtd, Sel.	NA	—
FOA63	48a	(1908)	2fr grn & black	"YUNNANFOU"	NA	
FOA64	49a		5fr bl & blk	"YUNNANFOU"	NA	
FOA65	50a		10fr pur & blk	"YUNNANFOU"	NA	
FOA66	51a	(1919)	2/5c on 1c	new dbl value	65.00	
FOA67	54a		2c on 5c	triple surch (u)	125.00	—
FOA68	60a		14c on 35c	closed "4,"	55.00	55.00
FOA69	65a		80c on 2fr (R)	triple surch, one invtd (u)	140.00	—

Offices in Egypt-Alexandria

FOA70	1a	(1899-1900)	1c blk, *lil bl* (R)	dbl ovpt	110.00	—
FOA71	1b			triple ovpt	110.00	—
FOA72	8a		20c red *grn*	dbl ovpt (vc)	—	—
FOA73	9a		25c blk, *rose* (R)	invtd ovpt (vc)	50.00	—
FOA74	9b			dbl ovpt, one invtd	100.00	—
FOA75	32a	(1921)	3m on 3c red org	larger numeral	60.00	40.00
FOA76	36a		6m on15c orange	larger numeral	50.00	50.00
FOA77	37a		8m on 20c brn vio	larger numeral	30.00	25.00
FOA78	38a		10m on 25c blue	invtd surch (vc)	25.00	25.00
FOA79	38b			dbl surch	25.00	25.00
FOA80	44a		60m on 2fr	larger numeral	NA	

Port Said

FOA81	9a	(1899-1900)	25c blk, *rose* (R)	dbl ovpt (vc)	125.00	—
FOA82	9b			invtd ovpt(vc)	175.00	—
FOA83	10a		30c brn, *bister*	invtd ovpt (vc)	175.00	—
FOA84	12b		50c car, *rose* (ll)	dbl ovpt ll (vc)	NA	
FOA85	16a		25c on 10c blk, *lav*	invtd surch	—	200.00
FOA86	17a		25c on 10c blk, *lav*	"25." invtd	NA	
FOA87	17b			"25," in black	—	NA
FOA88	17c			as b, "VINGT CINQ" invtd	—	NA
FOA89	17d			as b, "25," vertical	—	NA
FOA90	17e			as "c" and "d"	—	NA
FOA91	33a	(1921)	2m on 5c green	invtd surch (vc)	24.00	24.00
FOA92	34a		4m on 10c rose	invtd surch (vc)	24.00	24.00
FOA93	35a		5m on 1c	invtd surch (vc)	45.00	45.00
FOA94	35c			surcharged "2 Milliemes"	27.50	27.50
FOA95	36a		5m on 2c	surcharged "2 Milliemes"	32.50	32.50
FOA96	36b			as "a" invtd	60.00	60.00
FOA97	37a		5m on 3c	invtd surch (vc)	27.50	27.50
FOA98	37b			on Alexandria #18	200.00	200.00
FOA99	38a		5m on 43	invtd surch (vc)	50.00	50.00
FOA100	40a		10m on 4c	invtd surch (vc)	50.00	50.00
FOA101	41a		10m on 25c	invtd surch (vc)	50.00	50.00
FOA102	43a		15m on 4c	invtd surch (vc)	50.00	50.00
FOA103	44a		15m on 15c pale red	invtd surch (vc)	55.00	55.00
FOA104	45a		15m on 20c	invtd surch (vc)	55.00	55.00
FOA105	50a	(1902-03)	5m on 1c gray	"5," invtd	—	—
FOA106	52b		15m on 50c	bar below 15,	30.00	30.00
FOA107	J3a	(1921)	30m on 20c ol grn	invtd surch (vc)	NA	
FOA108	J5a		2m on 5c bl(R)	blue surch	165.00	165.00
FOA109	J6a		4m on 10c brn (bl)	surcharged "15 Milliemes"	NA	
FOA110	J7a		10m on 30c red (bl)	invtd surch (vc)	67.50	67.50
FOA111	J8a		15m on 50c brn vio (bl)	invtd surch (vc)	70.00	70.00

Offices in Turkish Empire (Levant)

FOA112	1a	(1885-1901)	1pi on 25c yel, *straw*	invtd surch (vc)	NA	
FOA113	2a	(1886)	1pi on 25c blk, *rose* (R)	invtd surch (vc)	200.00	175.00
FOA114	34a	(1903)	1pi on 25c bl	second "I" omitted	6.00	5.00
FOA115	34b			dbl surch (vc)	19.00	14.00
FOA116	39a	(1905)	1pi on 15c pale red	"Piastte"	NA	
FOA117	45a		4pi20pa on 30c org	"4," omitted	NA	—
FOA118	55a	(1923)	7pi 20pa on 35c vio	1pi 20pa on 35c vio	NA	
FOA119	16a	(1902-03)	2pi on 50c bis brn & lav	dbl surch	125.00	—

Offices in Zanzibar

FOA120	3a	(1896)	1-1/2 a on 15c bl	"ANNAS"	55.00	52.50
FOA121	5a		2-1/2 a on 25c blk, rose (bl)	dbl surch (vc)	125.00	—
FOA122	21a	(1896-1900)	2a on 20c red, grn	"ZANZIBAR" dbl	80.00	—
FOA123	21b			"ZANZIBAR" triple	85.00	—
FOA124	22a		2-1/2 a on 25c blk, rose (bl)	invtd surch (vc)	135.00	—
FOA125	27a		20a on 2fr brn, az	"ZANZIBAS"	NA	
FOA126	27b			"ZANZIBAR" triple	100.00	100.00
FOA127	28a		50a on 5fr lil, *lav*	"ZANZIBAS"	NA	
FOA128	44a	(1903)	3a on 30c lil	5a on 30c (error)	175.00	175.00
FOA129	56a	(1904)	25c & 2-1/2 a on 1a on 10c	invtd surch (vc)	NA	77.50
FOA130	57a		25c on 2-1/2 a on 3a on 30c	invtd surch (vc)	—	NA
FOA131	57b			dbl surch, both invtd	—	NA
FOA132	J2a	(1897)	1a on 10c brn (bl)	invtd surch (vc)	92.50	92.50
FOA133	J5a		5a on 50c lil (bl)	2-1/2 a on 50c lilac (bl)	NA	

Reunion

FOA134-141 are all NA

FOA135	4a		25c on 40c org, *yelsh*	invtd surch (vc)	NA	
FOA142	8a		5c on 40c ver, *straw* (vc)		90.00	70.00
FOA143	8b			dbl surch (vc)	NA	
FOA144	11a	(1891)	40c orange, *yelsh* (I) (vc)		NA	
FOA145	11b			dbl surch (vc)	NA	
FOA146	17a		1c blk, *lil bl*	invtd ovpt (vc)	27.50	27.50
FOA147	17b			dbl ovpt (vc)	35.00	35.00
FOA148	18a		2c brn, *buff*	invtd ovpt (vc)	20.00	20.00
FOA149	19a		4c claret, *lav*	invtd ovpt (vc)	55.00	50.00
FOA150	20a		5c grn *grnsh*	invtd ovpt (vc)	32.50	32.50
FOA151	20b			dbl ovpt (vc)	32.50	32.50
FOA152	21a		10c blk, *lav*	invtd ovpt (vc)	42.50	42.50
FOA153	22a		15c blue	invtd ovpt (vc)	70.00	65.00
FOA154	23a		20c red, *grn*	invtd ovpt (vc)	80.00	75.00
FOA155	23b			dbl ovpt (vc)	75.00	70.00
FOA156	24a		25c blk, *rose*	invtd ovpt (vc)	80.00	75.00
FOA157	25b		35c dp vio, *yel*	invtd ovpt (vc)	100.00	100.00
FOA158	26a		40c red, *straw*	invtd ovpt (vc)	125.00	125.00
FOA159	27a		75c car, *rose*	invtd ovpt (vc)	NA	
FOA160	28a		1fr brnz grn, *straw*	invtd ovpt (vc)	NA	
FOA161	28b			dbl ovpt (vc)	NA	
FOA162	29a	(1891)	02c on 20c red, *grn*	invtd surch (vc)	27.50	27.50
FOA163	30a		15c on 20c red, *grn*	invtd surch (vc)	32.50	32.50
FOA164	44a	(1900)	25c blk, *rose*	"Reunion" dbl	NA	
FOA165	48a		50c car, *rose*	"Reunion" in red & blue	NA	
FOA166	51a		75c dp vio, *org*	"Reunion" dbl	NA	
FOA167	52a		1fr brnz grn, *straw*	"Reunion" dbl	NA	
FOA168	56a	(1901)	5c on 40c re, *straw*	invtd surch (vc)	15.00	15.00
FOA169	56b			no bar	75.00	75.00
FOA170	56c			thin "5,"	—	—

ID	Cat.	Year	Description	Error		
FOA171	56d			"5," invtd, (vc)	NA	
FOA172	57a		5c on 50c car, *rose*	invtd surch (vc)	15.00	15.00
FOA173	57b			no bar	75.00	75.00
FOA174	57c			thin "5,"	75.00	75.00
FOA175	58a		15c on 75c vio, *org*	invtd surch (vc)	15.00	15.00
FOA176	58b			no bar	75.00	75.00
FOA177	58c			thin "5," and small "1,"	15.00	12.00
FOA178	58d			as "c" invtd	—	—
FOA179	59a		15c on 1fr brnz grn, *straw*	invtd surch (vc)	15.00	15.00
FOA180	59b			no bar	75.00	75.00
FOA181	59c			thin "5," and small "1,"	13.00	13.00
FOA182	59d			as "c" invtd	—	—
FOA183	100a	(1912)	5c on 15c gray (C)	invtd surch (vc)	60.00	60.00
FOA184	107a	(1917)	1c on 4c ol grn & red	invtd surch (vc)	30.00	30.00
FOA185	107b			dbl surch (vc)	50.00	50.00
FOA186	109Ab	(1933)	50c on 45c vio & red	dbl surch (vc)	NA	—
FOA187	116a	(1924-27)	25c on 5fr car & brn	dbl surch (vc)	75.00	—
FOA188	117a	(1926)	1.25 fr on 1fr bl (R)	dbl surch (vc)	32.50	32.50
FOA189	118a	(1927)	1.50fr on 1fr ind & ultra, *bluish*	dbl surch (vc)	90.00	90.00
FOA190	B1a	(1915)	10c + 5c (bk)	invtd surch (vc)	165.00	125.00
FOA191	B2a		10c + 5c (R)	invtd surch (vc)	45.00	45.00
FOA192	C1a	(1937)	50c red	vert. Pair, one without ovpt	NA	
FOA193	C1b			invtd ovpt (vc)	—	NA

Semi-Official Airs

ID	Cat.	Description	Error		
FOA194	San.525c (1923)	1F bl & brn,	Montpelier Avia. Mtg. R	up to 30.00	
FOA195	San.526b	2F red & bl,	Montpelier Avia. Mtg. R	30.00	70.00
FOA196	San.527c	5 bl & red,	Montpelier Avia. Mtg. R	70.00	130.00

France has turned out a large number of exquisite stamps but relatively few errors in the regular issues. Two "numerals printed separately" are inexpensive but one cliché and two values omitted are NA.

French Colonies

ID	Cat.	Description	Error		
FRC1	3a	10c bister, *yel*	pair, one sideways	NA	

French Congo

ID	Cat.	Year	Description	Error		
FRG1	2a	(1891)	5c on 1c blk, *lil bl*	dbl surch (vc)	NA	200.00
FRG2	3a		5c on 15c blue	dbl surch (vc)	NA	200.00
FRG3	5a		5c on 25c blk, *rose*	invtd surch (vc)	—	—
FRG4	7a	(1891-92)	5c on 25c blk, *rose*	surch vertical	150.00	45.00
FRG5	8a		10c on 25c blk, *rose*	invtd surch (vc)	NA	75.00
FRG6	8b			surch vertical	—	—
FRG7	8c			first "o" of "Congo" small	—	—
FRG8	8d			dbl surch (vc)	NA	80.00
FRG9	10a		15c on 25c blk, *rose*	surch vertical	150.00	45.00
FRG10	10b			invtd surch (vc)	—	—
FRG11	10c			dbl surch (vc)	NA	70.00
FRG12	17a	(1892)	10c on 1fr brn	dbl surch (vc)	—	NA
FRG13	19a	(1892-1900)	2c brn, *buff*	name dbl	100.00	90.00
FRG14	20a		4c claret, *lav*	name in blk & in blue	100.00	90.00
FRG15	22a		10c blk, *lav*	name dbl	NA	
FRG16	35a	(1900)	1c brn vio & gray lilac	background invtd (u) Sel. Q=100-200	42.50	42.50
FRG17	37b		4c scar & gray bl	background invtd (u) Sel. Q=100-200	47.50	47.50
FRG18	44b		40c org brn & brt grn	center invtd (u) Sel. Q=100-200)	95.00	95.00
FRG19	47a		1fr gray lil & ol	center invtd (u)	175.00	175.00
FRG19a	49a		1fr gray lilac & olive coconuts	center invtd (u) Sel. Q=100-200 R	70.00	100.00
FRG20	49b		5fr brn org & gray	center invtd (u) Sel. Q=100-200 R	130.00	200.00

FRG21-25 are all NA

French Equatorial Africa

FEA1-FEA18		(1940-41)		ALL DBL OVPT (VC)		
FEA1	94A		40c		16.00	—
FEA2	96a		45c		10.00	10.00
FEA3	98a		50c		15.00	—
FEA4	100a		55c		10.00	10.00
FEA5	100a b			one invtd	16.00	—
FEA6	102a		65c		10.00	—
FEA7	103a		70c		10.00	—
FEA8	105a		80c		10.00	—
FEA9	106a		90c		10.00	—
FEA10	106a b			one invtd	16.00	—
FEA11	110a		1.40fr		10.00	10.00
FEA12	111a		1.50fr		10.00	10.00
FEA13	114a		2.15fr		10.00	10.00
FEA14	115a		2.25fr		10.00	5.25
FEA15	116a		2.25fr		10.00	
FEA16	117a		2.50fr		10.00	
FEA17	119a		3fr		10.00	10.00
FEA18	123a		10fr			
FEA19	126a	(1940)	75c on 50c	dbl surch (vc)	—	—
FEA20	127a		1fr on 65c (C)	dbl surch (vc)	4.50	—
FEA20a	129a		80c brnty	ovpt without "2"	18.00	—
FEA21	141a		35c on dp grn & yel	dbl ovpt (vc)	10.00	—
FEA22	C6		green & black,imperf	value omitted, R	50.00	
FEA23	San 35a		green	value omitted R	50.00	
See Photo in Color Section						

French Guiana

FRG1	8a	(1887)	5c on 30c brn, *yelsh*	dbl surch (vc)	NA	
FRG2	8b			invtd surch (vc)	NA	
FRG3	8c			pair, one without surch	NA	
FRG4	10b	(1888)	5c on 30c brn, *yelsh*	dbl surch (vc)	—	—
FRG5	10c			invtd surch (vc)	—	—
FRG6	16a	(1892)	75c car, *rose*	invtd ovpt (vc)	NA	
FRG7	17a		1fr brnz gn, *straw*	invtd ovpt (vc)	NA	
FRG8	21a		5c grn, *grnsh*	invtd ovpt (vc)	67.50	67.50
FRG9	21b			dbl ovpt (vc)	67.50	
FRG10	22a		10c blk, *lavender*	invtd ovpt (vc)	100.00	100.00
FRG11	28a		40c red, *straw*	invtd ovpt (vc)	100.00	100.00
FRG12	85a	(1924)	10fr grn, *yel*	printed on both sides (u)	32.50	32.50
FRG13	93a		10c on 50c car, *rose*	dbl surch (vc)	275.00	—
FRG14	95a	(1922)	2c on 15c vio (bl)	invtd surch (vc)	50.00	—
FRG15	96a		4c on 15c vio (G)	dbl surch (vc)	45.00	—
FRG16	101a	(1924)	25c on 2fr bl	dbl surch (vc)	75.00	—
FRG17	101b			triple surch (u)	85.00	—
FRG18	108a	(1927)	3fr on 5fr vio	no period after "F"	5.00	5.00
FRG19	B1a	(1915)	10c + 5c rose	invtd surch (vc)	140.00	140.00
FRG20	B1b			dbl surch (vc)	140.00	140.00

French Guinea

FRN1	13a	(1892-1900)	40c red, straw	"GUINEE FRANCAISE" dbl	NA	
FRN2	54a	(1912)	10c on 75c dp vio, *org*	dbl surch, invtd (vc)	160.00	—
FRN3	55a		5c on 2c vio brn, *buff*	pair, one without surch	NA	—

French India

FRI1	70a	(1923-28)	1fa122ca on 75c bl & blk (bl)	dbl surch (vc)	80.00	—
FRI2	74a		3faca on 1fr yel & blk (R)	dbl surch (vc)	80.00	—
FRI3	77a		2r on 5fr rosse & blk (R)	dbl surch(vc)	70.00	—
FRI4	115a	(1941)	1fa3ca on 35c	horizontal ovpt	65.00	65.00
FRI5	116a		2fa9ca on 25c	ovpt "a" (bl)	NA	
FRI6	116b			ovpt "b" (C)	NA	—
FRI7	B1a		10c +5c rose & blk	invtd surch (vc)	100.00	100.00

Cat.	Ref.	Date	Description	Error		
FRI8	B2a		10c + 5c rose & blk	invtd surch (vc)	100.00	100.00
FRI9	B2b			dbl surch (vc)	100.00	100.00
French Morocco						
FRM1	5a	(1891-1900)	25c on 25c blk, *rose* (R)	dbl surch (vc)	110.00	—
FRM2	11a	(1908)	1c on 1c gray (R)	surch omitted	—	—
FRM3	15a		5c on 5c grn (R)	dbl surch (vc)	—	150.00
FRM4	41a	(1914-21)	5c on 5c grn	new value omitted	175.00	175.00
FRM5	42a		10c on 10c rose	new value omitted	NA	
FRM6	43a	(1917)	15c on 15c org	new value omitted	60.00	60.00
FRM7	44a		20c on 20c brn vio	"Protectorat Francais" dbl	175.00	175.00
FRM8	45a		25c on 25c blue	new value omitted	190.00	190.00
FRM9	46a		25c on 25c violet	"Protectorat Francais" omitted	40.00	40.00
FRM10	46b			"Protectorat Francais" dbl	95.00	95.00
FRM11	46c			"Protectorat Francais" dbl (R+bk)	90.00	90.00
FRM12	49a		40c on 40c red & pale bl	new value omitted	200.00	200.00
FRM13	51a		50c on 50c bis brn & lav	"Protectorat Francais" invtd	90.00	90.00
FRM14	51b			"Protectorat Francais" dbl	—	—
FRM15	52a		1p on 1fr cl & ol grn	"Protectorat Francais" invtd	200.00	200.00
FRM16	52b			new value dbl	95.00	95.00
FRM17	52c			new value dbl, one invtd	95.00	95.00
FRM18	53a		2p on 2fr gray vio & yel	new value omitted	100.00	100.00
FRM19	53b			"Protectorat Francais" omitted	70.00	65.00
FRM20	53c			new value dbl	—	—
FRM21	53d			new value dbl, one invtd	—	—
FRM22	81a	(1918-24)	25c blue	"TANGER" omitted	NA	—
FRM23	121a	(1931)	25c on 30c turq blue	invtd surch (vc)	70.00	70.00
FRM24	122a		50c on 60c lilac	invtd surch (vc)	80.00	80.00
FRM25	123a		1fr on 1.40fr rose	invtd surch (vc)	50.00	45.00
FRM26	B2a	(1914)	10c + 5c on 10c rose	dbl surch (vc)	85.00	85.00
FRM27	B2b			invtd surch (vc)	110.00	110.00
FRM28	B2c			"c" omitted	50.00	50.00
FRM29	B4a		10c+5c on 10c (V)	dbl surch (vc)	110.00	110.00
FRM30	B4b			invtd surch (vc)	110.00	110.00
FRM31	B4c			dbl surch one invtd	110.00	110.00
FRM32	B6a	(1915)	5c + 5c grn	invtd surch (vc)	165.00	165.00
FRM33	C12a	(1931)	1fr on 1.40fr (B)	invtd surch (vc)	200.00	200.00
FRM34	J3a		30c on 30c car	pair, one without surch	—	—
FRN35	J4a		50c on 50c lilac	"S" of "CENTIMOS" omitted	—	10.00
FRN36	J11a		10c on 10c choc (R)	dbl surch (vc)	90.00	90.00
French Polynesia						
FRP1	55a	(1915)	10c red	invtd ovpt (vc)	85.00	85.00
FRP2	64a		45c on 10c rose & org	invtd surch (vc)	NA	
FRP3	B1a		10c + 5c red	"e" instead of "c" 35.00	35.00	
FRP4	B1b			invtd surch (vc)	85.00	85.00
FRP5	B2a		10c + 5c rose & org	"e" instead of "c"	25.00	25.00
FRP6	B2b			"c" invtd	25.00	25.00
FRP7	B2c			invtd surch (vc)	150.00	150.00
FRP8	B3a		10c + 5c rose & org	"e" instead of "c"	15.00	15.00
FRP9	B3b			invtd surch (vc)	85.00	85.00

French Southern and Antarctic Territories has produced no errors

French Sudan

FRS1	48a	(1930)	3fr red vio	dbl ovpt (vc)	100.00	—

French West Africa has produced no errors

FUJEIRA

FUJ1	11B	(1969)	Michel Block	multicolor invert	45.00 (R)

See Photo in Color Section

FUNCHAL

FUN1	13	(1897)	2 -1/2 R gray & blk	value invtd Sel. Q=<200 R	up to 30.00

CHAPTER IV: G-I

GABON

GAB1	3e	(1886)	25c on 20c red, *grn*	56 dots around "GAB"	NA	
GAB2	16a	(1904-07)	1c blk, *lil bl*	"GABON" double	NA	—
GAB3	83a	(1912)	10c on 2fr vio, *rose*	invtd surch (vc)	175.00	175.00
GAB4	89a	(1924-31)	10c yel grn & bl grn	dbl ovpt (bk & bl) (vc)	90.00	90.00
GAB5	93a		20c ol brn & dk vio (C)	invtd ovpt (vc)	90.00	90.00
GAB6	B1a	(1916)	10c + 5c red & car	dbl surch (vc)	100.00	110.00
GAB7	B2a		10c + 5c red & car	dbl surch	100.00	110.00

Gabon is certainly not the place for the neophyte error collector to begin. The prices are high, all of the errors but one are surcharge errors, and the errors are not particularly attractive.

GAMBIA

GAM1	4b	(1874)	6p blue	panel sloping down from left to right	NA	
GAM2	18c	(1886-87)	6p slate grn	as "a" panel sloping down from left to right	120.00	75.00
GAM3	18d			as "b" panel sloping down from left to right	55.00	80.00
GAM4	66a	(1906)	1p on 3sh	dbl surch (vc)	NA	

Panel sloping errors and one vc
That's all Gambia offers thee. — The Bard

GEORGIA

GEO1	36a	(1923)	10,000r on 1000r	blk surch	10.00	15.00
GEO2	36b		20,000r on 1000r		200.00	—
GEO3	37a		15,000r on 2000r	blk surch, violet surch	15.00	15.00
GEO4	38a		20,000r on 500r	blk surch	10.00	4.00
GEO5	39a		40,000r on 5000r	blk surch	7.00	8.00
GEO6	40a		80,000r on 3000r	blk surch	6.50	10.00
GEO7	N17b	(1916)	5c grn & blk	invtd ovpt (vc)	72.50	35.00
GEO8	N101a		1/2 p green	dbl ovpt (R & bk)	—	
GEO9	N103a		3p vio *yel*	dbl ovpt (vc)	—	NA
GEO10	N109a		10c brown orange	invtd ovpt (vc)	—	—
from Sellinger:						
GEO11	17	(1919)	1r orange brn, St. George	invtd center, used Q=<100	70.00	130.00
GEO12	18	(1920)	2r red brn, Queen Thamar	invtd center, used Q=<100	70.00	130.00
GEO13	19		3r gray blue, Queen Thamar	invtd center, used Q=<100	70.00	130.00

Georgia is an interesting country in two respects: (1) it has produced three inverted centers that are all affordable and (2) there has been a philatelic debate as to whether certain early issues have been fraudulent. All errors are affordable.

GERMAN N. GUINEA

GNG1	5a	(1898)	25pf orange	invtd ovpt (vc)	NA	—

One vc is all we see. —The Bard

GERMAN S. W. AFRICA has produced no errors

GERMAN STATES

Baden

GER1	8a	(1858)	3kr blk, *bl*	printed on both sides	—	NA
GER2	23b	(1864)	9kr brown	printed on both sides	—	

Bavaria

GER3	16a	(1867-68)	3kr rose	printed on both sides	—	—
GER4	77a	(1911)	3pf brn, *gray brn*	"911," for "1911,"	NA	
GER5	79b			"911," for "1911,"	16.00	16.00
GER6	115a	(1916)	2-1/2 pf on 2pf gray	dbl surch (vc)	—	—

GER7	144a	(1919)	35pf orange	without ovpt (vc)	125.00	—
GER8	148a		75pf red brown	without ovpt (vc)	32.50	NA
GER9	164a		35pf orange	without ovpt (vc)	18.00	—
GER10	168a		75pf red brown	without ovpt (vc)	NA	—
GER11	118a	(1919)	15pf dk violet	dbl ovpt (vc)	NA	
GER12	191a		5m slate & car	invtd ovpt (vc)	NA	—
GER13	217a	(1919-20)	20pf blue	dbl ovpt (vc)	60.00	—
GER14	223a		75pf olive bis	without ovpt (vc)	8.00	—
GER15	234a	(1920)	1.25m on 1m yel grn	without surch	NA	—
GER16	235a		1.50m on 1m org	without surch (vc)	5.75	—
GER17	236a		2.50m on 1m gray	without surch	5.75	—
GER18	237a		20pf on 3pf brown	invtd surch (vc)	12.50	30.00
GER19	237b			dbl surch (vc)	70.00	100.00
GER20	256a		5pf yellow grn	invtd surch (vc)	16.00	—
GER21	259a		20pf violet	dbl ovpt (vc)	16.00	—
GER22	259a		20pf violet	invtd ovpt (vc)	16.00	—
GER23	260a		30pf deep blue	invtd ovpt (vc)	22.50	—
GER24	261a		40pf brown	invtd ovpt (vc)	22.50	—
GER25	266a		1m car & gray	invtd ovpt (vc)	22.50	—
GER26	269a		2m vio & ol bis	without ovpt (vc)	50.00	—
GER27	B1a	(1919)	10pf + 5pf car rose	invtd surch (vc)	12.00	30.00
GER28	B1b			surch on back	24.00	—
GER29	B2a		15pf + 5pf ver	invtd surch (vc)	12.00	30.00
GER30	B3a		20pf +5pf blue	invtd surch (vc)	12.00	30.00
GER31	J1a	(1862)	3kr black	"Empfange,"	NA	
GER32	J11b	(1888)	3pf gray, rose toned paper	invtd ovpt (vc)	NA	—
GER33	J13a		10pf gray	as "a" dbl ovpt (vc)	—	NA

Printed on both sides with Baden is all we see
Bavaria is laden with two errors, omitted overprints and vc's
Which is a greater sin we'll leave it to thee. —The Bard

Bergedorf has produced no errors
Bremen

| GER34 | 2a | (1856-60) | 5gr blk, *rose* | printed on both sides | — | — |

Bergedorf has none and Bremen one—
Printed on both sides
With price none
I want one. —The Bard

Brunswick has produced no errors
Hanover has produced no errors
Lubeck

| GER35 | 3a | (1859) | 2s brown | value in words reads "ZWEI EIN HALB" | NA | |

Wow! Here we can have lots of fun
Brunswick, Hamburg and Hanover none,
Lubeck's high price puts you on the run. —The Bard

Oldenburg
GER36-41 are all NA
Prussia has produced no errors
Saxony has produced no errors
Schleswig-Holstein

| GER42 | 2b | (1850) | 2s rose & pink | dbl embossing | NA | — |

Thurn and Taxis has produced no errors
Wurtemberg

GER42	72a	(1881)	5m bl & blk	dbl impression of figure of value	190.00	—
GER43	O157a		25pf brn & blk	invtd ovpt (vc)	100.00	*200.00*
GER44	O158a		30pf org & blk	invtd ovpt (vc)	NA	

North German Confederation has produced no errors

Prussia, Saxony, Thurn and Taxis did not produce a single error while Schleswig Holstein produced only one sky high NA! Wurtemberg did produce a few affordable errors. Try WUR2 for size. The North German Confederates produced none.

GERMANY

GRM1	45a	(1900)	2pf gray	"REIGHSPOST"	75.00	190.00
GRM2	65b		5m slate & car I	red & white retouched	NA	
GRM3	65c			white only retouched	NA	
GRM4	66a		3pf brown	"DFUTSCHES"	15.00	*50.00*
GRM5	95a		5m slate & car	center invtd	NA	
GRM6	155a		20m indigo & grn	green background invtd (u) Sel.	175.00	NA
GRM7	196b	(1922-23)	2m indigo & grn	green background invtd (u)	14.00	*140.00*
GRM8	241a	(1923)	8th m on 30pf	"8," invtd	30.00	NA
GRM9	244a		20th m on 12m	invtd surch (vc)	—	—
GRM10	246a		20th m on 200m	invtd surch (vc)	85.00	165.00
GRM11	248a		30th m on 10m dp bl	invtd surch (vc)	150.00	—
GRM12	249a		30th m on 200m pale bl (bl)	without surch	165.00	—
GRM13	252a		75th m on 1000m yel grn	without surch	165.00	—
GRM14	253a		100th m on 100m	dbl surch (vc) R		
GRM15	253b			invtd surch (vc)	15.00	
GRM16	254b		100th m on 400m bluish grn (G)	without surch	165.00	—
GRM17	256a		250th m on 200m	invtd surch (vc)	27.50	
GRM18	256b			dbl surch (vc)	50.00	—
GRM19	257a		250th m on 300m dp grn	invtd surch (vc)	21.00	—
GRM20	258a		250th m on 400m	invtd surch (vc)	27.50	—
GRM21	260a		250th m on 500m red org	dbl surch (vc)	21.00	—
GRM22	260b			invtd surch (vc)	37.50	—
GRM23	263a		800th m on 200m	dbl surch (vc)	85.00	—
GRM24	263b			invtd surch (vc)	50.00	—
GRM25	264a		800th m on 300m lt grn	blk surch (vc)	37.50	—
GRM26	265a		800th m on 400m dk brn	invtd surch (vc)	67.50	—
GRM27	265b			dbl surch (vc)	70.00	—
GRM28	270a		2mil m on 300m dp grn	invtd surch (vc)	67.50	—
GRM29	270b			dbl surch (vc)	85.00	—
GRM30	310a	(1923)	1 mird m on 100m vio	invtd surch (vc)	62.50	—
GRM31	311a		5mird m on 2mil m	invtd surch (vc)	30.00	—
GRM32	311b			dbl surch (vc)	62.50	—
GRM33	312a		5mird m on 4mil m	invtd surch (vc)	42.50	*165.00*
GRM34	312b			dbl surch (vc)	50.00	—
GRM35	313a		5mird m on 10mil m	invtd surch	27.50	*165.00*
GRM36	313b			dbl surch (vc)	30.00	—
GRM37	314a		10mird m on 20mil m	dbl surch (vc)	72.50	—
GRM38	314b			invtd surch	42.50	—

GRM14

GRM52A

GRE179

GRE199

GRE184

GRE185A

GRM39	315a		10mird m on 50mil m	invtd surch (vc)	30.00	—
GRM40	315b			dbl surch (vc)	72.50	—
GRM41	316a		10mird m on 100mil m	invtd surch (vc)	37.50	—
GRM42	316b			dbl surch (vc)	70.00	—
GRM43	319a		5mird m on 10 mil m	invtd surch (vc)	30.00	—
GRM44	319b			dbl surch (vc)	30.00	—
GRM45	321a		10mird m on 50mil m	invtd surch (vc)	35.00	—
GRM46	323b-328b	(1923)	328b 3pf	all value omitted	105.00	NA
GRM47	324b		5pf		140.00	—
GRM48	325b		10pf		105.00	—
GRM49	326b		20pf		100.00	—
GRM50	327b		50pf		100.00	—
GRM51	328b		100pf		140.00	—
GRM52	404b	(1933)	8pf dp orange	open "D"	27.50	4.00
GRM52A	589		39pf olive	dbl ovpt R?		
GRM53	730a	(1955)	10pf lemon, blk & grn	value omitted	NA	
GRM54	B6a	(1923)	25m + 500m	invtd surch (vc)	95.00	
GRM55	B7a		20m + 1000m	invtd surch (vc)	NA	—
GRM56	B7b			green background invtd (vc)	125.00	NA
GRM57	B32a	(1929)	50pf + 40pf choc, ocher & red	"PE" for "PF"	200.00	NA
GRM58	O29a	(1923)	5th m on 5m	invtd surch (vc)	55.00	
GRM59	O30a		20th on 30pf	invtd surch (vc)	70.00	—
GRM60	O31b		100th m on 15pf	invtd surch (vc)	55.00	—
GRM61	O32a		250th m on 10pf car rose	dbl surch (vc)	55.00	—
GRM62	O34a		75th m on 50m	invtd surch	55.00	—
GRM63	O48a	(1923)	5pf dk green	invtd ovpt (vc)	125.00	110.00
GRM64	O49a		10pf carmine	invtd ovpt (vc)	100.00	110.00
GRM65	O53a		3pf lt brown	invtd ovpt (vc)	60.00	160.00
GRM66	O54b		5pf lt green	invtd ovpt	110.00	—
GRM67	INJ7a		10c carmin	invtd ovpt (vc)	35.00	—

German Democratic Republic

GDR1	O22a	(1956)	20pf ol, arc at left	arc of compass project at right	.15	NA

GERMAN OFFICES ABROAD

Foochow Issue

GOA1	16a		5pf on 10pf, #3	on #3a	NA	

Offices in Morocco

GOA2	19b		6p25c on 5m sl & car, type 1	red & /or white retouched	190.00	NA

Offices in the Turkish Empire

GOA3	24a	(1900)	25pi on 5msl & car, type 1	dbl surch (vc)	—	NA
GOA4	24d			red and/or white retouched	200.00	NA
GOA5	24Bc		25pi on 5m sl & car, type II	dbl surch (vc)	NA	—
GOA6	30a	(1903-05)	25pi on 5m sl & car	dbl surch (vc)	NA	

GERMANY

Germany, its states, and its Democratic Republic by rough count have produced close to 7,000 stamps. As with most modern countries, only a few errors occurred in recent years. To wit, in Bavaria turned out about 30 vc's alone from 1914 to 1920. The 1923 issue is also loaded with vc's. There are also other types of errors—value omitted and would you believe the fabulous 1905 center inverted. Our last _serious_ analysis of Deutchland is too many vc's and not serious errors.

GERMAN E. AFRICA

A very few errors and vc's all
Their overprinters were really on the ball! —-The Bard

GHANA has produced no errors

GIBRALTAR

GIB1	24a	(1889)	25c on 2p brn vio	small "i" in "CENTIMOS"	NA	200.00
GIB2	24b			broken "N"	175.00	165.00
GIB3	25a		25c on 2 -1/2 p ultra	small "I" in "CENTIMOS"	NA	200.00
GIB4	25b			broken "N"	NA	165.00
GIB5	30a	(1889-95)	10c rose	value omitted	NA	—
GIB6	129a	(1950)	6p dl vio + carmine rose	dbl ovpt (vc)	NA	
GIB7	166a	(1964)	6p brown + green	no period in ovpt	15.00	12.50
GIB8	178a		7p olive, rose red + blk	value omitted	NA	—
GIB9	MR1a	(1918)	1/2 p green	dbl ovpt	NA	—

GILBERT ISLANDS has produced no errors

GILBERT AND ELLICE ISLANDS

GIL1	2a	(1911)	1p carmine	pair, one without ovpt	32.50	45.00

Gilbert and Ellice Islands
Produced an error with a price
How can we discuss it twice? — The Bard

GOLD COAST

GOL1	37a	(1901)	1p on 6p lilac + purple	"ONE" omitted	NA	

The one error here
Is lack of a "ONE"
Without a "ONE" we can't have fun! —The Bard

GRAND COMORO

GRA1	20a	(1912)	5c on 2c brown, buff	invtd surch (vc)	150.00	—

Grand Comoro has a vc
That should please both you and me. —The Bard

GREAT BRITAIN

GRB1	3d		1p red brown	"A" missing in lower right corner	—	NA
GRB2	37b	(1862)	3p pale rose	with white dots under side ornaments	—	NA
GRB3	39b		6p lilac	hair lines	NA	60.00
GRB4	39e			as "d" hair lines	—	—
GRB5	40b		9p straw	hair lines	NA	—
GRB6	45b		6p lilac	dbl impression (u)	NA	—
GRB7	159a	(1912-13)	1/2 p green	dbl impression (u)	—	—
GRB8	161b		1-1/2 p red brown	"PENCF"	150.00	75.00
GRB9	187c	(1924)	1/2 p green	dbl impression (u)	NA	—
GRB10	379a	(1961)	2-1/2 p scarlet + black	blk omitted	NA	—
GRB11	380a		3p purple + orange	orange omitted	150.00	75.00
GRB12-20 are all NA or not priced						
GRB21	411a	(1964)	4p black, vio, pink, ocher	violet ("4d") omitted	175.00	
GRB22	411b			ocher omitted	NA	—
GRB23	411c			violet + ocher omitted	200.00	—
GRB24-31 are all NA or not priced						
GRB32	459a	(1966)	6p bl, sep, red, yel, grn, blk	blk omitted	65.00	
GRB33	459b			yellow green omitted	NA	—
GRB34	459c			red omitted	NA	—
GRB35	460a		1sh3p blk, red, yel, bl, citron	blue omitted	175.00	
GRB36	467a		6p org, red, dk bl	red (mini-minors) omitted	NA	—
GRB37	467b		dark blue	(jaguar + imprint) omitted	NA	—
GRB38	478b		3p King	green omitted	—	NA
GRB39	479b		1shop snowman	pink omitted	NA	—
GRB40	508a	(1967-69)	1shop ind, grnsh bl	greenish blue omitted	110.00	—
GRB41	514a	(1967)	4p multicolored	gold (Queen's head + value) omitted	125.00	—

GRB42	515a		9p multicolored	black (Queen's head + value) omitted	NA	—
GRB43	515b			yellow omitted	NA	—
GRB44	516a		1shop multicolored	blue omitted	150.00	—
GRB45	516b			gray omitted	50.00	—
GRB46	516c			gold (Queen's head) omitted	NA	—
GRB47	521a		1sh9p multicolored	gray omitted	—	NA
GRB48	522a		3p multicolored	gold (Queen's head + value) omitted	55.00	—
GRB49	522b			pink omitted	60.00	—
GRB50	523a		4p multicolored	gold (Queen's head + value) omitted	60.00	—
GRB51	524a		1shop multicolored	gold (Queen's head + value) omitted	NA	—
GRB52	524b			blue omitted	NA	—
GRB53	561a	(1968)	9p gold + multi	blue omitted	—	—
GRB54	561b			gold (Queen's head) omitted	125.00	—
GRB55	562a		1shop gold + multi	gold (Queen's head) omitted	125.00	—
GRB56	562b			red omitted	—	—
GRB57	563a		1shop gold + multi	gold (Queen's head) omitted	125.00	—
GRB58	568a		4p multicolored	gold (Queen's head + value) omitted	100.00	—
GRB59	569a		1sh multicolored	gold (Queen's head + value) omitted	100.00	—
GRB60	570a		1shop multicolored	gold (Queen's head + value) omitted	100.00	—
GRB61	571a		1shop multicolored	gold (Queen's head + value) omitted	NA	—
GRB62	572a		4p gold + multi	gold omitted	NA	—
GRB63	573a		9p gold + multi	yellow omitted	60.00	—
GRB64	575a	(1969)	5p multicolored	blk omitted	NA	—
GRB65	575b			gray omitted	100.00	—
GRB66	575c			red omitted	37.50	—
GRB67	576a		9p multicolored	red & blue omitted	NA	—
GRB68	581a		4p multicolored	violet omitted	NA	—
GRB69	581b			orange omitted	125.00	—
GRB70	583a		1 shop multicolored	silver omitted	175.00	—
GRB71	587a		1 shop multicolored	black omitted	50.00	—
GRB72	587b			green omitted	50.00	—
GRB73	593a 9p		multicolored	black (9d) omitted	80.00	—
GRB74-79 are all NA or not priced						
GRB80	O54a	(1896)	1/2 p vermillion	"OFFICIAI"	30.00	16.00
GRB81	O55a		1p lilac	"OFFICIAI"	30.00	17.50
GRB82	O60a	(1902)	1p carmine	"ARMY" omitted	—	—

GREAT BRITAIN

Pink omitted, black omitted, gold omitted, green
What ever happened to the British Stamp Machine? —The Bard

GRO1	4a	(1942-43)	3p dark purple	dbl ovpt (vc)	—	—
GRO2	5a		5p lt brown (bl blk)	black ovpt	.15	.15
GRO3	J7		10c on 1p carmine rose	"C" of "CENTS" omitted	NA	—

East Africa Forces
Tripolitania has produced no errors
China has produced no errors
Morocco
GRO4-6 are all NA or not priced
British Currency has produced no errors
Tangier

GRO7	525a	(1948)	2 -1/2 p bright ultra	pair, one without ovpt	NA	—
GRO8	603a	(1957)	9p on deep olive green	"TANGIER" omitted	NA	—

Turkish Empire

GRO9	4a	(1887)	40pa on 2 -1/2 p vio, blue	dbl surch (vc)	NA	—
GRO10	5a		80pa on 5p lilac & blue	small "0," in "80,"	85.00	70.00

GRO11	9a	(1902-05)	80pa on 5p lilac & blue	small "0," in "80,"	NA	100.00
GRO12	55a	(1921)	30pa on 1/2 p green	invtd surch (vc)	100.00	—

Guernsey has produced no errors
Alderny has produced no errors
The Isle of Man has produced no errors
Jersey

JER1	20a		10sh gray & multi	10sh green & multi (error)	NA

GREECE

GRE1-22 are all NA or unpriced except for GRE7

GRE7	20d		20 l blue, *bluish*	"80,"on back	—	NA
GRE23	36b			dbl "20," on back	—	NA
GRE24	39b	(1872)	5 l green, *greenish*	dbl "5," on back	—	*100.00*
GRE25	40b		10 l red org, *greenish*	as #40, "10," on back invtd	—	40.00
GRE26	40c			dbl "10," on back	NA	
GRE27	40d			"0," on back	NA	
GRE28	40e			"01,"on back	—	NA
GRE29	46c		10 l orange	"00." on back	NA	70.00
GRE30	46d			"1," on back	—	100.00
GRE31	46e			"0," on back	—	70.00
GRE32	46f			"01," on back	—	200.00
GRE33	46g			dbl "10," on back	—	NA
GRE34	47c		20 l ultra	"02," on back	—	NA
GRE35	47d			"20," on back	—	NA
GRE36	47e			as "c," invtd	—	50.00
GRE37	47f			dbl "20," on back	—	NA
GRE38	92a	(1889-95)	5 l green	dbl impression (u)	—	—
GRE39	118a	(1896)	2 l rose	without engraver's name	15.00	10.00
GRE40	129c	(1900)	20 l on 25 l dp bl,	dbl surch (vc)	50.00	30.00
GRE41	129d			triple surch	70.00	—
GRE42	129e			invtd surch	60.00	—
GRE43	129f			"20," above word	50.00	30.00
GRE44	129g			pair, one without surch	100.00	—
GRE45	129h			"20," without word	—	—
GRE46	130b		30 l on 40 l vio	broad "0"in "30,"	10.00	8.00
GRE47	130c			first letter of word is "A"	70.00	45.00
GRE48	130d			dbl surch (vc)	NA	—
GRE49	132a		40 l on 2 l bister	broad "0," in "40,"	10.00	6.00
GRE50	132b			first letter of word is "A"	70.00	45.00
GRE51	133a		50 l on 40 l , salmon	broad "0," in "50,"	10.00	5.25
GRE52	133b			first letter of word is "A"	150.00	100.00
GRE53				"50," without word	—	—
GRE54				"50," above word	—	—
GRE55	140c		20 l on 25 l dk blue	dbl surch (vc)	50.00	25.00
GRE56	140d			triple surch	75.00	50.00
GRE57	140e			invtd surch (vc)	60.00	30.00
GRE58	140f			"20," above word	75.00	—
GRE59	141b		30 l on 40 l vio	broad "0," in "30,"	7.00	7.00
GRE60	141c			first letter of word "A,"	70.00	60.00
GRE61	141d			dbl surch (vc)	—	—
GRE62	142a		40 l on 2 l bister,	broad "0," in "40,"	6.00	4.00
GRE63	142b			first letter of word "A,"	70.00	60.00
GRE64	143a		50 l on 40 l salmon	broad "0," in "50,"	9.25	4.00
GRE65	143b			first letter of word "A"	70.00	60.00
GRE66	143c			"50,S" without word	—	—
GRE67	159a	(1900-01)	5 l on l d blue	wrong font "M" with serifs	100.00	80.00
GRE68	159b			dbl surch (vc)	NA	
GRE69	161a		50 l on 2d bister	broad "0," in "50,"	37.50	37.50
GRE70	162a		1d on 5d green	Greek "D" instead of "A" as 3rd letter	NA	
GRE71	163a		2d on 10d brown	Greek "D" instead of "A" as 3rd letter	NA	
GRE72	164a		50 l on 25 l on 40 l vio	broad "0," in "50,"	NA	

GRE73	191a	(1906)	30 l deep purple	dbl impression (u)	NA	—
GRE74	210a	(1921)	3d carmine rose size 20 1/4mm by 25 -1/2 mm		75.00	17.50
GRE75	211a		5d ultra on above size		150.00	17.00
GRE76	212a		10d deep blue	size 20mm by 26 -1/2 mm	NA	175.00
GRE77	214a	(1913)	1 l green	without period after "Ellas"	80.00	80.00
GRE78	221c		25 l ultra	dbl impression (u)	50.00	—
GRE79	240a	(1916)	30 l rose	pair, one without ovpt	—	—
GRE80	260a	(1923)	5 l on 10 l rose	invtd surch (vc)	25.00	—
GRE81	267a		5 l on 3 l orange	invtd surch (vc)	25.00	—
GRE82	268a		10 l on 20 l violet	invtd surch (vc)	80.00	—
GRE83	272a		50 l 0n 50 l dk blue	invtd surch (vc)	80.00	—
GRE84	282a		10 l on 25 l ultra	dbl surch (vc)	60.00	—
GRE85	288a		10 l on 10 l brown red	invtd surch (vc)	12.00	—
GRE86	290a		5 l on 1 l violet brown	invtd surch (vc)	25.00	12.00
GRE87	291a		5 l on 5 l green	invtd surch (vc)	35.00	—
GRE88	293a		10 l on 20 l blue green	invtd surch (vc)	35.00	—
GRE89	294a		10 l on 25 l ultra	invtd surch (vc)	35.00	12.00
GRE90	296a		50 l on 1 d rose carmine & brown	invtd surch (vc)	—	—
GRE91	296b			dbl surch (vc)	150.00	—
GRE92	296c			dbl surch, one invtd	—	—
GRE93	299a		5 l on 5 l red	invtd surch (vc)	35.00	5.00
GRE94	301a		10 l on 20 l red	invtd surch (vc)	10.00	10.00
GRE95	304a		50 l on 1 d red	dbl surch (vc)	—	—
GRE96	308a		5 l on 10 l red	"Ellas" invtd	5.00	—
GRE97	311a		5 l on 10 l red	invtd surch (vc)	10.00	—
GRE98	322c	(1927)	10 l orange red	dbl impression (u)	80.00	—
GRE99	328b		1d dk blue & bister brn	center invtd (u)	NA	
GRE100	328c			dbl impression of center (u)	NA	
GRE101	328d			dbl impression of frame (u)	NA	
GRE102	330a		3d dp violet & black	dbl impression of center (u)	—	NA
GRE103	330b			center invtd (u)	—	NA
GRE104	331b		5d yellow & black	center invtd (u)	—	NA
GRE105	334a		25d green & black	dbl impression of center (u)	—	—
GRE106	373a	(1932)	1.50d on 5d	dbl surch (vc)	100.00	—
GRE107	376a		2d on 3d	dbl surch (vc)	120.00	—
GRE108	383a	(1935)	50 l on 40 l indigo (R)	dbl surch (vc)	—	25.00
GRE109	389a	(1936)	3d black & brown	pair with printer's name in Greek	20.00	—
GRE110	389b			pair with printer's name in English	20.00	—
GRE111	396a	(1937)	5 l brown red & blue	dbl impression of frame (u)	140.00	—
GRE112	397a		10 l blue & brown red	dbl impression of frame (u)	20.00	—
GRE113	399a		40 l green & black	green impression doubled (u)	20.00	—
GRE114	403a		5d red	printer's name omitted	8.00	8.00
GRE115	438a	(1942-44)	5d lt blue greeen	"NAYO..."	10.00	10.00
GRE116	445a		200d ultramarine	imprint omitted	3.00	3.00
GRE117	455a	(1944-45)	50 l brown & black	dbl surch (vc)	30.00	30.00
GRE118	457a		5d red	invtd surch (vc)	40.00	—
GRE119	457b			dbl surch (vc)	40.00	—
GRE120	457c			printer's name omitted	10.00	10.00
GRE121	457d			pair, one without surch	15.00	—
GRE122	468a	(1945)	40d blue	dbl impression (u)	20.00	—
GRE123	469a		30 d black + red brown	center dbl (u)	25.00	—
GRE124	469c			invtd frame (u)	65.00	—
GRE125	470a		60 d black + gray	center dbl (u)	25.00	—
GRE126	470b		60d black + blue gray		10.00	10.00
GRE127	470d			invtd frame (u)	60.00	—
GRE128	471a		200d black + vio brown	center dbl (u)	25.00	70.00
GRE129	472a		10d on 10d	invtd surch (vc)	100.00	—
GRE130	472b			dbl surch (vc)	20.00	—
GRE131	473a		20d on 50d	invtd surch (vc)	120.00	—

GRE132	476b		130d on 20 l	dbl surch (vc)	25.00	—
GRE133	476Ac		250d on 20 l	dbl surch (vc)	110.00	
GRE134	477a		300d on 80 l	purple brown surch	20.00	7.00
GRE135	477b			dbl surch (vc)	110.00	
GRE136	478a		50d on 5,000,000d	invtd surch (vc)	100.00	—
GRE137	478b			dbl surch (vc)	100.00	
GRE138	479a		1000d on 500,000d	dbl surch(vc)	40.00	—
GRE139	481a		5000d on 15,000d	blue surch	75.00	45.00
GRE140	482a	(1946)	130d brown olive + beige	dbl impression of brown olive (u)	15.00	—
GRE141	483a		300d red brown + lt brown	dbl impression of red brown	15.00	—
GRE142	485a		250d on 3d	date omitted	25.00	—
GRE143	485b			invtd surch (vc)	50.00	—
GRE144	486a		600d on 8d	additional surch on back, invtd	30.00	—
GRE145	486b			carmine surch	150.00	—
GRE146	489a		600d dp blue + lt blue	dbl impress (u)	30.00	—
GRE147	498a	(1947)	50d on 1d green	dbl surch (vc)	90.00	—
GRE148	499a		250d on3d red brown	dbl surch (vc)	90.00	—
GRE149	499b			pair, one without surch	90.00	—
GRE150	500a		600d on 8d dp blue	dbl surch (vc)	90.00	—
GRE151	501a		20d on 500d	dbl surch (vc)	25.00	—
GRE152	524a	(1950)	1000d, ivory + dp green	without dates	NA	—
GRE153	524b			"1949," only	NA	—
GRE154	524c			dates invtd	NA	—
GRE155	524d			dates doubled	NA	—
GRE156	564a	(1954)	2400d green/blue	dbl impression (u)	125.00	—
GRE157	620a	(1956)	1.50d black + carmine	dbl impression of black (u)	150.00	—
GRE158	622a		3.50d lt blue, black+ red	dbl impression of black (u)	150.00	120.00
GRE159	684a		4.50d multi	dbl impression of black (u)	NA	160.00
GRE160	688a	(1960)	4.50d ultra	dbl impression (u)	165.00	—
GRE161	718a		2.50d vermillion + pink	pink omitted (inscriptions white)	10.00	10.00
GRE162	814a		1 d gray + multi	dbl impression of black (u)	—	—
GRE163	894a		4.50d multi	dbl impression of black (u)	—	—
GRE164	1041a	(1972)	2.50d picture	"1972," omitted	3.00	3.00
GRE165	B14a	(1944)	15d	pair, one without surch	50.00	—
GRE166	C48a	(1941-42)	1d on 2d lt red	invtd surch (vc)	40.00	—
GRE167	C49a		1d on 2d vermillion	invtd surch (vc)	30.00	—
GRE168	C49b			dbl surch (vc)	20.00	—
GRE169	C50a		5d gray blue	invtd ovpt (vc)	40.00	—
GRE170	C50b			dbl ovpt (vc)	30.00	—
GRE171	C50c			pair, one without ovpt (vc)	20.00	—
GRE172	C51a		10d gray green	invtd ovpt (vc)	15.00	—
GRE173	C52a		25d lt red	invtd ovpt (vc)	100.00	—
GRE174	C56b		5d red orange	dbl impression (u)	50.00	—
GRE175	C60a		50d gray black	dbl impression (u)	100.00	—
GRE176	CB3a	(1944)	100,000d on 50d	invtd ovpt (vc)	50.00	—
GRE177	J66b	(1913-26)	5 l green	dbl impression (u)	60.00	
GRE178	J66c			"o" for "p" in lowest word	3.00	3.00
GRE179	RA3a	(1917)	1 l on 1 l	dbl surch (vc) R ?		
GRE180	RA6a		1 l on 3 l	triple surch (u)	5.00	—
GRE181	RA6b			dbl surch, one invtd	5.00	—
GRE182	RA6c			"K.M." for "K.II"	20.00	—
GRE183	RA7a		5 l on 1 l	dbl surch (vc)	10.00	—
GRE184	RA7b			dbl surch, one invtd R ?		
GRE185	RA7c			invtd surch (vc)	10.00	—
GRE185A	RA8		on 20 l lavender	invtd R ?		
GRE186	RA8a		5 l on 20 l	dbl surch (vc)	10.00	—
GRE187	RA8b			dbl surch, one invtd	10.00	—
GRE188	RA10a		5 l on 50 l	dbl surch (vc)	25.00	—
GRE189	RA11b		5 l on 1 d	invtd surch (vc)	50.00	—
GRE190	RA12b		10 l on 30 l	dbl surch (vc)	20.00	—
GRE191	RA13a		30 l on 30 l	dbl surch (vc)	20.00	—

GRE193	RA14a		5 l on 25 l lt blue	triple surch, one invtd (u)	6.00	—
GRE194	RA14b			dbl surch (vc)	6.00	—
GRE195	RA15a		50 l on 40 l indigo	dbl surch, one invtd	6.00	—
GRE196	RA15b			dbl surch (vc)	6.00	—
GRE197	RA16a		5 l on 50 l dk blue	dbl surch (vc)	10.00	—
GRE198	RA16b			invtd surch (vc)	10.00	—
GRE199	RA20a		50 l on 60 l blue	perf vert through middle 7.50	4.00R	20.00
GRE200	RA21a		5 l on 80 l blue	perf vert through middle	7.50	4.00
GRE201	RA21b			invtd surch (vc)	—	—
GRE202	RA22a		10 l on 70 l blue	perf vert through middle	4.25	2.00
GRE203	RA23a		10 l on 90 l blue	perf vert through middle	12.50	11.00
GRE204	RA30a		20 l on 90 l blue	invtd surch (vc)	65.00	—
GRE205	RA32a		5 l on 10 l blue	invtd surch (vc)	60.00	—
GRE206	RA32b			left "5," invtd	60.00	—
GRE207	RA36a		20 l on 2 d blue	surcharged "20 lept. 30"	60.00	60.00
GRE208	RA44a		5 l on 10 l vio & red	"K" with serifs	10.00	3.50
GRE209	RA55a	(1937)	50 l violet	invtd ovpt (vc)	.75	.15
GRE210	RA56a		10 l carmine	invtd ovpt (vc)	50.00	—
GRE211	RA58a		50 l on 5 l green	"o" for "p" in lowest word	25.00	25.00
GRE212	RA65a	(1940)	50 l gray green	invtd ovpt (vc)	35.00	—
GRE213	RA65b			pair, one without surch	20.00	—
GRE214	RA66a		50 l on 5 l dk green	invtd surch (vc)	15.00	—
GRE215	RA68a		50 l on 10 l dp blue green, orange & ivory	invtd surch (vc)	40.00	—
GRE216	RA68b			dbl surch (vc)	40.00	—
GRE217	RA69a	(1942)	20 l brown	pair, one without surch	25.00	—
GRE218	RA69c			dbl surch (vc)	—	15.00
GRE219	RA70a	(1943)	10 d on 5 l	dbl surch (vc)	25.00	—
GRE220	RA71a		10 d on 25 l	invtd surch (vc)	25.00	—
GRE221	RA72a	(1944)	100d black	dbl ovpt (vc)	9.00	—
GRE222	RA72b			invtd ovpt (vc)	9.00	—
GRE223	RA73a		5000d on 75d	dbl surch (vc)	20.00	—
GRE224	RA74a		25000d on 2d	dbl surch (vc)	25.00	—
GRE225	RA74b			additional surch on back (u)	17.50	—
GRE226	RA75a	(1945)	1d on 40 l	dbl surch (vc)	15.00	—
GRE227	RA76a		2d on 40 l	vert pair, one without surch	15.00	—
GRE228	RA76b			surcharged on back	10.00	—
GRE229	RA76c			invtd surch (vc)	10.00	—
GRE230	RA77a	(1946)	20d on 40 l	pair, one without surch	25.00	—
GRE231	RA79a	(1947)	50 d on 50 l	invtd surch (vc)	25.00	—
GRE232	RA80a		50d on 1 d	violet black surch	4.00	4.00
GRE233	RA83a	(1950)	50d on 10 l	stamp with dbl frame	8.00	—
GRE234	RA83b			surch reading down	18.00	18.00
GRE235	RA84a		50d on 10 l	surch reading down	16.00	16.00
GRE236	RA86a	(1951)	50d on 3d red brown	pair, one without surch	30.00	—
GRE237	N1a 25		l ultra	invtd ovpt (vc)	200.00	150.00
GRE238	N1b			Greek "l" instead of "d"	200.00	150.00
GRE239	N33a		1 l green	without period after "Ellas"	120.00	120.00
GRE240	N49a		1 l green	without period after "Ellas"	125.00	125.00
GRE241	N64a		10pa blue green	dbl ovpt (vc)	35.00	—
GRE242	N68a		25 l on 2 pa	new value invtd (u)	40.00	—
GRE243	N69a		50 l on 20pa	new value invtd (u)	45.00	—
GRE244	N70a		1d on 20pa	new value invtd (u)	45.00	—
GRE245	N71a		2d on 1pi	new value invtd (u)	—	—
GRE246	N75a	(1912)	25 l blue	25 l green (error) (u)	NA	—
GRE247	N94a	(1915)	10 l rose	dbl ovpt (vc)	60.00	—
GRE248	N96a		50 l vio brown	dbl ovpt (vc)	100.00	—
GRE249	N97a		1 l gray (R)	black ovpt	125.00	—
GRE250	N98a		5 l blue green	red ovpt	125.00	—
GRE251	N98b		5 l blue green	dbl ovpt (vc)	125.00	—
GRE252	N99a		10 l rose	red ovpt	125.00	—
GRE253	N99b			invtd ovpt (vc)	125.00	—
GRE254	N100a		25 l blue	red ovpt	125.00	—

GRE255	N101a		50 l vio brn	red ovpt	125.00	—
GRE256	N102a		1d orange (R)	invtd ovpt (vc)	125.00	—
GRE257	N102b			black ovpt	100.00	—
GRE258	N102c			dbl black ovpt	150.00	—
GRE259	N103a		1 l on 1d org	black surch dbl	150.00	—
GRE260	N103b			black surch invtd	150.00	—
GRE261	N105a	(1915)	2d dp blue (R)	dbl ovpt	—	—
GRE262	N107a		10d yellow green	invtd ovpt (vc)	—	—
GRE263	N126b		1 l green	without period after "Ellas"	100.00	100.00
GRE264	N144a		25d dp blue, ovpt. Horiz.	vertical ovpt	200.00	200.00
GRE265	N145		1 l green	without period after "Ellas"	125.00	—
GRE266	N202a	(1940)	5 l brown red & blue	invtd ovpt (vc)	50.00	—
GRE267	N203a		10 l blue + brown red	dbl impression of frame (u)	10.00	—
GRE268	N204a		20 l black + green	invtd ovpt (vc)	50.00	—
GRE269	N205a		40 l green + black	invtd ovpt (vc)	50.00	—
GRE270	N208a		1d green	invtd ovpt (vc)	35.00	—
GRE271	N217a		25d dark blue	invtd ovpt (vc)	90.00	—
GRE272	N228a	(1941)	100d silver, ultra, red	invtd ovpt (vc)	175.00	—
GRE273	N229a		2d red orange, black	invtd ovpt (vc)	75.00	—
GRE274	N230a		4dark green, black	invtd ovpt (vc)	150.00	—
GRE275	N231a		6d lake, black	invtd ovpt (vc)	150.00	—
GRE276	NJ28a	(1940)	2d light red	invtd ovpt (vc)	40.00	—
GRE277	NJA2 50 l			invtd ovpt (vc)	50.00	—

Greece has perhaps the errors most,
Would you like to be its host? —The Bard

What does Greece have?
Inverted centers
Inverted overprints
Double surcharges
Double impressions—many affordable, even inverted centers
Typographic errors
Omissions
Centers doubled
Inverted frames
And don't go—hurry to the error store,
Greece as a starter is the very best
When you're buying your errors
With lots of zest —The Bard

GREENLAND

GRN1	22a	(1945)	10o	ovpt in carmine should be blue	200.00	NA
GRN2	23a		15o	ovpt in carmine should be blue	200.00	NA
GRN3	24a		30o	ovpt in carmine, should be blue	75.00	100.00
GRN4	25a		1 k	ovpt in blue, should be carmine	75.00	100.00
GRN5	26a		2k	ovpt in blue, should be carmine	75.00	100.00
GRN6	27a		5k	ovpt in carmine, should be blue	75.00	100.00

GRENADA

GRD1	3a		1p green	1p yellow green	110.00	25.00
GRD2	5g	(1871)	6p vermillion	dbl impression (u)	—	NA
GRD3	5De	(1875)	6p vermillion	dbl impression (u)	—	NA
GRD4	8a	(1881)	1/2 p purple	"OSTAGE"	175.00	140.00
GRD5	8c			"ALF"	NA	—
GRD6	8d			"PEN"	—	—
GRD7	8e			no hyphen between "HALF" & "PENNY"	160.00	110.00
GRD8	8f			dbl surch (vc)	NA	
GRD9	9c		2 -1/2 p lake	"PENCF"	NA	
GRD10	9d			no period after "PENNY"	200.00	110.00

GRD11	9e			"PENOE"	150.00	—

GRD12-48 are all NA or unpriced except for GRD30

GRD30	32a		4p on 2sh orange	"4d" & "POSTAGE" 5mm apart	50.00	30.00

Adam and Eve went out in the snow
Many thousands of years ago
Twas then I'm sure that you all know
That to the error store did Grenada go —The Bard

Grenada Grenadines has produced no errors

GRIQUALAND WEST

GRI1-5 are either NA or not priced

GRI6	83a	(1878)	1/2 p gray black, red ovpt (R)	dbl ovpt (vc)	35.00	—
GRI7	83b			invtd ovpt (vc)	6.00	—
GRI8	83c			dbl ovpt, invtd	55.00	—
GRI9	84a		4p blue (type II)	invtd ovpt (vc)	NA	100.00
GRI10	85a		1/2 p gray black	dbl ovpt (vc)	55.00	—
GRI11	85b		1/2 p gray black	invtd ovpt (vc)	6.00	7.50
GRI12	86a		4p blue(type II)	invtd ovpt (vc)	NA	60.00
GRI13	87a		1/2 p gray black	invtd ovpt (vc)	200.00	NA
GRI14	87b		with 2nd ovpt	s in red, invtd (u)	NA	
GRI15	87c		with second ovpt	t in red, invtd (u)	110.00	—
GRI16	88a		1p rose	dbl ovpt (vc)	125.00	30.00
GRI17	88b			invtd ovpt (vc)	6.00	6.00
GRI18	88c			dbl ovpt, invtd	125.00	45.00
GRI19	88d		with 2nd ovpt	s in red invtd (u)	22.50	25.00
GRI20	90a		4p blue type (II)	dbl ovpt (vc)	—	150.00
GRI21	90b			invtd ovpt (vc)	110.00	60.00
GRI22	90c			dbl ovpt invtd	—	—
GRI23	92a		1/2 p gray black	invtd ovpt (vc)	25.00	35.00
GRI24	92b			with 2nd ovpt invtd	125.00	—
GRI25	93a		1 p rose	dbl ovpt (vc)	—	60.00
GRI26	93b			invtd ovpt (vc)	55.00	20.00
GRI27	93c			dbl ovpt invtd	—	75.00
GRI28	93d		with 2nd ovpt in t in red invtd	55.00	50.00
GRI29	95a		(t) 4p blue type II	dbl ovpt (vc)	—	150.00
GRI30	95b			invtd ovpt (vc)	200.00	20.00
GRI31	95c			dbl ovpt invtd	—	—
GRI32	97a		1/2 p gray black	dbl ovpt (vc)	NA	—
GRI33	98a		t 1p rose	dbl ovpt (vc)	—	125.00
GRI34	98b			triple ovpt (u)	—	—
GRI35	98c			invtd ovpt (vc)	—	75.00
GRI36	99a		4p blue (type II)	dbl ovpt (vc)	—	100.00
GRI37	100a		6p brt violet	dbl ovpt	NA	140.00
GRI38	100b			invt ovpt	—	32.50
GRI39	101a		1sh green	dbl ovpt (vc)	200.00	100.00
GRI40	102a		5 sh orange	dbl ovpt (vc)	NA	60.00
GRI41	102b			triple ovpt (u)	—	275.

Griqualand West was part of South Africa, and quit issuing stamps in 1878. It is the story of overprints. GRI17 catalogues for only $6 while other overprints hit the NA level. Most are simple (vc's), whereas GRI15 adds a second overprint in red inverted ($110.00).

With all this variety:
Do your best and never rest
Take your pick from G.R.West. —The Bard

GUADELOUPE

GUA1	1a	(1884)	20c on 30c brown, *bister*	large "2,"	175.00	150.00
GUA2	2a		25c on 35c black, *orange*	large "2,"	175.00	150.00
GUA3	2b			large "5,"	90.00	70.00
GUA4	6a	(1889)	5c on 1c blk, *lil brown*	invtd surch (vc)	NA	
GUA5	6b			dbl surch (vc)	NA	
GUA6	7a		10c on 40c red, *straw*	dbl surch (vc)	NA	200.00

GUA7	8a		15c on 20c red, *grn*	dbl surch (vc)	NA	200.00
GUA8	9a		25c on 30c brown, *bister*	dbl surch (vc)	NA	200.00
GUA9	14a	(1891)	1c black, *lil blue*	dbl ovpt (vc)	18.00	14.00
GUA10	14b			invtd ovpt (vc)	70.00	70.00
GUA11	15a		2c brown, *buff*	dbl ovpt (vc)	18.00	14.00
GUA12	17a		5c green, *grnsh*	dbl ovpt (vc)	18.00	14.00
GUA13	17b			invtd ovpt (vc)	80.00	80.00
GUA14	19a		15c blue	dbl ovpt (vc)	55.00	55.00
GUA15	20a		20c red, *grn*	dbl ovpt (vc)	110.00	100.00
GUA16	21a		25c black, *rose*	dbl ovpt (vc)	110.00	100.00
GUA17	21b			invtd ovpt (vc)	100.00	100.00
GUA18	22a		30c brown, *bister*	dbl ovpt (vc)	110.00	110.00
GUA19	24a		40c red, *straw*	dbl ovpt (vc)	110.00	110.00
GUA20	45a	(1903)	5c on 30c	"C" instead of "G"	13.00	13.00
GUA21	45b			invtd surch (vc)	20.00	20.00
GUA22	45c			dbl surch (vc)	75.00	75.00
GUA23	45d			dbl surch, invtd	85.00	—
GUA24	46a		10c on 40c	"C" instead of "G"	15.00	15.00
GUA25	46b			"I" invtd	30.00	30.00
GUA26	46c			invtd surch (vc)	22.50	22.50
GUA27	47a		15c on 50c	"C" instead of "G"	18.00	18.00
GUA28	47b			invtd surch (vc)	57.50	57.50
GUA29	48a		40c on 1fr	"C" instead of "G"	20.00	20.00
GUA30	48b			"4,"invtd	70.00	70.00
GUA31	48c			invtd surch (vc)	60.00	60.00
GUA32	48d			dbl surch (vc)	100.00	100.00
GUA33	49a		1fr on 75c	"C" instead of "G"	75.00	75.00
GUA34	49b			"I" invtd	90.00	90.00
GUA35	49c			value above "G & D"	175.00	175.00
GUA36	49d			invtd surch (vc)	65.00	65.00
GUA37	166a	(1944)	1fr on 65c	dbl surch (vc)	82.50	—
GUA38	B2a	(1915-17)	15c + 5c violet	dbl surch (vc)	85.00	85.00
GUA39	J4a	(1879)	15c black, *blue*	period after "c" omitted	100.00	100.00
GUA40	J5a		30c black	period after "c" omitted	140.00	125.00
GUA41	J13a		30c on 60c brown, *cream*	"3," with flat top	NA	
GUA42	J13b			invtd surch (vc)	NA	
GUA43	J14b			"3," with flat top	NA	
GUA44	J14c			as "b" invtd	NA	

Guadeloupe produced a number of vc's and many typos. For instance, a "C" instead of "G." Another country that no longer produces stamps, this country integrated into France in 1947. Interest may continue in the country by French enthusiasts. Many prices affordable—some high, some low.

GUATEMALA

GUE1	1b	(1871)	1c ocher	printed on both sides, imperf (u)	75.00	—
GUE2	4b		20c rose	error, 20 c blue (u)	130.00	125.00
GUE3	17a	(1881)	1c on 1/4r brown + green	"ecntavo"	30.00	20.00
GUE4	17b			pair, one without surch	200.00	—
GUE5	18a		5c on 1/2r yel grn	"ecntavos"	35.00	35.00
GUE6	18b			"5," omitted	100.00	—
GUE7	18c			dbl surch (vc)	75.00	
GUE8	19a		10c on 1r black + green	"s" of "centavos" missing	75.00	75.00
GUE9	19b			"ecntavos"	40.00	45.00
GUE10	22a		2c brown + green	center invtd (u)	200.00	150.00
GUE11	23a		5c red + green	center invtd (u)	NA	
GUE12	25a		20c yellow + green	center invtd (u)	NA	200.00
GUE13	26a	(1886)	25c on 1p vermillion	"centovos"	1.00	—
GUE14	26b			"centanos"	1.00	—
GUE15	26c			"255," instead of "25,"	150.00	—
GUE16	26d			invtd "S" in "Nacionales"	20.00	—
GUE17	26f			"cen avos"	20.00	—

GUE18	26h			"Corre cionales"	20.00	—
GUE19	26i			invtd surch (vc)	75.00	—
GUE20	27a		50c on 1p vermillion	"centavos"	1.00	—
GUE21	27b			"centanos"	1.00	—
GUE22	27c			"Carreos"	1.00	—
GUE23	27d			invtd surch(vc)	50.00	—
GUE24	27e			dbl surch (vc)	75.00	—
GUE25	27f			invtd "S" in "Nacionales"	10.00	—
GUE26	27g			"centavo"	20.00	—
GUE27	27h			"cen avos"	20.00	—
GUE28	28a		75c on 1p vermillion	"centovos"	1.00	—
GUE29	28b			"centanos"	1.00	—
GUE30	28c			"Carreos"	1.00	—
GUE31	28d			"50," for "75," at upper right	1.50	—
GUE32	28e			invtd "S" in "Nacionales"	10.00	—
GUE33	28f			dbl surch (vc)	75.00	—
GUE34	28g			"ales" invtd	100.00	—
GUE35	29a		100c on 1p ver	"110," at upper left & "a" at lower left, instead of "100,"	4.00	—
GUE36	29b			invtd surch (vc)	75.00	—
GUE37	29c			"Guatemala" bolder; 23mm instead of 18-1/2 mm wide1	.50	—
GUE38	29d			dbl surch, one diagonal	100.00	—
GUE39	30a		150c on 1p vermillion	invtd "G"	5.00	—
GUE40	30b			"Guetemala" & italic '5' in upper 4 numerals	5.00	—
GUE41	30d			invtd surch (vc)	90.00	—
GUE42	30e			pair, one without surch	100.00	—
GUE43	30f			dbl surch	100.00	—
GUE44	42a	(1886)	1c on 2c brown,	I date invtd	75.00	—
GUE45	42b			date dbl, I (vc)	75.00	—
GUE46	42c			date omitted, I,	60.00	—
GUE47	42d			date dbl, one invtd, I,	100.00	—
GUE48	42e			date triple, one invtd, I,	100.00	—
GUE49	42f			setting II,	1.50	1.00
GUE50	42g			invtd surch, II (vc)	4.00	—
GUE51	42h			dbl surch, II (vc)	100.00	—
GUE52	51a	(1894)	10c on 75c car rose	dbl surch (vc)	75.00	—
GUE53	51b			invtd surch (vc)	100.00	—
GUE54	55c		10c on 200c	invtd surch (vc)	100.00	—
GUE55	52a		b 2c on 100c red brn (bk)	vert pair, one without surch	150.00	—
GUE56	55a		d 10c on 200c orange yellow (bk)	invtd surch (vc)	100.00	—
GUE57	55a		e—vert pair	one without surch	150.00	—
GUE58	56a		1c on 2c (bk)	"Centav"	5.00	5.00
GUE59	56b			dbl surch (vc)	75.00	—
GUE60	56c			as "a" dbl surch (vc)	150.00	—
GUE61	56d			blue black surch	20.00	20.00
GUE62	56e			dbl surch, one invtd (vc)	150.00	
GUE63	57a	(1895)	1c on 5c (R)	invtd surch	3.00	3.00
GUE64	57b			"1894," instead of "1895,"	3.50	3.00
GUE65	57c			dbl surch (vc)	—	50.00
GUE66	58a		1c on 5c (R)	invtd surch (vc)	50.00	50.00
GUE67	58b			dbl surch (vc)	—	50.00
GUE68	59a	(1896)	1c on 5c (R)	invtd surch (vc)	50.00	50.00
GUE69	59b			dbl surch (vc)	—	50.00
GUE70	74a	(1897)	1c on 12c rose red	invtd surch (vc)	30.00	30.00
GUE71	74b			pair, one without surch (vc)	75.00	—
GUE72	74c			dbl surch, one invtd (vc)	100.00	—
GUE73	75a (f)	(1898)	1c on 5c violet	invtd surch	75.00	—
GUE74	76a (f)		1c on 50c ol green	invtd surch (vc)	100.00	100.00
GUE75	77a (f)		6c on5c violet	invtd surch (vc)	75.00	—

GUE76	77b			dbl surch (vc)	100.00	—
GUE77	79a (g)		10c on 20c emerald	dbl surch, one invtd	125.00	125.00
GUE78	81a (f)		1c on 75c carmine rose	dbl surch (vc)	100.00	
GUE79	85a (f)		6c on 200c orange yel	invtd surch (vc)	50.00	50.00
GUE80	86a	(1898)	1c dark blue	invtd ovpt (vc)	12.50	12.50
GUE81	87a		2c on 1c dk blue	invtd surch (vc)	12.50	12.50
GUE82	88a		1c on 10c bl gray	"ENTAVO"	5.00	5.00
GUE83	90a		2c on 10c blue gray	dbl surch, carmine & black	100.00	75.00
GUE84	91a		2c on 50c dp blue	dbl surch, car & black	100.00	100.00
GUE85	97a	(1899)	1c on 5c violet	invtd surch (vc)	7.50	7.50
GUE86	97b			dbl surch (vc)	15.00	15.00
GUE87	97c			dbl surch, one invtd	15.00	15.00
GUE88	108a	(1901)	1c on 20c green	invtd surch (vc)	20.00	20.00
GUE89	108b			dbl surch, one diagonal	50.00	—
GUE90	110a		1c on 25c red orange	invtd surch (vc)	25.00	25.00
GUE91	110b			dbl surch (vc)	50.00	50.00
GUE92	111a		1c on 1c dk blue	dbl surch (vc)	20.00	—
GUE93	111b			invtd surch (vc)	20.00	—
GUE94	112a		2c on 1c dk blue	dbl surch (vc)	75.00	—
GUE95	112b			invtd surch (vc)	25.00	—
GUE96	113b		6c on 25c red (bk)	dbl surch (vc)	75.00	75.00
GUE97	124a	(1903)	124a 25c on 1c dk green	invtd surch (vc)	40.00	40.00
GUE98	126a		25c on 6c lt green	invtd surch (vc)	40.00	40.00
GUE99	133a		1c on 10c orange & blue	dbl surch (vc) R	15.00	

See Photo in Color Section

GUE100	133b			invtd surch (vc)	15.00	15.00
GUE101	133c			pair, one without surch	50.00	—
GUE102	134b		2c on 12 -1/2 c ultra & blk (R)	invtd surch (vc)	15.00	10.00
GUE103	134c			dbl surch (vc)	30.00	—
GUE104	135a		6c on 20c rose lilac & black	invtd surch (vc)	20.00	20.00
GUE105	137a		6c on 50c (R)	dbl surch (vc)	100.00	100.00
GUE106	139a		12-1/2 c on 2p vermillion & blk	invtd surch	25.00	25.00
GUE107	139b			period omitted after "1909,"	12.50	12.50
GUE108	141a	(1911)	25c blue & blk	center invtd (u)	NA	
GUE109	142a		5p red & blk	center invtd (u)	25.00	27.50
GUE110	143a (h)		1c on 6c	dbl surch (vc)	75.00	—
GUE111	145a		6c on 10c	dbl surch (vc)	50.00	—
GUE112	147a	(1912)	1c on 20c	invtd surch (vc)	7.50	7.50
GUE113	147b			dbl surch (vc)	15.00	15.00

GNA1

GNA2

GNA3

GNA7

GNA8

GNA16

GNA19

GNA20

GUE114	148a		2c on 50c	invtd surch (vc)	10.00	10.00
GUE115	148b			dbl surch (vc)	12.50	—
GUE116	148c			dbl invtd surch	25.00	—
GUE117	149a		5c on 75c	"191," for "1912,"		
GUE118	149b			dbl surch (vc)	15.00	15.00
GUE119	149c			invtd surch (vc)	10.00	—
GUE120	151a	(1913)	1c on 50c (bl)	invtd surch (vc)	10.00	—
GUE121	151b			dbl surch (vc)	17.50	—
GUE122	153a		12-1/2 c on 2p (bk)	invtd surch (vc)	15.00	15.00
GUE123	153b			dbl surch (vc)	40.00	—
GUE124	166a	(1920)	2c on 30c red & black	invtd surch (vc)	12.50	12.50
GUE125	166b			"1920," dbl	10.00	10.00
GUE126	166c			"1920," omitted	15.00	15.00
GUE127	166d			"2 centavos" omitted	15.00	15.00
GUE128	167a		2c on 60c (bk & R)	invtd surch (vc)	10.00	10.00
GUE129	167b			"1920," invtd	7.50	7.50
GUE130	167c			"1920," omitted	10.00	10.00
GUE131	167d			"1920," only	10.00	—
GUE132	167e			dbl surch (vc)	25.00	—
GUE133	168a		25c on 2p (bk)	"35," for "25,"	7.50	7.50
GUE134	168b			large "5," in "25,"	7.50	7.50
GUE135	168c			invtd surch (vc)	15.00	15.00
GUE136	168d			dbl surch (vc)	25.00	—
GUE137	169a		25c green	dbl ovpt (vc)	—	50.00
GUE138	169b			dbl ovpt, invtd	75.00	—
GUE139	170a	(1921)	12-1/2 c on 20c	dbl surch (vc)	15.00	—
GUE140	170b			invtd surch (vc)	15.00	—
GUE141	171a		50c on 75c lilac & blk	dbl surch (vc)	17.50	—
GUE142	171b			invtd surch (vc)	23.00	25.00
GUE143	178a	(1922)	12 -1/2 c on 20c	invtd surch (vc)	10.00	—
GUE144	179a		12 -1/2 c on 60c (R)	invtd surch (vc)	25.00	—
GUE145	180a		12 -1/2 c on 90c	invtd surch (vc)	25.00	—
GUE146	181a		25c on 60c	invtd surch (vc)	20.00	—
GUE147	183a		25c on 90c	invtd surch (vc)	25.00	—
GUE148	188d		25c on 3p (I) (R)	invtd surch (vc)	40.00	—
GUE149	193e		25c on 1p (V)	invtd surch 9vc)	40.00	—
GUE150	198e		25c on 3p (R) (V)	invtd surch (vc)	50.00	—
GUE151	199e		25c on 1.50p (V)	invtd surch (vc)	40.00	—
GUE152	208a	(1924)	1.25p on 5p orange	"UN PESO 25 CENTS." omitted	40.00	—
GUE153	230 a	(1928)	1/2 c on 2p (bl)	invtd surch (vc)	12.50	—
GUE154	231a		1/2 c on 5p(bk)	invtd surch	10.00	10.00
GUE155	231b			dbl surch (vc)	50.00	—

GNA23

GNA25

GNA26

GNA27

GNA28

GNA29 front

GNA29 back

GNA31

GNA32

GUE156	231c			blue surch	45.00	45.00
GUE157	231d			blue & black surch	50.00	50.00
GUE158	232b		1c on 2.50p (R)	dbl surch (vc)	—	50.00
GUE159	245a	(1929)	3c on 3p dk green (bk)	invtd surch	15.00	15.00
GUE160	246a		5c on 3p dk green (R)	invtd surch (vc)	15.00	15.00
GUE161	C3a		15c on 15p blk	dbl surch (G & R)	100.00	—
GUE162	C4a		20c on 15p blk	invtd surch (vc)	100.00	
GUE163	C4b			dbl surch (vc)	100.00	—
GUE164	C7a	(1930)	6c rose red	dbl impression (u)	25.00	25.00
GUE165	C8a		1c on 3p green (bk)	dbl surch (vc)	100.00	—
GUE166	C12a		10c on 15p blk (R)	dbl surch (vc)	125.00	—
GUE167	C13a	(1931)	4c orange	dbl ovpt (vc)	40.00	50.00
GUE168	C14a		6c rose red	on #C7a dbl imperf (u)	30.00	30.00
GUE169	C14b			invtd ovpt (vc)	6.00	6.00
GUE170	C15a		15c ultra	dbl ovpt (vc)	100.00	100.00
GUE171	C16a		30c green	dbl ovpt (vc)	75.00	75.00
GUE172	C21a		3c on 3p green (V)	invtd surch (vc)	40.00	40.00
GUE173	C23a		10c on 15p black (R)	first "I" of "Interior" missing	10.00	10.00
GUE174	C24a		15c on 15p black (bl)	first "I" of "Interior" missing	15.00	15.00
GUE175	C25a	(1933)	4c orange	dbl ovpt (vc)	40.00	40.00
GUE176	C61a	(1937)	25c bl green	Quetzal omitted	—	NA
GUE177	C69a	(1936)	5q orange & ind	quetzal omitted	NA	
GUE178	C109a	(1939)	50c orange & brt violet	quetzal omitted	—	NA
GUE179	C133a	(1945)	5c carmine rose	triple ovpt, one invtd (u)	50.00	25.00
GUE180	C133b			dbl ovpt, one invtd	65.00	—
GUE181	C177a	(1950)	5c rose violet & carmine	dbl impression (frame)	25.00	—

Guatemala, like Greece, has produced a plethora of errors—affordable vc's, centers inverted (2), a handful of double impressions, printed on both sides, and 650,282 (approximately) typos. Prices will vary, but a number of interesting items are available.

GUINEA catalogued no errors, but many exist

GNA1A	M243x	(1959)	10f indg, yel, grn & red #123	dbl ovpt	—	—
GNA1B	M244x		45f on 20f magenta, black green & olive green (R)	dbl ovpt	—	—

GNA36-38   GNA39   GNA41

GNA42   GNA43   GNA44   GNA45

GNA47   GNA48   GNA49

GNA1,2	201-2	(1960)	50, 100f multicolor	dbl ovpt (vc) R?	
GNA3-6	309-12	(1963)	5, 10, 15, 25f	different colors, semi-perf R	75.00
GNA7	325	(1964)	5fr, multicolored	invtd center R	75.00
GNA8-15,	325-7	(1964)		eight Kennedy missing	90.00
	& C56			colors errors R	
GNA16	349	(1964)	75f rose red & dark brown	invtd center R?	
GNA17	372	(1965)	30f orange & green	invtd center R?	
GNA18,19	372, 374 or 5	(1965)	green, violet	frame colors missing R?	
GNA20	373	(1965)	10f red & green	heart of picture shows outside frame R	
GNA21-24			100fr & C75	2 normal color & 2 error of color R	110.00
GNA25-28.	394-6,	(1965)	394,2 5fr yel grn & org; 395,45 fr vio & org; 366, C75 75fr red brn & org; C75 100 fr blue & org	error is that all have org design of wreath & hands missing R?	
GNA29,30	396		75fr red brn & org	face of stamp has org design missing; back has the missing "speck" R ?	
GNA31,32	410, 413		5 & 50c	multicolor imperfs, R?	
GNA33	434		25fr green & orange	invtd R ?	
See Photo in Color Section					
GNA34	432		100fr, lavender & orange	invtd R ?	
See Photo in Color Section					
GNA36-38	433-5			orange UNESCOand circle printed on 4th stamp missing from 1st three, R	set 125.00
GNA39-40	B21,3	(1961)	multicolor 25f lav, green, brown; 50fr verm, green, brn	dbl ovpt R ?	
GNA41	C26	(1960)	500fr multi	dbl ovpt, R ?	
GNA42	C36	(1962)	50f orange on green	dbl ovpt R	50.00
GNA43	C36var	(1962)	50f vertical orange on green	dbl ovpt R ?	
GNA44-45	C47,49	(1963)	100fr 500fr multicolored	both dbl ovpts, R ?	
GNA46-47	C52, 53	(1963)	100, 200fr multi	invtd dbl ovpt R ?	
See Photo in Color Section					
GNA48,49			like GNA 59,60	but simply invtd R	75.00

Many errors dark and light
A color carousel
Inverts and color errors
Guinea rings the bell. —The Bard

GUINEA-BISSAU has produced no errors

GUY1   GUY2

of Questa

GUY3   GUY4

GUY5

GUYANA

Guyana's errors are probably the most difficult to catalogue of those of any nation. Dozens of overprints abound and are cross-referenced further in one well-known catalogue. However, a majority of them are not priced. We have been able to obtain, list and describe a number of Guyana errors. They are as follows:

GUY1	SG236	$5 multicolored	ovpt invtd R	10.00
GUY2	335	$7 gold & multi	triple surch (u) R	70.00
GUY3	353	15c maroon & silver	invtd "1981" R ?	
GUY4	430a	3 multi	invtd ovpt (pair) R ?	
GUY5	502	2c grey	invtd "20," R ?	
GUY6		B. Guyana 541 multicolor	dbl ovpt R	60.00
GUY7	781	5c multicolor	dbl ovpt R	75.00
GUY8	SG860	4c red, blue & black	two error types R ?	
GUY9	794A	multi 50c on 5c	invtd R ?	
GUY10	SG825	100 invtd Y on pale orange R		50.00
GUY11	SG833	light green	dbl ovpt R	45.00
GUY12	847	12 multi	dbl ovpt R ?	
GUY13	1076	100 tan & red	invtd ovpt (pair) R ?	
GUY14	2056	grey with red ovpt	dbl ovpt R ?	

The Guyanama is a strange anima
It feeds its kids errors on bananamas
Error prices are benignama
And overprints hitting the millennia. —The Bard

H

HAITI

HAI1A		(1974)	Unused "Centenaire de UPU"	overprints invtd, set of 11 R	200.00

See 1 part of set in Color Section

HAI1	83	(1904)	2c rose & blk	invtd center (u) Q=>200 R	up to 30.00
HAI2A	86		10c pale yellow & black	invtd center (u) Q=>200 R	up to 30.00

GUY10

GUY6

GUY7

GUY9

GUY11

GUY12

GUY8

GUY13

GUY14

HAI2	87		20c dull blue & blk	invtd center (u) Q=>200 R	up to 30.00	
HAI3			50c olive & blk	invtd center (u) Q=>200 R	up to 30.00	
HAI4	108a	(1906)	1c on 20c orange	1c on 50c claret	NA	—
HAI4A			10c on orange red	invtd ovpt R	30.00	
HAI4B			1c on orange	dbl impression R.	30.00	
HAI5	503a		50c emerald & yel	claret ovpt, horiz	.35	.35
HAI6	C24b	(1944)	10c on 60c chocolate	dbl surch (vc)	52.50	—
HAI7	C49a		30c on 25c dk green	30c on 1g gray black	70.00	—
HAI8	C50a		1g gray black	"P" of ovpt omitted	42.50	42.50
HAI9	C61a	(1953)	50c on 60c purple	dbl surch (vc)	50.00	50.00
HAI10	C62a		50c on 1.35g black	dbl surch (vc)	50.00	—
HAI11	C168	(1960)	50c red orange & black	invtd center (u) R ?		

See Photo in Color Section

HAI12-14	469		50c org; C168, 100c grn; C169, 150c blue	blk building centers missing from all set R	90.00	
HAI15,16,	469	C169		error of color R ?		
HAI17,18	B2-B3		1 purple, 1.5 orange	invtd R ?		

See Photo in Color Section

HAI19	B20		100g blue	color error R	35.00	
HAI20	C221E		100g blue	color error, dbl impression R ?		
HAI21	CB8-9		50c imperf pair	surch only (red cross) R	50.00	

A few errors exist that are not too exciting
But a number of unlisted are really inviting
We'll list as many as we've seen.
Out of the Haiti error machine

HATAY

HAT1	1a		10s on 20pa dp orange	"Sent" instead of "Sant"	20.00	20.00
HAT2	2a		25s on 1ku dk slate green	small "25,"	.40	.40
HAT3	3a		50s on 2ku dk violet	small "50,"	.40	.40

HAI1A Set of 11

HAT4	25a	(1939)	10p orange & aqua	ovpt reading up	20.00	—
HAT5	30a		5ku chocolate	ovpt invtd (vc)	20.00	—
HAT6	35a		17-1/2 ku brown carmine	ovpt invtd (vc)	20.00	—
HAT7	J13a		5ku slate black	ovpt invtd (vc)	20.00	—

It has been said that there are two groups of people familiar with that which was Hatay: (1) those who lived in Hatay and (2) error collectors. Out of 50 total stamps issued (all in 1939), 10 percent were errors—a high percentage compared to most countries. Further, 60 percent of Hatay's errors were of the common inverted overprint type. Still, Hatay's errors are relatively inexpensive.

HELIGOLAND
All Sellinger and all six unpriced

HONDURAS

HON1	62aSel	(1891)	2p brown & black	head invtd (u) Q=54 used	140.00	NA
HON2	63a Sel		5p purple & black	head invtd (u) Q=100-200	30.00	70.00
HON3	64a Sel		10p green & black	head invtd (u) Q=100-200	50.00R	—
HON4	105b	(1898)	5c dull ultra	5c red violet (error) (u)	1.50	.70
HON5	106b		6c red violet	6c dull rose (error)	—	—
HON6	127b	(1909)	1c green	printed on both sides	7.50	—
HON7	139a	(1911)	2c green	invtd ovpt (vc)	22.50	22.50
HON8	141a	(1913)	2c on 1c violet	dbl surch (vc)	—	3.25
HON9	141b			invtd surch (vc)	4.50	—
HON10	141c			dbl surch, one invtd	6.75	—
HON11	141d			red surch	40.00	40.00
HON12	142a		2c on 1c violet	invtd surch (vc)	14.00	—
HON13	143a		2c on 10c blue	dbl surch (vc)	5.75	5.75
HON14	143b			invtd surch (vc)	—	—
HON15	166a	(1914)	10c on 6c gray violet	dbl surch (vc)	10.00	—
HON16	183a	(1918)	5c bright blue	invtd ovpt (vc)	5.00	5.00
HON17	184a	(1919)	1c brown	printed on both sides (u)	2.00	—
HON18	193b		1p yellow green	printed on both sides	7.50	—
HON18a	198Sel	(1920)	2c red imperf min. Sheet	invtd center, Spurious		
HON19	202a		6c on 2c carmine	"ALE" for "VALE"	2.00	2.00
HON20	202b			comma after "CTS"	2.00	2.00
HON21	202c			without period after "CTS"	2.00	2.00
HON22	202d			"CT" for "CTS"	2.00	2.00
HON23	202e			dbl surch (vc)	4.25	—

HAI1

HAI2

HAI2A

HAI3

HAI4

HAI13

HAI14

HAI16

HAI17

HAI19

HON24	202f			invtd surch (vc)	4.25	—
HON25	204a	(1923)	50c on 2c carmine	invtd surch (vc)	10.00	10.00
HON26	204b			"HABILTADO"	6.00	6.00
HON27	205a		1p on 5c lilac rose (bk)	"PSEO"	20.00	20.00
HON28	205b			invtd surch (vc)	20.00	20.00
HON29	206a		1p on 5c lilac rose (VB)	"PSEO"	70.00	—
HON30	208a		10c on 1c brown	"DIES" also "Dies", R, DE12	4.00	—
HON31	208b			"DEIZ"	4.00	—
HON32	208c			"DEIZ CAS"	4.00	—
HON33	208d			"TTS" for "CTS"	4.00	—
HON34	208e			"HABILTADO"	4.00	—
HON35	208f			"HABILTAD"	4.00	—
HON36	208g			"HABITA"	4.00	—
HON37	208h			invtd surch (vc)	20.00	—
HON38	209a		50c on 2c carmine	"CAT" for "CTA"	7.50	—
HON39	209b			"TCA" for "CTA"	7.50	—
HON40	209c			"TTA" for "CTS"	7.50	—
HON41	209d			"CAS" for "CTS"	7.50	—
HON42	209e			"HABILTADO"	7.50	—
HON43	210a		1p on 5c lilac rose	"PFSO"	75.00	—
HON44	210Cd		10c on 1c brown	"DIFZ"	55.00	55.00
HON45	231a	(1926)	6c deep purple (bk)	invtd ovpt (vc)	5.50	5.50
HON46	231b			dbl ovpt (vc)	5.50	5.50
HON47	232a		6c deep purple (R)	dbl ovpt (vc)	5.00	—
HON48	233b		6c lilac	invtd ovpt (vc)	5.00	5.00
HON49	235a		6c violet	"1926," invtd	16.00	16.00
HON50	235b			"Habilitado" triple, one invtd	16.00	16.00
HON51	236c-k		6c on 10c blue (R)	mostly minor typos & inexpensive		
HON52	237b-h		2c carmine	inexpensive typos, a dbl ovpt, triple ovpt		
HON53	238a		2c carmine	"HARILITADO"	.90	.90
HON54	238b			dbl ovpt (vc)	1.40	1.40
HON55	238c			invtd ovpt (vc)	2.00	2.00
HON56	239a	(1927)	6c deep purple	"1926," over "1927,"	35.00	35.00
HON57	240c		6c on 20c brown	invtd surch (vc)	2.00	2.00
HON58	240d			dbl surch (vc)	8.50	8.50
HON59	241a		6c on 15c blue	"c" of "cts" omitted	—	—
HON60	242a		6c on 15c violet	dbl surch (vc)	1.75	1.75
HON61	242b			dbl surch, one invtd	2.00	2.00
HON62	243a		6c on 20c yel brown	6c on 20c deep brown	—	—
HON63	243b			"6," omitted	1.75	1.75

HAI20

HAI21

HON98A

HON227

HON64	243c			"Vale" & "cts" omitted	3.50	3.50
HON65	259b	(1929)	1c blue (R)	dbl ovpt (vc)	2.50	1.75
HON66	259c		ultramarine color	dbl ovpt (vc)	2.50	1.75
HON67	261a		2c carmine (R br)	dbl ovpt (vc)	—	
HON68-72 all unpriced					—	—
HON73	269a		6c gray blk (R)	dbl ovpt (vc)	6.00	6.00
HON74	272b		6c dk blue (R)	dbl ovpt (vc)	2.00	2.00
HON75	272c			dbl ovpt (R+V)	—	
HON76	273a		10c blue (R)	dbl ovpt(vc)	2.50	1.75
HON77	274a		15c dp blue (R)	dbl ovpt (vc)	3.50	2.50
HON78	276a		30c dark brown (R)	dbl ovpt (vc)	3.50	2.50
HON79	279a		1c on 6c lilac rose	"1992," for "1929,"	—	
HON80	279b			"9192," for "1929,"	—	—
HON81	279c			surch reading down	—	
HON82	279d			dbl surch, one reading down	—	
HON83	280a		1c on 10c blue	"1093," for "1930,"	1.40	
HON84	280b			"tsc" for "cts"	1.40	
HON85	281a		2c on 10c blue	" tsc" for "cts"	2.00	
HON86	281b			"Vale 2" omitted	—	
HON87	282a	(1930)	1c blue (R)	dbl ovpt (vc)	2.00	2.00
HON88	285a		1c chocolate	dbl ovpt (vc)	1.00	1.00
HON89	285b			invtd ovpt	1.40	1.40
HON90	285c			dbl ovpt, one invtd	—	
HON91	287a		1c brown	dbl ovpt (vc)	—	
HON92	287c			invtd ovpt (vc)	—	
HON93	289b		50c on 2c carmine	invtd surch (vc)	—	
HON94	290a		1c olive green	dbl ovpt (vc)	1.75	1.75
HON95	290b			invtd ovpt (vc)	1.75	1.75
HON96	290d			on no. 075	12.00	
HON97	291a		2c carmine rose	dbl ovpt (vc)	1.75	1.75
HON98	291b			invtd ovpt (vc)	1.75	1.75
HON98A	295type (1930)		2c green	unissued color & pair imperf vert, R	60.00	
HON99	342a	(1944)	1c orange yellow	invtd ovpt (vc)	5.00	5.00
HON100	343a		2c red orange	invtd ovpt (vc)	5.00	5.00
HON101-114 all NA or not priced						
HON115	C15a	(1929)	5c on 20c yellow brown (G)	dbl surch (R+G)	45.00	—
HON116	C19a		20c on 50c vermillion	"1299," for "1929,"	190.00	—
HON117	C19b			"cts. Cts." for "cts oro."	190.00	—
HON118	C19c			"r" of "Aereo" omitted	2.00	—
HON119	C20a	(1930)	5c on 10c (R)	"1930," reading down	3.50	—
HON120	C20b			"1903," for "1930,"	3.50	—
HON121	C20c			surch reading down	10.00	—
HON122	C20d			dbl surch (vc)	14.00	—
HON123	C20e			dbl surch., one downward	14.00	—
HON124	C23a		10c on 20c (Bk)	"0," for "10,"	3.50	—
HON125	C23b			dbl surch (vc)	8.75	—
HON126	C23c			dbl surch , one downward	12.00	—
HON127	C24a		10c on 20c (V)	"0," for "10,"	NA	—
HON128	C25a		25c on 50c (bk)	"Internaoicnal"	3.50	—
HON129	C25b			"o" for "oro"	3.50	—
HON130	C25c			invtd surch (vc)	17.50	—
HON131	C25d			as "a" invtd surch	175.00	—
HON132	C25e			as "b" invtd surch	175.00	—
HON133	C26a		5c on 10c blue	dbl surch (vc)	9.50	—
HON134	C26b			"Servicioa,"	3.50	—
HON135	C27a		15c on 20c yellow brown	dbl surch (vc)	7.00	—
HON136	C28a		20c on 50c red,surch reading down	surch reading up	7.00	—
HON137	C29a		10c on 5c on 20c, (bl + R)	"1930," reading down	9.00	9.00
HON138	C29b			"1903," for "1930,"	9.00	9.00

HON139	C30a	10c on 10c on 20c (bk +R)	"0,"for "10,"	87.50	87.50
HON140	C31a	50c on 25c on 1p green	"Internaoicnal"	7.00	—
HON141	C31b		"o" for "oro"	7.00	—
HON142	C31c	25c	surch invtd (vc)	17.50	17.50
HON143	C31d	50c	surch invtd (vc)	17.50	17.50
HON143	C31e		as "a" & "c"	—	—
HON144	C31f		as "a" & "d"	—	—
HON145	C31g		as "b" & "c"	—	—
HON146	C31h		as "b" & "d"	—	—
HON147	C32a	5c on 20c yel brown	dbl surch (vc)	5.25	5.25
HON148	C33a	5c on 10c (R)	"1930," reading down	NA	—
HON149	C33b		"1903," for "1930,"	NA	—
HON150	C35a	25c on 50c (bk)	55c on 50c vermillion	NA	
HON151	C36a	20c on 50c red	dbl surch, reading down	NA	
HON152	C37a	50c yel, grn, & blue	"Internacional"	5.25	—
HON153	C37b		"luternacional"	5.25	—
HON154	C37c		dbl ovpt (vc)	5.25	—
HON155	C38a	20c dark blue (R)	dbl ovpt (vc)	8.75	—
HON156	C38b		triple ovpt	12.00	—
HON157	C40a	1p buff (bl)	dbl ovpt (vc)	10.50	—
HON158	C56b	15c on 20c yel brown	green surch	20.00	20.00
HON159	C57a	15c on 50c red	invtd surch (vc)	10.50	10.50
HON160	C59b	15c on 1p buff	"Sevricio"	14.00	14.00
HON161	C60a	(1931)	15c on 20c (G)	invtd surch (vc)	6.25	—
HON162	C60b		"XI" omitted	6.25	—
HON163	C60c		"X" for "XI"	6.25	—
HON164	C60d		"Pi" for "XI"	6.25	—
HON165	C61a	15c on 50c (R)	"XI" omitted	6.75	—
HON166	C61b		"PI" for "XI"	6.75	—
HON167	C61c		dbl surch (vc)	20.00	20.00
HON168	C62a	15c on 50c (bk)	"1391," for "1931,"	10.50	10.50
HON169	C62b		dbl surch (vc)	8.75	8.75
HON170	C63a	15c on 1p (bk)	"1391," for "1931,"	12.50	—
HON171	C63b		surch on both side (u)	7.00	—
HON172	C73a	(1933)	10c on 2c	dbl surch (vc)	5.50	—
HON173	C73b		invtd surch (vc)	4.25	—
HON174	C73c		"Ae" of "Aero" omitted	1.00	—
HON175	C73d		on #212 , no "Official"	—	—
HON176	C74a	15c on 6c	dbl surch (vc)	3.50	—
HON177	C74c		"Aer" omitted	—	—
HON178	C74d		"A" omitted	1.00	—
HON179	C74e		invtd surch (vc)	3.50	—
HON180	C75a	15c on 10c (R)	dbl surch (vc)	5.50	—
HON181	C75b		invtd surch (vc)	3.50	—
HON182	C75c		"r" of "Aereo" omitted	1.00	—
HON183	C110a	(1941)	8c dp blue & brown	ovpt invtd (vc)	—	NA
HON184	C118a	(1942)	8c on 15c	"Cerreoo"	2.00	2.00
HON185	C118b		dbl surch (vc)	25.00	25.00
HON186	C118c		as "a" dbl surch (vc)	175.00	—
HON187	C119a	16c on 46c	"Cerreo"	2.00	2.00
HON188	C181a	(1951)	16c green	invtd ovpt (vc)	45.00	45.00
HON189	C182a	22c orange yel	invtd ovpt (vc)	45.00	—
HON190	C185a	2 1 lilac	invtd ovpt (vc)	60.00	—
HON191	C209a	(1953)	10c on 1c	invtd surch (vc)	45.00	45.00
HON192	C213a	24c on 2c	invtd surch (vc)	45.00	45.00
HON193	C221a	5 1 red org & blk	date invtd	150.00	—
HON194	C490a	10c on 3c (#c224)	invtd surch (vc)	—	—
HON195	CO5a	5c on 6c red violet	"1910," for "1930,"	2.75	2.75
HON196	CO5b		"1920," for "1930,"	2.75	2.75
HON197	CO9a	(1931)	6c orange red	invtd ovpt (vc)	24.00	24.00
HON198	CO11a	15c olive brown	invtd ovpt (vc)	24.00	24.00

HON199	CO11a		15c olive brown	invtd ovpt (vc)		20.00	20.00
HON200	CO90a	(1957)	5c pink & ultra	invtd ovpt (vc)		—	—
HON201	CO99a	(1959)	2c gray olive	invtd ovpt (vc)		—	—
HON202	CO102a		10c dull purple	ovpt omitted (vc)		—	—
HON203	O28a	(1911-15)	1c violet	invtd ovpt (vc)		2.00	—
HON204	O28b			dbl ovpt (vc)		2.00	—
HON205	O29a		6c ultra	invtd ovpt (vc)		2.50	—
HON206	O30a		10c blue	"OFICAIL"		2.50	—
HON207	O30b			dbl ovpt (vc)		3.50	—
HON208	O34a		2c green	"CFICIAL"		5.00	—
HON209	O42a	(1913-14)	10c on 1c violet	"OFICIAL" invtd		7.50	—
HON210	O44a		10c on 20c on 1c	maroon surch		20.00	20.00
HON211	O48a	(1915)	1c brm (R)	"OFICAIL"		5.00	—
HON212	O49a		2c car (bk)	"OFICAIL"		5.00	—
HON213	O49b			dbl ovpt (vc)		4.00	—
HON214	O50a		5c ultra (bk)	"OFIC"		—	—
HON215	O51a		5c ultra (R)	"OFIC"		—	—
HON216	O51b			"OFICAIL"		5.00	—
HON217	O55a		20c brown (R)	dbl ovpt (R+bk)(vc)		10.00	—
HON218	O55b			"OFICAIL"		5.00	—
HON219	O57a		1c on 2c car	"0.10," for "0.01,"		4.25	4.25
HON220	O57b			"0.20," for "0.01,"		4.25	4.25
HON221	O57c			dbl surch (vc)		8.50	8.50
HON222	O57d			as "a" dbl surch(vc)		77.50	—
HON223	O57e			as "b," dbl surch (vc)		77.50	—
HON224	O99a	(1936-37)	2c black brown	invtd ovpt (vc)		10.00	—
HON225	O103a		15c olive brown	invtd ovpt (vc)		5.00	—
HON226	O104a		20c red brown	"1938-35,"		—	—
HON227	San86	(1931)	20c light brown, pair	2diff "1," in 1931 R		20.00	—

Honduras has produced tons of errors. Many are overprint errors involving vc's or typos. There are exceptions such as the affordable inverted heads in the 1891 issue. Stamps printed on both sides may be found in the 1919 issue, although they are priced at prohibitively high levels.

Tequcialpa is our home
Because it sits upon the throne
Of stamps which are so error-prone. —The Bard

HONG KONG

HOK1-8, 11-16 all NA or not priced

HOK9	66c			"J" of "JUBILEE" shorter	NA	175.00
HOK10	66d			tall "K" in "KONG" NA		
HOK17	213a		$1.30 sky blue	ocher (sash) omitted	150.00	—
HOK18	213b			yellow omitted	150.00	—
HOK19	214a		$2 fawn	yellow & ocher (sash) omitted	200.00	—
HOK20	214b			yellow omitted	—	—
HOK21	215a		$5 orange	ocher sash omitted	155.00	—
HOK22	249a		10c brown, blk, org & red	red omitted	—	—

Early surcharges, all NA
Later color omissions
Just like their commonwealth friends
These are their commissions —The Bard

HORTA has produced no errors

HUNGARY

HUN1	22Ac	(1888-98)	1k black, one plate	"1," printed separately	10.50	.90
HUN2	96a	(1913-16)	50f lake, blue	cliche of 35f in plate of 50f	165.00	—
HUN2a	386a Sel.(1923)		5000k dk grn & yel grn	invtd center (u) Q=100 38 in museum,	NA	
HUN3	1262a	(1959)	60f dull blue & lemon	ovpt omitted	NA	—
HUN4	F1a	1946)	"Ajl.1. on 20f	"Alj.1	6.00	—
HUN5	J16c Sel (1908)		20f green & black	center invtd(u) Q=100 or less	—	NA

HUN6	J16b d	(1906)	50f green & black	center invtd (u) Q=100 or less	—	NA
HUN7	J38a	(1915)	50f green & red	center invtd (u) Q=100 or less)	60.00	—
HUN8	J46a	(1918-19)	3f green & red	"KOZTARSASAG" omitted	NA	—
HUN9	J49a		40f green & red	invtd ovpt	4.00	4.00
HUN10	J50a	(1918)	50f green & red	center & ovpr invtd (u)Q=>200,	10.00	10.00
HUN11	J65a	(1919)	2f green & black	invtd center (u) Q=100 or less,	NA	
HUN12	J194Ci	(1951)	20f magenta	"fiellr"	—	3.75
HUN13	J227a	(1953)	2fo dull green	small "2," (3mm high)	1.00	.60
HUN14	O1	(1921)	10f brn violet & blk	invtd center (u) Q=100 or less	—	—
HUN14a	O2a	(1921)	2f olive brown & black	invtd center(u) Q=100 or less	130	200
HUN15	P2b	(1872)	rose red	printed on both sides	—	—
HUN16	P4b	(1881)	1k orange	printed on both sides	—	—
HUN17	PR1a	(1868)	1k blue	pair, one sideways	—	—
HUN18	IN4a	(1919)	6f grnsh bl (R)	invtd ovpt (vc)	1.00	1.00
HUN19	IN6a		15f violet (R)	dbl ovpt (vc)	3.00	_R ?
HUN20	1N14a		2k of brown & bister	invtd ovpt (vc)	3.25	_ R
HUN20A	IN20		3f violet	red imprint, dbl imprints R ?		
HUN21	IN24a	(1918)	25f brt blue	invtd ovpt (vc)	1.00	1.00
				ovpt on 1918 issue		
HUN22	IN26a	(1918-19)	2f brown orange	invtd ovpt (vc)	1.50	1.50
HUN23	IN29a		6f grnsh bl	invtd ovpt, red, Occupation	4.50	4.50
			(KOZTARSASAG ovpt)	Francaise (vc)		
See Photo in Color Section						
HUN23A	IN30a		rose red 10f (KOZovpt)	invtd ovpt, red, Occ. Fr, R	12.50	
				set of these 3	(29a-34a)	
See Photo in Color Section						
HUN24	IN32a		25f brt blue	invtd ovpt (vc)	4.00	4.00
HUN25	IN34a		40f olive grn	invtd ovpt (vc)	12.50	—
See Photo in Color Section						
HUN26	INJ8a		30f on 2f orange	dbl surch (vc)	4.50	—
				(1914 stamp surcharged)		
HUN27	2N29a	(1918)	20f dk brown (R)	black ovpt	6.00	6.00
HUN28	2N29b			blue ovpt	6.50	6.50
HUN29	2N30a		25f brt blue (R)	black ovpt	4.00	4.00
HUN30	2N42b		20f dk brown (bk)	red ovpt	7.00	7.00
HUN31	2N46a		3k dk vio & indigo (R)	blue ovpt	3.50	3.50
HUN32	2N46b			black ovpt	52.50	52.50
HUN33	2N49a		25f brt bl (R)	black ovpt	4.00	4.00
HUN34	2NP1a	(1919)	(2f) orange (bl)	invtd ovpt	—	—
HUN35	2NP1b			dbl ovpt (vc)	—	—
HUN36	4N1a		30f on 2f brown	red surch	.65	.65
			orange (bl)			
HUN37	4N1b			invtd surch (vc) (R)	—	—
HUN38	4N5a		3k on 2f gray		.50	.50
			grn & red (bk)			
HUN39	4NJ1a		40f on 15f+2f vio (bk)	red surch	.70	.70
HUN40	4NJ2a		60f on 2f grn & red (bk)	red surch	3.50	3.50
HUN41	4NJ3a		60f on 10f grn & red (bk)	red surch	3.00	3.00
HUN42	5N20a		20b dk brown	gold ovpt	32.50	32.50
HUN43	5N20b			silver ovpt	32.50	32.50
HUN44	9N1a		10f on 2f brn org (bl)	black surch	25.00	25.00

HUN18

HUN19

HUN20

HUN20A

HUN45	9N2a		30f on 2f brn org	invtd surch (vc)	—	—
HUN46	9N3a		50f on 20f dk brn (bl)	invtd surch (vc)	—	—
HUN47	9N4a		1k 50f on 15f vio	brown surch	—	—
HUN48	9N4b			dbl surch (bk)	—	—
HUN49	10N12a		2k of brn & bister	red ovpt	6.00	6.00
HUN50	Folderer 1 Sel.	(1868)		1/2 kr, Revenue	invtd center (u)	
HUN51	Folderer 2 Sel.	(1868)		1 kr, Revenue	invtd center (u)	

I

ICELAND

ICE1	31b	(1897)	3a on 5a green	invtd surch (vc)	NA	
ICE2	32a		3a on 5a green	invtd surch (vc)	NA	
ICE3	40a	(1902-04)	20a deep blue	inscribed "PJONUSTA"	70.00	70.00
ICE4	45a		5a green	invtd ovpt (vc)	25.00	—
ICE5	45b			"I" before Gildi omitted	40.00	—
ICE6	45c			'03.'03	80.00	—
ICE7	45d			02'.'03	80.00	—
ICE8	45e			pair, one without ovpt	32.50	—
ICE9	46a		6a gray	dbl ovpt (vc)	40.00	—
ICE10	46b			invtd ovpt (vc)	40.00	—
ICE11	46c			'03-'03	110.00	—
ICE12	46d			02-'03	110.00	—
ICE13	46e			pair, one without ovpt	40.00	—
ICE14	46g			as "f," invtd	80.00	—
ICE15	47a		20a dull blue	invtd ovpt (vc)	25.00	—
ICE16	47b			"I" before Gildi omitted	25.00	—
ICE17	47c			02'-'03	110.00	—
ICE18	48a		25a yel brown & blue	invtd ovpt (vc)	32.50	52.50
ICE19	48b			'03-'03	80.00	—
ICE20	48c			02'-'03	80.00	—
ICE21	49b		3a orange	invtd ovpt (vc)	200.00	—
ICE22	49c			"I" before Gildi omitted	NA	—
ICE23	49d			'03-'03	NA	—
ICE24	49e			02'-'03	NA	—
ICE25	50a		3a yellow	dbl ovpt (vc)	75.00	—
ICE26	50b			invtd ovpt (vc)	25.00	—
ICE27	50c			"I" before Gildi omitted	NA	—
ICE28	50d			02'-'03	110.00	—
ICE29	51a		4a rose & gray	dbl ovpt (vc)	100.00	—
ICE30	51b			invtd ovpt (vc)	70.00	—
ICE31	51c			dbl ovpt, one invtd	140.00	—
ICE32	51d			"I" before Gildi omitted	80.00	—
ICE33	51e			'03-'03,	95.00	—
ICE34	51f			02'-'3,	100.00	150.00
ICE35-39 all NA or not priced						
ICE40	53b			pair, one without ovpt	NA	—
ICE41	54a		10a carmine	invtd ovpt (vc)	29.00	40.00
ICE42	54b			pair, one without ovpt	42.50	—
ICE43	55a		16a brown	invtd ovpt (vc)	27.50	55.00
ICE44	55b			"I" before Gildi omitted	100.00	—
ICE45	55c			'03-'03,	125.00	—
ICE46	55d			02'-'03,	125.00	—
ICE47	56a		20a dull blue	invtd ovpt (vc)	NA	—
ICE48	57a		25a yel brown & blue	invtd ovpt (vc)	NA	—
ICE49	58a		40a red violet	invtd ovpt (vc)	27.50	100.00
ICE50	59a		50a blue & carmine	dbl ovpt (vc)	85.00	85.00
ICE51	59b			02'-'03,	100.00	

ICE#	No.	(Year)	Description	Variety	Price1	Price2
ICE52	59c			'03-'03	100.00	—
ICE53-61 all NA or not priced						
ICE62	66a		40a red violet	invtd ovpt, (vc)	40.00	—
ICE63	66b			'03-'03	110.00	—
ICE64	66c			02'-'03	125.00	—
ICE65	67a		50a blue & carmine	invtd ovpt (vc)	100.00	200.00
ICE66	67b			'03-'03,	175.00	—
ICE67	67c			02'-'03,	100.00	—
ICE68	67d			as "c" invtd (vc)	NA	—
ICE69	68a		100a brown & violet	invtd ovpt (vc) 100.00	—	
ICE70	68b			02'-'03	100.00	—
ICE71	68c			'03-'03,	150.00	—
ICE72	283a	(1954)	5a on 35a carmine rose	bars omitted	70.00	—
ICE73	283b			invtd surch (vc)	150.00	—
ICE74	O20a	(1902-03) 3a yellow		"I" before Gildi omitted	20.00	—
ICE75	O20b			invtd ovpt (vc)	13.00	18.00
ICE76	O20c			as "a" invtd	100.00	—
ICE77	O20d			pair, one with invtd ovpt	50.00	—
ICE78	O20e			'03-'03,	100.00	—
ICE79	O20f			02'-'03,	100.00	—
ICE80	O21a		4a gray	"I" before Gildi omitted	40.00	—
ICE81	O21b			invtd ovpt (vc)	25.00	14.00
ICE82	O21e			'03-'03	125.00	—
ICE83	O21f			02'-'03,	40.00	—
ICE84	O21g			pair, one without ovpt	40.00	—
ICE85	O21h			pair, one with invtd ovpt	67.50	35.00
ICE86	O21i			"L" only of "I GILDI" invtd	160.00	—
ICE87	O23a		10a ultramarine	"I" before Gildi omitted	25.00	—
ICE88	O23b			invtd ovpt (vc)	20.00	—
ICE89	O23c			'03-'03,	150.00	—
ICE90	O23d			02'-'03,	90.00	—
ICE91	O23e			"L" only of "I GILDI"	25.00	—
ICE92	O23f			as "e" invtd	35.00	—
ICE93	O23g			"IL" only of "I GILDI"	26.00	—
ICE94	O25a		3a yellow	02'-'03,	NA	—
ICE95	O26a		5a brown	invtd ovpt (vc)	20.00	*140.00*
ICE96	O26b			'03-'03,	140.00	—
ICE97	O26c			02'-'03,	125.00	—
ICE98	O26d			"L" only of "I GILDI" invtd	175.00	—
ICE99	O27a		10a blue	"I" before Gildi omitted	NA	—
ICE100	O27b			invtd ovpt (vc)	NA	
ICE101	O27c			'03-'03,	NA	
ICE102	O27d			02'-'03,	NA	—
ICE103	O28a		16a carmine	"I" before Gildi omitted	140.00	
ICE104	O28b			dbl ovpt (vc)	70.00	110.00
ICE105	O28c			dbl ovpt, one invtd	80.00	—
ICE106	O28d			invtd ovpt (vc)	50.00	100.00
ICE107	O28e			'03-'03,	170.00	—
ICE108	O29a		20a yellow green	invtd ovpt (vc)	70.00	110.00
ICE109	O29b			'03-'03,	125.00	—
ICE110	O29c			02'-'03,	125.00	—
ICE111	O29d			"I" before Gildi omitted	80.00	—
ICE112	O30a		50a red lilac	"I" before Gildi omitted	30.00	—
ICE113	O30b			invtd ovpt (vc)	80.00	—
ICE114	O50a	(1922)	2k rose	larger letters, no period	80.00	60.00

**Lots of o'erprints in `02 and `03
Led to errors for you and me
Some NA but as we can see
There's much affordability.
But whether or not we have I GILDI** *("valid")*
I'd prefer more variety. —The Bard

IFNI

IFN1	5a		10c dk carmine (bl)	red ovpt	13.00	6.50

One single error
We can't evaluate
Too bad they didn't
Make more mistakes. — The Bard

INDIA

IND1-7 all NA or not priced

IND8	81a	(1911-23)	1/2a green	dbl impression (u)	175.00	—
IND9	82a		1a carmine rose	printed on both sides (u)	—	—
IND10	M34a	(1914)	3p gray	dbl ovpt (vc)	30.00	25.00
IND11	M42a		12a claret	dbl ovpt (vc)	—	—
IND12	O1a	(1866)	1/2 a blue	invtd ovpt (vc)	—	—
IND13	O5a		1/2 a blue	invtd ovpt (vc)	—	—
IND14	O5b			without period	—	165.00

IND15-19 all NA or not priced

IND16	O8b		2a yellow	invtd ovpt (vc)	—	—
IND17	O9a		4a green	invtd ovpt (vc)	—	—
IND18	O15a	(1866)	1/2 p violet	dbl ovpt (vc)	NA	—
IND19	O17a		1/2 a blue, re-engraved	dbl ovpt (vc)	—	—
IND20	O19a		2a orange	2a yellow	6.00	1.75
IND21	O22a	(1874-82)	1/2 a re-engraved	blue ovpt	NA	37.50
IND22	O23a		1a brown	blue ovpt	NA	85.00

IND23-30, 32-35 all NA or not priced

IND31	O53a	(1912-22)	1/2 a green	dbl ovpt (vc)	90.00	—
IND36	O76a	(1926)	1a on 1 -1/2 a choc	dbl surch (vc)	30.00	—

INDOCHINA

INC1	1a	(1889)	5c on 35c dp vio, org	without date	165.00	140.00
INC2	1b			invtd surch (vc)	—	—
INC3	2a		5c on 35c dp vio, org (R)	date in smaller type	125.00	125.00
INC4	2b			invtd surch #2 (vc)	NA	
INC5	2c			invtd surch #2a, (vc)	NA	
INC6	68a	(1919)	2c on 5c	invtd surch (vc)	62.50	—
INC7	69a		4c on 10c (bl)	closed "4,"	3.50	.60
INC8	69b			dbl surch (vc)	65.00	
INC9	70a		6c on 15c	invtd surch (vc)	70.00	
INC10	74a		14c on 35c	closed "4,"	5.00	3.00
INC11	80a		80c on 2fr (R)	dbl surch (vc)	200.00	150.00
INC12	94a	(1922-23)	1/10c blk & salmon '23	dbl impression of frame (u)	—	—
INC13	96a		2/5c of brown & blk	head & value dbl (u)	150.00	150.00
INC14	101a		4c orange & blk	head & value dbl (u)	80.00	80.00
INC15	102a		5c carmine: & blk	head & value dbl (u)	200.00	200.00
INC16	109a		12c brown & blk	head & value dbl (11c + 12c) (u)	NA	
INC17	B2a	(1917)	5c+5c green & blk	dbl surch	125.00	125.00
INC18	B4a		15c+5c vio & blk	triple surch (u)	125.00	125.00
INC19	B4b			quadruple surch (u)	110.00	110.00
INC20	B5a		4c on 5c+5c (bl)	closed "4,"	150.00	150.00
INC21	B7a	(1919)	8c on 15c+5c	dbl surch (vc)	150.00	150.00
INC22	B10a	(1918?)	24c on 35c+25c	dbl surch (vc)	NA	
INC23	J27a	(1919)	24c on 60c org	closed "4,"	12.00	9.00
INC24	J28a		40c on 1fr gray	closed "4,"	12.50	10.00
INC25	J30a		2pi on 5fr red	dbl surch (vc)	125.00	100.00
INC26	J30b			triple surch (u)	125.00	90.00
INC27	J36a		4c orange	"4 CENTS," omitted	NA	
INC28	J36b			"4 CENTS," dbl	50.00	50.00
INC29	O3a	(1933)	3c deep brown (bl)	invtd ovpt (vc)	75.00	—
INC30	O4a		4c dark blue (R)	invtd ovpt (vc)	75.00	—
INC31	Q3a	(1902)	10c black, lavender	invtd ovpt (vc)	65.00	27.50
INC32	Q4a		10c red	invtd ovpt (vc)	45.00	27.50
INC33	Q4b			dbl ovpt (vc)	45.00	27.50

INDONESIA

INE1	B164		multi, birds,	value missing R	30.00	
INE2	777	(1969)	30r multi, Communications Satellite & earth	color missing R ?		

INHAMBANE

INH1	47a	(1914)	50r on 65r dull blue	"Republica" (vc) invtd	—	—
INH2	50a	(1913)	1c on 2a red vio	invtd surch (vc)	35.00	35.00
INH3	64a		1/4c on 1/2 a blue green	invtd surch (vc)	35.00	35.00
INH4	32var.		2 -1/2 r Red on grey	invtd surch (vc) R	8.00	

Four inverted surcharges
That's all for Inhambane
That's not many errors
When they're all the same. —The Bard

ININI has produced no errors

IONIAN ISLANDS

ION1	N2a		10 l blue & red brown	(#413) (H) on #397	40.00	45.00
ION2	N3a		20 l black & green (H)	ovpt invtd (vc) 90oldst	.00	—
ION3	N6a		80 l ind & yel brown (H)	ovpt invtd (vc)	75.00	80.00
ION4	N8a		1.50d green (H)	ovpt invtd (vc)	75.00	75.00
ION5	N16a		25d dark blue (H)	ovpt invtd (vc)	125.00	110.00
ION6	N17a		30d orange brown (H)	ovpt invtd	165.00	165.00
ION7	N22a	(1941)	30c olive brown (R)	"SOLE" for "ISOLE"	25.00	—
ION8	N26a	(1943)	25c deep green	carmine ovpt	40.00	90.00
ION9	N27a		50c purple	carmine ovpt	40.00	90.00
ION10	NC3a	(1941)	25d rose (H)	ovpt invtd (vc)	190.00	190.00
ION11	NC4a		30d dark green	ovpt reading up	70.00	70.00
ION12	NC4b			horizontal ovpt on single stamp	*125.00*	*125.00*
ION13	NC4c			as "b" invtd	NA	
ION14	NC6a		100d brown	ovpt reading up	NA	
ION15	NC12a		50c olive brown	"SOLE" for "ISOLE"	18.50	—
ION16	NC13a	(1943)	50c olive brown	"SOLE" for "ISOLE"	NA	—
ION17	NC13b			carmine ovpt.	135.00	NA
ION18	NRA1a	(1941)	10 l carmine (bl+bk)	blue ovpt dbl	27.50	22.50
ION19	NRA1b			invtd ovpt (vc)	60.00	60.00
ION20	NRA2a		10 l brt rose, *pale rose*	ovpt on horiz pair	40.00	40.00
ION21	NRA2b			horizontal ovpt on single stamp	*100.00*	—
ION22	NRA2c			ovpt reading up	11.00	11.00
ION23	NRA3a		50 l gray green, *pale green*	ovpt reading up	5.00	5.00
ION24	NRA3b			ovpt on horiz. pair	15.00	15.00
ION25	NRA3c			horiz ovpt on single stamp	*100.00*	—
ION26	NRA4a		1d dl blue, lt blue	ovpt reading up	20.00	20.00
ION27	NRA5a		50 l gray green, *pale green*	ovpt reading up	200.00	—

IRAN

IRA1-7 all NA or not priced

IRA8	169a		12c on 1k red	blue surch	25.00	6.00
IRA9-16 all NA or not priced						
IRA17	247a	(1902)	1c gray & buff	with Persian numerals "2,"	25.00	—
IRA18	282a		3c dk green & yel	"Persans"	22.50	3.25
IRA19A	485		6k grey grn & carmine	invtd center R ?		
See Photo in Color Section						
IRA19	635a	(1921)	3c dark green	center & ovpt invtd (u)	40.00	—
IRA20	646a	(1922)	1c green & orange	invtd ovpt (vc)	*40.00*	—
IRA21	707a	(1926)	1c orange & maroon	invtd ovpt (vc)	100.00	—
IRA22	709a		3c yellow green & maroon	invtd ovpt (vc)	100.00	—
IRA23	927a	(1950)	10r carmine & blue green	invtd center (u)	NA	—

IRA24	1059Ab	(1956-57)	50d brown & olive brown	invtd center (u)	—	—
IRA25	1827a	(1974-75)	10r deep lilac	value in Persian omitted	25.00	3.00
IRA26	2110a	(1982)	10r multicolored	missing dot in Arabic numeral	1.00	1.00
IRA27	C22b	(1928-29)	1c emerald	dbl ovpt (vc)	16.00	—
IRA28	C25a		5c olive brown	"5," omitted	NA	
IRA29	C26a		10c dark green	"10," omitted	7.00	—
IRA30	C26b			"l" inverted	15.00	—
IRA31	C27a		1k dull violet	"l" invtd	5.00	—
IRA32	O15a		2k ultra	violet ovpt	6.00	5.00
IRA33	O17a		10k rose red	violet ovpt	—	12.50

Lots of inverted centers
And printed on both sides
Most all of these are NA´s
Except one lonely guy —The Bard

IRAQ

IRQ1	29a		3f on 1/2 a (R)	dbl surch (vc)	165.00	
IRQ2	29b			invtd surch (vc)	*165.00*	—
IRQ3	31a		5f on 1a	dbl surch (vc)	NA	—
IRQ4	31b			invtd Arabic "5,"	*30.00*	*35.00*
IRQ5	32a		8f on 1-1/2 a	invtd surch (vc)	*150.00*	—
IRQ6	36a		25f on 4a	"Flis" for "Fils"	NA	
IRQ7	36b			invtd Arabic "5,"	NA	
IRQ8	42a		1/2 d on 10r	bar in "1/2," omitted	NA	
IRQ9	173a	(1957)	28f blue	dbl ovpt (vc)	200.00	NA
IRQ10	260a	(1960)	10f maroon & black	invtd ovpt (vc)	75.00	60.00
IRQ11	O41a	(1932)	5f on 1a	invtd Arabic "5,"	*40.00*	*35.00*
IRQ12	O48a		40f on 8a	"Flis" for "Fils"	NA	
IRQ13	O53a		1/2 d on 10r	bar in "1/2," omitted	NA	—

Iraq has no inverted center
Nor printed on both sides
But its numerous o´erprint errors
Are really bona fides. —The Bard

IRELAND

IRE1	1a	(1922)	1/2 p green	invtd ovpt (vc)	NA	
IRE2	15a		1-1/2 p red brown	"PENCF"	NA	
IRE3	16a		2p orange (II)	invtd ovpt (vc)(II)	NA	
IRE4	16c			invtd ovpt (I) (vc)	165.00	*150.00*
IRE5	26a		2p orange (II)	invtd ovpt (II)(vc)	NA	
IRE6	44a	(1922-23)	1/2 p green	accent omitted	NA	
IRE7	44b			accent added	125.00	*125.00*
IRE8	45a		1p scarlet	accent omitted	NA	
IRE9	45b			accent added	125.00	*125.00*
IRE10	45c			accent & final "t" omitted	NA	
IRE11	45d			accent & final "t" added	200.00	NA
IRE12	48a		2 -1/2 p ultra (R)	accent omitted	125.00	*150.00*
IRE13	49a		3p violet	accent omitted	NA	

HUN23A

HUN25

INE1

INE2

INH4

IRE14	50a		4p sl green (R)	accent omitted	140.00	165.00
IRE15	52a		6p dull violet	accent added		NA
IRE16-22 are all NA or not priced						
IRE23	60a		1p scarlet	tall "I"	55.00	90.00
IRE24	61a		1 -1/2 p red brown	tall "I"	80.00	165.00
IRE25	62a		2p orange (II)	tall "I"	15.00	27.50
IRE26	389a	(1976)	7p ultra, silver & red	silver (inscription) omitted		NA
IRE27	392b		15p red, silver & blue	silver (inscription) omitted		NA

ISRAEL

ISR1	168b	(1960)	1a brown, *pinkish*	black ovpt omitted (u)	—	—
ISR2	173a		12a grnsh blue, *lt bl*	black ovpt omitted(u)	—	—
ISR3	Bale IV. Rev. 50	(1961)	50 p Revenue	invtd numeral (u)	NA	—
ISR4	215a	(1962)	3a on 1a light lilac	without ovpt (u)	80.00	—
ISR5	217a		30a on 32a emerald	without ovpt (u)	32.50	—
ISR6	Bale IV. Rev.65a	(1979)		invtd numeral (u) R.	30.00	70.00
ISR7	Bale IV. Rev. 66a			invtd numeral (u) R.	30.00	70.00

Overprints omitted dominate the Israel postal stamp error scene while inverted numerals do likewise for the revue issue scene. If you are interested in the latter, both IRS6 and IRS7 seem reasonable, while an ISR5 would be an unusual and inexpensive item to add to the ordinary stamp error array.

Four overprints omitted
That is the story
Of Israel's
Fame and Glory. —The Bard

ITALIAN COLONIES has produced no errors

ITALIAN E. AFRICA has produced no errors

ITALIAN STATES
Because this volume is on affordable errors and so many errors cost more than $200, and because so many errors are typos and the states no longer exist, we have eliminated listings for the Italian States.

ITALY

ITA1	22a		15c blue	head invtd (u)	—	NA
ITA2	22b			dbl head (u)	55.00	50.00
ITA3	22c			head omitted	250.00	—
ITA4-12 are all NA or not priced						
ITA13	58a	(1890)	2c on 10c ol gray	invtd surch (vc)	175.00	—
ITA14	60a		2c on 50c claret	invtd surch (vc)	—	NA
ITA15	62a		2c on 1.25 l org	invtd surch (vc)	NA	
ITA16	64a	(1891)	2c on 5c bl grn	"2." with thin tail	80.00	190.00
ITA17	77a	(1901-26)	2c org brown	dbl impression (u)	125.00	*185.00*
ITA18	92a	(1905)	15c on 20c org	dbl surch (vc)	—	NA
ITA19	147a	(1923-25)	7 -1/2 c on 85c	dbl surch (vc)	150.00	NA
ITA20	148a		10c on 1c	invtd surch (vc)	45.00	*55.00*
ITA21	149a		10c on 2c	invtd surch (vc)	9.00	*18.00*
ITA22	156a		50c on 40c	invtd surch (vc)	135.00	*175.00*
ITA23				dbl surch (vc)	77.50	100.00
ITA24	157a		50c on 55c	invtd surch (vc)	NA	
ITA25	203a		30c bl grn & red brn	center invtd (u)	NA	
ITA26	421a	(1942)	50c brn vio & vio	frame missing	NA	—
ITA27	B4	(1916)	20c on 15c+5c	dbl ovpt (vc)	200.00	—
ITA28	B4b			invtd ovpt (vc)	200.00	NA
ITA29	B8a	(1921)	40c brown (bl)	invtd ovpt (vc)	12.00	15.00
ITA30	B9a	(1922-23)	10c cl ('23) (bk)	blue ovpt (vc)	30.00	7.50
ITA31	B9b			brown ovpt (vc)	30.00	7.50
ITA32	B10a		15c slate (bl)	red ovpt	100.00	30.00
ITA33	B11a		20c brn org (bk)	blue ovpt (vc)	200.00	30.00
ITA34	B12a	(1923)	25c bl (bk or bl)	red ovpt	90.00	25.00

ITA35	B13a		40c brn (bl)	black ovpt	40.00	7.50
ITA36	B13b			as "a" invtd ovpt	30.00	—
ITA37	B14a		50c vio (bk)	blue ovpt	—	—
ITA38	B16a		1 brn & grn (bk)	invtd ovpt	NA	—
ITA39	C10a	(1927)	50c on 60c gray	pair, one without surch	NA	
ITA40	C27a	(1930)	7.70 Prus bl & gray	7 stars instead of 6	NA	
ITA41	C48a		5.25 l + 19.75 l red, grn & ultra	left stamp without ovpt	NA__	
ITA42	C115a	(1949)	6 l on 3.20 l	pair, one without surch	NA	—
ITA43	C115b			invtd surch (vc)	—	NA
ITA44	E13a	(1925)	70c on 60c dull red	invtd surch (vc)	32.50	65.00
ITA45	J3a D3	(1870-1925)	1c		NA	
ITA46	J4a D3		2c		NA	
ITA47	J5a D3		5c		1.75	1.75
ITA48	J6a D3		10c		3.25	3.25
ITA49	J7b D3		20c		15.00	15.00
ITA50	J8a D3		30c		4.50	5.50
ITA51	J9a D3		40c			NA
ITA52	J10a D3		50c		16.00	18.00
ITA53	J11a D3		60c		180.00	180.00
ITA54-61 are all NA or not priced						
ITA62	P1	(1862)	2c buff	numeral dbl	165.00	NA
ITA63	Q22a	(1914-22)	1.50l on 5c brown	dbl surch (vc)	25.00	—
ITA64	Q33a	(1927-39)	3 l bister	printed on both sides (u)	15.00	—

Too many poems
Maybe so
But let's try just one mo':
What do we see in Italy:
Many, many, many vc's —The Bard

ITALIAN OFFICES ABROAD
Due to an abundance of costly errors, their uninteresting nature and subsequent lack of interest in these offices, we are not listing errors of Italian Offices Abroad.

IVORY COAST

IVC1	23a	(1906-07)	4c choc, *gray black*	name dbl	125.00	125.00
IVC2	39a	(1912)	10c on 40c red, *straw*	pair, one without surch	62.50	—
IVC3	B1a	(1915)	10c+5c	dbl surch (vc)	45.00	45.00
IVC4	Q5a	(1903)	50c lilac	invtd red ovpt (vc)	NA	
IVC5	Q6a		1fr rose, *buff*	invtd bl black ovpt	200.00	200.00
IVC6	Q7a		50c on 15c pale grn	invtd surch (vc)	100.00	100.00
IVC7	Q8a		50c on 60c brn, *buff*	invtd surch (vc)	125.00	125.00
IVC8	Q11a		1fr on 5c blue	invtd surch (vc)	150.00	150.00
IVC9	Q17a		c1fr on 10c gray brn	invtd surch (vc)	125.00	125.00
IVC10	Q18a		d 1fr on 10c gray brn	invtd surch (vc)	125.00	125.00
IVC11	Q21a		4fr on 60c brn, *buff*	dbl surch (vc)	—	—
IVC12	Q24a		4fr on 15c green	one large star	NA	
IVC13	Q24b			two large stars	150.00	150.00
IVC14	Q25a		4fr on 30c rose	one large star	NA	
IVC15	Q25b			two large stars	150.00	150.00
IVC16	Q26a	(1904)	50c lilac	invtd ovpt (vc)	—	—
IVC17	Q27a		1fr rose, *buff*	invtd ovpt	—	—
IVC18	Q28a		50c lilac	invtd ovpt (vc)	125.00	125.00
IVC19	Q29a		1fr rose, *buff*	invtd ovpt	150.00	150.00
IVC20	Q35a	(1905)	4fr on 1fr rose, *buff*	italic "4,"	NA	

Ivory Coast has a "split personality." Among all regular issues, three overprint errors exist, all of which are affordable. Among the 36 officials, on the other hand, seventeen overprint errors exist. Most are vc's with only four NA.

STV14.1018

STV15.1017

STV16.1020

STV17.1019

POL28 111

SPA55 C56

IRA19A

GUE99 133a

CRE3A 85

ADEN QUATI MINKUS274

CAF22 C61

CTR53c C156

UBS1254
normal stamp

UBS 1254a

BRU4 46

HAI 1A. UPU
(Set of 11)

DUB7 C34

HUN23 IN29a

HUN23A 30a

HUN25 IN34a

CRE3B 88

LIB216. 280

PAR85 430

HAI11 C168

HAI B3

TIM18 302a

GNA33 434

GNA34 435

ECU117 SAN211a

ECU118 SAN209a

ECU119 SAN210a

PER63 220b

EQG1 R25

GNA46.C52

AJMAN STATE - "History of Space" unlisted

CRE9B J1

VIR14 O14

CHD21 244A-F

MOS6 471

CAF3 70fr

POL103 1474

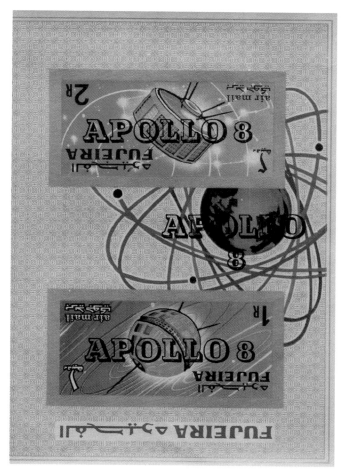

FUGI MICHEL11b block

PAN139A 434

FRA1b 111

PUE7A 155

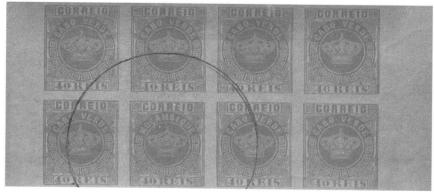

CPV4. 13c

FRA1a Caillie issue

LIB214-17 B16

CHD20 233C

FEA23 SAN35a

EAF2 62b

PAR89 C272

CHAPTER V: J-O

JAMAICA

JAM1	27b	(1890)	2-1/2p on 4p orange brn	dbl surch (vc)	NA	
JAM2	27d			"PFNNY"	100.00	70.00
JAM3	27f			as "d" dbl surch	—	—
JAM4	33b	(1903-04)	1/2 p green & black	(JAM-JAM), typo, "SERv ET" for "SERVIET")	40.00	42.50
JAM5	34b	(1904)	1p car & black		35.00	35.00
JAM6	35a		2-1/2 p ultra & black		60.00	70.00
JAM7	36a		5p yel & black		NA	
JAM8	37b	(1905)	1/2 p green & black		35.00	35.00
JAM9	41a	(1907)	5p yel & black		NA	
JAM10	182a	(1962)	4p multicolored	yellow omitted	—	
JAM11	223a	(1964)	6p multicolored	ultramarine omitted	30.00	—
JAM12	224a		8p multicolored	red omitted	—	—
JAM13	226a		1sh yel brown & black	yellow brown omitted	200.00	—
JAM14	226b			black omitted	NA	—
JAM15	231a		10sh multicolored	blue ("Jamaica" etc.) omitted	150.00	—
JAM16	271a	(1968)	3p multicolored	gold (flame) omitted	110.00	—
JAM17	273a		3sh multicolored	gold (flame) omitted	110.00	—
JAM18	283a	(1969)	5c on 6p multi	blue (wing dots) omitted	*40.00*	—
JAM19	MR1a	(1916)	1/2 p green	without period	11.00	11.00
JAM20	MR1b			dbl ovpt (vc)	200.00	200.00
JAM21	MR1c			invtd ovpt (vc)	95.00	95.00
JAM22	MR1d			as "c" without period	NA	—
JAM23	MR2a		3p violet, *yel*	without period	21.00	30.00
JAM24	MR4		1/2 p green	without period	11.00	11.00
JAM25	MR4b			pair, one without ovpt	NA	
JAM26	MR4c			"R" inserted by hand	NA	210.00
JAM22	MR4d			"WAR" only	125.00	—
JAM23	MR5a		1-1/2 p orange	without period		
JAM24	MR5b			"TAMP"	90.00	90.00
JAM25	MR5c			"S" inserted by hand	NA	—
JAM26	MR5d			"R" omitted	NA	
JAM27	MR5e			"R" inserted by hand	NA	200.00
JAM28	MR6a		3p violet, yel	without period	17.00	18.00
JAM29	MR6b			"TAMP"	NA	140.00
JAM30	MR6c			"S" inserted by hand	150.00	140.00
JAM31	MR6d			invtd ovpt (vc)	NA	175.00
JAM32	MR6e			as "a" invtd		
JAM33	MR7a		1/2 p green	without period	7.50	6.00
JAM34	MR7b			ovpt on back instead of face	125.00	—
JAM35	MR7c			invtd ovpt (vc)	13.00	10.00
JAM36	MR8		1-1/2 p orange	without period	7.00	5.25
JAM37	MR8b			dbl ovpt (vc)	90.00	90.00
JAM38	MR8c			invtd ovpt (vc)	90.00	90.00
JAM39	MR8d			as "a" invtd	—	—
JAM40	MR9		3p violet, yel	without period	13.00	12.00
JAM41	MR9b			vertical ovpt (vc)	NA	
JAM42	MR9c			invtd ovpt (vc)	150.00	—
JAM43	MR9d			as "a" invtd	—	—
JAM44	O1	(1890)	1/2 p green (II)	type I,	25.00	25.00
JAM45	O1b			invtd ovpt (II) (vc)	75.00	80.00
JAM46	O1c			dbl ovpt (vc) (II)	80.00	90.00

JAM47-50 are all NA or not priced

Omitted colors like the rest
Of the commonwealth's very best —The Bard

JAPAN

JAP1-4 and 6-9 are all NA or not priced

JAP5	407b			ovpt on No. 401 (vc)	175.00	—
JAP6	453b	(1949)	16y blue	as "a" 10y stamp omitted	—	—

JORDAN

JOR1	1a	(1920)	1 m dark brown	invtd ovpt (vc)	125.00	—
JOR2	1c			as "b" invtd ovpt (vc)	110.00	—
JOR3	14a	(1922)	2/10 pi on 2m bl grn	1?/10i on 2m bl grn (error)	85.00	85.00?
JOR4	54a	(1923)	2m blue grn (G)	dbl ovpt (vc)	NA	—
JOR5	54b			invtd ovpt (vc)	NA	—
JOR6	55a		3m lt brn (G)	blk ovpt (vc)	70.00	75.00
JOR7	58a		1pi dk blue (G)	dbl ovpt (vc)	NA	—
JOR8	58b			ovpt on back	175.00	—

JOR9-14 are all NA or not priced

JOR15	65a		1/2 pi red	invtd ovpt (vc)	100.00	—
JOR16	66a		1pi dark blue	invtd ovpt (vc)	105.00	—
JOR17	67a		1-1/2 pi violet	dbl ovpt (vc)	125.00	—
JOR18	68a		2 pi orange	invtd ovpt (vc)	—	—
JOR19	68b			pair, one without ovpt	—	—
JOR20	69a		3 pi olive brown	invtd ovpt (vc)	125.00	—
JOR21	69b			dbl ovpt (vc)	150.00	—

JOR22-26 are all NA or not priced

JOR27	91a		1/2 pi on 1-1/2 pi vio	surch typographed	30.00	32.50
JOR28	121a	(1924)	10pi vio & dk brn (R)	pair, one without ovpt	—	—
JOR29	B1a	(1930)	2(m) prus blue	invtd ovpt (vc)	200.00	—
JOR30	B4a		5(m) orange	dbl ovpt (vc)	NA	—
JOR31	B6a		15(m) ultra	invtd ovpt (vc)	NA	—
JOR32	B12a		500(m) brown	"C," of "Locust" omitted	NA	—
JOR33	J1a	(1923)	1/2 pi on 3pi of brn	invtd ovpt (vc)	175.00	175.00
JOR34	J1b			dbl ovpt (vc)	175.00	175.00
JOR35	N19a	(1949)	4m green	"PLAESTINE"	20.00	—
JOR36	N22a		50m dull green	"PLAESTINE"	20.00	—
JOR1A	M7x	(1920)	2pi olive	ovpt 17 x	—	—
JOR2A	M12x	(1922)	1/10 pi on 1m bist brown	red ovpt	40.00	40.00
JOR3A	M12x1			violet ovpt	—	—
JOR4A	M12x2			pair, one no ovpt	160.00	—
JOR5A	M13x		2/10 pi on 2m blue green	3/10 for 2/10	—	55.00
JOR6A	M13x1			red ovpt	60.00	75.00
JOR7A	M13x2			violet ovpt	75.00	75.00
JOR8A	M14x		3/10 on 3m yel brn	violet ovpt	—	—
JOR9A	M14x			violet ovpt	—	—
JOR10A	M16x		5/10pi on 5m orgn		70.00	60.00
JOR11A	M16x1			violet ovpt	—	—
JOR12A	M17x		1pi on 1pi	violet ovpt	150.00	160.00
JOR13A	M18x		2pi on 2pi olive	red ovpt	—	—
JOR14A	M19x		5pi dp red pur	violet ovpt	—	—
JOR15A	M20x		9pi on 9pi ochre (R)	black ovpt	120.00	120.00
JOR16A	M22x		20pi	violet ovpt	NA	—
JOR17A	M25x	(1922)	1m bistre brown	red ovpt	17.50	17.50
JOR18A	M25x1			violet ovpt	22.00	22.00
JOR19A	M26x		2m blue green	red ovpt	18.00	18.00
JOR20A	M26x1			violet ovpt	6.00	6.00
JOR21A	M27x13m		yellow brown	red ovpt	—	—
JOR22A	M27x1			violet ovpt	—	—
JOR23A	M28x		4m scarlet	red ovpt	—	—
JOR24A	M28x1			violet ovpt	—	—
JOR25A	M29x		5m orange (V)	red ovpt	40.00	30.00
JOR26A	M30x	(1922)	1pi indigo (V)	red ovpt	14.00	14.00
JOR27A	M31x		2pi	olive red ovpt	—	—
JOR28A	M31x1			violet ovpt	40.00	40.00

JOR29A	M31x2			on #7x , (R)	—	—
JOR30A	M31x3			on 7#, (V)	30.00	30.00
JOR31A	M33x	(1922)	9pi ochre	red ovpt	—	—
JOR32A	M33x1		9pi ochre	red ovpt	—	—
JOR33A	M34x		10pi cobalt (R)	violet ovpt,	NA	
JOR34A	M35x		20pi gray (R)	violet ovpt,	NA	

Mostly vc's early
Very few errors late
I wonder what's happening
A better printing plate? —The Bard

K

KARELIA has produced no errors

KATANGA has produced no errors

KAZAKHSTAN has produced no errors

KENYA, UGANDA, TANZANIA

KEN1	103b	(1954-59) 5c choc & black	dam inverted	—	—

A dam is inverted, missing is blue
There's not more than these errors true. —The Bard

KHOR FAKKAN Dependency of Sharja (Trucial States)

KHO1	M11x	(1965)	2r boy scouts #96	invtd oovpt	—	5.00
KHO2	M90x	(1967)	Souvenir sheet # 79 ovpt	Death Aniversary/22 Anov. 1967 in carmine-black ovpt.	—	—
KHO3	M 93x	(1968)	Sharja ovpt KHOR FAKKAN in red or silver (5r) 3d Hobbema	invtd ovpt	5.00	—

KIACHAU

KIA1	Ac	(1900)	5pfg on 10pf car	dbl surch, one invtd	NA	—
KIA2	2c		5pfg on 10pf car	dbl surch, one invtd	NA	—
KIA3	3c		5pfg on 10pf car	dbl surch (vc)	NA	—
KIA4	1ab		5pfg on 10pf car	dbl surch (vc)	NA	
KIA5	2ab		5pfg on 10pf car	dbl surch (vc)	NA	
KIA6	4a		5pf on 10pf car	dbl surch (vc)	NA	
KIA7	5a		5pf on 10pf car	dbl surch (vc)	NA	
KIA8	6a		5pf on 10pf car	dbl surch (vc)	NA	
KIA9	6b		5pf		—	NA
KIA10	6c			as "b" dbl surch	—	—
KIA11	8a		5pf on 10pf car	on No. 6B	—	—
KIA12	9a		5pf on 10pf car	dbl surch (vc)	—	NA
KIA13	9b			on No. 6a	—	—
KIA14	9c			on 6b	—	—
KIA15	9d			on 6c	—	—

Kiachau offers many vc's, typos, and some affordable overprint errors. Quite a few more are NA. Kiachau no longer issues stamps and probably not much interest lies here.

KIONGA has produced no errors

KIRIBATI has produced no errors

KOREA

KOR1	10b	(1897)	5p green	invtd ovpt (vc)	150.00	150.00
KOR2	10c			without ovpt at bottom	140.00	140.00
KOR3	10d			without ovpt at top	140.00	140.00
KOR4	10f			dbl ovpt at top	150.00	150.00
KOR5	10g			ovpt at bottom in blk	175.00	175.00
KOR6	10h			pair, one without ovpt	NA	

KOR7	10i			dbl ovpt at top, invtd at bottom	NA	
KOR8	11a		10p deep blue	without ovpt at bottom	150.00	150.00
KOR9	11b			without ovpt at top	150.00	150.00
KOR10	11c			dbl ovpt at top (vc)	165.00	165.00
KOR11	11d			bottom ovpt invtd	150.00	150.00
KOR12	11e			top ovpt, dbl, one in blk	NA	
KOR13	11f			top ovpt omitted, bottom ovpt invtd	NA	
KOR14	12a		25p maroon	ovpt at bottom invtd	150.00	150.00
KOR15	12b			ovpt at bottom in blk	NA	
KOR16	12c			bottom ovpt omitted	150.00	150.00
KOR17	12e			top ovpt, dbl, one in blk	NA	
KOR18	12f			top & bottom ovpts double, one of each in blk	NA	
KOR19	12g			pair, one without ovpt	NA	
KOR20	13a		50p purple	without ovpt at bottom	125.00	125.00
KOR21	13b			without ovpt at top	110.00	110.00
KOR22	13Gh	(1900)	10p deep blue	without ovpt at bottom	NA	—
KOR23	14a		25p maroon	without ovpt at bottom	NA	—
KOR24	14b			without ovpt at top	NA	—
KOR25	14c			dbl ovpt at bottom (vc)	NA	—
KOR26	15a		50p purple	without ovpt at bottom	NA	—
KOR27	17a	(1900)	1 ch on 25p (#12)	figure "1," omitted	80.00	—
KOR28	17b			on #12c	70.00	70.00
KOR29	36e	(1902)	2ch on 25p maroon	2ch on 50p purple	165.00	150.00
KOR30	36f			as "e" character "cheun" unabbreviated (in two rows instead of one)		
KOR31	56a		5ch on 14s rose like & pale rose	5ch on 40s dark violet (error)	110.00	—
KOR32	58a		20ch on 6s lt ultra	20ch on 27s rose brown (error)	80.00	—
KOR33	58b			dbl surch (vc)	30.00	—
KOR34	127a	(1951)	100wn on 4wn rose car	invtd surch (vc)	35.00	—
KOR35	128a		200wn on 15wn	invtd surch (vc)	10.00	10.00
KOR36	129a		300wn on 10wn (br)	invtd surch	17.50	—
KOR37	130a		300wn on 20wn	invtd surch (vc)	17.50	—
KOR38	154a	(1952)	500wn grn (Italy)	flag without crown (u)	11.50	—
KOR39	155a	(1952)	500wn blue	flag without crown(u)	11.50	—
KOR40	174a	(1951)	300wn on 4wn	invtd surch (vc)	70.00	50.00
KOR41	175a		300wn on 10wn br	invtd surch (vc)	50.00	40.00
KOR42	176a		300wn on 14wn br	300wn on 14wn lt bl	NA	
KOR43	176b			invtd surch (vc)	50.00	50.00
KOR44	177a		300wn on 15wn	invtd surch (vc)	40.00	40.00
KOR45	178a		300wn on 30wn br	invtd surch (vc)	42.50	40.00
KOR46	180a		300wn on 65wn br	invtd monad	52.50	50.00
KOR47	181a		300wn on 100wn	invtd surch (vc)	50.00	40.00
KOR48	C5a	(1951)	500wn on 150wn bl	"KORFA"	15.00	12.50
KOR49	C5b			surch invtd (vc)	125.00	—

Imperf sheets of one
Never errors be
The real errors mostly
Are the early vc. —The Bard

KUWAIT

KUW1	6a	(1923-24) 3a brown org		invtd ovpt (vc)	—	—
KUW2	56a	(1939) 10r rose car & dk vio		dbl ovpt (vc)	NA	
KUW3	77a	(1948-49) 3a on 3p violet		pair, one without surch	—	—

Three overprint errors for Kuwait
For more action we'll just have to wait. —The Bard

KYRGYZSTAN has produced no errors

AFFORDABLE FOREIGN ERRORS

L

LABUAN

LAB1	12a	(1880-83)	8c on 12c car	original value not obliterated	NA	
LAB2	12b			additional surch "8" across original value	NA	
LAB3	12c			"8," invtd	NA	
LAB4	14a		8c on 12c car	"Eight"	NA	
LAB5	14b			invtd surch (vc)	NA	
LAB6	14c			dbl surch (vc)	NA	
LAB7	26a	(1885)	2c on 8c car	dbl surch (vc)	—	
LAB8	27a		2c on 16c blue	dbl surch (vc)	—	NA
LAB9	29b	(1891)	29b 6c on 8c violet	dbl surch (vc)	NA	—
LAB10	29c			"Cents" omitted	NA	
LAB11	29d			invtd surch (vc)	45.00	50.00
LAB12	29e			dbl surch, one invtd	NA	—
LAB13	29g			"6," omitted	NA	—
LAB14	31a		6c on 16c blue	invtd surch (vc)	NA	
LAB15	32a		6c on 40c ocher	invtd surch (vc)	NA	
LAB16	40a	(1893)	2c on 40c ocher	invtd surch (vc)	200.00	
LAB17	41a		6c on 16c gray	invtd surch (vc)	NA	175.00
LAB18	41b			surch sideways	—	—
LAB19	41c			"Six" omitted	—	—
LAB20	41d			"Cents" omitted	—	—
LAB21	63a	(1896)	25c blue green	without ovpt	11.00	2.00
LAB22	64a		50c claret	without ovpt	10.00	2.00
LAB23	65a		$1 dark blue	without ovpt	15.00	2.00
LAB24	66a	(1896)	1c lilac & blk	orange ovpt	160.00	20.00
LAB25	66b			dbl ovpt (vc)	190.00	190.00
LAB26	66c			"JEBILEE"	250.00	
LAB27	67b		2c blue & black	"JEBILEE"	NA	—
LAB28	68a		3c bister & black	dbl ovpt (vc)	200.00	125.00
LAB29	68b			triple ovpt (u)	—	NA
LAB30	68c			"JEBILEE"	—	NA
LAB31	69a		5c green & black	dbl ovpt (vc)	NA	
LAB32	70a		6c brown red & black	dbl ovpt (vc)	NA	
LAB33	91a	(1899)	4c on 18c bister & black	dbl surch (vc)	NA	
LAB34	117a	(1904)	4c on 50c claret	dbl surch (vc)	200.00	
LAB35	J1a	(1901)	2c green & black	dbl ovpt (vc)	140.00	—
LAB36	J3a		4c car & black	dbl ovpt (vc)	—	200.00
LAB37	J6a		8c red & black	center invtd, ovpt, reading down few exist, only used	—	NA

Lots of vc's for a country that ceased
Some prices so low, others high
Others unpriced and reached the sky. —The Bard

LAGOS

LAG1	6a	(1875)	1sh orange	value 15-1/2 mm instead of 16-1/2 mm long	NA	—
LAG2	39a	(1893)	1/2 p on 4p lilac & black	dbl surch (vc)	60.00	60.00
LAG3	39b			triple surch (u)	95.00	—
LAG4	39c		1/2 p on 2p lilac & blue (#18)		—	NA

Very few errors for an obsolete land
A triple surcharge is its wedding band —The Bard

LAOS has produced no errors

LATAKIA

LAT1	C1a	(1931-33)	50c ocher	invtd ovpt (vc)	NA

One error—inverted overprint—NA
What in heaven's else can we say? —-The Bard

LATVIA

LAT1	109a	(1921-22)	15r ultra	printed on both sides (u)	37.50	—
LAT2	857a	(1930)	2s (4s) org & red org	cliche of 1s (2s) in plate of 2s(4s)	NA	
LAT3	2N23a	(1909-12)	10k on 2k grn	invtd surch (vc)	25.00	—
LAT4	2N27a		70k on 15k red brown & blue	invtd surch (vc)	50.00	
LAT5	2N31a		2r on 50k vio & grn	invtd surch (vc)	30.00	—
LAT6	2N36a	(1917)	10r on 3.50r mar & lt grn	invtd surch (vc)	100.00	—

Printed on both sides and a cliche
Two bad the latter is an NA. —The Bard

LEBANON

LEB1	1a	(1924)	10c on 2c vio brn	invtd surch (vc)	15.00	9.00
LEB2	5a		1p on 20c red brn	dbl surch (vc)	15.00	9.00
LEB3	5b			invtd surch (vc)	15.00	9.00
LEB4	9a		2.50p on 50c dl bl	invtd surch (vc)	15.00	9.00
LEB5	10a		2p on 40c red & pale bl	invtd surch (vc)	20.00	12.00
LEB6	13a		10p on 2fr org & pale bl	invtd surch (vc)	30.00	18.00
LEB7	14a		25p on 5fr bl & buff	invtd surch (vc)	57.50	35.00
LEB8	15a		50c on 10c green	invtd surch (vc)	17.50	11.00
LEB9	17a		2.50p on 50c blue	invtd surch (vc)	17.50	11.00
LEB10	18a		50c on 10c gray grn & yel grn	invtd surch (vc)	100.00	—
LEB11	19a		1.25p on 25c rose & dk rose	invtd surch (vc)	100.00	—
LEB12	20a		1.50p on 30c brn red & blk	invtd surch (vc)	100.00	—
LEB13	21a		2.50p on 50c ultra & dk bl	invtd surch (vc)	100.00	—
LEB14	39a	(1923-24)	50c on 10c green	invtd surch (vc)	12.50	12.50
LEB15	39b			dbl surch (vc)	17.50	17.50
LEB16	41a		1.50p on 30c red	invtd surch (vc)	16.00	16.00
LEB17	42a		2p on 45c red	invtd surch (vc)	13.00	12.00
LEB18	43a		2.50p on 50c blue	invtd surch (vc)	13.00	13.00
LEB19	43b			dbl surch (vc)	12.00	12.00
LEB20	49a		4p on 75c *bluish*	invtd surch (vc)	35.00	18.00
LEB21	72a	(1927)	10c dark violet (R)	black ovpt	20.00	11.00
LEB22	86a	(1928)	10c dark vio (R)	French ovpt omitted, on #50	—	—
LEB23	87a		50c yel grn (bk	Arabic ovpt invtd	18.00	18.00

LEB33A

LIB46A

LIB113A

LIB114A

LIB97A

LIB131A

LIB124A

LEB24	88a		1p magenta (bk)	invtd ovpt (vc)	18.00	18.00
LEB25	93a		5p violet (RS)	French ovpt below Arabic	14.00	14.00
LEB26	94a		10p vio brn (bk)	dbl ovpt (vc)	—	—
LEB27	94b			dbl ovpt invtd		
LEB28	94c			invtd ovpt (vc)	70.00	70.00
LEB29	100a		15p on 25p (II) (bk+R)	Arabic ovpt invtd	—	—
LEB30	104a	(1928-29)	4p on 25c olive black	dbl surch (vc)	18.00	9.00
LEB31	105a		7.50p on 2.50 pck bl	dbl surch (vc)	18.00	9.00
LEB32	105b			invtd surch (vc)	18.00	9.00
LEB33	B6a	(1926)	1.50p+50c rose red (B)	dbl surch (vc)	14.00	14.00
LEB33A	Bf	(1926)	2p +75c dark brown	surch invtd (vc) R	20.00	
LEB34	C1a	(1924)	2p on 40c	dbl surch (vc)	—	—
LEB35	C3a		5p on 1fr	dbl surch & ovpt	—	—
LEB36	C4a		10p on 2fr	invtd surch & ovpt	70.00	—
LEB37	C7a		5p on 1fr	ovpt reversed	25.00	—
LEB38	C8a		10p on 2fr	ovpt reversed	25.00	—
LEB39	C8b			dbl surch (vc)	25.00	—
LEB40	C11a	(1925)	5p violet	invtd ovpt (vc)	—	—
LEB41	C21a	(1928)	2p dark brown	dbl ovpt (vc)	20.00	—
LEB42	C21b			invtd ovpt (vc)	20.00	—
LEB43	C22a		3p orange brown	dbl ovpt (vc)	20.00	—
LEB44	C23a		5p violet	dbl ovpt (vc)	13.00	—
LEB45	C24a		10p violet brown	dbl ovpt (vc)	13.00	—
LEB46	C33a	(1929)	50c yellow green (R)	invtd ovpt (vc)	17.50	14 .00
LEB47	C34a		1p magenta (bk)	invtd ovpt (vc)	17.50	14.00
LEB48	C35a		25p ultra (R)	invtd ovpt (vc)	NA	190.00
LEB49	C36a		15p on 25p ultra (I)	type II (#106)	NA	
LEB50	C37a		50c on 75c	airplane invtd	30.00	—
LEB51	C37b			French & Arabic surch, invtd	—	—
LEB52	C37c			"P" omitted	—	—
LEB53	C37d			airplane omitted	—	—
LEB54	C38a	(1930)	2p on 1.25p dp green	invtd surch (vc)	16.00	14.00

Lebanon is known for its cedar trees
Lebanon is known for its mass of vc's. —The Bard

LEEWARD ISLANDS

LEE1	10ab	(1897)	1p	triple ovpt (u)	NA	—
LEE2	17a	(1902)	1p on 4p lilac & org	tall narrow "O" in "One"	27.50	60.00
LEE3	18a		1p on 6p lilac & brn	tall narrow "O" in "One"	37.50	70.00

Triple overprints are time to play
It's much too bad they are NA. —The Bard

LESOTHO

LES1	20a	(1966)	1r dp claret & blk	"Lseotho"	50.00	—
LES2	J1a	(1966)	1c carmine	"Lseotho"	50.00	—
LES3	J2		5c dark purple	"Lseotho"	85.00	—

LIBERIA

LIB1	33a	(1892-96)	1c vermillion	1c blue (error)(u)	37.50	—
LIB2	34a		2c blue	2c vermillion (error)(u)	37.50	—
LIB3	35a		4c green & blk	center invtd (u)	92.50	—
LIB4	37a		8c brown & blk	center invtd (u)	NA	
LIB5	37b		center sideways (u)		—	—
LIB6	41a		16c lilac	16c deep greenish blue (error) (u)	—	—
LIB7	M44b	(1892)	32c slate blue green	32c lilac (error)	70.00	—
LIB8	49a		$5 carmine & blk	center invtd (u)	NA	—
LIB9	50a	(1893)	5c on 6c blue grn	"5," with short flag	5.00	5.00
LIB9A	M50x		1c red salmon	addl ovpt 63, O S (R)	7.50	—
LIB10	50b			both 5's with short flags	2.50	2.50
LIB11	50c			"I" dot omitted	19.00	19.00
LIB12	50d			surch "b"	30.00	30.00
LIB12A	M51x	(1892-93)	2c gray blue	addl ovpt 63, O S (R)	7.50	—

LIBERIA

LIB12B	M52x		4c emerald green & black (R)	addl ovpt 63, O S (R)	8.00	—
LIB12C	M53x		5c on 6c emerald green, "93	5 with short flag	5.00	5.00
LIB12D	M53x1			both 5, short flag	5.00	5.00
LIB12E	M53x2			ovpt 48 x 2	20.00	20.00
LIB12F	M53x3			not dot over i	20.00	20.00
LIB12G	M55x		8c deep brown & black (R)	addl ovpt 63, O S (R)	9.00	—
LIB12H	M56		12c brown lake	addl ovpt 63, O S	9.00	—
LIB12I	M57x		16c lilac	addl ovpt 63, O S (B)	9.00	—
LIB12J	M57x1			OFFICSL	—	—
LIB12K	M58x		24c dp yellow green on cream	addl ovpt 63, O S (R)	10.00	—
LIB12L	M59x		32c slate blue green	addl ovpt 63, O S (R)	12.00	—
LIB12M	M59x1			OFFICSL	—	—
LIB13	62a	(1905)	5c ultra & blk	center invtd(u)	NA	—
LIB14	71a	(1901-02)	10c yel & blue blk	"O S" omitted	—	—
LIB14A	M121x	(1902)	5c blue gray & black	ORDINARY dbl ovpt	30.00	30.00
LIB14B	M125x		15c gray black	ORDINARY dbl ovpt	30.00	30.00
LIB14C	M130x		30c dark blue	dbl ovpt	—	—
LIB14D	M132x		$1 gray blue & black	on #60 optd OFFICIAL	NA	—
LIB14E	M136x		1c dark green	O S dbl ovpt	50.00	—
LIB14F	M136x1			dbl ovpt	75.00	—
LIB14G	M137x		2c red salmon & black	O S dbl ovpt	95.00	—
LIB14H	M137x1			dbl ovpt	95.00	—
LIB14I	M139x		10c bist yel & blue bllk	dbl ovpt (R)	—	—
LIB14J	M142x		25c yellow green	invtd ovpt (R)	100.00	—
LIB14K	M145x	(1902)	75c on $1 #45a	large c & comma	12.00	12.00
LIB14L	M145x1			invtd ovpt	35.00	35.00
LIB14M	M145x2			as x, invtd ovpt addl ovpt OFFICIAL (#146) O S	—	—
LIB15		(1901-02)	76a 25c yellow grn	"O S" omitted	—	—
LIB16	79a		$1 ultra & blk	"O S" omitted	—	—
LIB17	81a		$5 car & blk	"O SS" omitted	NA	—
LIB18	91a	(1902)	75c on $1 #47	thin "C" & comma	19.00	19.00
LIB19	91b			invtd surch (vc)	62.50	62.50
LIB20	91c			as "a" invtd	—	—
LIB21	92a		75c on $1 #O10	thin "C" & comma	NA	—
LIB22	93a		75c on $1 #O23a	thin "C" & comma	NA	—
LIB23	94a	(1903)	3c black	printed on both sides (u)	45.00	—
LIB23A	M149x	(1903)	3c deep green	no ovpt (from full sheet)	4.25	—
LIB23B	M149x1			pair, one no ovpt	20.00	—
LIB24	98a	(1904)	1c on 5c on 6c bl grn	"5," with short flag	4.25	4.25
LIB25	98b			both 5's with short flags	8.75	8.75
LIB26	98c			"i" dot omitted	—	—
LIB27	98d			surch on #50d	12.50	12.50
LIB28	98e			invtd surch (vc)	6.75	6.75
LIB28A	M158x2	(1904)	1c on 5c on 6c emerald green	ovpt 48 x 2	1.00	—
LIB28B	M161x2		1c on 5c on 6c emerald green	ovpt 48 x 2	9.00	—
LIB28C	M161x3			no dot over I	6.00	6.00
LIB29	99a		2c on 4c grn & blk	pair, one without surch	35.00	—
LIB30	99b			dbl surch (vc)	—	—
LIB31	99c			dbl surch, red & blk	62.50	—
LIB32	99d			surcharged on back also	19.00	—
LIB33	99e			"Official" ovpt missing	30.00	—
LIB34	101a	(1906)	1c	(101a to 123a, all invtd center)	37.50	37.50
LIB35	102a		2c		27.50	27.50
LIB36	103a		5c		125.00	125.00
LIB37	104a		10c		57.50	57.50

LIB38	105a		15c		125.00	125.00
LIB39	106b		20c		125.00	125.00
LIB40	107a		25c		55.00	55.00
LIB41	109b		50c		55.00	55.00
LIB42	110b		75c		92.50	92.50
LIB43	111a		$1		75.00	75.00
LIB44	112a		$2		72.50	72.50
LIB45	116a	(1909-12)	2c		70.00	60.00
LIB46	117a		5c		62.50	55.00
LIB46A	118a	(1909-12)	10c plum & black	imperf pair R ?		
LIB47	119a		15c		47.50	47.50
LIB48	120a		20c		70.00	55.00
LIB49	121b		25c		47.50	42.50
LIB50	123a		50c		75.00	62.50
LIB51	126a	(1912)	3c on plum & blk (bl)	"3," invtd	—	
LIB52	127b		3c on 10c plum & blk (bl)	dbl surch, one invtd	22.50	—
LIB53	127c			dbl vertical surch	—	—
LIB54	128a	(1913)	8c on 3c red & grn (I)	surch on No 64a	3.00	.15
LIB55	128b			dbl surch (vc)	6.25	—
LIB56	128d			invtd surch (vc)	25.00	
LIB57	139a	(1915-16)	5c on 30c (R)	dbl surch (vc)	14.00	14.00
LIB58	141a		10c on 50c (R)	dbl surch, one invtd	—	
LIB59	142a		10c on 50c (R)	dbl surch red & blk	35.00	35.00
LIB60	142b			blue surch	35.00	35.00
LIB61	146a		50c on $2 (R)	"Cents"	17.00	17.00
LIB62	148a		$1 on $5 (bk)	dbl surch (vc)	85.00	85.00
LIB63	152a		2c on 15c	dbl surch (vc)	92.50	—
LIB64	153a		1c on 2c lake & blk	strip of 10 types	35.00	
LIB65	154a		2c on 5c ultra & blk (R)	black surch	14.00	14.00
LIB66	154b			strip of 10 types (R)	35.00	—
LIB67	154c			strip of 10 types (bk)	165.00	—
LIB68	157a	(1916)	3c on 6c violet	invtd surch (vc)	75.00	75.00
LIB69	158a		5c on 12c yellow	invtd surch (vc)	12.50	12.50
LIB70	158b			surch sideways	12.50	
LIB71	159a		10c on 24c rose red	invtd surch (vc)	15.00	15.00
LIB72	159b			surch sideways	—	—
LIB73	160a	(1917)	4c on 25c yel grn	"OUR"	25.00	25.00
LIB74	160b			"FCUR"	25.00	25.00
LIB75	162a		3c on 10c plum & blk	"3," invtd	9.25	9.25
LIB76	176a	(1920)	176a 3c on 1c grn & blk	"CEETS"	17.00	17.00
LIB77	176b			dbl surch (vc)	7.00	7.00
LIB78	176c			triple surch (u)	8.50	8.50
LIB79	177a		4c on 2c rose & blk	invtd surch (vc)	14.00	14.00
LIB80	177b			dbl surch(vc)	5.50	5.50
LIB81	177c			dbl surch, one invtd	14.00	—
LIB82	177d			triple surch,(u) one invtd	14.00	14.00
LIB83	177e			quadruple surch (u)	17.00	17.00
LIB84	177f			typewritten surch	—	—
LIB85	177h			printed & typewritten surcharges, both invtd	—	—
LIB86	178a		5c on 10c bl & blk	invtd surch (vc)	5.25	5.25
LIB87	178b			dbl surch (vc)	8.25	8.25
LIB88	178c			dbl surch, one invtd	8.25	8.25
LIB89	178d			typewritten surch, ("five")	—	72.50
LIB90	178e			printed & typewritten surch	72.50	—
LIB91	179a		5c on 10c orange red & blk	5c on 10c org & blk	4.00	2.75
LIB92	179b			invtd surch (vc)	8.25	—
LIB93	179c			dbl surch (vc)	8.25	—
LIB94	179d			dbl surch, one invtd	10.50	9.50
LIB95	179e			typewritten surch in violet	72.50	72.50
LIB96	179f			typewritten surch in black	—	—

LIB97	179g			printed & typewritten surch	72.50	—
LIB97A	180		5c on 10c green & blk	dbl ovpt one only R ?		
LIB98	180a		5c on 10c grn & blk	dbl surch (vc)	8.25	8.25
LIB99	180b			dbl surch, one invtd	12.50	12.50
LIB100	180c			invtd surch (vc)	—	12.50
LIB101	180d			quadruple surch (u)	21.00	21.00
LIB102	180e			typewritten surch	—	72.50
LIB103	180f			typewritten & printed surch	—	—
LIB103A	181			violet & blk, invtd "5" R ?		
LIB104	181a		5c on 10c vio & blk (Monrovia)	dbl surch, one invtd	12.50	12.50
LIB105	182a		5c on 10c magenta & blk (Robertsport)	dbl surch (vc)	12.50	12.50
LIB106	182b			dbl surch, one invtd	12.50	12.50
LIB107	182c			dbl surch, both invtd	21.00	
LIB108	191a	(1921)	75c red & blk brn	center invtd (u)	—	70.00
LIB109	229a	(1927)	2c on 1c dp grn & blk	"Ceuts"	10.00	—
LIB110	229b			"Vwo"	10.00	—
LIB111	229c			"twc"	10.00	—
LIB112	229d			dbl surch (vc)	20.00	—
LIB113	229e			wavy lines omitted	12.50	—
LIB113A	263		20c grey, lilac & black	invtd ovpt (vc) R ?		
LIB114	264a	(1936)	12c on 30c (V)	"193," instead of "1936,"	9.50	—
LIB114A	266		25c choc + green	invtd ovpt R ?		
LIB115	292Ab	(1944-46)	4c on 10c (bk)	dbl surch, one invtd	—	—
LIB115A	312 var`		5c multi	black color has dramatic 2mm shift R	5.00	
LIB116	B1a		2c + 3c on 10c	dbl red surch	—	—
LIB117	B1b			dbl blue surch	—	—
LIB118	B1c			both surcharges dbl	—	—
LIB119	B1d			pair, one without "2c"	—	—
LIB120	B2a		2c + 3c on 10c	blk & ultra dbl surch (vc)	—	—
LIB121	B4a	(1918)	2c + 2c rose & blk	dbl surch, one invtd	—	—
LIB122	B4b			invtd surch, cross dbl	—	—
LIB123	B4c			invtd surch, cross omitted	17.00	—
LIB124	B6a		10c + 2c dk green	invtd surch (vc)	5.75	27.50
LIB124A	1313		$1 yel brown + blue	invtd ovpt R ?		
LIB125	C68var	(1952)	25c lilac rose & blk	center invtd (u)	50.00	

LIB218

LIB219

LIB220

LIB221

LIB222

LIB223

LIB224

LIB126	C89var		50c dk blue &car	center invtd	50.00	
LIB127	F10a	(1903)	10c bl &blk (Buchanan)	center invtd (u)	100.00	
LIB128	F11a		10c org red & blk ("Grenville")	center invtd (u)	100.00	—
LIB129	F12a		10c grn & blk (Harper)	center invtd (u)	100.00	—
LIB130	F13a		10c vio & blk (Monrovia)	center invtd (u)	100.00	—
LIB131	F14a		10c mag & blk (Robertsport)	center invtd (u)	100.00	—
LIB131A	F20		10c black & blue Buchanan, triangles	semi-perf R ?		
LIB132	J1b	(1892)	3c on 3c violet	invtd surch (vc)	45.00	45.00
LIB133	J1c			as "a" invtd surch	110.00	—
LIB134	J2b		6c on 6c olive gray	invtd surch (vc)	52.50	35.00
LIB135	J8a	(1893)	20c vio, *gray*	center invtd (u)	110.00	110.00
LIB136	M1a	(1916)	1c on 1c lt grn	2nd "F" invtd	NA	
LIB137	M1b			"FLF"	NA	
LIB138	M1c			invtd surch (vc)	NA	
LIB139	M2a		1c on 1c grn & blk	2nd "F" invtd	NA	
LIB140	M2B			"FLF"	NA	
LIB141	M3a		1c on 1c yel grn & blk	2nd "F" invtd	7.50	.50
LIB142	M3b			"FLF"	7.50	7.50
LIB143	M4a		1c on 2c lake & blk	2nd "F" invtd	7.50	7.50
LIB144	M4b			"FLF"	7.50	7.50
LIB145	M5a		1c on 1c	2nd "F" invtd	NA	
LIB146	M5b			"FLF"	NA	
LIB147	M6a		1c on 1c	2n "F" invtd	7.50	7.50
LIB148	M6b			"FLF"	7.50	7.50
LIB149	M6c			"LFF 1c" invtd	10.00	10.00
LIB150	M6d			as "a" & "1c" invtd	—	14.00
LIB151	M7a		1c on 2c	2nd "F" invtd	5.75	5.75
LIB152	M7b			"FLF"	5.75	5.75
LIB153	M7c			pair, one with "LFF 1c"	5.75	5.75
LIB154	O13a	(1893)	5c on 6c bl grn (no. 50)	"5," with short flag	5.00	5.00
LIB155	O13b			both 5's with short flags	5.00	5.00
LIB156	O13c			I dot omitted	19.00	19.00
LIB157	O13d			ovpt on #50d	45.00	45.00
LIB158	O23a		$1 bl & blk	$1 ultra & black	15.00	15.00
LIB159	O31a	(1898-1905)	2c bis & blk	pair, one without ovpt	62.50	—
LIB160	O43a		3c green	ovpt omitted	5.00	—
LIB161	O43b			invtd ovpt	—	—
LIB162	O44a	(1904)	1c on 5c on 6c bl grn	"5," with short flag	4.25	—
LIB163	O44b			both "5s," with straight flag	8.00	8.00
LIB164	O45a		2c on 30c steel blue	dbl surch, red & black	—	—

LIB225

LIB226

LIB227

LIB228

LIB232

LIB233

LIB234

LIB235

LIB165	O45b			surch also on back	—	—
LIB166	O47a	(1906)	2c car & blk (bl)	center & ovpt invtd (u)	16.00	11.00
LIB167	O47b			invtd ovpt (vc)	4.50	
LIB167A	M177x1	(1906)	2c carmine red & black	dbl ovpt	5.00	5.00
LIB168	O48a		5c ultra & blk (bk)	invtd ovpt (vc)	4.50	4.50
LIB169	O48b			center & ovpt invtd (u)	27.50	
LIB170	O49a		10c dl vio & blk (R)	invtd center (u)	—	—
LIB171	O49b			center & ovpt invtd (u)	32.50	—
LIB172	O50a		15c brn & blk (bk)	invtd ovpt (vc)	4.50	—
LIB173	O50b			ovpt omitted	—	—
LIB174	O50c			center & ovpt invtd	40.00	—
LIB175	O51a		20c dp grn & blk (R)	ovpt omitted	—	—
LIB176	O52a		25c plum & gray (bl)	with 2nd ovpt in blue, invtd	—	—
LIB177	O54a		50c org brn & dp grn (G)	invtd ovpt (vc)	2.75	—
LIB177A	M184t	(1906)	50c org brown & dk green (G)	center invtd	15.00	—
LIB178	O55a		75c ultra & blk (bk)	invtd ovpt (vc)	9.50	5.75
LIB179	O55b			ovpt omitted	22.50	—
LIB180	O56a		$1 dp grn & gray (R)	invtd ovpt	—	—
LIB181	O57a		$2 plum & blk (bl)	ovpt omitted	22.50	—
LIB182	O58a		$5 org & blk (bk)	ovpt omitted	11.00	—
LIB183	O58b			invtd ovpt (vc)	6.25	4.00
LIB184	O60a	(1909-12)	2c car rose & brn (bl)	ovpt omitted	—	—
LIB185	O61a		5c turq & blk (bk)	dbl ovpt, one invtd	7.50	—
LIB186	O65a		25c ultra & grn (bk)	dbl ovpt	4.75	4.75
LIB187	O67a		50c brn & grn (bk)	center invtd (vc)	27.50	—
LIB188	O67b			invtd ovpt (vc)	4.00	2.75
LIB189	O71a	(1912)	3c on 10c blk & ultra	pair, one without surch, the other with dbl surch, one invtd	—	—
LIB190	O71b			dbl surch, one invtd	1.75	—
LIB191	O82a	(1915-16)	25c on $1 (R)	"25" dbl	22.50	—
LIB192	O82b			"OS" invtd	22.50	—
LIB193	O96a		5c on 30c dk brn	"FIV"	27.50	27.50
LIB193A	M237x	(1915-16)	10c on 50c (R)	dbl ovpt , one in black	40.00	40.00
LIB193B	M237x1			black ovpt	10.00	10.00
LIB193C	Mx2			blue ovpt handstamped	40.00	40.00
LIB193D	M239x		25c on $1	ovpt 239x	30.00	30.00
LIB193E	M240x1		50c on $2 (R)	ceuts for Cents	15.00	15.00
LIB193F	M240x2			ovpt 240 x 2	NA	
LIB193G	M241x		$1 on $5	ovpt 241x (R)		
LIB193H	M246x		10c on 50c opvt 237	blue ovpt 237, handstamped	2.00	2.00
LIB193I	M248x		25c on $1 ovpt 239	O S omitted	—	—
LIB193J	M248x1			O S invtd ovpt	13.00	13.00

LIB253

LIB254

LIB255

LIB256

LIB236 front

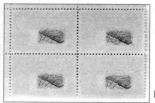
LIB236 back

LIB193K	M249x1		50c on $2 ovpt 240	ovpt 240 x 2 (R)	15.00	15.00
LIB193L	M262x1	(1916)	Official; 1c on 1c dp green & black	LFF (2nd F upside-down)	200.00	200.00
LIB194	O106a	(1918)	50c maroon & blk (bl)	ovpt omitted	11.00	—
LIB195	O111a		3c on 1c grn & red brn	"CEETS"	9.50	—
LIB196	O111b			dbl surch (vc)	2.75	2.75
LIB197	O111c			dbl surch, one invtd	5.75	5.75
LIB198	O112a		4c on 2c red & blk	invtd surch(vc)	4.50	4.50
LIB199	O112b			dbl surch (vc)	4.50	4.50
LIB200	O112c			dbl surch, one invtd	7.00	7.00
LIB201	O112d			triple surch (u)	7.00	7.00
LIB202	O119a	(1921)	15c blk & grn	dbl ovpt (vc)	—	—
LIB203	O122a		50c grn & blk	ovpt "S" only	—	—
LIB204	O149a		30c dp ultra & brn	ovpt omitted	—	—
LIB205	O152a		$1 red org & grn	ovpt omitted	11.00	—
LIB206	O155a	(1926)	2c on 1c	"Gents"	7.25	—
LIB207	O155b			surch in blk	5.75	—
LIB208	O155c			as "b" "Gents"	9.50	—
LIB209	O156a	(1926)	2c on 1c	invtd surch (vc)	—	—
LIB210	O156b			"Gents"	10.00	—
LIB211	O157a	(1927)	2c on 1c	"Ceuts"	40.00	—
LIB212	O157b			"Vwo"	40.00	—
LIB213	O157c			"twc"	40.00	—
LIB214,215	B16,B17		(Red Cross ovpt)	3c blue, 5c brown invtd R ?		
See Photo in Color Section						
LIB216,217	280-281		5c brown, 10c green	Rowland Hill invtd ovpts R	45.00 pair	
See Photo in Color Section						
LIB218-223, 347-9,	C88-90		3c red-org, 5c black, 25c purple, airm.10c blue, 12c brown, 25c fuschia	missing colors, imperf, R set of 6	100.00	
LIB224-228	(368)			5 diff. mixed flags all on same 5c value on brown (should be diff. values) R ?		
LIB229-31	(370)		5c rose (Tubman)	normal & 2 diff colors R	95.00	
LIB232	(369)		5c blue (Tubman)	red missing in flag R ?		
LIB233	(370)		5c on red, blue & yel flag	invtd flag R ?		
LIB234-235	C68-69		25c magenta & black, 50c blue & magenta	invtd centers (u) R	50.00	

LIB237

LIB257

LIB258

LIB259

LIB260

LUX8

LOU3A

LIB236	C69	50c blue & blk, block of 4	frame only, map missing (printed on back in red) R	200.00	
LIB237	C68	25c magenta	imperf, frame only R	50.00	
LIB238- LIB252	C68-9 plus unlisted	(1) frame only, imperf; (2) perf only full designs, plus air mails 25c, 50c, perf reg. & imperf center missing. R		125.00	
LIB253	C115	15c on green, red, white, blue flag	invtd flag R ?		
LIB254-8	C114	15c blue with colored	flags on same value R ?		
LIB259	C114	10c gray with red, white, blue flag	dbl French flag on Italy R	40.00	
LIB260	O133 20c		brown with blue	invtd ovpt R	16.00

Liberia is a maze of errors—spelling, vc's, triple overprints, quadruple overprints, inverted centers, etc. Many of the error varieties are NA. Still, many are not. One stamp in the 1906 series with center and overprint inverted sells for less than $20. Also many Liberian errors are unlisted as given above so that there will be an even broader choice of the errors from this country.

LIBYA

LBA1	1a	(1912-22) 1c brown-('15)	dbl ovpt (vc)	150.00	150.00
LBA2	3a	5c green	dbl ovpt (vc)	30.00	30.00
LBA3	3c		invtd ovpt (vc)	—	NA
LBA4	3d		pair, one without ovpt	125.00	125.00
LBA5	4a	10c claret	pair, one without ovpt	45.00	45.00
LBA6	6a	20c orange	dbl ovpt (vc)	90.00	90.00
LBA7	6b		pair, one without ovpt	NA	—
LBA8	10a	45c olive grn	invtd ovpt (vc)	150.00	—
LBA9	16a	(1912) 15c slate	blue blk ovpt	NA	3.75
LBA10	22a	(1921) 5c blk & green 5c black & red brm (error)	center invtd (u)	NA	—
LBA11	22b		center invtd (u)	40.00	21.00
LBA12	23a	10c blk & rose	center invtd (u)	40.00	21.00
LBA13	24a	15c blk brn & brn org	center invtd (u)	149.00	37.50
LBA14	25a	25c dk bl & bl	center invtd (u)	12.00	6.00
LBA15	26a	30c blk & blk brn	center invtd (u)	NA	
LBA16	27a	50c blk & olive green	50c blk & brn (error)	NA	—
LBA17	27b		center invtd (u)	—	NA
LBA18	33a	(1921) 5c olive green	dbl ovpt (vc)	190.00	90.00
LBA19	34a	10c red	dbl ovpt (vc)	150.00	90.00
LBA20	34b		invtd ovpt (vc)	125.00	90.00
LBA21	51b	(1924-40) 10c blk & dl red	center invtd (u)	25.00	—
LBA22	52b	15c blk brn & org	center invtd, perf 11 (u)	NA	
LBA23	53a	25c dk bl & bl	center invtd (u)	25.00	37.50
LBA24	55b	50c blk & olive grn	center invtd (u)	NA	
LBA25	106a	6mal on 12m red	invtd surch (vc)	25.00	25.00
LBA26	107a	10 mal on 20m dp bl	Arabic "20," for "10,"	20.00	20.00
LBA27	E11b	(1926-36) 2.50 l on 60c	black surch	NA	
LBA28	J3a	(1915) 20c buff & magenta	dbl ovpt (vc)	50.00	50.00
LBA29	J3b		invtd ovpt (vc)	50.00	50.00
LBA30	J5a	40c buff & magenta	dbl ovpt (vc)	NA	
LBA31	J8a	1 l blue & magenta	dbl ovpt (vc)	NA	
LBA32	J28a	(1951) 10mal on 20m org yel	Arabic "20," for "10,"	200.00	—

A center inverted and a lot of vc
These explain most of this country. —The Bard

LIECHTENSTEIN

LIE1	11a	(1920) 5h yellow green	invtd ovpt (vc)	70.00	—
LIE2	11b		dbl ovpt (vc)	22.50	45.00
LIE3	12a	10h claret	invtd ovpt (vc)	70.00	—
LIE4	12b		dbl ovpt (vc)	22.50	45.00
LIE5	13a	25h deep blue	invtd ovpt (vc)	70.00	—
LIE6	14a	40h on 3h violet	invtd surch (vc)	70.00	—
LIE7	15a	1k on 15h dull red	invtd surch (vc)	70.00	—
LIE8	15b		ovpt type "a"	62.50	150.00

LIE9	16a		2-1/2 k on 20h dk grn	invtd surch (vc)	70.00	—
LIE10	51a	(1921)	2rp on 10h dp org	dbl surch (vc)	30.00	*65.00*
LIE11	51b			invtd surch (vc)	30.00	*80.00*
LIE12	51c			dbl surch, one invtd (vc)	30.00	*65.00*
LIE13	52a		2rp on 10h dp org	dbl surch (vc)	57.50	*150.00*
LIE14	52b			invtd surch (vc)	57.50	*150.00*
LIE15	52c			dbl surch, one invtd	57.50	*150.00*

LITHUANIA

LIT1	10a	(1919)	15sk black	"5," for "15,"	50.00	50.00
LIT2	15a		20 sk black	"astas" for "pastas"	60.00	55.00
LIT3	80a		5auk green & red	right "5," dbl, grn & red	67.50	62.50
LIT4	114a	(1922)	4auk on 75sk bis & red	invtd surch (vc)	20.00	20.00
LIT5	115a		4auk on 75sk bis & red	dbl surch (vc)	25.00	25.00
LIT6	117c		2auk dp bl & yel brn	center invtd (u)	70.00	70.00
LIT7	119a		6auk dk bl & grnsh bl	cliche of 8 auk in sheet of 6 auk	30.00	25.00
LIT8	140b		1c on 50sk olive (C)	invtd surch (vc)	25.00	—
LIT9	140c			dbl surch, one invtd	—	—
LIT10	151a		10c on 1auk	invtd surch (vc)	32.50	—
LIT11	152a		10c on 2auk	invtd surch (vc)	25.00	—
LIT12	153a		15c on 4auk	invtd surch (vc)	25.00	—
LIT13	157a		30c on 8auk (C)	invtd surch (vc)	25.00	15.00
LIT14	B16a	(1926)	1+1c on #B1	invtd surch (vc)	10.00	—
LIT15	B19a		2+2c on #B3	dbl surch, one invtd	10.00	—
LIT16	B31a		2+2c on #B2	invtd surch (vc)	6.00	—
LIT17	B32a		2+2c on #B3	invtd surch (vc)	—	—
LIT18	C23a	(1922)	10c on 60sk	invtd surch (vc)	22.50	—
LIT19	C26a		20c on2auk	without "CENT"	165.00	125.00
LIT20	C27a		25c on 2auk	invtd surch (vc)	22.50	17.50
LIT21	C28a		30c on 4auk (C)	dbl surch (vc)	26.00	20.00
LIT22	C30a		50c on 10auk	invtd surch (vc)	26.00	20.00
LIT23	C31a		1 l on 5auk	dbl surch (vc)	35.00	—
LIT24	L1a	(1919)	50sk on 3k red	dbl surch (vc)	—	—

Spelling errors or vc's
Not very much to please. —The Bard

LOURENCO MARQUES

LOU1	36b	(1898-1903)	25 sea green	25r light green (error)	*32.50*	*32.50*
LOU2	55a	(1899)	50r on 30r grn & brn	invtd surch (vc)	—	—
LOU3	74a	(1903)	75r rose	invtd ovpt (vc)	35.00	35.00
LOU3A	78var.		5 orange—w/marqu	"f"s errpr R	5.00	
LOU4	78a	(1911)	5r orange	dbl ovpt (vc)	10.00	10.00
LOU5	78b			invtd ovpt (vc)	10.00	10.00
LOU6	80a		15r gray grn	invtd ovpt (vc)	10.00	10.00
LOU7	98a	(1913)	10c on 16a bis brn	invtd surch (vc)	—	—
LOU8	117a		1/2 c black	value omitted	—	—
LOU9	132a	(1914)	115r on 10r red vio	"Republica" invtd	—	—
LOU10	145a	(1915)	2c on 15r gray grn	new value invtd	22.50	—
LOU11	147a	(1916)	147A 50r brown	invtd ovpt (vc)	—	—
LOU12	161a	(1921)	1c on 2-1/2 c vio (bk)	invtd surch (vc)	25.00	—
LOU13	P2a	(1895)	2-1/2 r brown	invtd ovpt (vc)	30.00	30.00

Some scattered errors and vc's
Enough to please the Portuguese —The Bard

LUXEMBOURG

LUX1	26a	(1873)	1fr on 37-1/2c bister	surch invtd (vc)	—	NA
LUX2	39a	(1879)	1 fr on 37-1/2 c bis	"Pranc"	NA	
LUX3	39b			without surch	NA	—
LUX4	39c			as "b" imperf	NA	—
LUX5	121a	(1923)	25c on 37-1/2 c	dbl surch (vc)	75.00	—
LUX6	155a	(1928)	15c on 20c yel grn	bars omitted	—	—

LUX7	477a	(1969)	3fr multicolored	green omitted (u)	*150.00*	*150.00*
LUX8	B242a	(1964)	2fr+25c multi	values omitted R	300.00*	

*NA from author's personal collection

LUX9	O39a	(1881)	40c orange	invtd ovpt (vc)	185.00	NA
LUX10	O41a		4c green	invtd ovpt (vc)	NA	—
LUX11	O46a		5c yellow	invtd ovpt (vc)	200.00	—
LUX12	O52a	(1882)	1c gray lilac	"S" omitted	—	—
LUX13	O80a	(1908-26)	1c gray	invtd ovpt	110.00	—
LUX14	O82a		4c bister	dbl ovpt (vc)	125.00	—
LUX15	O82a		4c bister	dbl ovpt (vc)	125.00	—

Luxembourg has produced among other things a value omission, a color omission and several vc's in the Officials.

M

MACAO

MAC1	16a	(1884)	80r on 100r lilac	invtd surch (vc)	*80.00*	*30.00*
MAC2	16b			without accent on "e" of "reis"	62.50	55.00
MAC3	16d			as "b" perf 13-1/2	35.00	32.50
MAC4	17a	(1885)	5r on 5r rose, perf 12-1/2 (bk)	with accent on "e"of "Reis"	12.50	12.00
MAC5	17b			dbl surch (vc)	140.00	125.00
MAC6	17c			invtd surch (vc)	125.00	100.00
MAC7	18a		10r on 25r rose (bl)	accent on "e" of "Reis"	—	—
MAC8	18b			pair, one without surch	—	—
MAC9	20a		20r on 50r green (bk)	dbl surch (vc)	—	100.00
MAC10	20b			accent on "e" of "Reis"	—	—
MAC11	22a	(1885)	5r on 25r rose (bk)	original value not obliterated	—	—
MAC12	23a		10r on 50r green (bk)	invtd surch (vc)	—	—
MAC13	24a	(1887)	5r on 80r gray	"R" of "Reis" 4mm high	55.00	47.50
MAC14	26a		10r on 80r gray	"R" 4mm high	55.00	47.50
MAC15	27a		10r on 200r orange	"R" 4mm high	75.00	45.00
MAC16	28a		20r on 80 gray	"R" 4mm high	60.00	47.50
MAC17	32a	(1887)	5r green & buff	with labels, 5r on 20r	65.00	65.00
MAC18	32b			with labels, 5r on 20r	75.00	65.00
MAC19	332c			with labels, 5r on 60r	65.00	65.00
MAC20	33a			with labels, 10r on 10r	80.00	75.00
MAC21	33b			with labels, 10r on 60r	90.00	75.00
MAC22	34a		40r green & buff	with labels, 40r on 20r	125.00	*110.00*
MAC23	45a	(1892)	30r on 200r gray lilac	invtd surch (vc)	75.00	40.00
MAC24	58a	(1894)	1a on 5r black (r)	short "l"	4.25	2.25
MAC25	58b			invtd surch (vc)	27.50	27.50
MAC26	58c			dbl surch (vc)	*125.00*	—
MAC27	58d			surch on back instead of face	35.00	35.00
MAC28	59a		3a on 20r carmine (G	invtd surch (vc)	—	—
MAC29	60a		4a on 25r violet (bk)	invtd surch (vc)	32.50	32.50
MAC30	62a		8a on 50r blue (R)	dbl surch, one invtd	—	—
MAC31	62b			invtd surch (vc)	50.00	45.00
MAC32	63a		13a on 80r gray (bk)	dbl surch (vc)	—	—
MAC33	64a		16a on 100r brown (bk)	invtd surch (vc)	—	—
MAC34	65a		31a on 200r gray lil (bk)	invtd surch (vc)	75.00	40.00
MAC35	66a		47a on 300r orange (G)	dbl surch (vc)	—	—
MAC36	108a	(1902)	6a on 10r orange	dbl surch (vc)	55.00	50.00
MAC37	110a		6a on 5r black	invtd surch (vc)	45.00	35.00
MAC38	112a		6a on 40r choc	dbl surch (vc)	50.00	35.00
MAC39	113a		18a on 20r rose	dbl surch (vc)	60.00	35.00
MAC40	115a		18a on 80r gray	dbl surch (vc)	85.00	85.00
MAC41	119a	(1902-10)	6a on 5r yellow	invtd surch (vc)	30.00	30.00
MAC42	144a	(1910)	1/2 a gray green	invtd ovpt (vc)	18.00	18.00
MAC43	145a		1a yellow green	invtd ovpt (vc)	18.00	18.00

MAC44	146a		2a slate	invtd ovpt (vc)	18.00	18.00
MAC45	147a		1/2 a gray	invtd ovpt (vc)	5.00	5.00
MAC46	147B1		1a orange	invtd ovpt (vc)	5.00	5.00
MAC47	150a		4a carmine (G)	4a pale yel brn (error)	*50.00*	*50.00*
MAC48	158a	(1911)	1a on 5r brn & buff	"I" omitted	37.50	37.50
MAC49	158b			invtd surch (vc)	24.00	24.00
MAC50	159a		2a on half of 4a car	"2," omitted	40.00	40.00
MAC51	159b			invtd surch (vc)	32.50	35.00
MAC52	159d			entire stamp	32.50	32.50
MAC53	159Ca		5a on half of 10a sl bl(#89)	entire stamp	—	—
MAC54	160a		5a on half of 10a sl bl (#89)	invtd surch (vc)	*200.00*	*200.00*
MAC55	160b			entire stamp	—	—
MAC56	161a		5a on half of 10a sl bl (#135)	invtd surch (vc)	100.00	100.00
MAC57	161b			entire stamp	80.00	80.00
MAC58	162a		1a black	"Corrieo"	NA	—
MAC59	163a		2a black	"Corrieo"	NA	—
MAC60	196a	(1913)	5a yellow brn	invtd ovpt (vc)	*40.00*	*40.00*
MAC61	199a		13a violet	invtd surch (vc)	75.00	—
MAC62	206a		1/2 a on 5a yel brn (R)	"1/2 Avo" invtd	35.00	35.00
MAC63	207a			"4 Avos" invtd	40.00	35.00
MAC64	209a		1a on 13a gray lil (R)	"REPUBLICA" omitted	—	—
MAC65	210a	(1913-24)	1/2 a olive brown	inscriptions invtd	50.00	—
MAC66	211a			inscriptions invtd	50.00	—
MAC67	211b			inscriptions invtd	50.00	—
MAC68	213a		2a blue green	inscriptions invtd	40.00	—
MAC69	254a		10a slate blue	"Provisorio" dbl	30.00	—
MAC70	J1	(1904)	1/2 a gray green	name & value invtd	27.50	15.00
MAC71	J30a	(1914)	40a car (G)	dbl ovpt, red & green (u)	35.00	8.00
MAC72	P1a	(1892-93)	2-1/2 r on 40r choc	invtd surch (vc)	40.00	30.00
MAC73	P2a		2-1/2 r on 80r gray	invtd surch (vc)	40.00	35.00
MAC74	P2b			dbl surch (vc)	40.00	35.00
MAC75	P3a		2-1/2 r on 10r grn (1893)	dbl surch (vc)	—	—
MAC76	P5a	(1894)	1/2 a on 2-1/2 r brn (bk)	dbl surch (vc)	—	—

MACEDONIA has produced no errors

MADAGASCAR - British Consular

MAD1	1b	(1884)	1p violet	seal omitted	NA
MAD2	4a		4p violet 1 oz	"1 oz" corrected to "4 oz" in mss.	NA
MAD3	4b			seal omitted	NA

**Forgetting the types, the errors are three
And refreshingly none are a vc
But mucho cash must be shelled out
NA, NA, NA ouch. —The Bard**

MADEIRA

MAR1	2a	(1868)	20r bister	invtd ovpt (vc)	—	—
MAR2	4a		80r orange	dbl ovpt (vc)	—	–
MAR3	10a	(1868-70)	25r rose	invtd ovpt (vc)	—	–
MAR4	11a		50r greem	invtd ovpt (vc)	—	—
MAR5	13a		100r lilac	invtd ovpt (vc)	—	—
MAR6	16a	(1871-80)	5r black (R)	invtd ovpt (vc)	—	—
MAR7	16b			dbl ovpt (vc)	55.00	55.00
MAR8	23a		25r rose	invtd ovpt (vc)	32.50	32.50
MAR9	23b			dbl ovpt (vc)	32.50	32.50
MAR10	24a	(1872)	50r green	dbl ovpt (vc)	—	—
MAR11	24b			invtd ovpt (vc)	155.00	155.00
MAR12	34a	(1880-81)	25r pearl gray	invtd ovpt (vc)	52.50	52.50
MAR13	P1a	(1876)	2-1/2 r olive	invtd ovpt (vc)	30.00	—

MALAGASY (Madagascar)

MAL1	1a	(1889)	1a 05c pm 10c blk, *lav*	invtd surch (vc)	NA	
MAL2	2a		05c on 25c blk, *rose*	invtd surch (vc)	NA	
MAL3	2b		25c on 10c lavender (error)			NA
MAL4	3a		25c on 40c red, *strawi*	invtd surch (vc)	NA	
MAL5	5a	(1891)	15c on 25c blk, *rose*	surch vertical	*155.00*	*97.50*
MAL6	6a		5c on 10c blk, *lav*	dbl surch (vc)	NA	—
MAL7	29a	(1896-1906)	2c brn, *buff*	name in blue black	3.50	3.50
MAL8	46a	(1899)	1fr brnz grn, *straw*	name in blue	17.50	10.00
MAL9	48a	(1902)	05c on 50c car, *rose*	invtd surch (vc)	67.50	67.50
MAL10	49a		10c on 5fr red lil, *lav*	invtd surch (vc)	80.00	—
MAL11	50a		15c on 1fr ol grn, *straw*	invtd surch (vc)	80.00	—
MAL12	50b			dbl surch (vc)	NA	—
MAL13	51a		0,01 on 2c brn, *buff*	invtd surch (vc)	50.00	50.00
MAL14	51b			"00,1," instead of "0,01,"	65.00	65.00
MAL15	51c			as "b" invtd	—	—
MAL16	51d			comma omitted	145.00	150.00
MAL17	51e			name in blue black	7.50	7.50
MAL18	52a		0,05 on 30c brn, *bister*	invtd surch (vc)	50.00	50.00
MAL19	52b			"00,5," instead of "0,05,"	65.00	65.00
MAL20	52c			as "b" invtd	NA	
MAL21	52d			comma omitted	145.00	150.00
MAL22	53a		0,10 on 50c car, *rose*	invtd surch (vc)	50.00	50.00
MAL23	53b			comma omitted	145.00	150.00
MAL24	54a		0,15 on 75c vio, *org*	invtd surch (vc)	60.00	60.00
MAL25	54b			comma omitted	160.00	160.00
MAL26	55a		0,15 on 1fr ol grn, *straw*	invtd surch (vc)	75.00	75.00
MAL27	55b			comma omitted	175.00	175.00
MAL28	56a		0,05 on 30c brn, *bister*	"00,5." instead of "0,05,"	NA	
MAL29	56b			invtd surch (vc)	NA	
MAL30	58a		0,01 on 2c brn, *buff*	invtd surch (vc)	47.50	47.50
MAL31	58b			comma omitted	145.00	150.00
MAL32	59a		0,05 on 30c brn, *bis*	invtd surch (vc)	47.50	47.50
MAL33	59b			comma omitted	145.00	150.00
MAL34	60a		0,10 on 50c car, *rose*	invtd surch (vc)	145.00	150.00
MAL35	63a	(1903)	63a 1c dk violet	on bluish paper	5.00	4.00
MAL36	68a		15c carmine	on bluish paper	95.00	—
MAL37	116a	(1912)	5c on 20c red, *grn*	invtd surch (vc)	90.00	90.00
MAL38	118a		10c on75c vio, *org*	dbl surch (vc)	165.00	165.00
MAL39	124a		10c on 75c org yel	invtd surch (vc)	140.00	140.00
MAL40	127a	(1921)	60c on 75c (R)	invtd surch (vc)	140.00	140.00
MAL41	135a	(1925)	25c on 15c dl vio & rose	dbl surch (vc)	55.00	—

MALAWI

MAW1	23a	(1965)	9p rose	silver omitted (u)	—	—

Color omitted - commonwealth
Therein lies all error wealth. —The Bard

FEDERATION OF MALAYA

Johore

MFM1	2a	(1884-86)	2c rose	dbl ovpt (vc)	—	NA
MFM2	16a	(1891)	2c on 24c green	"CENST"	NA	
MFM3	26a		3c on 4c lilac & blk	no period after "Cents"	35.00	35.00
MFM4	27a		3c on 5c lilac & grn	no period after "Cents"	42.50	55.00
MFM5	28a		3c on 6c lilac & bl	no period after "Cents"	60.00	65.00
MFM6	29a		3c on $1 green & car	no period after "Cents"	150.00	NA
MFM7	52a	(1903)	3c on 4c yel & red	without bars	2.50	*4.25*
MFM8	53a		10c on 4c grn & car rose	without bars	22.50	*35.00*
MFM9	55a		$1 on $2 lilac & car rose	invtd "e" in "one"	NA	—
MFM10	56a	(1904)	10c on 4c yel & red	dbl surch (vc)	NA	—
MFM11	86a	(1912)	3c on 8c vio & blue	"T"of "CENTS" omitted	NA	—

Kedah

MFM12	21a		50c on $2 dk brn & dk grn	"C" of ovpt inserted by hand	NA	
MFM13	13a		b 25c red vio & blue	invtd ovpt (vc)	NA	—
MFM14	N4a	(1942)	5c yellow (R)	black ovpt	NA	
MFM15	N9a		25c brn vio & ultra	black ovpt	100.00	100.00
MFM16	N13a		$1 dk grn & blk	invtd ovpt (vc)	NA	
MFM17	N15a		$5 dp car & blk	black ovpt	NA	

Kelantan—Stamps of 1911-21 ovpt in black: "MALAYA BORNEO EXHIBITION" in 3 lines

MFM18	3a	(1922)	4c black & red		2.75	25.00
MFM19	4a		5c green & red, yel		4.25	27.50
MFM20	7a		30c violet & red		5.50	50.00
MFM21	8a		50c black & orange		7.00	55.00
MFM22	10a		$1 green & brown		22.50	75.00
MFM23	12a		$5 green & ultra		140.00	325.00
MFM24	14a		1c green		2.00	25.00
MFM25	23a		10c black & violet		4.75	45.00

Malacca

MFM26	15a	(1899)	4c on 8c lil & blue	dbl surch grn (vc)	NA	
MFM27	15b			pair, one without surch	—	NA
MFM28	15c			dbl surch, 1 green, 1 red	NA	
MFM29	19a		4c on 3c lil & car rose	dbl surch (vc)	NA	
MFM30	19b			pair, one without surch	NA	
MFM31	19d			bar dbl	—	NA
MFM32	20a	(1900)	1c on 15c grn & vio	invtd period (vc)	NA	
MFM33	N17a	(1942)	1c black	invtd ovpt, black (vc)	12.50	20.00
MFM34	N21a		6c gray	invtd ovpt, black (vc)	—	NA
MFM35	N28a	(1943)	1c black	invtd ovpt, black (vc)	12.50	17.50
MFM36	N30a		6c on 5c choc	"6 cts" invtd, black	NA	

Pahang—stamps of the Straits Settlements overprinted in black "PAHANG"

MFM37	21a	(1897)	2c on half of 5c blue	black surch	NA	
MFM38	22a		3c on half of 5c blue	blk surch	NA	
MFM39	25b	(1899)	4c on 8c lilac & blue	invtd surch (vc)	NA	

Penang has produced no errors

Perak

MFM40	6a	(1883)	2c rose	invtd ovpt (PERAK) (vc)	NA	
MFM41	6b			dbl ovpt (PERAK)(vc)	NA	
MFM42	7a	(1886-90)	2c rose	"FERAK" corrected by pen	165.00	200.00
MFM43	14a		1c on 2c rose	without period after "PERAK"	NA	
MFM44	16a		1c on 2c rose	dbl surch (vc)	NA	—
MFM45	18b		1c on 2c rose	dbl surch, one invtd (vc)	—	—
MFM46	18c			"PREAK"	—	—
MFM47	19a		1c on 2c rose	dbl surch, one invtd (vc)	—	—
MFM48	19b			invtd surch (vc)	—	—
MFM49	19c			"One" invtd	NA	
MFM50	19d			dbl surch (vc)	NA	
MFM51	20a	(1889-90)	1c on 2c rose	italic Roman "K" in "PERAK"	125.00	150.00
MFM52	20b			dbl surch (vc)	—	—
MFM53	23a		1c on 2c rose	"PREAK"	NA	
MFM54	28a	(1891)	1c on 2c rose	bar omitted	125.00	
MFM55	31a		1c on 2c rose	bar omitted	NA	—
MFM56	35a		1c on 2c rose	bar omitted	150.00	—
MFM57	65a	(1900)	3c on 8c lilac & blue	no period after "Cent"	80.00	100.00
MFM58	65b			dbl surch (vc)	NA	
MFM59	66a		3c on 50c grn & blk	no period after "Cent"	70.00	110.00
MFM60	O3a	(1890)	2c rose	no period after "S"	40.00	40.00
MFM61	O3b			dbl ovpt (vc)	NA	
MFM62	O4a		4c brown	no period after "S"	72.50	100.00
MFM63	O10a	(1894)	5c blue	invtd ovpt (vc) NA		
MFM64	O11a	(1897)	5c lilac & olive	dbl ovpt (vc)	NA	
MFM65	N17a		2c brown orange	invtd ovpt (vc)	R 20.00	21.00
MFM66	N18a		3c green	invtd ovpt (vc) R	11.00	
MFM67	N19a		8c rose red	invtd ovpt (vc)	7.50	7.50
MFM68	N19b			dbl ovpt, one invtd	175.00	200.00

MFM69	N19c			pair, one without ovpt	NA	
MFM69A	N20a		2c orange	invtd ovpt (vc) R	5.00	
MFM70	N24a		$5 red, *emerald*	invtd ovpt (vc)	NA	
MFM71	N26a		1c black	invtd ovpt (vc)	25.00	30.00
MFM72	N27a		8c rose red	invtd ovpt (vc)	15.00	17.50
MFM73	N28a		2c on 5c chocolate	invtd ovpt (vc) R	13.00	
MFM74	N28b			as "a" "2 Cents" omitted	37.50	42.50
MFM75	N31a	(1943)	2c on 5c choc	"2 Cents" invtd	25.00	30.00
MFM76	N31b			entire surch invtd	25.00	30.00
MFM77	N32a		2c on 5c choc	vertical characters invtd R	13.00	
MFM78	N32b			entire surch invtd (vc)	25.00	30.00
MFM79	N34a		5c choc	invtd ovpt (vc)	37.50	45.00
MFM80	N36a		8c rose red	invtd ovpt (vc)	25.00	30.00

Perlis has produced no errors
Selangor

MFM81	5a	(1881)	2c brown	dbl ovpt (vc)	—	—
MFM82	8a		2c rose	dbl ovpt (vc)	—	—
MFM83	43a	(1900)	1c on 50c grn & blk	dbl surch (vc)	NA	

Sungei Ujong

MFM84	15a	(1881-84)	2c rose	"Ujong" printed sideways	—	—
MFM85	15b			"Sungei" printed twice	—	—
MFM86	21a	(1885-90)	2c rose	"UNJOG"	NA	

Trengganu

MFM87	B1a	(1917)	3c +2c rose red	"CSOSS"	40.00	*65.00*
MFM88	B1b			comma after "2c"	2.50	*6.50*
MFM89	B1c			pair, one without surch	NA	
MFM90	B2a		4c +2c brn org	"CSOSS"	165.00	*165.00*
MFM91	B2b			comma after "2c"	10.00	*26.00*
MFM92	B3a		8c+2c ultra	"CSOSS"	110.00	*125.00*
MFM93	B3b			comma after "2c"	8.25	*32.50*

MALAYA

FEDERATED MALAY: JOHORE, KEDAH, KELANTAN, MALACCA (no errors), NEGRI SEMBILAN, PAHANG, PENANG (no errors), PERAK, PERLIS (no errors), SELANGOR, SUNGEI UJONG,TREGANNU

We did not list all the errors as it would be a foolish endeavor, but those states with the absence of errors are listed. It appears Perak has the greatest number. A cursory listing is provided above including vc's, misspellings, one inverted (NA), and a black surcharge where red is called for (NA).

Malaysia

MLY1	1a	(1963)	10s violet & yellow	yellow omitted (u)	100.00	—
MLY2	18a	(1965)	15c blue, blk & grn	green omitted (u)	18.00	—
MLY3	21a		30c tan & multi	blue omitted (u)	87.50	—
MLY4	22a		50c rose & multi	rose omitted (u)	42.50	—

MFM66

MFM69A

MFMF73

MAL1

MAL2

MFM77

MLT19

AFFORDABLE FOREIGN ERRORS

Johore

MLY5	169a	(1965)	1c blk & lt grnsh bl	black omitted (u)	50.00	—
MLY6	171a		5c black & prus bl	yellow omitted (u)	24.00	—

Kedah

MLY7	106a	(1965)	1c blk & lt grnsh bl	black omitted (u)	50.00	—

Kelantan has produced no errors
Malacca has produced no errors
Negri Sembilan has produced no errors
Pahang has produced no errors

Penang

MLY8	69a	(1965)	5c black & Prus blue	Prus blue omitted (u)	—	—
MLY9	69b			yellow omitted (u)	—	—

Perak

MLY10	141a	(1965)	5c black & Prus blue	yellow omitted (u)	20.00	—
MLY11	144a		15c blk, lil rose &	lilac rose omitted (u)	80.00	—

Perlis has produced no errors
Sabah has produced no errors

Selangor

MLY12	122a	(1965)	2c black, red & gray	rose carmine omitted (u)	—	—

Trengganu has produced no errors
Wilayah Persekutuan has produced no errors
Maldive Islands has produced no errors

Colors omitted, that's all we get
But many of them cost a bit.
Here's the Commonwealth once more
Kedah, Penang and Johore. —The Bard

MALI (REPUBLIC OF)

MAL1	C224		100r multicolored	date error 5, R	22.00
MAL2	C327	(1978)	250fr multi	spelling error, Repu(p)lique R	155.00

MALTA

MLT1	20a	(1902)	llp on 2-1/2 p.	Ultra-pnney	_25.00_	_27.50_
MLT2				dbl surch	NA	
MLT3	122a	(1926)	3p black, _yel_,	inv. out	175.00	NA
MLT4	2236a	(1953)	1-1/2 p. green	ovpt omitted	NA	
MLT5	275a	(1960)	1-1/2 bister, brt blue & gold	gold dates and crosses omitted	75.00	_57.50_
MLT6	280a		2sh 6p on brt greenish blue & gold	gold omitted	NA	
MLT7	298a	(1964)	2p dk grn, black & brown	black omitted		
MLT8	315a	(1965-70)	2p multi	gold omitted	25.00	
MLT9	316a		2-1/2 p multi-gold	("SARACENIC") omitted		
MLT10	3317b		3p multi-gold	(windows) omitted	37.50	
MLT11	318a		4p multi-black	(arms shading omitted)	47.50	—
MLT12	318b			silver omitted	45.00	—
MLT13	320a		6p multi	black omitted	60.00	—
MLT14	324a		16s 6p	queen's head omitted	NA	
MLT15	330a		£lmulti-pink	(shading on figures) omitted	30.00	—
MLT16	336a	(1965)	6p ol.gr, red org, el, blk & gold	black omitted	140.00	—
MLT17	336b			gold omitted	165.00	—
MLT18	346a	(1966)	ish deep ol, gold & red	gold omitted	NA	
MLT19	354 var.	(1966)	Kennedy Memorial: white, gold, black instead of normal	misplaced gold R	50.00	
MLT20	375a		lp slate gold & red	red omitted (stars)	50.00	—
MLT21	J5a		2-1/2 p, black, _white_	2 of 1/2 omitted	NA	

Malta reminds us of Australia with its large number of "colors omitted." There is one big difference between the errors of these two commonwealth nations. Generally, the price of Australian errors is much higher and falls within the not affordable (NA) category, while the mint copies of Maltese color errors often fall under $100 (e.g. MLT5, MLT8, MLT9, MLT10, MLT11, etc.).

MANCHUKUO

MAN1	36a	(1934)	1f on 4f olive green	brown surch	26.00	16.00
MAN2	36b			upper left character of surch omitted	—	—
MAN3	36c			invtd surch (vc)	90.00	90.00
MAN4	105a	(1937)	2-1/2 f on 2f	invtd surch (vc)	110.00	85.00
MAN5	105b			vert. Pair, one without surch.	95.00	—
MAN6	135a	(1940)	4f black & green	dbl impression of green (u)	30.00	—

A few errors such as impressions double
A scattering of things cause the rest of the trouble. —The Bard

MARIANA ISLANDS

MAR1	15b	(1900)	25pf orange	invtd ovpt (vc)	NA	—
MAR2	11a	(1899)	3pf light brown	11a-16a, ovpt at 48 degree angle	NA	
MAR3	12a		5pf green		NA	
MAR4	13a		10pr carmine		200.00	NA
MAR5	14a		20pf ultra		200.00	NA
MAR6	15a		25pf orange		NA	
MAR7	16a		50pf red brown		NA	

Inverts, angles, costs are high
If you buy them take a sigh. —The Bard

MARIENWERDER

MAW1	24a	(1920)	5pf green	invtd ovpt (vc)	130.00	NA
MAW2	26a		20pf bl vio	invtd ovpt (vc)	80.00	130.00
MAW3	26b			dbl ovpt (vc)	80.00	150.00
MAW4	29a		75pf grn & black	invtd ovpt (vc)	80.00	100.00
MAW5	31a		1m car rose	invtd ovpt (vc)	NA	
MAW6	33a		2m on 2-1/2 pf gray	invtd surch (vc)	45.00	90.00
MAW7	34a		3m on 3pf brown	dbl surch (vc)	45.00	90.00
MAW8	34b			invtd surch (vc)	45.00	90.00
MAW9	35a		5m on 7-1/2 pf org	invtd surch (vc)	45.00	90.00
MAW10	35b			dbl surch (vc)	45.00	90.00

MARSHALL ISLANDS has produced no errors

MARTINIQUE

MRT1	1a	(1886-91)	5 on 20c	dbl surch (vc)	NA	
MRT2	3a	(1887)	15c on 20c	invtd surch (vc)	NA	
MRT3	4a		15c on 20c	invtd surch (vc)	NA	
MRT4	5a	(1888)	01 on 20c	invtd surch (vc)	200.00	200.00
MRT5	7c		15 on 20c	invtd surch (vc)	NA	
MRT6	8a	(1887)	015 on 20c	invtd surch (vc)	NA	
MRT7	9a	(1888)	01c on 20c	invtd surch (vc)	NA	
MRT8	12a	(1890)	05c on 10c	slanting "5,"	150.00	110.00
MRT9	13a	(1888)	05c on 20c	slanting "5,"	60.00	50.00
MRT10	13b			invtd surch (vc)	NA	190.00
MRT11	14a	(1891)	05c on 30c	slanting "5,"	70.00	60.00
MRT12	15a		05c on 35c	slanting "5,"	65.00	60.00
MRT13	15b			invtd surch (vc)	175.00	140.00
MRT14	16A		05c on 40c	slanting "5,"	110.00	85.00
MRT15	18a	(1887)	15c on 20c	slanting "5,"	NA	
MRT16	19a	(1890)	15c on 25c	slanting "5,"	60.00	60.00
MRT17	19b			invtd surch (vc)	NA	
MRT18	20a	(1891)	15c on 75c	slanting "5,"	NA	
MRT19	22a	(1891-92)	05c on 5c blk	slanting "5,"	45.00	35.00
MRT20	23b		05c on 15c blk	slanting "5,"	40.00	35.00
MRT21	24a		15c on 20c blk	invtd surch (vc)	175.00	175.00
MRT22	24b			dbl surch (vc)	175.00	175.00
MRT23	25a		15c on 30c blk	invtd surch (vc)	175.00	175.00
MRT24	25b			slanting "5,"	40.00	35.00
MRT25	26a		05c on 10c blk	invtd surch (vc)	175.00	175.00
MRT26	28a		15c on 20c blk	invtd surch (vc)	NA	

MRT27	29a		05c on 25c	slanting "5,"	*160.00*	*160.00*
MRT28	30a		15c on 25c	slanting "5,"	*160.00*	*160.00*
MRT29	31a		05c on 25c	"1882," instead of "1892,"	NA	
MRT30	31b			"95,I" instead of "05,"	NA	
MRT31	31c			slanting "5,"	*150.00*	*150.00*
MRT32	32a		15c on 25c	"1882," instead of "1892,"	NA	
MRT33	32b			slanting "5,"	*90.00*	*90.00*
MRT34	33a	(1892-1906)	1c blk, *lil bl*	"MARTINIQUE" in blue	NA	
MRT35	54a	(1904)	10c on 30c brn, *bister*	dbl surch (vc)	—	—
MRT36	57a		10c on 40c red, *straw*	dbl surch (vc)	NA	
MRT37	60a		10c on 1fr brnz grn, *straw*	dbl surch (vc)	150.00	150.00
MRT38	105a	(1920)	5c on 1c	dbl surch (vc)	17.00	17.00
MRT39	105b			invtd surch (vc)	17.00	17.00
MRT40	106a		10c on 2c	invtd surch (vc)	17.00	17.00
MRT41	107a		25c on 15c	dbl surch (vc)	27.50	27.50
MRT42	107b			invtd surch (vc)	27.50	27.50
MRT43	114a	(1924)	1c on 2c	dbl surch (vc)	200.00	200.00
MRT44	114b			invtd surch (vc)	45.00	45.00
MRT45	115a		5c on 20c	invtd surch (vc)	45.00	45.00
MRT46	116a		15c on 30c (#76)	surch reading down	21.00	21.00
MRT47	117a		15c on 30c (#77)	surch reading up	30.00	30.00
MRT48	119a		25c on 50c (#85)	surch reading down	22.50	22.50
MRT49	Q1a	(1903)	5fr on 60c brn, *buff*	invtd surch (vc)	NA	

Some "slanting 5's" and massive vc's,
The Gods of War shall ne'er be pleased. —The Bard

MAURITANIA

MAU1	C11a (Sanabria 15a)	(1942)	10fr Caravan, (50 exist)	invtd center (u)	NA
MAU2	C12 (Sanabria 16a)		20fr caravan & plane	invtd center (u) Q=100 or less	NA
MAU3	C16		500f multi	no frame around "MIFERMA" dbl ovpt R	25.00
MAU4,5	C16		500f multi	1 invtd, 1 dbl R	75.00

MAURITIUS

MUR1	4d	(1848)	2p dark blue	"PENOE" (u)	NA	
MUR2	4ae		2p blue	"PENOE" (u)	NA	
MUR3	6c		2p blue	"PENOE" (u)	NA	
MUR4	4bf		2p blue	"PENOE" (u)	NA	
MUR5	6ad		2p blue	"PENOE" (u)	NA	
MUR6	6AF			dbl impression (u)	—	—
MUR7	3cd		1p orange red	1p brownish red	NA	
MUR8	4cg		2p blue	"PENOE"	NA	
MUR9	5bc		1p orange red	1p brownish red	NA	
MUR10	5bd			pair, dbl impression (u)	—	—
MUR11	6be		2p blue	"PENOE"	NA	
MUR12	4hi		2p blue	"PENOE"	NA	
MUR13	6gh		2p blue	"PENOE"	NA	
MUR14	43a	(1876)	1/2 p on 9p	invtd surch (vc)	NA	

MAU3

MAU4

MUR15	43b			dbl surch (vc)	—	—
MUR16	76a	(1883)	16c on17c rose	dbl surch (vc)	—	—
MUR17	83a	(1995-87)	2c on 38c violet	invtd surch (vc)	NA	
MUR18	83b			dbl surch (vc)	NA	
MUR19	83c			without bar	—	55.00
MUR20	84a	(1887)	2c on 13c sl (R)	invtd surch (vc)	100.00	125.00
MUR21	84b			dbl surch (vc)	—	NA
MUR22	84c			as "b," one on back	NA	—
MUR23	85a	(1891)	2c on 17c rose	invtd surch (vc)	175.00	175.00
MUR24	85b			dbl surch (vc)	NA	
MUR25	86a		2c on 38c vio	dbl surch (vc)	75.00	75.00
MUR26	86b			dbl surch, one invtd	75.00	75.00
MUR27	86c			invtd surch (vc)	NA	
MUR28	87a		2c on 38c on 9p vio	dbl surch (vc)	NA	
MUR29	87b			invtd surch (vc)	125.00	125.00
MUR30	87c			dbl surch, one invtd	75.00	75.00
MUR31	88a		2c on 4c rose	dbl surch (vc)	65.00	65.00
MUR32	88b			invtd surch (vc)	65.00	65.00
MUR33	88c			dbl surch, one invtd	70.00	70.00
MUR34	113a	(1899)	6c on 18c	invtd surch (vc)	175.00	150.00
MUR35	127a	(1902)	12c on 36c	invtd surch(vc)	NA	

Color Omitted Errors on Interesting Bird Series

MUR36	276a	(1965)	2c brt yel & brn	gray (leg, etc) omitted	50.00	
MUR37	277a		3c brn & dk brn	black eye & beak omitted	45.00	—
MUR38	278a		4c dl rose lil & blk	rose lilac omitted	30.00	—
MUR39	281a		15c lt gray & dk brn	carmine (beak) omitted	45.00	—
MUR40	287a		1r lt yel grn & blk	pale gray ground omitted	80.00	—
MUR41	287b		pale orange omitted		80.00	—

End of Series

MUR42	E2a	(1904)	15c on 15c ultra	"INLAND" invtd	175.00	175.00
MUR43	E2b			invtd "A" in "INLAND"	NA	
MUR44	E3a		1115c on 15c ultra	dbl surch (vc)	175.00	—
MUR45	E3b			invtd surch (vc)	—	175.00
MUR46	E3c			no period after "c"	150.00	150.00
MUR47	E4a		15c green & red	dbl surch (vc)	150.00	150.00
MUR48	E4b			invtd surch (vc)	100.00	100.00
MUR49	E4d			as "c" dbl surch (vc)	NA	
MUR50	E5a		18c green & black	exclamation point (!) Instead of "I" in ""FOREIGN"	200.00	—

No ode to say for thee today
We'd rather see a trilogy:
Mauritius:
1. Has its share of vc's
2. Has the famous (NA) "PENOE" error
3. Like commonwealth colleagues—has colors omitted. —The Bard

MAYOTTE - One of the Comorro Islands

MAY1	2a	(1892-1907)	2c brn, *buff*	name double	NA	
MAY2	26a	(1912)	5c on 25c blk, *rose* (C)	dbl surch (vc)	125.00	
MAY3	28a		10c on 40c red, *straw*	dbl surch (vc)	175.00	—
MAY4	29a		10c on 45c blk, *gray grn* (C)	dbl surch (vc)	175.00	—

Three vc's and a name that's double
Will all that make for a bust and bubble.— The Bard

MEMEL - Off the Baltic Sea, in northern Europe

MEM1	43a	(1921-22)	15pf on 10pf on 10c	invtd surch (vc)	60.00	85.00
MEM2	44a		15pf on 20 pf on 25c	invtd surch (vc)	60.00	85.00
MEM3	45a		15pf on 50pf on 35c (R)	invtd surch (vc)	60.00	85.00
MEM4	46a		60pf on 50pf on 20c	invtd surch (vc)	60.00	85.00
MEM5	49a		5.00m on 2m on 1fr	invtd surch (vc)	NA	
MEM6	93a	(1922-23)	10m on 10pf on 10c	dbl surch (vc)	125.00	140.00

MEM7	C4a	(1921)	2m on 1fr	"Flugpost" invtd	200.00	NA
MEM8	C6a		60pf on 40c	"Flugpost" invtd	200.00	NA
MEM9	C7a		3M on 60c	"Flugpost" invtd	200.00	NA
MEM10	N1a	(1923)	10m on 5c bl (bk)	"Memel" & bars omitted	7.50	_17.00_
MEM11	N12a		10m on5c bl (R)	"Markes" instead of "Markiu"	22.50	50.00
MEM12	N15a		50m on 25c red (bl)	invtd surch (vc)	40.00	
MEM13	N16a		100m on 1 l brn (bk)	invtd surch (vc)	40.00	—
MEM14	N46a	(1923)	10c on 25m (bk)	dbl surch (vc)	65.00	—
MEM15	N50a		50c on 500m (G)	invtd surch (vc)	125.00	—
MEM16	N53a		3c on 40mviolet	dbl surch (vc)	65.00	—
MEM17	N54a		3c on 300m ol grn	dbl surch (vc)	65.00	—
MEM18	N63a		thick figures on next 4-3c on 10m lt brn	dbl surch (vc)	60.00	—
MEM19	N65a		5c on 100m carmine	dbl surch (vc)	60.00	—
MEM20	N68a		50c on 1000m blue	dbl surch (vc)	60.00	—
MEM21	N69a		1 1 on 1000m blue	dbl surch (vc)	90.00	—
MEM22	N88a	(1923)	15c on 100m on 25c red (G)	invtd surch (vc)	140.00	NA

Flugppost, Flugpost in the air
Vc, vc all elsewhere. —The Bard

MESOPOTAMIA

MES1	N1a	(1917)	1/4a on 2pa red lil	"IN BRITISH" omitted	NA	
MES2	N2a		1/4a on 5pa vio brown	"1/4 an" omitted	NA	
MES3	N8a		1a on 20pa red	"OCCUPATION" omitted	NA	
MES4	N11a		on 20pa ultra	"1 An" omitted	NA	
MES5	N12a		2a on 1pi vio & black	"BAGHDAD" omitted	NA	
MES6	N17a		1a on 20pa car rose	"1 An" omitted	NA	
MES7	N21a		1/2 a on 10pa dull grn	"OCCUPATION" omitted	NA	
MES8	N25a		2a on 1pi ultra	"OCCUPATION" omitted	NA	
MES9	N25b			"BAGHDAD" omitted	NA	
MES10	N26a		1/2 a on 10pa car	"BAGHDAD" double	NA	
MES11	N32a	(1918-20)	2-1/2 a on 1pi blue	invtd surch (vc)	NA	
MES12	N33a		3a on 1-1/2 pi car & black	dbl surch red & black (vc)	NA	
MES13	N34a		4a on 1 3/4pi slate & red brn	center invtd (u)	—	NA
MES14	N43a		1a on 20pa rose	"POSTAGE" omitted	—	—
MES15	N44a		1a on 20pa rose	dbl surch (vc)	—	—
MES16	N48a		4a on 1pi dull vio	dbl surch (vc)	—	—
MES17	N48b			"4," omitted	NA	—
MES18	N48c			as "b" dbl surch (vc)	—	—
MES19	N49a		8a on10pa claret	dbl surch (vc)	NA	—
MES20	N49b			invtd surch (vc)	NA	
MES21	N49c			8a on 1pi dull violet	NA	—

A little here and a little there
Then comes an inverted center rare (NA! NA!). —The Bard

MEXICO

MEX1	1b	(1856)	1/2 r blue	without ovpt 4	40.00	35.00
MEX2	1c			dbl impression (u)	—	150.00
MEX3	2c		1r yellow	without ovpt	12.50	15.00
MEX4	2d			1r green (error)	—	—
MEX5	3d		2r yellow grn	without ovpt	35.00	20.00
MEX6	3e			printed on both sides (yel green)	200.00	NA
MEX7	4c		4r red	without ovpt	125.00	150.00
MEX8	5b		8r red lilac	without ovpt	200.00	200.00
MEX9	6a	(1861)	1/2 r black, _buff_	without ovpt	30.00	35.00
MEX10	7a		1r black, _green_	impression of 2r on back	—	NA
MEX11	7b			without ovpt	5.00	4.50
MEX12	7c			printed on both sides (u)	—	NA
MEX13	7d			as "b" blk, pink (error)	—	NA

MEX14	7f			dbl impression (u)	—	150.00
MEX15	8a		2r black, *pink*	impression of 1r on back	NA	—
MEX16	8c			without ovpt	3.00	6.50
MEX17	8d			printed on both sides (u)	—	NA
MEX18	8e			dbl impression (u)	—	100.00
MEX19	9b		4r black, *yellow*	without ovpt	45.00	70.00
MEX20	10b		4r dull rose, *yel*	without ovpt	100.00	125.00
MEX21	10c			printed on both sides (u)	—	NA
MEX22	11d		8r black, *red brn*	without ovpt	100.00	200.00
MEX23	12b		8r grn, *red brn*	without ovpt	125.00	160.00
MEX24	12d			printed on both sides (u)	NA	
MEX25	14a	(1864)	1r red	without district name	.75	—
MEX26	15a		2r blue	without district name	.75	—
MEX27	16a		4r brown	without district name	1.25	—
MEX28	17a		1p black	without district name	2.00	—
MEX29	18a	(1864-66)	3c brn (IV, V)	without ovpt	NA	—
MEX30	19a		1/2 r brown (I)	without ovpt	150.00	NA
MEX31	20e		1/2 r lilac (IV)	without ovpt	4.00	—
MEX32	21b		1r blue (IV, V)	without ovpt	2.00	—
MEX33	22b		1r ultra (I, II)	without ovpt	130.00	120.00
MEX34	23c		2r org (III,IV,V)	2r dp org, without ovpt, early plate	150.00	50.00
MEX35	24b		4r grn (III, IV, V	4r dk grn, without ovpt	3.50	275.00
MEX36	25c		8r red (IV, V)	8r dk red, without ovpt	5.25	NA
MEX37	27c	(1866)	13c blue	without ovpt	80.00	—
MEX38	31a		7c lilac	without ovpt	3.25	—
MEX39	32a		13c lilac	without ovpt	1.25	—
MEX40	33a		25c orange brown	without ovpt	1.25	—
MEX41	34a		50c green	without ovpt	2.50	—
MEX42	37a	(1867)	2r blk, *pink*	printed on both sides (u)	—	140.00
MEX43	38a		4r red, *yel*	printed on both sides (u)	—	150.00
MEX44	42a		1/2 r gray	without ovpt	175.00	175.00
MEX45	43b		1r blue	without ovpt	NA	75.00
MEX46	44a		2r green	printed on both sides	—	NA
MEX47	44b			without ovpt	75.00	20.00
MEX48	45a		4r rose	without ovpt	NA	—
MEX49	47a	(1868)	12c blk, *green*	period after "12,"	—	50.00
MEX50	48a		25c bl, *pink*	without ovpt	125.00	
MEX51	52a		6c blk, *buff*	without ovpt	140.00	—
MEX52	52b			period after "6,"	—	70.00
MEX53	53a		12c blk, *green*	period after "12,"	85.00	30.00
MEX54	53c			without ovpt	110.00	—
MEX55	54b		25c blue, *pink*	without ovpt	150.00	—
MEX56	56c		100c blk, *brown*	without ovpt	NA	—
MEX57	57a		100c brn, *brown*	printed on both sides (u)	NA	—
MEX58	61a		25c blue, *pink*	no period after "25,"	—	100.00
MEX59	61d			"85," for "25,"	60.00	30.00
MEX60	61e			"35," for "25,"	—	47.50
MEX61	62a		50c blk, *yellow*	no period after "50,"	175.00	25.00
MEX62	62b		50c blue	*lt pink* (error)	NA	
MEX63	64a		100c blk, *brown*	no period after "100,"	140.00	47.50
MEX64	68a		25c blue, *pink*	no period after "25,"	—	75.00
MEX65	68d			"85," for "25,"	60.00	37.50
MEX66	69a		50c blk, *yellow*	no period after "50,"	200.00	30.00
MEX67	70a		100c blk, *brown*	no period after "100,"	200.00	65.00
MEX68	73b	(1872)	25c bl, *pink*	"85," for "25,"	—	125.00
MEX69	74a		50c blk, *yellow*	no period after "50,"	NA	
MEX70	75a		100c blk, *brown*	no period after "100,"	—	NA
MEX71	79a		50c blk, *yellow*	no period after "50,"	—	NA
MEX72	84a		50c yellow	50c blue (error) (u)	—	NA
MEX73	84c			as "a" without ovpt (u)	65.00	—
MEX74	83bc		25c red	without ovpt	NA	—

MEX75	90a		50c yellow	50c blue (error) (u)	NA	
MEX76	90b			as "a" without ovpt	100.00	—
MEX77	93a	(1872)	6c green	without moire on back, without ovpt	60.00	65.00
MEX78	94a		12c blue	without moire on back, without ovpt	24.00	35.00
MEX79	95a		25c red	without moire on back, without ovpt	24.00	35.00
MEX80	96b		50c yellow	without moire on back, without ovpt	47.50	65.00
MEX81	96d			50c blue (u) (error)	—	NA
MEX82	96e			as "d" without ovpt	42.50	—
MEX83	96f			as "e" without moire on back	65.00	—
MEX84	98b		100c gray lilac	without moire on back, without ovpt	47.50	110.00
MEX85	102b		50c yellow	50c blue (error) (u)	165.00	50.00
MEX86	102c			as "b" without ovpt	45.00	—
MEX87	105b	(1874-80)	4c orange('80)	without ovpt	6.50	12.50
MEX88	106e		5c brown	without ovpt	37.50	
MEX89	107c		10c black	without ovpt	27.50	27.50
MEX90	108c	('78)	10c orange	without ovpt	55.00	55.00
MEX91	109d		25c blue	without ovpt	35.00	—
MEX92	109h			printed on both sides (u)	—	—
MEX93	110a		50c green	without ovpt	47.50	—
MEX94	111b		100c carmine	without ovpt	50.00	—
MEX95	117a	(1881)	4c orange	without ovpt	18.00	18.00
MEX96	118a		5c brown	without ovpt	.50	19.00
MEX97	119c		10c orange	without ovpt	.75	4.00
MEX98	120b		25c blue	without ovpt	.50	
MEX99	120c			dbl impression (u)	—	65.00
MEX100	121a		50c green	without ovpt	45.00	40.00
MEX101	122a		100c carmine	without ovpt	6.00	
MEX102	123a	(1879)	1c brown	without ovpt	72.50	140.00
MEX103	124a		2c dk violet	without ovpt	75.00	90.00
MEX104	124b			printed on both sides (u)	—	—
MEX105	125a		5c orange	without ovpt	45.00	65.00
MEX106	126a		10c blue	without ovpt	50.00	75.00
MEX107	127a		25c rose	without ovpt	1.65	
MEX108	128a		50c green	without ovpt	1.25	—
MEX109	128b			printed on both sides (u)	—	165.00
MEX110	129a		85c violet	without ovpt	2.50	—
MEX111	130a		100c black	without ovpt	2.50	—
MEX112	131a	(1882)	1c brown	without ovpt	125.00	—
MEX113	132a		2c dk violet	without ovpt	95.00	—
MEX114	133a		5c orange	without ovpt	1.25	—
MEX115	134a		10c blue	without ovpt	1.25	—
MEX116	136a		12c brown	without ovpt	2.50	—
MEX117	137b		18c orange brn	without ovpt	2.25	12.50
MEX118	138a		24c violet	without ovpt	2.25	16.00
MEX119	139a		25c rose	without ovpt	4.50	
MEX120	141a		50c green	without ovpt	125.00	—
MEX121	142a		50c yellow	without ovpt	6.25	—
MEX122	144a		100c black	without ovpt	4.75	—
MEX123	145a		100c orange	without ovpt	150.00	—
MEX124	146a	(1882-83)	2c green	without ovpt	27.50	18.00
MEX125	147a		3c car lake	without ovpt	5.25	6.00
MEX126	148a	('83)	6c blue	without ovpt	27.50	35.00
MEX127	149a		6c ultra	without ovpt	3.50	6.00
MEX128	150b	(1884)	1c green	1c blue (error) (u)	NA	
MEX129	321a	(1913)	5c black & red	"CENTAVOB" embossed "CONSTITUCIONAL" COLORLESS ROULETTE		

MEX130	322a		1c black & red	with green seal	NA	
MEX131	323a		2c black & red	with green seal	NA	
MEX132	324a		2c black & red	with green seal	NA	
MEX133	325a		3c black & red	with green seal	NA	
MEX134	326a		5c black & red	"CENTAVOB"	175.00	42.50
MEX135	329a		BLACK ROULETTE 5c black & red	"MARO" with green seal	85.00	50.00
MEX136	338a		5c black & red	"CENTAVOB" colorless roulette	NA	
MEX137	340b		5c brnsh blk & red	dbl seal	NA	
MEX138	340c			red printing omitted	—	NA
MEX139	341a	(1913-14)	1c black & red	"erano" ('14) black roulette		
MEX140	342a		2c black & red	"erano" ('14)	35.00	35.00
MEX141	343a		3c black & red	"CENTAVO"	25.00	25.00
MEX142	343b			"erano" ('14)	35.00	35.00
MEX143	344b		5c black & red	heavy black penetrating roulette	2.75	1.75
MEX144	344c			as "b" "MARO"	7.50	5.00
MEX145	347a	(1913)	1c yellow grn	with coupon	5.00	5.00
MEX146	348a		2c violet	with coupon	12.00	12.00
MEX147	349a		5c brown	with coupon	1.25	1.25
MEX148	350a		10c claret	with coupon	10.00	10.00
MEX149	351a		20c gray grn	with coupon	15.00	15.00
MEX150	352a		50c ultra	with coupon	50.00	40.00
MEX151	353a		1p orange	with coupon inscribed "SONORA" in black	125.00	100.00
MEX152	394a	(1914)	1c blue & red	dbl seal	—	—
MEX153	394b			without seal	20.00	—
MEX154	395a		2c green & orange	without seal	100.00	—
MEX155	396b		5c yellow & grn	without seal	—	200.00
MEX156	397a		10c lt bl & red	10c blue & red	40.00	15.00
MEX157	413a		50c gray green & org	without seal, "PLATA" added to inscription		
MEX158	413b			as "a"- "P" of "PLATA" missing	150.00	—
MEX159	438a		10c blue	dbl ovpt (vc)	—	—
MEX160	452a	(1915)	5c orange	invtd ovpt (vc)	27.50	—
MEX160A	504		5c orange, 1 block of 8	semi perf. R	60.00	
MEX161	509a	(1915-16)	4c carmine	PS"CEATRO"	7.50	7.50
MEX162	513a		1p brown & blk	invtd center (u)	200.00	—
MEX163	514a		5p cl & ultra ('16)	invtd center (u)	NA	
MEX164	519a	(1916)	3c orange brn (bl)	dbl ovpt (vc)	—	NA
MEX165	521a		5c carmine (bl)	dbl ovpt (vc)	75.00	—
MEX166	538a		5p carmine & blk	tablet invtd	200.00	—
MEX167	541a		2c green (R)	monogram invtd	40.00	—
MEX168	546a		15c gray bl & cl (bk)	tablet dbl	NA	
MEX169	546b			monogram dbl	—	NA
MEX170	548a		50c red brn & blk (R)	monogram invtd	65.00	—
MEX171	548b			tablet invtd	75.00	—
MEX172	549a		1p blue & blk (R)	tablet dbl	175.00	—
MEX173	549b			monogram invtd	60.00	—
MEX174	556a		10c bl & org (R)	monogram invtd	125.00	—
MEX175	557a		15c gray bl & cl (bk)	monogram invtd	90.00	—
MEX176	558a		20c red & bl (bk)	monogram invtd	82.50	—
MEX177	562a		10c red (bl)	vertical ovpt	125.00	—
MEX178	577a	(1916)	5c on 1c dl vio (br)	vertical surch	1.25	1.25
MEX179	577b			dbl surch (vc)	150.00	—
MEX180	578a		10c on 1c dl vio (bl)	dbl surch (vc)	100.00	—
MEX181	579a		20c on 5c org (br)	dbl surch (vc)	90.00	—
MEX182	582a		5c on 1c (br)	dbl tablet, one vertical	100.00	—
MEX183	582b			invtd tablet	NA	
MEX184	584a		25c on 5c (G)	invtd tablet	NA	
MEX185	587a		5c on 1c (br)	vertical tablet	100.00	125.00
MEX186	589a		25c on 5c (G)	invtd tablet	NA	
MEX187	592a		60c on 2c lt grn (br)	invtd surch (vc)	NA	—
MEX188	614a	(1917-20)	10c blue	without imprint	5.00	.50

MEX189	623a		10c blue	without imprint ('17)	15.00	15.00
MEX190	627a		1p blue & blk	with center of 5p	NA	—
MEX191	627a		1p bl & dark blue	(error) (u)	NA	25.00
MEX192	628b		5p green & blk	with center of 1p	NA	—
MEX193	632a	(1921)	10c blue & brn	center invtd (u)	—	NA
MEX194	665a	(1926)	1p brown & blue	1p red & blue	35.00	15.00
MEX195	667a	(1930)	2c red	reading down	15.00	15.00
MEX196	668a		4c green	reading down	15.00	15.00
MEX197	669a		5c orange	reading down	15.00	—
MEX198	669b			dbl ovpt	75.00	75.00
MEX199	672a		30c dk green	reading down	47.50	—
MEX200	673a		40c violet	reading down	47.50	—
MEX201	674a		1p red brn & bl	dbl ovpt (vc)	140.00	—
MEX202	674b			triple ovpt (u)	200.00	—
MEX203	682a	(1931)	1p brown & bl	1p red & blue	40.00	45.00
MEX204	C29a	(1930)	5c ol grn & sepia	dbl ovpt (vc)	NA	—
MEX205	C32a		10c sep & brn red	dbl ovpt (vc)	50.00	50.00
MEX206	C39a	(1931)	15c on 20c brn ol	invtd surch (vc)	150.00	—
MEX207	C39b			dbl surch (vc)	150.00	—
MEX208	C39c			pair, one without surch	NA	
MEX209	C47a		40c on 25c (#C3)	invtd surch (vc)	NA	—
MEX210	C49a		30c on 20c brn ol	invtd surch (vc)	—	NA
MEX211	C118a	(1942)	40c grnsh blk (C)	without ovpt	7.50	7.50
MEX212	C237a	(1956-63)	1.20p dk grn & pur	dark green omitted	110.00	—
MEX213	237c			purple omitted	125.00	—
MEX214	C427a	(1974)	80c black & multi	red omitted	100.00	—
MEX215	CO1a	(1929)	25c dk grn & gray brn	without period	11.00	11.00
MEX216	CO2a		25c dk grn & gray brn (R)	without period	13.00	15.00
MEX217	CO2Bc		25c brn car & gray brn	without period	17.50	20.00
MEX218	CO11a	(1930)	20c black violet	without period	13.00	15.00
MEX219	CO11b			invtd ovpt (vc) R	10.00	—
MEX220	CO11C			as "a" invtd ovpt	140.00	—
MEX221	CO30a	(1934)	10c violet	dbl ovpt (vc)	NA	—
MEX222	O2a	(1887)	olive brn	blue ruled lines on paper	—	—
MEX223	O95a	(1915-16)	4c carmine	"CEATRO"	7.00	15.00
MEX224	O97a		10c ultra, type II	dbl ovpt (vc)	NA	—
MEX225	O98a		40c slate	invtd ovpt (vc)	12.00	12.50
MEX226	O99a		1p brown & black	invtd ovpt (vc)	14.00	17.50
MEX227	O100a		5p claret & ultra	invtd ovpt (vc)	40.00	—
MEX228	O120a	(1918)	10c blue (R)	dbl ovpt (vc)	200.00	200.00
MEX229	O124a	(1919)	1c dull vio (R)	"OFICIAN"	35.00	40.00
MEX230	O125a		2c gray grn (R)	"OFICIAN"	35.00	40.00

MEX160A

MEX219

MEX295A
front

MEX295A
back

MTG2

MTG1

MEX231	O126a		3c bister brn (R)	"OFICIAN"	47.50	50.00
MEX232	O127Ab		4c carmine (bk)	"OFICIAN"	NA	—
MEX233	O128a		10c blue (R)	"OFICIAN"	42.50	30.00
MEX234	O129a		20c rose (bk)	"OFICIAN"	—	70.00
MEX235	O130a		1c dull violet (R)	"OFICIAN"	72.50	50.00
MEX236	O131a		5c ultra (R)	"OFICIAN"	72.50	50.00
MEX237	O139a	(1921)	10c bl, reading down (R)	ovpt reading up	30.00	30.00
MEX238	O147a	(1921-30)	3c bister brn	"OFICAL"	24.00	12.50
MEX239	O147b			"OIFCIAL"	24.00	12.50
MEX240	O147c			dbl ovpt (vc)	72.00	—
MEX241	O150a		10c blue	"OIFCIAL"	25.00	—
MEX242	O153a		40c violet	" OFICAL"	30.00	30.00
MEX243	O153b			"OICIFAL"	30.00	30.00
MEX244	O153c			invtd ovpt (vc)	45.00	—
MEX245	O2a	(1887)	olive brown	blue ruled lines on pager	—	—
MEX246	O95a	(1915-16)	4c carmine	"CEATRO"	7.00	15.00
MEX247	O97a		10c ultra, type II	dbl ovpt (vc)	NA	—
MEX248	O98a		40c slate	invtd ovpt (vc)	12.00	12.50
MEX249	O98b			dbl ovpt (vc)	20.00	—
MEX250	O99a		1p brown & black	invtd ovpt (vc)	14.00	17.50
MEX251	O100a		5p claret & ultra	invtd ovpt (vc)	40.00	—
MEX252	O120a	(1918)	10c blue (R)	dbl ovpt (vc)	200.00	200.00
MEX253	O124a		1c dull vio (R)	"OFICIAN"	35.00	40.00
MEX254	O125a		2c gray grn (R)	"OFICIAN"	35.00	40.00
MEX255	O126a		3c bister brn (R)	"OFICIAN"	47.50	50.00
MEX256	O127c		4c carmine (bk)	"OFICIAN"	—	—
MEX257	O127Ab		5c ultra	"OFICIAN"	NA	—
MEX258	O128a		10c blue (R)	"OFICIAN"	42.50	30.00
MEX259	O129a		20c rose (bk)	"OFICIAN"	—	70.00
MEX260	O130a		1c dull violet (R)	"OFICIAN"	72.50	50.00
MEX261	O131a		5c ultra (R)	"OFICIAN"	72.50	50.00
MEX262	O139a	(1921)	10c bl, reading down (R)	ovpt reading up (vc)	30.00	30.00
MEX263	O147a	(1921-30)	3c bister brn	"OFICAL"	24.00	12.50
MEX264	O147b			"OIFCIAL"	24.00	12.50
MEX265	O147c			dbl ovpt (vc)	72.00	—
MEX266	O150a		10c blue	"OIFCIAL"	25.00	—
MEX267	O153a		40c violet	"OFICAL"	30.00	30.00
MEX268	O153b			"OICIFAL"	30.00	30.00
MEX269	O153c			invtd ovpt (vc)	45.00	—
MEX270	O159a	(1921-24)	10c blue	dbl ovpt	—	—
MEX271	O162a		40c violet	vert. Pair, imperf.b	—	—
MEX272	O166a	(1926-27)	3c bis brn, ovpt horiz (R)	period omitted	15.00	15.00
MEX273	O168a		2c scarlet (bl)	ovpt reading up	15.00	15.00
MEX274	O169a		3c bis brn, ovpt horiz. (R)	invtd ovpt (vc)	30.00	—
MEX275	O171a		20c deep blue (R)	ovpt reading up	7.00	6.00
MEX276	O174a		40c violet (R)	invtd ovpt (vc)	40.00	—
MEX277	O178a	(1927-31)	2c scarlet	"OFICAIL	15.00	15.00
MEX278	O178b			ovpt reading down	.75	1.00
MEX279	O179a		3c bis brn	"OFICAIL"	20.00	15.00
MEX280	O180a		4c green	"OFICAIL"	20.00	20.00
MEX281	O180b			ovpt reading down	5.00	1.00
MEX282	O181a		5c orange	ovpt reading down	2.00	1.25
MEX283	O182a		8c orange	ovpt reading down	3.50	3.00
MEX284	O183a		10c lake	ovpt reading down	1.00	1.00
MEX285	O184a		20c dark blue	"OFICAIL"	20.00	20.00
MEX286	O184b			ovpt reading down	10.00	10.00
MEX287	O185a	(1927-33)	4c green	invtd ovpt (vc)	15.00	15.00
MEX288	O187a		30c dark green	invtd ovpt	15.00	15.00
MEX289	O187b			pair, tete beche ovpt	17.50	17.50
MEX290	O187c			"OFICAIL"	17.50	17.50
MEX291	O193a	(1927-28)	5p grn & blk (bk)	invtd ovpt	120.00	120.00
MEX292	O204a	(1932-33)	20c dark blue	dbl ovpt (vc)	100.00	45.00
MEX293	O208a		50c olive brn	"OFICIAL OFICIAL"	25.00	25.00
MEX294	O217a	(1934-37)	2c scarlet	dbl ovpt (vc)	75.00	—

MEX295	RA4a	(1929)	1c brown	ovpt reading down	40.00	40.00
MEX295A	RA9		8c orange yellow	printed both sides R	25.00	
MEX296	RA13a	(1931)	1c dull violet	"PRO INFANCIA" double	50.00	—

Guadalajara

MEX297	42a	(1868)	un r blk, green	"nu" instead of "un"	—	80.00
MEX298	47a		un r blk, green	"nu" instead of "un"	—	70.00

**Mexico has so many errors we don't know what to do.
With the overprint most common, but there are others too.
Typos of all types, printing both sides
Give the color buff lots of exciting rides. —The Bard**

MICRONESIA, FEDERATED STATES OF has produced no errors

MIDDLE CONGO

MIC1	39a	(1924-30)	45c vio & pale red (bl)	invtd ovpt (vc)	75.00	75.00
MIC2	41a	('25)	50c org & blk	without ovpt (vc)	100.00	—
MIC3	45a		1fr green & vio	dbl ovpt (vc)	125.00	110.00
MIC4	57a	(1927)	1.50fr on 1fr ultra & bl	new value omitted	80.00	—
MIC5	58a		3fr on 5fr org brn & dl red	new value omitted	150.00	—
MIC6	B1a	(1916)	10c+5c car & blue	dbl surch (vc)	70.00	70.00
MIC7	B1b			invtd surch (vc)	60.00	60.00

MOHELI

MOH1	21a	(1912)	10c on 45c blk, gray grn (C)	"Moheli" double	NA	
MOH2	21b			"Moheli" triple	NA	

**"Moheli" double, "Moheli" triple
Both an NA cripple. —The Bard**

MOLDOVA has produced no errors

MONACO

MON1	57a	(1924)	45c on 50c brn ol, buff	dbl surch (vc)	NA	
MON2	58a		75c on 1fr blk yel	dbl surch (vc)	NA	
MON3	59a		85c on 5fr dk green	dbl surch (vc)	NA	
MON4	95a	(1928)	50c on 1.05fr red vio	dbl surch (vc)	—	—
MON5	B9a	(1920)	2c + 3c on #B4	"c" of "3c"invtd	NA	
MON6	B10a		2c +3c on #B5	"c" of "3c" invtd	NA	
MON7	B11a		2c + 3c on #B6	"c" of "3c" invtd	NA	
MON8	C9a	(1946)	100fr red	invtd ovpt (vc)	NA	
MON9	C9b			dbl ovpt (vc)	NA	
MON10	C49a	(1956)	100fr on 20fr	dbl surch (vc)	NA	
MON11	C50a		100fr on 20fr	dbl surch (vc)	NA	
MON12	J19a	(1918)	20c on 10c lt vio	dbl surch (vc)	NA	
MON13	J27a	1925)	1fr on 50c brn, org	dbl surch (vc)	NA	

**Mostly vc's and some so rare
They fly up only in the air.
Poste Aerienne—NA we say
We study vc's night and day
And all we get is a BIG NA!***

*Nearly all Monaco stamps from 1940 exist imperforate.

MONGOLIA

MON1	48a	(1931)	1c blue	blue ovpt	8.00	5.50
MON2	50a		5c brown vio	blue ovpt	8.50	6.00
MON3	51a		10c green	blue ovpt	11.00	9.50
MON4	59a		5m on 5c brn vio (bk)	invtd surch (vc)	—	7.50
MON5	60A		10m on 10c green (R)	invtd surch (vc)	15.00	12.50
MON6	61a		20m on 20c bis brn (bl)	invtd surch (vc)	—	18.00

**Three blue o'erprints and three vc's
The country's total errors are these. —The Bard**

MONTENEGRO

MTG1	Mich.1		black, grayish white,	dbl impression R	30.00
MTG2	J-7	(1894)	3 on emerald	dbl impression R	20.00

MONTSERRAT

MOS1	1c	(1876)	1p red	"S" invtd	NA
MOS2	2c		6p green	"S" invtd	NA
MOS3	2e		6p blue green	"S" invtd	NA
MOS4	6b	(1884)	1p rose red	"S" invtd	NA
MOS5	11a		1p red	"S" invtd	NA
MOS6	471	(1981)	$5 multi	invtd ovpt R ?	

See Photo in Color Section

MOS7	574	(1985)	$1 multi	dbl ovpt, gutter pair R	80.00
MOS8	504	(1983)	75c multi	invtd ovpt (vc) R ?	

Five "S's" inverted, all NA
One orange omitted—A-OK. —The Bard

MOROCCO has produced no errors

MOZAMBIQUE

MOZ1	39a	(1895)	25r violet	dbl ovpt (vc)	—	
MOZ2	47a	(1898)	2-1/2 r on 20r rose	invtd surch (vc)	55.00	45.00
MOZ3	48a		5r on 40r choc	invtd surch (vc)	90.00	45.00
MOZ4	73a	(1902)	65r on 20r rose	dbl surch (vc)	30.00	30.00
MOZ5	82a		65r on 15r red brn	pair, one without surch	—	—
MOZ6	84a		115r on 5r yel	invtd surch (vc)	—	
MOZ7	128a	(1913)	2-1/2 c on 4a yel grn	dbl surch (vc)	35.00	35.00
MOZ8	135a		1c on 10r red vio	invtd surch (vc)	30.00	30.00
MOZ9	160a	(1921)	6c lilac	name & value printed twice	—	—
MOZ10	222a	(1918)	2-1/2 c on 5c red	"PETRIA"	2.00	2.00
MOZ11	222b			"REPUBLICA"	2.00	2.00
MOZ12	222c			"1910." for "1916"	7.50	4.00
MOZ13	224a	(1919)	1c on 1c gray grn	"REPUBLICA"	4.75	4.00
MOZ15	225a		1-1/2 c on 5c red	"PETRIA"	3.00	2.00
MOZ16	225b			"REPUBLLICA"	3.00	2.50
MOZ17	225c			"1910," for "1916,"	5.00	3.75
MOZ18	229a		6c on 5c red	"1910," for "1916,"	8.00	5.00
MOZ19	229b			"PETRIA"	2.50	2.00
MOZ20	229c			"PEPUBLICA"	2.50	2.00
MOZ21	235a	(1921)	2e on 5c red	"PETRIA"	2.00	2.25

MOS7

MOS8

MOZ33

MOZ34

MOZ35

MOZ36

MOZ22	235b			"PEPUBLICA"	4.25	2.50
MOZ23	235c			"1910," for "1916,"	8.00	6.50
MOZ24	301a	(1946)	10c on 15c dk vio brn	invtd surch (vc)	15.00	
MOZ25	511	(1975)	1e pink & multi		.15	.15
MOZ26	C10a	(1946)	3e on 5e red brn	invtd surch (vc)	—	—
MOZ27	J32a	(1918)	5c rose	invtd ovpt (vc)	8.25	7.50
MOZ28	J33a		1c gray green	"PEPUBLICA"	15.00	15.00
MOZ29	MR3a	(1918)	1c gray green	"PEPUBLICA"	8.50	4.75
MOZ30	MR4a		5c red	"PETRIA"	2.25	2.25
MOZ31	MR4b			"PEPUBLICA"	2.50	2.25
MOZ32	MR4c			"1910," for "1916,"	6.50	5.00
MOZ33	390		1c multi, block of 4	with red printing 5 mm high R	8.00	
MOZ34-36	466, 471	(1966-67)		color error, background, color of 471-normal 466 & 471 included for reference R	50.00	
MOZ37	506	(1973)	1e multi, block of 4	"CORREIOS" omitted R	20.00	
MOZ38	511	(1975)	1e pink & multi	horiozontal pair with value omitted R	7.50	
MOZ39	512	(1975)	1.5e multi on yellow, block of 4	value omitted R	12.50	
MOZ40	514	(1975)	3.50e lemon & multi, block of 4	value omitted R	12.50	
MOZ41	521var.	(1975)	2e maroon block of 4	ovpt vertically upward R	12.00	
MOZ42	522var.		250e multicolor, block of 4	ovpt vertically upward R	10.00	
MOZ43	529var.		20e multi, block of 6	ovpt split R	9.00	

"PEPUBLICA" is scorned by philatelists
And other scholars too
But the country's "value omitted"
Is something for the errorist true. —The Bard

MOZAMBIQUE COMPANY

MCZ1	1a	(1892)	5r black (C)	pair, one without overprint	22.50	22.50
MCZ2	4a		25r black	dbl ovpt (vc)	27.50	—
MCZ3	5a		40r chocolate	dbl ovpt (vc)	20.00	—
MCZ4	12a	(1895-1907)	5r orange	value omitted	10.00	—
MCZ5	14a	(1907)	10r yel grn	value invtd at top of stamp	14.00	10.00

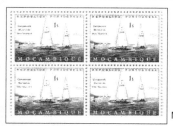

MOZ37

MOZ40

MOZ41

MOZ42

MOZ43

MCZ6	19a		25r carmine	value omitted	11.00	8.00
MCZ7	21a		50r brown	value omitted	9.00	—
MCZ8	39a		500r blk & red, *bl*	500r pur & red, yel, (error) (u)		
MCZ9	45a	(1898)	2-1/2 r olive yel (bl)	dbl ovpt (vc)	*18.00*	*18.00*
MCZ10	45b			red ovpt	*25.00*	*25.00*
MCZ11	48a		15r red brown (V)	red ovpt	—	—
MCZ12	50a		25r green (G)	invtd ovpt (vc)	27.50	16.00
MCZ13	51a		50r blue (bk)	invtd ovpt (vc)	27.50	20.00
MCZ14	52a		75r rose (V)	invtd ovpt (vc)	30.00	25.00
MCZ15	52b			red ovpt	—	—
MCZ16	53a		80r yellow grn (g)	invtd ovpt (vc)	—	—
MCZ17	55a		150r org brn, *pink* (O)	invtd ovpt (vc)	19.00	16.00
MCZ18	55b			dbl ovpt (vc)	—	—
MCZ19	57a		300r dk blue, *sal* (bk)	invtd ovpt (vc)	27.50	25.00
MCZ20	57b			green ovpt	—	—
MCZ21	61b	(1900)	50r on half of 1907) 1907)	entire stamp	12.00	5.00
MCZ22	64a	(1911)	15r dk green (C)	dbl ovpt (vc)	17.00	9.50
MCZ23	80a		25r carmine (G)	value invtd at top of stamp	18.00	—
MCZ24	82a		75r red lilac	value omitted	15.00	—
MCZ25	85a		130r brown, *yel*	dbl ovpt (vc)	18.00	—
MCZ26	91a	(1916)	1/2 c on 5r org	1/2 c double	11.00	
MCZ27	98a		10c on 100r dk bl, *bl*	invtd surch (vc)	20.00	20.00
MCZ28	99a		11-1/2 c on 115r org brn, *pink*	invtd surch (vc)	30.00	30.00
MCZ29	B1a	(1917)	2-1/2 r gray	dbl ovpt (vc)	40.00	*40.00*
MCZ30	P1a	(1894)	2-1/2 r brown	invtd ovpt (vc)	12.00	12.00

A purple, red and yellow error
Fills the heart with certain terror
But way and way too many vc's
Does not the errorist please.

N

NAMIBIA has produced no errors

NATAL - Southern Coast of Africa, on Indian Ocean

NAT1	6a	(1858)	1p rose	No.1 embossed over No.6	—	—
NAT2	18a	(1869)	1p rose red (#15)	dbl ovpt (vc)	—	NA
NAT3	23a		3p blue (#12)	invtd ovpt (vc)	—	—
NAT4	30a		1p rose red (#15)	1p carmine red	120.00	25.00
NAT5	30b			invtd ovpt (vc)	—	—
NAT6	31a		3p blue (#12)	dbl ovpt (vc)	—	NA
NAT7	36a		6p violet (#16)	invtd ovpt (vc)	—	—
NAT8	42a	(1870)	1sh green (bk)	dbl ovpt (vc)	NA	
NAT9	45a	(1874)	1p rose red	dbl ovpt (vc)	—	—
NAT10	46b	(1875)	1p carmine	dbl ovpt (vc)	NA	
NAT11	48a		1p rose red	invtd ovpt (vc)	NA	
NAT12	49a		6p violet	invtd ovpt (vc)	NA	175.00
NAT13	49b			dbl ovpt (vc)	—	NA
NAT14	50a		1sh green	dbl ovpt (vc)	—	NA
NAT15	59a	(1877)	1/2 p on 1p rose	dbl surch "1/2"	—	—
NAT16	61a		1/2 p on 1p yel	dbl surch (vc)	NA	175.00
NAT17	61b			invtd surch (vc)	NA	175.00
NAT18	61c			pair, one without surch	NA	
NAT19	61d			"POTAGE"	200.00	175.00
NAT20	61e			"POTAGE"	200.00	175.00
NAT21	61f			"POSTAGE" omitted	NA	—
NAT22	62a		1p on 6p vio	"POSTAGE" omitted	—	—
NAT23	62b			"POTAGE"	NA	150.00
NAT24	63a		1p on 6p rose	invtd surch (vc)	—	NA
NAT25	63b			dbl surch	—	NA

NAT26	63c			dbl surch, one invtd	NA	190.00
NAT27	63d			triple surch, one invtd	—	—
NAT28	63e			quadruple surch	NA	—
NAT29	63f			"POTAGE"	NA	—
NAT30	76a	(1888)	1sh orange	dbl ovpt (vc)	—	—
NAT31	77a	(1891)	2-1/2 p on 4p brown	"PENGE"	40.00	32.50
NAT32	77b			"PENN"	NA	—
NAT33	77c			dbl surch (vc)	175.00	100.00
NAT34	77d			invtd surch (vc)	185.00	110.00
NAT35	79a	(1895)	1/2 p on 6p vio (R)	"Ealf"	12.50	20.00
NAT36	79b			"Pennv"	10.00	16.00
NAT37	79c			dbl surch, one vertical	NA	—
NAT38	80a		1/2 p on 1p rose (bk)	pair, one without & the other with dbl surch	—	—

Too many overprints get in the way
Too many vc's too many NA
Surcharges both quadruple and triple
Shakes to the errorist not even a ripple —The Bard

NAURU

NAU1	8a	(1916-23)	4p slate green	dbl ovpt	—	—

NEPAL

NEP1	17b	(1898-1904)	4a dull green	cllice of 1a in plaate of 4a ('04)	NA	—

Nepal has a real cliche
It's too bad it is NA.
That's about all we have to say. —The Bard

NETHERLANDS

NET1	166c	(1925-27)	1-1/2 c red vio ('28)	"CEN" for "CENT"	165.00	NA
NET2	244a	(1943)	10c on 2-1/2 c yel	surch omitted	NA	
NET3	374a	(1958)	12c on 10c	dbl surch (vc)	NA	
NET4	374b			invtd surch (vc)	NA	
NET5	J77a	(1924)	5c on 1c red	surch reading down	NA	

A very few errors for this land
"CEN" for cent and surcharge reading down
Are two key ones of great renown
Why are dutch so error-free?
Perhaps the dykes keep out the sea. —The Bard

NETHERLANDS ANTILLES

NEA1	74b	(1918)	5c on 12-1/2 c blue	dbl surch (vc)	—	NA
NEA2	90a	(1927)	15c on 1.50g dk bl	dbl surch	NA	—
NEA3	106a		6c on 7-1/2 c org red	invtd surch (vc)	NA	
NEA4	CB25a		30c+50c	dbl impression of denomination (u)	NA	

A double impression and 3 vc's
The impression would certainly please.
But all four are NA
Can't afford any today. —The Bard

NETHERLANDS EAST INDIES

NEI1	46a	(1902)	1/2 c on 2c yel brn	dbl surch (vc)	175.00	150.00
NEI2	50a	(1902-08)	15c chocolate	ovpt with 1 horiz bars	1.50	.75
NEI3-NEI8	63a-80a	(1908)		ovpt reading down		
NEI3	63a		1/2 c		.55	3.25
NEI4	64a		1c		.55	2.50
NEI5	65a		2c		2.25	4.50
NEI6	66a		2-1/2 c		.95	3.00
NEI7	67a		3c		15.00	40.00
NEI8	68a		5c		2.25	2.50

NEI9	70a		10c		.65	*1.90*
NEI10	71a		12-1/2 c		4.50	*8.00*
NEI11	72a		15c		25.00	*62.50*
NEI12	74a		20c		7.25	8.00
NEI13	75a		22-1/2 c		NA	
NEI14	76a		25c		5.50	7.25
NEI15	77a		30c		11.00	15.00
NEI16	78a		50c		7.50	9.00
NEI17	79a		1g		175.00	NA
NEI18	80a		2-1/2 g		NA	
NEI19	81a		1/2 c violet	invtd ovpt (vc)	.55	*2.25*
NEI20	81b			dbl ovpt (vc)	NA	—
NEI21	82a		1c olive green	invtd ovpt (vc) R ?		
NEI22	83a		2c yellow brn	invtd ovpt (vc)	1.50	6.00
NEI23	84a		2-1/2 c green	invtd ovpt (vc)	2.00	3.25
NEI24	85a		3c orange	invtd ovpt (vc)	17.00	22.50
NEI25	86a		5c rose red	invtd ovpt (vc)	2.25	.15
NEI26	88a		10c slate	invtd ovpt (vc) R?		
NEI27	89a		12-1/2 c deep blue	invtd ovpt (vc)	2.75	5.00
NEI28	89b			dbl ovpt, one invtd	125.00	125.00
NEI29	90a		15c choc(on No. 50a)	invtd ovpt (vc)	2.75	9.00
NEI30	92a		20c olive grn	invtd ovpt (vc)	9.00	10.00
NEI31	94a		25c violet	invtd ovpt (vc)	4.50	9.00
NEI32	95a		30c orange brn	invtd ovpt (vc)	18.00	26.00
NEI33	96a		50c red brown	invtd ovpt (vc)	12.00	19.00
NEI34	97a		1g dull lilac	invtd ovpt (vc)	150.00	150.00
NEI35	98a		2-1/2 g slate blue	invtd ovpt (vc)	NA	
NEI36	139a	(1918)	17-1/2 c on 22-1/2 c	invtd surch (vc)	NA	
NEI37	158a		12-1/2 c on 20c bl (R)	invtd surch (vc)	NA	
NEI38	194a	(1937)	10c on 30c (R)	dbl surch (vc)	NA	—
NEI39	269a	(1947)	3c on 7-1/2 c ultra	dbl surch (vc)	150.00	150.00
NEI40	B57a	(1948)	15c+10c on 10c	invtd surch	NA	
NEI41	C17a		50c on 1.50g org	invtd surch (vc)	NA	
NEI42	J2a	(1945-46) black		"Maill" instead of "Mail"	NA	
NEI43	O8b	(1911)	5c rose red	dbl ovpt (vc)	—	NA
NEI44	O12a		15c chocolate	ovpt with 2 bars	32.50	—
NEI45	O12b			as "a" "Dienst" invtd	52.50	—
Overprints, inverted no's O1a -O20a						
NEI46	O1a		1/2 c		435.00	125.00
NEI47	O2a		1c		3.00	19.00
NEI48	O3a		2c		3.00	20.00
NEI49	O5a		2-1/2 c		9.00	30.00
NEI50	O6a		3c		110.00	40.00
NEI51	O8a		5c		3.00	20.00
NEI52	O10a		10c		3.00	7.00

NEI21

NEI26

NCG1

NCG2

NCL43

NEI53	O11a		12-1/2 c		32.50	55.00
NEI54	O14a		20c		175.00	70.00
NEI55	O16a		25c		NA	
NEI56	O17a		30c		NA	140.00
NEI57	O18a		50c		32.50	32.50
NEI58	O19a		1g		NA	
NEI59	O20a		2-1/2 g		NA	

Mostly vc's and little more
The Indies become a horrid bore. —The Bard

NETHERLANDS NEW GUINEA has produced no errors

NEVIS

NEV1	31a	(1883)	1/2 p on half of 1p	dbl surch (vc)	—	NA
NEV2	31b			unsevered pair	NA	
NEV3	32a		1/2 p on half of 1p (V)	dbl surch (vc)	—	NA

NEW BRITAIN

NEW1	4a		2p on 20pf ultra	"2d" dbl, "G.R.I." omitted	NA	—
NEW2	4b			invtd surch (vc)	—	—
NEW3	6a		2-1/2 p on 20pf ultra	invtd surch (vc)	—	—
NEW4	8a		3p on 30pf org & blk, *sal*	dbl surch (vc)	175.00	190.00
NEW5	8b			triple surch (u)	—	—
NEW6	9a		4p on 40pf lake & black	dbl surch (vc)	NA	—
NEW7	9b			invtd surch (vc)	NA	—
NEW8	9c			"4d" omitted	—	—
NEW9	10a		5p on 50pf pur & blk, *sal*	dbl surch (vc)	NA	—
NEW10	11a		8p on 80pf lake & black, *rose*	no period after "8d"	NA	—
NEW11	15a		5sh on 5m slate & car	no period after "I"	—	—
NEW12	16a		1p on 3pf brown	dbl surch (vc)	NA	
NEW13	16b		"I" omitted		—	NA
NEW14	16c			as "b" dbl surch (vc)	NA	
NEW15	16d			invtd surch (vc)	NA	
NEW16	16e			"4" for "I"	—	—
NEW17	16f			small "I"	200.00	—
NEW18	17a		1p on 5pf green	dbl surch (vc)	NA	—
NEW19	17b			"G.I.R."	NA	
NEW20	17c			"d" invtd	—	NA
NEW21	17d			no periods after "G R I"	—	—
NEW22	17e			small "I"	90.00	125.00
NEW23	17f			"Id" double	—	—
NEW24	17g			no period after "Id"	—	—
NEW25	17h			triple surch (u)	—	—
NEW26	18a		2p on 10pf car	dbl surch (vc)	NA	
NEW27	18b			dbl surch, one invtd	—	NA
NEW28	18c			surcharged "G.I.R., 3d"	NA	—
NEW29	18d			surch "Id"	NA	—
NEW30	18e			period before "G"	NA	—
NEW31	18f			no period after "2d"	100.00	150.00
NEW32	18g			invtd surch (vc)	—	—
NEW33	18h			"2dd"dbl, one invtd	—	—
NEW34	18i			"Id" on "2d"	—	—
NEW35	19a		2p on 20pf ultra	dbl surch (vc)	NA	
NEW36	19b			dbl surch, one invtd	NA	
NEW37	19c			"R" invtd	—	NA
NEW38	19d			surch "Id"	NA	
NEW39	19f			invtd surch (vc)	NA	
NEW40	19g			"Id" on "2d"	—	NA
NEW41	19h			pair, one without surch	—	
NEW42	21a		2-1/2 p on 20pf ultra	dbl surch, one invtd	—	—
NEW43	21b			"2-1/2 ," triple	—	—
NEW44	21c			surch "3d"	—	—

NEW45	22a		3p on 25pf org & blk, *yel*	dbl surch (vc)	NA	
NEW46	22b			invtd surch (vc)	NA	
NEW47	22c			"G.R.I." only	—	—
NEW48	22d			"G.I.R."	NA	
NEW49	22e			pair, one without surch	—	—
NEW50	22f			surch "G.I.R., 5d"	—	—
NEW51	23a		3p on 30pf org & blk, *sal*	dbl surch (vc)	NA	
NEW52	23b			dbl surch, one invtd	NA	
NEW53	23c			"d" invtd	—	NA
NEW54	23d			surch "ld"	NA	—
NEW55	23e			triple surch (u)	—	—
NEW56	23g			dbl invtd surch	NA	—
NEW57	23h			pair, one without surch	NA	—
NEW58	24a		4p on 40pf lake & blk	dbl surch (vc)	NA	
NEW59	24b			dbl surch, one invtd	NA	
NEW60	24e		surch "ld"	NA		
NEW61	24f			"I" on "4,"	—	—
NEW62	25a		5p on 50pf pur & blk, *sal*	dbl surch (vc)	NA	—
NEW63	25b			dbl surch, one invtd	NA	—
NEW64	25c			"5," omitted	NA	—
NEW65	25d			invtd surch (vc)	NA	—
NEW66	25e			dbl invtd surch	NA	—
NEW67	25f			"G.I.R."	—	—
NEW68	26a		8p on 80pf lake & blk, *rose*	dbl surch (vc)	NA	
NEW69	26b			dbl surch, one invtd	NA	
NEW70	26c			triple surch (u)	—	—
NEW71	26d			no period after "8d"	—	—
NEW72	26e			invtd surch (vc)	NA	
NEW73	26f			surch "3d"	NA	
NEW74	28a		2sh on 2m bl	surch "5s"	—	—
NEW75	28b			dbl surch (vc)	—	—
NEW76	29a		3sh on 3m blk vio	no periods after "R I"	—	—
NEW77	29b			"G.R.I." double	—	—
NEW78	29Cd		5sh on 5m sl & car	no periods after "R I"	—	—
NEW79	29Ce			surch "ls"	—	—
NEW80	30a	(1914)	1p on 3pf brown	invtd surch (vc)	NA	
NEW81	31a		1p on 5pf green	dbl surch (vc)	NA	
NEW82	31b			no period after "d"	—	—
NEW83	31c			invtd surch (vc)	NA	—
NEW84	32a		2p on 10pf car	dbl surch (vc)	NA	
NEW85	32b			dbl surch, one invtd	NA	
NEW86	32c			surch sideways	NA	—
NEW87	32d			no period after "2d"	—	—
NEW88	32e			no period after "G"	NA	—
NEW89	33a		2p on 20pf ultra	no period after "d"	35.00	*75.00*
NEW90	33b			dbl surch (vc)	NA	—
NEW91	33c			dbl surch, one invtd	NA	—
NEW92	33d			invtd surch (vc)	—	—
NEW93	33e			"I" omitted	—	—
NEW94	34a		3p on 25pf org & blk, *yel*	dbl surch (vc)	NA	
NEW95	34b			dbl surch, one invtd	NA	—
NEW96	34c			no period after "d"	NA	—
NEW97	34d			invtd surch (vc)	NA	—
NEW98	35a		3p on 30pf org & blk, *sal*	no period after "d"	NA	
NEW99	35b			invtd surch (vc)	—	—
NEW100	35c			dbl surch (vc)	NA	—
NEW101	35d			dbl surch, one invd	—	—
NEW102	36a		4p on 40pf lake & blk	no period after "d"	NA	
NEW103	36b			dbl surch (vc)	NA	
NEW104	36c			"4d" omitted	—	—
NEW105	36d			"ld" on "4d"	—	—
NEW106	36e			no period after "R"	—	—

NEW107	36f			invtd surch (vc)	NA	—
NEW108	36g			surch "ld"	NA	—
NEW109	37a		5p on 50pf pur & blk, sal	"d" omitted	NA	—
NEW110	37b			dbl surch (vc)	NA	—
NEW111	37c			"5d" dbl	NA	—
NEW112	38a		8p on 80pf lake & blk, rose	invtd surch (vc)	—	—
NEW113	38b			dbl surch (vc)	NA	
NEW114	38c			dbl surch, one invtd	—	—
NEW115	38d			triple surch (u)	—	—
NEW116	39a		1s on 1m car	dbl surch (vc)	—	—
NEW117	39b			dbl surch, one with "sl" for "ls"	—	—
NEW118	39c			no period after "l"	NA	—
NEW119	40a		2sh on 2m blue	dbl surch , one invtd	—	NA
NEW120	40b			dbl surch (vc)	—	—
NEW121	40c			large "S"	—	—
NEW122	40d			no period after "l"	NA	
NEW123	41a		3sh on 3m blk vio—	dbl surch (vc)	—	—
NEW124	41b			no period after "l"	NA	
NEW125	41c			no period after "R l"	NA	—
NEW126	41d			invtd surch (vc)	—	—
NEW127	42a		5sh on 5m sl & car	dbl surch, one invtd	—	NA
NEW128	43a		3p black & red (Rabaul)	"Friedrich Wilhelmshaven"	150.00	NA
NEW129	43b			"Herbertshohe"	165.00	NA
NEW130	43c			"Kawieng"	NA	
NEW131	43d			"Kieta"	NA	
NEW132	43e			"Manus"	200.00	NA
NEW133	43f			dbl surch (vc) (Rabaul)	NA	
NEW134	43g			as "c", dbl surch (vc)	NA	—
NEW135	43h			as "e" dbl surch (vc)	NA	—
NEW136	44a	(1915)	1p on 2p on 10pf	"l" double	—	—
NEW137	44b			"l" invtd	—	—
NEW138	45a		1p on 2p on 20pf	"l" invtd	—	—
NEW139	O1a	(1915)	1p on 3pf brown	dbl surch (vc)	NA	—

NEW CALEDONIA - An island in the So. Pacific Ocean, East of Queensland, Australia

NCL1	2a	(1882)	5c on 40c red, straw	invtd surch (vc)	NA	
NCL2	4a		25c on 35dp vio, yel	invtd surch (vc)	NA	
NCL3	5a		25c on 75c rose caar, rose	invtd surch (vc)	NA	
NCL4	6a	(1884)	5c on 40c red, straw	invtd surch (vc)	12.00	12.00
NCL5	7a	(1883)	5c on 75c rose car, rose	invtd surch (vc)	35.00	35.00
NCL6	8a	(1886)	5c on 1fr	invtd surch (vc)	15.00	15.00
NCL7	9a		5c on 1fr	invtd surch (vc)	25.00	25.00
NCL8	11a	(1892)	10c on 40c red, straw	invtd surch (vc)	20.00	20.00
NCL9	11b			dbl surch (vc)	40.00	40.00
NCL10	11c			no period after "10c"	20.00	16.00
NCL11	12a		10c on 30c brn, bis	invtd surch (vc)	9.25	9.25
NCL12	12b			dbl surch (vc)	25.00	25.00
NCL13	12c			dbl surch, invtd	30.00	25.00
NCL14	13a		10c on 40c red, straw	invtd surch, (vc)	9.25	9.25
NCL15	13b			no period after "10c"	8.75	8.75
NCL16	13c			dbl surch (vc)	25.00	25.00
NCL17	35a	(1892-93)	5c on 20c red, grn (bk)	invtd surch (vc)	55.00	52.50
NCL18	35b			dbl surch, invtd (vc)	—	—
NCL19	36a		5c on 75c car, rose (bk)	invtd surch (vc)	55.00	52.50
NCL20	37a		5c on 75c car, rose (bl)	invtd surch (vc)	55.00	52.50
NCL21	38a		10c on 1fr brnz grn, straw (bk)	invtd surch (vc)	NA	
NCL22	39a		10c on 1fr brnz grn, straw (bl)	invtd surch (vc)	55.00	52.50
NCL23	59a	(1900-01)	5c on 2c	dbl surch (vc)	80.00	80.00

NCL24	59b			invtd surch (vc)	80.00	80.00
NCL25	60a		5c on 4c	invtd surch (vc)	50.00	50.00
NCL26	60b			dbl surch (vc)	50.00	50.00
NCL27	61a		15c on 30c	invtd surch (vc)	40.00	40.00
NCL28	61b			dbl surch (vc)	40.00	40.00
NCL29	62a		15c on 75c	pair, one without surch (vc)	—	—
NCL30	62b			invtd surch (vc)	90.00	90.00
NCL31	62c			dbl surch (vc)	90.00	90.00
NCL32	63a		15c on 1fr	dbl surch (vc)	90.00	90.00
NCL33	63b			invtd surch (vc)	90.00	90.00
NCL34	64a	(1902)	5c on 30c		22.50	22.50
NCL35	65a		15c on 40c	invtd surch (vc)	22.50	22.50
NCL36	66a	(1905)	1c blk, lil bl (bl)	invtd ovpt	165.00	165.00
NCL37	68a		4c cl, lav (bl)	dbl ovpt (vc)	200.00	200.00
NCL38	75a		25c blk, rose (bl)	dbl ovpt (vc)	—	—
NCL39	78a		50c car, rose (bl)	pair, one without ovpt	—	—
NCL40	79a		75c vio, org (bk)	dbl ovpt in blk & red	NA	
NCL41	80a		1fr brnz grn, straw (bl)	dbl ovpt, one in red	NA	
NCL42	81a		1c on 2c brown#67	numeral dbl	—	—
NCL43	81b			numeral only (2) R?	—	
NCL44	83a		4c on 5c #69	small "4"	NA	
NCL45	84a		4c on 5c #70	pair, one without numeral	—	—
NCL46	117a		5c on 15c gray (C)	invtd surch (vc)	100.00	100.00
NCL47	122a		5c on 15c violet	dbl surch (vc)	40.00	40.00
NCL48	122b			invtd surch (vc)	22.50	22.50
NCL49	123a	(1922)	5c on 15c vio (R)	dbl surch (vc)	40.00	40.00
NCL50	124a		25c on 15c vio	dbl surch (vc)	40.00	
NCL51	126a		25c on 5fr blk, straw	dbl surch (vc)	60.00	60.00
NCL52	C1a		65c deep violet	"65c" omitted	110.00	—

A little here and a little there
But vc's come from everywhere
Some crawl up and others crawl down
Some even wear the royal crown. —The Bard

NEW GUINEA has produced no errors

NEW HEBRIDES, FRENCH- Islands in the So. Pacific, north of New Caledonia

NEH1	8a	(1908-09)	1p carmine	pair, one without ovpt	NA	—
NEH2	26a	(1921)	1p on 5p ol green	invtd surch (vc)	NA	—
NEH3	39a	(1924)	5p on 2-1/2 p ultra	invtd surch (vc)	NA	—

NEW REPUBLIC- No. Part of Natal, So. Africa

NER1	2a	(1886)	2p violet, *yel*	without date	—	—
NER2	3a		3p violet, *yel*	dbl impression	—	—
NER3	4a		4p violet, *yel*	without date	—	—
NER4	5a		6p violet, *yel*	dbl impression	—	—
NER5	7a		1sh violet, *yel*	"1/S"	NA	—
NER6	8a		1/6 violet, *yel*	without date	—	—
NER7	8b			"1shop"	NA	—
NER8	10a		2shop violet, *yel*	without date	—	—
NER9	10b			"2/6,"	135.00	—
NER10	12a		5sh violet, *yel*	without date	—	—
NER11	13a		5/6 violet, *yel*	5shop	150.00	—
NER12	14a		7shop violet, *yel*	"7/6,"	150.00	—
NER13	20a		2p violet, gray	without "ZUID AFRIKA"	—	—
NER14	26b		1shop violet, *gray*	"1/6,"	140.00	—
NER15	28a		2shop violet, *gray*	"2/6,"	175.00	—
NER16	30a		5shop violet *gray*	"5/6,"	190.00	
NER17	32Bc		10sh 6p vio, *gray*	without date	—	—
NER18	37a		1p violet, *yel*	arms invtd	25.00	25.00
NER19	38a		2p violet, *yel*	arms invtd	25.00	27.50
NER20	39a		4p violet, *yel*	arms invtd	100.00	—

NER21	41b		1p violet, *gray*	arms invtd	30.00	35.00
NER22	42b		2p violet, *gray*	arms invtd	45.00	—
NER23	43a	(1887)	3p violet, *yel*	arms invtd	24.00	24.00
NER24	43d			arms omitted	—	—
NER25	44a		4p violet, *yel*	arms invtd	27.50	27.50
NER26	45a		6p violet, *yel*	arms invtd	52.50	52.50
NER27	45b			arms omitted	200.00	—
NER28	47a		1sh violet, *yel*	arms invtd	65.00	—
NER29	47b			arms omitted	55.00	—
NER30	49a		2sh violet, *yel*	arms invtd	75.00	—
NER31	49b			arms omitted	100.00	100.00
NER32	50a		2shop violet, *yel*	arms invtd	24.00	24.00
NER33	50Bc		3sh violet *yel*	arms invtd	47.50	47.50
NER34	51a		4sh violet, *yel*	arms invtd	—	—
NER35	52b		5sh violet, *yel*	arms invtd	90.00	—
NER36	54a		7shop violet, *yel*	arms invtd	80.00	—
NER37	55a		10sh violet, *yel*	arms invtd	21.00	21.00
NER38	55b			arms omitted	75.00	75.00
NER39	56b		10shop violet, *yel*	arms invtd	—	—
NER40	56c			arms omitted	—	—
NER41	57a		£1 violet, *yel*	arms invtd	52.50	—
NER42	59a		1p violet, *gray*	arms omitted	110.00	110.00
NER43	59b			arms invtd	21.00	21.00
NER44	60a		2p violet, *gray*	arms omitted	100.00	100.00
NER45	60b			arms invtd	22.50	22.50
NER46	61a		3p violet, *gray*	arms invtd	65.00	65.00
NER47	62a		4p violet, *gray*	arms invtd	85.00	85.00
NER48	63a		6p violet, *gray*	arms invtd	100.00	100.00
NER49	64a		1shop violet, *gray*	arms invtd	—	—

NEW ZEALAND

NEZ1	90b	(1900)	4p yel brown & bl	dbl impression of center (u)	—	—
NEZ2	93b		6p rose	dbl impression (u)	NA	—
NEZ3	113b		4p yel brn & bl	center invtd (u)	—	—
NEZ4	333b	(1960-66)	1/2 p dp car, grn & pale bl (u)		70.00	—
NEZ5	333c			pale blue omitted (u)	55.00	—
NEZ6	334b		1p brn, org & grn	orange omitted (u)	150.00	—
NEZ7	335b		2p grn, rose car, blk & yel	black omitted (u)	200.00	—
NEZ8	335c			yellow omitted (u)	NA	—
NEZ9	336a		2-1/2 p blk, grn, red & brn	brown omitted (u)	50.00	—
NEZ10	336b			green & red omitted (u)	160.00	—
NEZ11	336c			green omitted (u)	75.00	—
NEZ12	336d			red omitted (u)	90.00	—
NEZ13	337b		3p prus bl, yel, brn & grn	yellow omitted (u)	45.00	—
NEZ14	337c			brown omitted (u)	45.00	—
NEZ15	337d			green omitted (u)	45.00	—
NEZ16	338a		4p bl, grn, yel & lilac	yellow omitted (u)	100.00	—
NEZ17	338b			lilac omitted (u)	45.00	—
NEZ18	339a		5p pur, blk, yel & grn	yellow omitted (u)	125.00	—
NEZ19	340a		6p dp grn, lt grn & lil	light green omitted (u)	60.00	—
NEZ20	340b		6pdp grn, lt grn & lil	lilac omitted (u)	70.00	—
NEZ21	342a		9p ultra & car	carmine omitted (u)	150.00	—
NEZ22	344a		1sh3p bl, brn & carmine	carmine omitted (u)	150.00	—
NEZ23	348a		2 shop red brn & yellow	yellow omitted (u)	NA	—
NEZ24	353a	(1960)	2p dp brown & red, cream	red omitted (u)	NA	—
NEZ25	356a	(1962)	3p dk brown & green	green omitted (u)	—	—
NEZ26	357b		8p dk red & gray	gray omitted (u)	NA	—
NEZ27	359b	(1963)	2-1/2 p multicolored	yellow omitted(u)	NA	—
NEZ28	362a		3p multicolored	blue (sky) omitted (u)	NA	—

NEZ29	363a		1sh9p bl, blk, yel & carmine	carmine omitted (value) (u)	NA	—
NEZ30	374a	(1965)	3p multicolored	gold omitted (u)	NA	—
NEZ31	375a	(1965)	4p multicolored	blue omitted (u)	NA	—
NEZ32	378a	(1966)	4p green & gold	gold omitted (u)	NA	—
NEZ33	408a	(1968)	3c multicolored	gold omitted (u)	100.00	—
NEZ34	465a	(1970)	3c multicolored	green omitted (u)	*200.00*	—
NEZ35	B56a	(1959)	3p+1p ultra & car	Red Cross omitted (u)	NA	—
NEZ36	B58b		3p+1p blue, black & pink	pink omitted (u)	*150.00*	*50.00*
NEZ37	B64b	(1962)	3p+1p salmon, blk, green & org	orange omitted (u)	—	—
NEZ38	B67b	(1964)	2-1/2 p + 1p lt bl, pale yel, red & blk	red omitted (u)	—	—
NEZ39	B67c			yellow omitted (u)	—	—
NEZ40	B72b	(1966)	4p +1p lt grn & multi	brown omitted (u)	—	—

NICARAGUA

From 1901 to 1936 the number of Nicaraguan errors was fantastic. We have narrowed these down to a small sampling.

1. The 1901 issue has numerous vc's, as simple as a bar below value, and most values are lower than $25.00.
2. The second 1901 issue has lots of affordable vc's; one triple overprint less than $25.00.
3. 1902-only two errors—162a (vc);162b blue surcharge. Prices are higher but affordable.
4. 1903-no errors
5. 1904-05 some vc's, some others trivial—e.g. without ornaments. All prices under $15.00
6. 1905- June, July, two vc's under $5.00
7. 1906-8; May 1908; more variety—e.g. surcharge reading up—prices higher ($50.00 or more).
8. June 1908-more variety (wrong dates, spelling)—prices low.
9. Nov. 1908- high prices, one NA
10. Dec. 1908- few vc's- one priced over $75.00
11. Feb., Mar. 1909-only one vc at about $10.00
12. July 1910, 1910, Dec. 19, 1910-lots of vc's; prices very high on 1910 issue; very low in Dec. 1910.
13. Mar.11-some vc's, some others (without period)
14. April, June 1911—very low price—not as dominated by vc's as in certain other issues.
15. July, Oct., Nov., Dec. 1911; these issues have their share of vc's but have: (1) some higher but affordable "new value in red or yellow on face" ($50.00 or more) (2) some low "TIMBRE FISCAL" on the face for a dollar or so.
16. 1912 Issue—no errors.
17. 1913-15-(several issues) (May 13, 1914 issue—no errors) many other than vc errors—e.g. 0.12 for 0.02. Prices generally low (few in $20.00 to $30.00 range).
18. 1918-19; considerable vc's. An exception: "rordobo" rather than "cordoba." A few high-priced items (e.g. blue surcharge over $100.00).
19. 1910-1921-few inexpensive vc's and others.
20. Sept. 1921-Nov. 1922; no errors.
21. 1923-4; two inexpensive vc's.
22. 1927; mostly vc's or variations such as over 1927 only—mostly inexpensive.
23. 1928; majority vc's- some variation (double overprint, one inverted, mostly inexpensive).
24. 1928-29-no errors.
25. 1929-about half vc's—mostly inexpensive except double surcharged, one inverted (R) and (B).
26. 1929-31-no errors.
27. 1931, May, June-majority vc's mostly inexpensive
28. 1932, Jan.-no errors.
29. 1932, Dec.-2 vc's inexpensive
30. 1933-About half vc's-inexpensive (Aug. 1933 - no errors).
31. 1935-36-a number of vc's, also "1939," instead of "1936,"; inexpensive.

NICARAGUA

Two sample pieces

NCG1	319a	2c on 20c red	middle stamp "do" instead of "de" R ?
NCG2	C22	1bf block of 4 different colors & value in brown/tan sheet	s/s invtd center R ?

NIGER - No. of Nigeria, No. Africa

NIG1	22a	(1922-26) 25c on 15c red brn & org ('25)	multiple surch (u)	80.00	—
NIG2	22b		"25c" invtd	70.00	—
NIG3	24a	25c on 5fr vio & blk (R) ('24)	dbl surch (vc)	80.00	—
NIG4	28a	(1926) 1.25fr on 1fr dp bl & lt bl (R)	surch omitted	140.00	—

NIGER COAST PROTECTORATE
(Oil Rivers Protectorate)

NCP1	2a	(1892) 1p lilac	"OIL RIVERS' at top	NA	—
NCP2	7d	(1893) 1/2 p on half of 1p (R)	"1/2 " omitted	—	—
NCP3	7Ab	1/2 p on half of 1p (V)	surch dbl (vc)	NA	—
NCP4	49a	(1894) 1/2 p on half of 1p (R)	invtd surch (vc)	NA	—
NCP5	50a	1p on half of 2p (R)	dbl surch (vc)	NA	—
NCP6	50b		invtd surch (vc)	—	NA
NCP7	54a	(1894) 1/2 p on 2-1/2 p (bl)	dbl surch (vc)	—	—
NCP8	54a	1/2 p on 2-1/2 p blue	dbl surch (vc)	NA	—

NIGERIA

NIG1	107b	(1961) 6p black & yuel	yellow omitted (u)	—	NA
NIG2	132a	(1962) 3p ultra & emerald	emerald omitted (u)	—	—
NIG3	151a	(1963) 1sh3p brown & bister	bister (head) omitted (u)	—	—
NIG4	192a	(1965-66) 1sh gray & multi	red omitted (u)	—	—

One little color was lost on the floor
One little color just added more
One little color we've not committed
One little color we've surely omitted. —The Bard

NIUE - Island in the So. Pacific, N.E. of New Zealand

NIU1	3a	(1902) 1/2 p green (C)	invtd surch (vc)	NA	
NIU2	4a	1p carmine (bl)	no period after "PENI"	140.00	150.00
NIU3	7a	1p carmine (bl)	no period after "PENI"	9.00	16.00
NIU4	7b		dbl surch (vc)	NA	—
NIU5	8a	2-1/2 p blue (C)	no period after "PENI"	45.00	47.50
NIU6	9a	2-1/2 p blue (V)	no period after "PENI"	20.00	25.00
NIU7	13c	(1903) 1sh brown red	orange red with "b" surch "h"(error)	NA	
NIU8	19a	(1917) 1p carmine (br)	no period after "PENI"	140.00	150.00
NIU9	20a	3p violet brn (bl)	no period ater "Pene"	NA	
NIU10	39a	(1920) 6p dp grn & red brn	center invtd (u)	NA	—

Niue has some errors five
No period following pence
But from there things get better
We even have an inverted center. —The Bard

NORFOLK ISLAND has produced no errors

NORTH BORNEO - N.E. part of island of Borneo, Malay archipelago

NOB1	4a	(1883-84) 4a 8c on 2c brown	dbl surch (vc)	—	NA
NOB2	17a	(1886) 5c on 8c green	invtd surch (vc)	NA	—
NOB3	20a	3c on 4c rose	dbl surch, both types of "3,"	—	—
NOB4	28a	4c rose	cliche of 1c in plate of 4c (u)	165.00	NA
NOB5	28c		as "a", imperf. In pair with #28 (u)	NA	—
NOB6	50a	(1890) 2c on 25c slate blue	invtd surch (vc)	NA	
NOB7	50b		with additional surch "2 cents" in black	—	—
NOB8	52a	(1891-92) 6c on 8c green	"c" of "cents" invtd	NA	
NOB9	52b		"cetns"	NA	
NOB10	52c		invtd surch (vc)	200.00	NA
NOB11	55a	6c on 10c blue	invtd surch (vc)	140.00	*140.00*
NOB12	55b		dbl surch (vc)	NA	—
NOB13	55c		triple surch (vc)	NA	—

NOB14	56a	(1892)	1c on 4c rose	dbl surch (vc)	NA	—
NOB15	56b			surch on face & back	—	NA
NOB16	74a	(1895)	4c on $1 red	dbl surch (vc)	NA	—
NOB17	101a	(1899)	4c on $5 red vio	"CENTS" 8-1/2 mm below "4,"	11.00	18.00
NOB18	102a		4c on $10 brown	"CENTS" 8-1/2 mm below "4,"		
NOB19	115a	(1901-05)	25c slate blue (r)	invtd ovpt (vc)	NA	
NOB20	118a		$1 red (bk)	dbl ovpt (vc)	—	NA
NOB21	119a		$2 gray green (R)	dbl ovpt (vc)	NA	—
NOB22	122a	(1902)	10c sl & dk brn (R)	dbl ovpt (vc)	NA	
NOB23	125a	(1904)	4c on 6c ol brn & blk	invtd surch (vc)	NA	
NOB24	126a		4c on 8c brn lil & blk	invtd surch (vc)	NA	
NOB25	135a		4c pm #10 brown	invtd surch (vc)	NA	—
NOB26	160a	(1916)	2c on 3c dp rose	invtd "S"	87.50	87.50
NOB27	161a		4c on 6c ol grn (R)	invtd "S"	100.00	100.00
NOB28	162a		10c on 12c bl (R)	invtd "S"	110.00	110.00
NOB29	166a	(1923)	3c on 4c dull red & blk	dbl surch (vc)	—	
NOB30	221a	(1945)	$2 ol green & pur	dbl ovpt (vc)	—	—
NOB31	B17a	(1918)	4c + 2c dull red	invtd surch (vc)	NA	—
NOB32	B22a		12c + 2c deep blue	invtd surch	NA	—
NOB33	J3a	(1895)	5c org red & blk (V)	period after "DUE" (V)	45.00	—
NOB34	J5a		8c lilac & blk (H)	dbl ovpt (vc) (H)	—	
NOB35	J6a		12c blue & blk (H)	dbl ovpt (vc)	—	NA
NOB36	J7a		18c green & blk (V)	ovpt reading down	NA	
NOB37	J7b			ovpt hoizontally	20.00	2.75
NOB38	J7c			same as "b" invtd	NA	
NOB39	J9a	(1897)	2c dp rose & blk (V)	ovpt horizontally	12.00	15.00
NOB40	J10a		8c brn lil & blk (H)	period after "DUE"	30.00	60.00
NOB41	J11a	(1901)	2c green & blk	ovpt horiz.		27.50
NOB42	J12a		3c lilac & ol grn	period after "DUE"	18.00	30.00
NOB43	J14a		5c orange & blk	period after "DUE"	30.00	
NOB44	J16a		8c brown & blk	ovpt horiz.	30.00	—
NOB45	J16b			period after "DUE" (H)	60.00	—
NOB46	J20a	(1903-11)	1c bis brn & blk, period after "DUE"	period omitted	—	—
NOB47	J22a		3c lilac & ol grn	ovpt vertical	110.00	110.00
NOB48	J23a		4c dp rose & blk,	"Postage Due" dbl. Perf 15	110.00	—
NOB49	J24a		5c orange & blk	ovpt vert. Perf 15	165.00	110.00
NOB50	J25a		6c olive brn & blk	"Postage Due" double	—	
NOB51	J25b			"Postage Due" invtd	—	110.00
NOB52	J26a		8c brown & blk	ovpt vertical	150.00	125.00
NOB53	J30a		18c green & blk	"Postage Due" dbl	—	80.00
NOB54	J31a		24c claret & blue	"Postage Due" dbl	—	125.00
NOB55	J31b			ovpt vertical	—	85.00

A nice cliche for every day
And a surcharge triple which is no cripple
Other than that lots of vc's
Hanging in the Borneo trees. —The Bard

NORTHERN NIGERIA has produced no errors

NORTHERN RHODESIA

NOR1	75a	(1963)	1/2 p violet & blk	value omitted	NA	—
NOR2	76a		1p blue & blk	value omitted	11.50	—
NOR3	78b		3p orange & blk	value omitted	90.00	—
NOR4	79a		4p green & blk	value omitted	NA	—
NOR5	80a		6p yellow grn & blk	value omitted	NA	—
NOR6	81a		9p ocher & blk	value omitted	150.00	—
NOR7	82a		1sh dk gray & blk	value omitted	—	—
NOR8	88a		20sh dk blue & blk	value omitted	NA	—

Nine little Indians, value committed
Eight little Indians, value omitted
I'd rather have the omit, wouldn't you?
They're much more rare and valuable too. —The Bard

AFFORDABLE FOREIGN ERRORS

NORTH INGERMANLAND

NRI1	14a	(1920)	10m brn & vio	center invtd	NA	—

NORTH WEST PACIFIC ISLANDS

NWP1	11a	(1915-16)	1/2 p emerald	dbl ovpt (vc)	—	—
NWP2	12a		1p car (Die 1)		5.00	5.00
NWP3	12b		1p carmine (Die 1a)		125.00	125.00
NWP4	28a	(1919)	2-1/2 p dk bl	"1," of fraction omitted	NA	

NORWAY

NOW1	1a	(1855)	4s blue	dbl foot on right hind leg of lion	—	NA
NOW2	16b	(1872-75)	1s yel green	"E.EN"	25.00	*55.00*
NOW3	24c	(1877-78)	5o ultra	no period after "Postfrim"	57.50	13.00
NOW4	24d			retouched plate	100.00	17.50
NOW5	24e			as "c" retouched plate	125.00	27.50
NOW6	25a		10o rose	no period after "Postfrim"	—	—
NOW7	25b			retouched plate	60.00	2.50
NOW8	29a		35o bl green ('78)	retouched plate	NA	110.00
NOW9	35a	(1882-93)	1o black brn ('86)	no period after "Postfrim"	60.00	60.00
NOW10	35b			small "N" in "NORGE"	60.00	60.00
NOW11	44b		20o blue ('85)	no period after "Postfrim"	NA	15.00

NOSSI-BE - Island in the Indian Ocean, off the N.W. coast of Madagascar

NOS1	1a	(1889)	25 on 40c red, *straw*	dbl surch (vc)	—	NA
NOS2	12a		0.25 on 1fr	without ornament	NA	165.00
NOS3	24a	(1893)	50 on 10c (bk)	invtd surch (vc)	175.00	125.00
NOS4	26a		1fr on 5c (bk)	invtd surch (vc)	165.00	150.00
NOS5	27a		10c (C)	invtd ovpt (vc)	55.00	50.00
NOS6	29a		15c (bk)	invtd ovpt (vc)	55.00	50.00
NOS7	30a		20c (bk)	dbl ovpt (vc)	—	—
NOS8	31a		20c (bl)	invtd ovpt (vc)	80.00	75.00
NOS9	J1a		20 on 1c blk, *lil bl*	invtd surch (vc)	NA	
NOS10	J1b			surcharged vertically	NA	
NOS11	J1c			surch on back	NA	
NOS12	J2a		30 on 2c brn, *buff*	invtd surch (vc)	NA	
NOS13	J2b			surch on back	NA	
NOS14	J3a		50 on 30c brn, *bister*	invtd surch (vc)	NA	
NOS15	J3b			surch on back	NA	

NYA7A

NYA7B

NYA7C

NYA7D

NYA7E

NYA7F

NYA7G

NYA7H

NOS16	J4a		35 on 4c cl, *lav*	invtd surch (vc)		NA	
NOS17	J4b			surch on back		NA	
NOS18	J4c			pair, one without surch		NA	
NOS19	J5a		35 on 20c red, *green*	invtd surch (vc)		NA	
NOS20	J6a		1fr on 35c vio, *orange*	invtd surch (vc)		NA	
NOS21	J6b			surch on back		NA	
NOS22	J14a	(1891)	0.15c on 20c	25c on 20c (error)		NA	
NOS23	J7a		5c on 20c	invtd surch (vc		200.00	200.00
NOS24	J8a		5c on 20c	invtd surch (vc		200.00	200.00
NOS25	J10a		10c on 15c	invtd surch (vc		200.00	200.00
NOS26	J11a		10c on 15c	invtd surch (vc		200.00	200.00
NOS27	J12a		15c on 10c	invtd surch (vc		200.00	200.00
NOS28	J13a		15c on 10c	invtd surch (vc		200.00	200.00
NOS29	J15a		25c on 5c	invtd surch (vc		200.00	200.00
NOS30	J16a		25c on 5c	invtd surch (vc		200.00	200.00
NOS31	J17a		0.25c on 75c	invtd surch (vc		850.00	750.00

If you go to NOSSI-BE
You're sure to find vc
The problem is today
They're likely to be NA. —The Bard

NYASALAND PROTECTORATE has produced no errors

NYASA

NYA1	6a	(1898)	50r light blue	invtd ovpt (vc)		—	—

Nos. 26-38 are known with inverted centers but are believed to be purely speculative and never regularly issued. Valued at $25.00 each.

NYA2	50a	(1910)	50r on 100r	"50 REIS" omitted		125.00	—
NYA3	61a	(1911)	400 blk & dk brn, red ovpt	pair, one without ovpt		—	—
NYA4	83a	(1921)	1/2 c on 5r (R)	1/2 c on 2-1/2 r (R) (error)		200.00	200.00
NYA5	84a		1c on10r	pair, one without surch		—	—
NYA6	88a		3c on 400r	"Republica" omitted		—	—
NYA7	102a		7-1/2 c on 75r	invtd surch (vc)		—	—

NYASA has "produced" many other inverts that have little or no philatelic value. Photos of some of these invert types are presented here for purposes of illumination.

NYA7A	Camel
NYA7B	Giraffe
NYA7C	Giraffe ovpt (invtd)

NYA8

NYA8A

NYA8B

NYA8C

NYA8D

HYA8E

NYA8F

NYA8G

NYA7D			Camel invtd ovpt (block)		
NYA7E			Camel invtd ovpt (block)		
NYA7F			Camel surch invtd		
NYA7G			Waterlow punched trval. Spec.		
NYA7H			Camel 10 invtd giraffe standing		

Several (red overprint) stamps are issued without overprint. These (51-62) are:

NYA8			2-1/2 r Camels		
NYA8A			5r Camels		
NYA8B			10r Camels		
NYA8C			20r Zebra		
NYA8D			25r Zebra		
NYA8E			50r Zebra		
NYA8F			75r giraffe		
NYA8G			100r Giraffe		
NYA8H			200r Giraffe		
NYA8I			300r Ship		
NYA8J			400r ship		
NYA8K			500r Ship		

Lots of pretty stamps
Lots of speculation
For inverted centers
For this smallish nation. —The Bard

O

OBOCK

OBO1	29a	(1892)	35c on 25c blk, rose	"3," instead of "35,"	NA	
OBO2	30b		75c on 1fr brnz grn, *straw*	"57," instead of "75,"	NA	
OBO3	30c			"55,"instead of "75,"	NA	
OBO4	43a	(1892)	75c vio, org	name double	175.00	175.00
OBO5	43b			name invtd	NA	

OLTRE GIUBA - A strip of land near the Juba River in East Africa

| OLT1 | 1a | (1925) | 1c brown | invtd ovpt (vc) | 65.00 | — |
| OLT2 | Q6a | | 1 1 violet | dbl ovpt | 65.00 | — |

Be it inverted or be it double
It's sure to be paid lots of trouble
Some call them both a good vc
But this abbreviation bothers me. —The Bard

OMAN - S. E. CORNER OF THE ARABIAN PENINSULA

OMA1	5a	(1944)	1-1/2 a dark purple	dbl ovpt (vc)	NA	—
OMA2	30a	(1948)	1r on 1sh dk brown	dbl surch	NA	—
OMA3	101a		50b red brn & brt grn	value in "baizas" in Arabic	18.00	9.50

ORANGE RIVER COLONY has produced no errors

| NYA8H | NYA8I | NYA8J | NYA8K |

CHAPTER VI: P-S

PAKISTAN

PAK1	14a	(1947)	1r brown & slate	invtd ovpt (vc)	110.00	—
PAK2	14b			pair one without ovpt,	NA	—
PAK3	O28a	(1949-50)	1-1/2 a gray green (C)	invtd ovpt (vc)	35.00	—
PAK4	O66a	(1961)	1p on 1-1/2 a red	invtd ovpt (vc)	8.25	—
PAK5	O67a		1p on 1-1/2 a red	ovpt type "b"	6.00	4.00
PAK6	O68a		2p on 3p orange red	ovpt type "b"	6.00	4.00
PAK7	O70a		7p on 1a car rose	ovpt type "b"	2.25	2.25

Bahawalpur has produced no errors

PALAU has produced no errors

PALESTINE

PAL1	17e	(1920)	3m lt brown	invtd ovpt (vc)	NA	
PAL2	16ae		2m blue green	"PALESTINE" omitted	NA	
PAL3	48a	(1922)	1m dark brown	invtd ovpt (vc)	—	NA
PAL5	48b			dbl ovpt (vc)	NA	
PAL6	58a		2pi olive green	invtd ovpt (vc)	NA	

PANAMA

PAN1	22a	(1894)	1c on 2c rose	invtd surch (vc)	2.50	2.50
PAN2	22b			dbl surch (vc)	—	—
PAN3	23a		1c on 2c rose	"CCNTAVO," 2.50	2.50	—
PAN4	23b			invtd surch (vc)	2.50	2.50
PAN5	23c			dbl surch (vc)	—	—
PAN6	24a		5c on 20c black, lil	invtd surch (vc)	12.50	12.50
PAN7	24b			dbl surch (vc)	—	—
PAN8	24c			without "HABILITADO"	—	—
PAN9	25a		5c on 20c black, lil	"CCNTAVOS" 7.50	7.50	—
PAN10	25b			invtd surch (vc)	12.50	12.50
PAN11	25c			dbl surch (vc)	—	—
PAN12	25d			without "HABILITADO"	—	—
PAN13	26a		5c on 20c black, lil	invtd surch (vc)	12.50	12.50
PAN14	26b			dbl surch (vc)	—	—
PAN15	27a		10c on 50c brown	"1894," omitted	—	—
PAN16	27b			invtd surch (vc)	—	—
PAN17	27c			"CCNTAVOS"	—	—
PAN18	28a		10c on 50c brown	"CCNTAVOS"	—	—
PAN19	28b			invtd surch (vc)	—	—
PAN20	29a		10c on 50c brown	"1894," omitted 7.50	—	—
PAN21	29b			invtd surch (vc)	12.50	12.50
PAN22	29c			dbl surch (vc)	—	—
PAN23	30a		10c on 50c brown	"CCNTAVO	—	—
PAN24	30b			without "HABILITADO"	—	—
PAN25	30c			invtd surch (vc)	25.00	25.00
PAN26	30d			dbl surch (vc)	—	—
PAN27	65a	(1903)	2c rose	"PANAMA" 15mm long	3.50	—
PAN28	65b			violet bar	5.00	—
PAN29	66a		5c blue	"PANAMA" 15mm long	100.00	—
PAN30	67a		10c yellow	"PANAMA" 15mm long	6.00	—
PAN31	67b			horizontal ovpt	17.50	—
PAN32	68a		2c rose	"PANAMA" 15mm long	2.50	—
PAN33	69a		5c blue	"PANAMA" 15mm long	3.50	—
PAN34	69b			bar only	75.00	75.00
PAN35	69c			dbl ovpt (vc)	—	—
PAN36	70a		20c violet	"PANAMA" 15mm long	10.00	—
PAN37	70b			dbl ovpt, one in black	150.00	—
PAN38	71a	(1903)	1c green	"PANAMA" 15mm long	1.25	—
PAN39	71b			"PANAMA" reading down	3.00	.75
PAN40	71c			"PANAMA" reading up & down	3.00	—

PAN41	71d		dbl ovpt (vc)	8.00	—
PAN42	72a	2c rose	"PANAMA" 15mm long	1.00	—
PAN43	72b		"PANAMA" reading down	.75	.50
PAN44	72c		"PANAMA" reading up & down	4.00	—
PAN45	72d		dbl ovpt (vc)	8.00	—
PAN46	73a	20c violet	"PANAMA" 15mm long	2.25	—
PAN47	73b		"PANAMA" reading down	—	—
PAN48	73c		"PANAMA" reading up & down	8.00	8.00
PAN49	73d		dbl ovpt (vc)	18.00	18.00
PAN50	74a	50c bister brn	"PANAMA" 15mm long	5.00	—
PAN51	74b		"PANAMA"reading up & down	12.50	12.50
PAN52	74c		dbl ovpt (vc)	6.00	6.00
PAN53	75a	1p lake	"PANAMA" 15mm long	6.25	—
PAN54	75b		"PANAMA" reading up & down	15.00	15.00
PAN55	75c		dbl ovpt (vc)	15.00	—
PAN56	75d		invtd ovpt (vc)	—	25.00

Overprinted in red, one word (PANAMA) reading up, one down, is a common theme here.

PAN57	76a	(1904-05) 1c green	both words reading up	1.50	—
PAN58	76b		both words reading down	2.75	—
PAN59	76c		dbl ovpt (vc)	—	—
PAN60	76d		pair, one without ovpt.	15.00	—
PAN61	76e		"PANAAM"20.00	—	
PAN62	76f		invtd "M" in "PANAMA"	5.00	—
PAN63	77a	2c rose	both words reading up,	2.50	—
PAN64	77b		both words reading down	2.50	—
PAN65	77c		dbl ovpt (vc)	10.00	—
PAN66	77d		dbl ovpt, one invtd	14.00	—
PAN66	77e		invtd "M" in "PANAMA"	5.00	—
PAN67	78a	5c blue	both words reading up	3.00	—
PAN68	78b		both words reading down	4.25	—
PAN69	78c		invtd ovpt (vc)	12.50	—
PAN70	78d		"PANAAM"	25.00	—
PAN71	78e		"PANANA"	8.00	—
PAN72	78f		"PAMANA"	5.00	—
PAN73	78g		invtd "M" in "PANAMA"	5.00	—
PAN74	78h		dbl ovpt (vc)	20.00	—
PAN75	79a	10c yellow	both words reading up	5.00	—
PAN76	79b		both words reading down	5.00	—
PAN77	79c		dbl ovpt (vc)	15.00	—
PAN78	79d		invtd ovpt (vc)	6.75	—
PAN79	79e		"PAMANA"	8.00	—
PAN80	79f		invtd "M" in "PANAMA"	15.00	—
PAN81	79g		red brown ovpt	7.50	3.50
PAN82	80a	20c violet	both words reading up	5.00	—
PAN83	80b		both words reading down	10.00	—
PAN84	81a	50c bister brn	both words reading up	10.50	—
PAN85	81b		both words reading down	10.00	—
PAN86	81c		dbl ovpt	—	—
PAN87	82a	1p lake	both words reading up	12.50	—
PAN88	82b		both words reading down	12.50	—
PAN89	82c		dbl ovpt (vc)	—	—
PAN90	82d		dbl ovpt, one invtd	20.00	—
PAN91	81e		invtd "M" in "PANAMA"	45.00	—

Republico de Panama Carmine overprint

PAN92	129a	1c green	invtd ovpt (vc)	6.00	—
PAN93	129b		dbl ovpt (vc)	2.25	—
PAN94	129c		dbl ovpt, one invtd	6.00	—

Black overprints

PAN96	132a	1c green	vertical ovpt	42.50	—
PAN97	132b		invtd ovpt (vc)	42.50	—
PAN98	132c		dbl ovpt, one invtd	42.50	—
PAN99	133a	2c rose	invtd ovpt (vc)	4.00	—

PANAMA

PAN100	134a		10c yellow	invtd ovpt (vc)	4.00	—
PAN101	134b			dbl ovpt (vc)	16.00	—
PAN102	134c			dbl ovpt, one invtd	6.00	—
PAN103	135a		20c violet	invtd ovpt (vc)	4.00	—
PAN104	135b			dbl ovpt (vc)	5.50	—
PAN105	136a		50c brown, blue ovpt	dbl ovpt (vc)	14.00	—
PAN106	181a	(1906)	vermillion surch 1c on 20c violet	"Panrma" 2.25	2.25	
PAN107	181b			"Panama" 2.25	2.25	
PAN108	181c			"Panama" 2.25	2.25	
PAN109	181d			invtd surch (vc)	4.00	4.00
PAN110	181e			dbl surch, one invtd	—	—
PAN111	182a		2c on 50c bister brn	3rd "A: of "PANAMA" invtd	2.25	2.25
PAN112	182b			both "PANAMA" reading down	—	—
PAN113	182c			dbl surch (vc)	—	—
PAN114	182d			invtd surch	2.50	—
Carmine Surcharge						
PAN115	183a		5c on 1p lake	both "PANAMA" reading down	6.00	6.00
PAN116	183b			"5," omitted__	—	
PAN117	183c			dbl surch (vc)	—	—
PAN118	183d			invtd surch (vc)	—	—
PAN119	183e			3rd "A" of "PANAMA" invtd	5.50	5.50
PAN120	184a		5c on 1p lake	"PANAMA" 15mm long	—	—
PAN121	184b			"PANAMA" reading up & down	—	—
PAN122	184c			both "PANAMA" reading down	—	—
PAN123	184d			invtd surch (vc)	—	—
PAN124	184e			dbl surch (vc)	—	—
PAN125	184f			3rd "A" of "PANAMA" invtd	—	—
PAN126	189a		5c blue & black	5c ultramarine & black	2.00	.50
PAN127	210a	(1915-16)	5c blue & black	center invtd (u)	NA	—
PAN128	212a		20c brown & blk	center invtd (u)	NA	—
PAN129	217a		2c on 2-1/2c scar & blk	invtd surch (vc)	10.00	8.25
PAN130	217b			dbl surch (vc)	12.00	10.00
PAN131	261a	(1932)	1c dark green (R)	dbl ovpt (vc)	18.00	—
PAN132	263a		10c on 15c ultra	dbl surch (vc)	55.00	—
PAN133	277a	(1936)	2c on 24c yellow brn	dbl surch (vc)	20.00	—
PAN134	298a	(1937)	1/2 c orange (R)	invtd ovpt (vc)	30.00	—
PAN135	299a		1c green	invtd ovpt (vc)	30.00	—
PAN136	321Ab	(1938)	2c carmine	invtd ovpt (vc)	22.50	—

PAN47

PAN126

PAN129

PAN130

PAN138

AFFORDABLE FOREIGN ERRORS

PAN137	352a		50c on 24c yel brn	"Habilitada" 2.50	2.50	
PAN138	353a		1/2c on 8c gray blk	"B/.0.0.1-1/2 CORREOS" transposed	2.50	2.50
PAN139	367a		2c vermillion	invtd ovpt (vc)	2.00	2.00
PAN139A	434					
See Photo in Color Section						
PAN140	C1a	(1929)	25c on 10c org	invtd surch (vc)	22.50	22.50
PAN141	C2a		10c orange	invtd ovpt (vc)	16.00	14.00
PAN142	C2b			dbl ovpt (vc)	16.00	14.00
PAN143	C4a		25c on 20c dk brn	dbl surch (vc)	14.00	14.00
PAN144	C20a	(1936)	5c on 50c org	dbl surch (vc)	60.00	60.00
PAN145	C27a	(1937)	5c blue (R)	invtd ovpt (vc)	35.00	—
PAN146	C29a		20c red (bl)	dbl ovpt (vc)	35.00	—
PAN147	C31a		50c car rose (bl)	dbl ovpt (vc)	120.00	—
PAN148	C38a		10c on 50c blk	invtd surch (vc)	20.00	—
PAN149	C39a		5c dark blue	dbl ovpt (vc)	18.00	—
PAN150	C53Ac	(1938)	7c on 30c dp vio	dbl surch (vc)	18.00	—
PAN151	C53Ad			invtd surch (vc)	27.50	—
PAN152	C53B		8c on 15c dp grn	invtd surch (vc)	22.50	
PAN153	C63a	(1940)	5c on 15c lt ultra	"7 AEREO 7" on 15c	40.00	40.00
PAN154	C82a	(1947)	5c on 8c gray blk	dbl ovpt (vc)	25.00	
PAN155	C84a		5c on 7c rose car (bk)	dbl surch (vc)	NA	
PAN156	C86a		10c on 15c dk vio	dbl surch (vc)	30.00	30.00
PAN157	C107a		10c purple & blk	invtd ovpt (vc)	50.00	—
PAN158	C108a	(1949)	2c carmine	dbl ovpt (vc)	5.00	—
PAN159	C114a		2c carmine	invtd ovpt (vc)	14.00	—
PAN160	C114b			dbl ovpt (vc)	14.00	—
PAN161	C115a		5c orange (G)	invtd ovpt (vc)	8.00	—
PAN162	C115b			dbl ovpt (vc)	20.00	—
PAN163	C115c			dbl ovpt, one invtd	20.00	—
PAN164	C127a	(1952)	2c on 10c	pair, one without surch	NA	—
PAN165	C128b		5c on 10c (O)	pair, one without surch	NA	—
PAN166	C129a		5c on 2c ver & blk	invtd surch (vc)	22.50	—
PAN167	E1a	(1926)	10c org & blk	"EXRPESO"	40.00	—
PAN168	E2a		20c brn & blk	"EXRPESO"	40.00	—
PAN169	E2b			dbl ovpt (vc)	35.00	35.00
PAN170	F29a	(1916-17)	5c pm 8c pur & blk	"5" invtd,	55.00	—
PAN171	F29b			large round "5,"	50.00	—
PAN172	F29c			invtd surch (vc)	12.50	11.00
PAN173	F29d			tete beche surch	—	—
PAN174	F30a	(1917)	5c on 8c vio & blk	invtd surch (vc)	10.00	8.25
PAN175	F30b			tete beche surch	—	
PAN176	F30c			dbl surch (vc)	—	40.00
PAN177	H23a		1/2 c red orange	"R.A." for "A.R."	50.00	—
PAN178	H23b			dbl ovpt (vc)	8.00	—
PAN179	H23c			invtd ovpt (vc)	8.00	—
PAN180	16a	(1917)	1c on 1/2c orange	"UN CENTESIMO" invtd,	50.00	—
PAN181	16b			dbl surch (vc)	10.00	—

PAN139

PAN161

PAR78

PAN182	16c			invtd surch (vc)	6.50	6.50
PAN183	RA28a		1c on 5c	invtd surch (vc)	10.00	—
PAN184	RA41a	(1961)	1c on 10c emerald	invtd surch (vc)	—	—

Weep no more my sons
For a lack of vc's
They're here, they're there, they're everywhere
On land, in air, by sea
Air errors are especially strong
Why this is true nobody can see. —The Bard

PAPUA NEW GUINEA

PAP1	19a	(1907)	1/2p yellow green	dbl ovpt (vc)	NA	
PAP2	20a		1p carmine	vertical ovpt, up (vc)	NA	
PAP3	22a		2-1/2p ultra	dbl ovpt (vc)		
PAP4	24a		6p dk green	dbl ovpt (vc)	NA	—
PAP5	25a		1sh orange	dbl ovpt (vc)	NA	
PAP6	26b		2 shop brown	vert ovpt, down	NA	
PAP7	26d			dbl horizontal, ovpt	—	NA
PAP8	C1b	(1929)	3p blue grn & dk gray	vert pair, one without ovpt	NA	—
PAP9	C1c			horiz pair, one without ovpt	NA	
PAP10	C1d		3p blue grn & sepia black		50.00	62.50
PAP11	C1e			ovpt on back, vert	NA	
PAP12	C2b	(1936)	3p blue grn & blk	dbl ovpt (vc)	NA	
PAP13	C4a		1sh ol green & ol brn	invtd ovpt (vc)	NA	—
PAP14	J2a	(1960)	3p on 1/2p (bl)	dbl surch (vc)	NA	
PAP15	J3a		6p on 7-1/2p (R)	dbl surch (vc)	NA	
PAP16	J6a		6p on 7-1/2p	dbl surch (vc)	NA	

PARAGUAY

PAR1	47a	(1896)	5c on 2c brown & gray	invtd surch (vc)	10.00	10.00
PAR2	48a		5c on 4c yellow & gray	invtd surch (vc)	7.50	7.50
PAR3	49a	(1899)	10c on 15c org	invtd surch (vc)	14.00	14.00
PAR4	49b			dbl surch (vc)	9.00	9.00
PAR5	69a	(1902)	20c on 24c dp blue	invtd surch (vc)	6.25	—
PAR6	73a	(1903)	1c on 1p slate	no period after "cent"	1.65	1.50
PAR7	74a		5c on 8c gray brown	no period after "cent"	.90	.75
PAR8	74b			dbl surch (vc)	3.50	3.00
PAR9	76a		5c on 28c orange	no period after "cent"	.90	.75
PAR10	76b			comma after "cent"	.38	.30
PAR11	129a	(1907)	5c on vermillion	"5," omitted	1.00	1.00
PAR12	129b			invtd surch (vc)	1.25	1.25
PAR13	129c			dbl surch (vc)	—	
PAR14	129d			dbl surch, one invtd	1.00	1.00
PAR15	129e			dbl surch, both invtd	6.00	6.00
PAR16	130a		5c on 2c olive grn	"5," omitted	1.00	1.00
PAR17	130b			invtd surch (vc)	1.00	1.00
PAR18	130c			dbl surch (vc)	2.00	2.00
PAR19	130d			bar omitted	2.00	2.00
PAR20	131a	(1908)	5c on 10c bister	dbl surch (vc)	3.00	3.00
PAR21	132a		5c on 10c violet	invtd surch (vc)	1.50	1.50
PAR22	134a		5c on 20c violet	invtd surch (vc)	1.50	1.50
PAR23	136a		5c on 30c turq bl	invtd surch (vc)	—	—
PAR24	136b			dbl surch (vc)	6.00	6.00
PAR25	137a		5c on 60c choc	dbl surch (vc)	6.00	6.00
PAR26	138a		5c on 60c red brown	invtd surch (vc)	.38	.38
PAR27	140a		5c on 60c purple	dbl surch (vc)	2.50	2.50
PAR28	141a		5c deep blue	invtd ovpt (vc)	1.50	1.50
PAR29	141b			bar omitted	4.50	4.50
PAR30	141c			dbl ovpt (vc)	2.00	2.00
PAR31	142a		5c slate blue	invtd ovpt (vc)	1.25	1.25
PAR32	142b			dbl ovpt (vc)	1.75	1.75
PAR33	142c			bar omitted	4.50	4.50

PAR34	143a		5c greenish blue	invtd ovpt (vc)	1.25	1.25
PAR35	143b			bar omitted	3.75	3.75
PAR36	144a		1p brown org & blk	dbl ovpt (vc)	1.00	1.00
PAR37	144b			dbl ovpt, one invtd	1.25	1.25
PAR38	144c			triple ovpt, two invtd	2.25	2.25
PAR39	145a		1p brt rose & blk	bar omitted	—	—
PAR40	149a	(1908)	5c on 1c grnsh bl	invtd surch (vc)	.50	.50
PAR41	149b			dbl surch (vc)	.75	.75
PAR42	149c			"51," omitted	1.50	1.50
PAR43	147a		5c on 2c car rose	invtd surch (vc)	.50	.50
PAR44	147b			"5,"	1.25	1.25
PAR45	147c			dbl surch (vc)	—	—
PAR46	147d			dbl surch, one invtd	—	—
PAR47	148a		5c on 60c org brn	invtd surch (vc)	.75	.75
PAR48	148b			"5," omitted	1.00	1.00
PAR49	149a		5c on 60c sal pink	dbl surch (vc)	.50	.50
PAR50	149b			dbl surch, one invtd	3.50	3.50
PAR51	150a		5c on 60c choc	invtd surch (vc)	1.25	1.25
PAR52	151a		20c on 1c grnsh bl	invtd surch (vc)	1.50	1.50
PAR53	153a		20c on 2c car rose	invtd surch (vc)	12.50	
PAR54	154a		20c on 30c dl lil	invtd surch (vc)	1.50	1.50
PAR55	154b			dbl surch (vc)	—	—
PAR56	157a		5c on 40c dk bl	invtd surch (vc)	1.50	1.50
PAR57	158a		5c on 10c emerald	dbl surch (vc)	—	—
PAR58	159a		5c on 10c red lil	dbl surch (vc0	2.00	2.00
PAR59	159b			"5." omitted	1.50	1.50
PAR60	160a		5c on 20c bis	dbl surch (vc)	1.25	1.25
PAR61	161a		5c on 20c sal pink	"5," omitted	1.75	1.75
PAR62	163a		5c on 30c yel	"5,"omitted	1.50	1.50
PAR63	163b			invtd surch (vc)	1.25	1.25

PAR83

PAR84

PAR85

PAR86

PAR87

PAR88

PAR89

PAR90

PAR64	164a		5c on 60c org brn	dbl surch (vc)	5.00	5.00
PAR65	165a		5c on 60c dp ultra	invtd surch (vc)	2.50	2.50
PAR66	165b			"5," omitted	1.50	—
PAR67	166a		20c on 5c blue	invtd surch (vc)	3.00	3.00
PAR68	167a	(1908)	20c on 2c car	invtd surch (vc)	7.50	—
PAR69	170Ab		20c on 5c blue	invtd surch (vc)	8.75	8.75
PAR70	208a	(1912)	20c on 50c car rose	invtd surch (vc)	1.00	1.00
PAR71	208b			dbl surch (vc)	1.00	1.00
PAR72	208c			bar omitted	1.75	1.75
PAR73	229a	(1920)	1p yellow brown	invtd surch (vc)	.65	.65
PAR74	229e			"AABILITADO"	.75	.75
PAR75	229f			"1929," for "1920,"	.75	.75
PAR76	229g			ovpt lines 8mm apart	.20	.15
PAR77	243b		50c car & dk blue	center invtd (u)	10.00	10.00
PAR78	244b			center invtd (u)	12.50	12.50
PAR79	L23a	(1927-39)	1.50p brown	dbl ovpt (vc)	1.50	—
PAR80	O6a	(1886)	15c slate blue	wavy lines on face of stamp	—	—
PAR81	O6b			"OFICIAL" omitted	1.25	—
PAR82	O49a		1p olive grn	invtd ovpt (vc)	10.00	—
PAR85	430					

See Photo in Color Section
PAR89   C272
See Photo in Color Section

PENRHYN ISLAND

PEN1	1a	(1902)	1/2p green	no period after "ISLAND"	90.00	100.00
PEN2	5a		1/2p green	no period after "ISLAND"	60.00	65.00
PEN3	6a		1p carmine (bl)	no period after "ISLAND"	37.50	40.00
PEN4	8a		2-1/2p blue	"1/2," & "PENI" 2mm apart	10.50	16.00
PEN5	9a		2-1/2p blue	"1/2," & "PENI" 2mm apart	10.50	16.00
PEN6	13a	(1914-15)	1/2p yellow grn	no period after "ISLAND"	32.50	50.00
PEN7	13b			no period after "PENI"	75.00	90.00
PEN8	14a	(1915)	1/2p yel grn	no period after "ISLAND"	16.00	22.50
PEN9	14b			no period after "PENI"	37.50	50.00
PEN10	25a	(1920)	1/2p emerald & blk	center invtd (u)	NA	—
PEN11	26a		1p red & black	center invtd (u)	NA	—

PERU

PER1	9B	(1860-61)	1d blue	cornucopia on white ground	NA	47.50
PER2	9c			zigzag lines broken at angles	125.00	14.00
PER3	10b		1p rose	cornucopia on white ground	NA	22.50

PAR91

PAR92

PAR93

PER55

PER80A

PAR94

PER4	14a	(1868-72)	1d green	arms embossed	invtd	NA
PER5	32a	(1880)	1c green	invtd ovpt (vc)	10.00	10.00
PER6	32b			dbl ovpt (vc)	13.50	13.50
PER7	33a		2c rose (bl)	invtd ovpt (vc)	10.00	10.00
PER8	33b			dbl ovpt (vc)	14.00	12.00
PER9	34a		2c rose (bk)	invtd ovpt (vc)	—	—
PER10	34b			dbl ovpt (vc)		
PER11	35a		5c ultra	invtd ovpt (vc)	10.00	10.00
PER12	35b			dbl ovpt (vc)	14.00	14.00
PER13	36a		50c green	invtd ovpt (vc)	45.00	45.00
PER14	37a		1s rose (bl)	invtd ovpt (vc)	110.00	110.00
PER15	37b			dbl ovpt (vc)	110.00	110.00
PER16	38a	(1881)	1c green	invtd ovpt (vc)	8.25	8.25
PER17	38b			dbl ovpt (vc)	14.00	14.00
PER18	39a		2c rose (bl)	invtd ovpt (vc)	17.50	15.00
PER19	39b			dbl ovpt (vc)	25.00	20.00
PER20	40a		5c ultra (red)	invtd ovpt (vc)	14.00	14.00
PER21	40b			dbl ovpt	20.00	20.00
PER22	41a		50c green(red)	invtd ovpt (vc)	NA	
PER23	42a		1s rose (bl)	invtd ovpt (vc)	150.00	—
PER24	80a	(1883)	1c grn (red & blk)	oval ovpt invtd	—	—
PER25	80b			dbl ovpt of oval	—	—
PER26	86a		1c grn (bk & bk)	horseshoe invtd	10.00	—
PER27	96a		2c vermillion	dbl ovpt (vc)	—	—
PER28	103a	(1884)	5c blue	dbl ovpt (vc)	5.00	5.00
PER29	116a		1c green	horseshoe invtd	7.50	—
PER30	118a		1c orange	invtd ovpt (vc)	7.00	7.00
PER31	118b			dbl ovpt (vc)	7.00	7.00
PER32	119a		1c green	invtd ovpt (vc)	3.50	3.50
PER33	119b			dbl invtd ovpt	5.00	5.00
PER34	120b		2c violet	invtd ovpt (vc)	7.00	7.00
PER35	120c			dbl ovpt (vc)	7.00	—
PER36	121a		2c rose	dbl ovpt (vc)	7.00	7.00
PER37	121b			invtd ovpt (vc)	7.00	7.00
PER38	122Ab		5c ulltra	invtd ovpt (vc)	10.00	10.00
PER39	123a		10c green	invtd ovpt (vc)	7.00	7.00
PER40	124a		50c green	invtd ovpt (vc)	10.00	10.00
PER41	125a		2c vermillion	head invtd	2.50	2.50
PER42	125b			head dbl	5.00	5.00
PER43	126a		5c blue	head invtd	7.00	7.00
PER44	127a		50c rose	head dbl	55.00	45.00
PER45	128a		1s ultra	both ovpts invtd	125.00	110.00
PER46	128b			head dbl	125.00	110.00
PER47	157a	(1897)	1c bister	invtd ovpt (vc)	2.50	2.50
PER48	157b			dbl ovpt (vc)	10.00	10.00
PER49	166a	(1907)	1c on 12c (red)	invtd surch (vc)	8.00	8.00
PER50	166b			dbl surch (vc)	8.00	8.00
PER51	167a		2c on 12c (vc)	dbl surch (vc)	8.00	8.00
PER52	167b			invtd surch (vc)	8.00	8.00
PER53	187a	(1915)	1c on 1c	invtd surch (vc)	22.50	18.00
PER54	189a		2c on 12c	invtd surch (vc)	—	—

PER80B

PHI8

PER55	192a		1c on 4c	invtd surch (vc)	6.00	6.00
PER56	193a		1c on 10c	invtd surch (vc)	2.50	2.50
PER57	196a	(1916)	1c on 12c (red)	dbl surch (vc)	2.00	2.00
PER58	196b			green surch (vc)	4.50	4.50
PER59	198a		1c on 50c(grn)	invtd surch (vc)	2.00	2.00
PER60	200a		10c on 1c (grn)	"VALF"	3.50	3.50
PER61	208a	(1917)	1c on 4c ver	dbl surch (vc)	4.00	4.00
PER62	208b			invtd surch (vc)	4.00	4.00
PER63	220b	(1919)	5c bl & blk	center invtd (u)	11.00	11.00
See Photo in Color Section						
PER64	221b		5c brn & blk	center invtd (u)	11.00	11.00
PER65	222a	(1921)	1c ol brn & red brn	center invtd (u)	NA	
PER66	233a	(1923-24)		invtd surch (vc)	5.00	5.00
PER67	233b			dbl surch, one invtd (vc)	6.00	6.00
PER68	252a	(1925)	2c on 20c blue	invtd surch (vc)	35.00	35.00
PER69	252b			dbl surch, one invtd (vc)	50.00	50.00
PER70	253a		10c org red	invtd ovpt (vc)	17.50	17.50
PER71	257a		15c on 20c yellow	invtd surch (vc)	7.50	7.50
PER72	261a	(1930)	2c dk violet	invtd surch (vc)	2.50	2.50
PER73	263a		2c on 50c dk grn	"Habitada"	1.00	1.00
PER74	268a	(1930)	10c orange red (bk)	invtd ovpt (vc)	10.00	10.00
PER75	268b			without ovpt (vc)	6.50	6.50
PER76	268c			dbl surch (vc)	5.00	5.00
PER77	269a		2c on 10c org red	invtd surch (vc)	12.00	—
PER78	270a		4c on 10c org red	dbl surch (vc)	8.25	8.25
PER79	271a		15c on 10c org red	invtd surch (vc)	10.00	10.00
PER80	271b			dbl surch (vc)	10.00	10.00
PER81	388a	(1940)	5c on 10c scarlet	invtd surch (vc)	—	—
PER82	J7a	(1881)	5c ver (bl)	dbl ovpt (vc)	—	—
PER83	J7b			invtd ovpt (vc)	17.00	17.00
PER84	J8a		10c org (bl)	invtd ovpt (vc)	17.00	17.00
PER85	J28a	(1896-97)	1c bister	dbl ovpt (vc)	—	—
PER86	J29a		5c vermillion	dbl ovpt (vc)	—	—
PER87	J29b			invtd ovpt (vc)	—	—
PER88	J30a		10c orange	invtd ovpt (vc)	—	—
PER89	J31a		20c blue	dbl ovpt (vc)	—	—
PER90	J33a	(1896)	1s brn	dbl ovpt (vc)	—	—
PER91	J33b			invtd ovpt (vc)	—	—
PER92	J36a	(1902)	5c on 10s bl grn	dbl surch (vc)	—	—
PER93	J37a		1c on 20c blue	"DEFICIT" omitted	6.50	2.00
PER94	J37b			"DEFICIT" dble	6.50	2.00
PER95	J37c			"UN CENTAVO" dble	6.00	2.00
PER96	J37d			"UN CENTAVO" omitted	8.25	6.00
PER97	O2a	(1890)	1c dl vio	dbl ovpt (vc)	8.25	8.25
PER98	O3a			invtd ovpt (vc)	—	—
PER99	O3b			invtd ovpt (vc)	8.25	8.25
PER100	O4a		5c orange	invtd ovpt (vc)	8.25	8.25
PER101	O4a			dbl ovpt (vc)	8.25	8.25
PER102	O5a		10c slate	dbl ovpt (vc)	8.25	8.25
PER103	O5b			invtd ovpt (vc)	8.25	8.25
PER104	O6a		20c blue	dbl ovpt (vc)	8.25	8.25
PER105	O6b			invtd ovpt (vc)	8.25	8.25
PER106	O7a		50c red	invtd ovpt (vc)	12.00	—
PER107	O7b			dbl ovpt (vc)	—	—
PER108	O8a		1s brown	dbl ovpt (vc)	17.00	17.00
PER109	O8b			invtd ovpt (vc)	17.00	17.00
PER110	O9a	(1894)	1c green	"Goblerno" and head invtd	6.50	5.50
PER111	O9b			dbl ovpt of "Goblerno"	—	—
PER112	O11a		2c rose	ovpt head invtd	10.00	10.00
PER113	O11b			both ovpts invtd	—	—
PER114	O12a		2c violet	"Golerno" dbl	—	—
PER115	O13a		5c ultra	both ovpts invtd	—	—

PER116	O24a	(1896-1901)	10c yellow	dbl ovpt (vc)	—	—
PER117	Q9a	(1903-04)	5c on 10c vio brn	invtd surch (vc)	120.00	110.00
PER118	Q9b			dbl surch (vc)		
PER119	RA14a	(1931)	2c on 4c red	invtd surch (vc)	3.50	3.50
PER120	RA15a		2c on 10c bl grn	invtd surch (vc)	3.50	3.50
PER121	RA16a		2c on 15c sl gray	invtd surch (vc)	3.50	3.50
PER122	RA27a	(1936)	2c brn vio	dbl ovpt	1.40	—
PER123	RA27b			ovpt reading down	1.40	—
PER124	RA27c			ovpt dbl, reading down	1.40	—
PER125	N11a	(1881-82)	1c org (bl)	invtd ovpt (vc)		
PER126	N12a		2c dk vio (bk)	invtd ovpt (vc)	16.50	—
PER127	N12b			dbl ovpt (vc)	22.50	—
PER128	N13a		2c rose (bk)	invtd ovpt (vc)		
PER129	N14a		5c bl (R)	invtd ovpt (vc)	—	—
PER130	N16a		10c grn (r)	invtd ovpt (vc)	6.50	6.50
PER131	N16b			dbl ovpt (vc)	12.00	12.00
PER132	N19a	(1882)	1c grn (r)	arms invtd	8.25	10.00
PER133	N19b			arms dbl	5.50	6.50
PER134	N19c			horseshoe invtd	12.00	13.50
PER135	N20a		5c bl (r)	arms invtd	13.50	15.00
PER136	N20b			arms dbl	13.50	15.00
PER137	N21b		50c rose (bk)	arms invtd	10.00	—
PER138	N23a		1s ultra (r)	arms invtd	13.50	—
PER139	N23b			horseshoe invtd	16.50	—
PER140	N23c			arms & horseshoe invtd	20.00	—
PER141	N23d			arms dbl	13.50	—
PER142	3N1b	(1881)	10c blue	dbl ovpt (vc)	12.00	13.50
PER143	3N1c			ovpt on back of stamp	8.25	10.00
PER144	3N2a		25c rose	"2," in upper left corner invtd	8.25	—
PER145	3N2b			"Cevtavos"	8.25	10.00
PER146	3n2c			dbl ovpt (vc)	12.00	13.50

Who is who in Peru
Is it me or is it you
Not a one for error is King
The praises of inverted center sing
Even though the lowly typo's ring
All for one and one for all
Peru's the lively error ball. —The Bard

PHILIPPINES

PHI1	4c	(1854)	1r slate blue	"CORROS"	NA	
PHI2	72a	(1879)	2c on 25m grn	dbl surch (vc)	—	—
PHI3	72b			invtd surch (vc)	NA	150.00
PHI4	73a		8c on 100m car	"COREROS"	82.50	50.00
PHI5	213a	(1899-1900)	1c yellow grn	invtd ovpt (vc)	NA	
PHI6	216a		5c blue	invtd ovpt (vc)	—	NA
PHI7	321c	(1926)	16c olive grn & blk	dbl impression of center	NA	
PHI8	322a		18c lt brown & blk	dbl impression of center	NA	
PHI9	EO1a	(1931)	20c dull violet	no period after "B"	20.00	15.00
PHI10	EO1b			dbl ovpt (vc)	—	—
PHI11	O5a	(1931)	2c green	no period after "B"	15.00	5.00
PHI12	O5b			no period after "O"		
PHI13	O6a		4c carmine	no period after "B"	15.00	5.00
PHI14	O10a		12c red orange	no period after "B"	32.50	—
PHI15	O12a		20c orange yel	no period after "B"	22.50	15.00
PHI16	O25a	(1937-38)	2c rose	no period after "B"	4.25	2.25
PHI17	O27a	(1938-40)	2c rose	hyphen omitted	20.00	20.00
PHI18	O27b			no period after "B"	25.00	25.00
PHI19	O31a		10c rose car	no period after "O"	30.00	30.00
PHI20	O50a	(1948)	4c black brown	invtd ovpt (vc)	25.00	—

PHI21	O50b		dbl ovpt (vc)	25.00	—
PHI22	N1a	(1942-43) 2c apple green	pair, one without ovpt	—	—
PHI22	N4a	5c on 6c golden brown	top bar shorter, thinner	.20	.20
PHI23	N4b	5(c) on 6c dk brn		.20	.20
PHI24	N4c		as "b" top bar shorter & thinner	—	—
PHI25	N6a	(1943) 50c on 1p	dbl surch (vc)	—	NA
PHI26	N28a	12c on 20c lt ol grn	dbl surch (vc)	—	—
PHI27	NO1a	2c apple green	dbl ovpt (vc)	NA	—
PHI28	NO3a	(1944) 5(c) on 6c golden brn	narrower spacing between bars	.15	.15
PHI29	NO3b	5(c) on 6c dk brn		.15	.15
PHI30	NO3c		as "b" narrower spacing between bars		
PHI31	NO3d		dbl ovpt (vc)	—	—
PHI32	NO4a	16c on 30c org red	wider spacing between bars	.30	.30

PITCAIRN ISLAND

PIT1	45a	(1964-65) 8p multicolored	gray beak omitted	100.00	—
PIT2	72a	(1967) 1/2c on 1/2p	brown omitted	—	NA
PIT3	78a	10c on 8p	"10c," omitted	NA	—
PIT4	105a	(1969) 15c gold & multi gold	Queen's head omitted	NA	—

POLAND

POL1	11a	(1918) 5f on 2gr brn & buff	invtd surch (vc)	37.50	32.50
POL2	12a	10f on 6gr grn & buff	invtd surch (vc)	4.50	4.00
POL3	13a	25f on 10gr rose & buff	invtd surch (vc)	9.00	8.00
POL4	14a	50f on 20gr bl & buff	invtd surch (vc)	130.00	100.00
POL5	27a	(1918) 10h gray green	invtd ovpt (vc)	17.50	19.00
POL6	28a	20h magenta	invtd ovpt (vc)	17.50	19.00
POL7	29a	45h blue	invtd ovpt (vc)	17.50	19.00
POL8	30a	(1918-19) 3hal on 3h ol gray	invtd surch (vc)	NA	
POL9	31a	3hal on 15h brt rose	invtd surch (vc)	20.00	20.00
POL10	32a	10h on 30h sl grn	invtd surch (vc)	20.00	20.00
POL11	32b		brown surch (error)	60.00	50.00
POL12	34a	25hal on 40h ol bis	invtd surch (vc)	30.00	30.00
POL13	35a	45hal on 60h rose	invtd surch (vc)	20.00	20.00
POL14	36a	45hal on 80h lt blue	invtd surch (vc)	30.00	30.00
POL15	37a	50hal on 60h rose	invtd surch (vc)	20.00	20.00

POL4A

POL46A

POL47A

POL47B

POL47C

POL50B

POL52

POL16	38a		45hal on 80h lt blue	invtd surch (vc)	20.00	20.00
POL17	39a		50hal on 80h lt blue	invtd surch (vc)	20.00	20.00
POL18	40a		90h dark violet	invtd ovpt (vc)	20.00	20.00
POL19	43a	(1919)	6h deep orange	invtd ovpt (vc)	NA	—
POL20	46a		40h olive green	invtd ovpt (vc)	100.00	100.00
POL21	46b			dbl ovpt (vc)	NA	
POL22	47a		50h blue green	invtd ovpt (vc)	—	NA
POL23	48a		60h deep blue	invtd ovpt (vc)	100.00	75.00
POL24	49a		80h orange brown	invtd ovpt (vc)	100.00	100.00
POL25	49b			dbl ovpt (vc)	125.00	125.00
POL26	60a	(1919)	25h on 80h org brn	invtd surch (vc)	60.00	60.00
POL27	73a		5pf on 7-1/2pf org	invtd surch (vc)	100.00	—
POL28	111		5pf on 2pf (r)	invtd surch (vc)	NA	—
See Photo in Color Section						
POL29	153a	(1921)	3m on 40f brt vio	dbl surch (vc)	20.00	20.00
POL30	153b			invtd surch (vc)	20.00	20.00
POL31	158a		4m red	4m carmine rose (error)	200.00	—
POL32	193a	(1923)	3000m brown	"Konapski" 9.00	9.00	
POL33	195a		10000m on 25m	dbl surch (vc)	5.00	
POL34	195b			invtd surch (vc)	7.50	—
POL35	196a		25000m on 20m red	dbl surch (vc)	5.00	5.00
POL36	196b			invtd surch (vc)	10.00	—
POL37	197a		50000m on 10m grnsh bl	dbl surch (vc)	5.00	5.00
POL38	197b			invtd surch (vc)	7.50	7.50
POL39	198a		25000m on 20m carmine	dbl surch (vc)	5.00	5.00
POL40	198b			invtd surch (vc)	7.50	—
POL41	199a	(1924)	20000m on 2m gray grn	invtd surch (vc)	7.50	7.50
POL42	199b			dbl surch (vc)	5.00	5.00
POL43	200a		100000m on 5m red brn	dbl surch (vc)	5.00	5.00
POL44	200b			invtd surch (vc)	7.50	7.50
POL45	286a	(1934)	1z on 1.20z indigo (r)	figure "1," in surch 5mm high instead of 4-1/2mm	20.00	20.00
POL46	751a		20g lt brn & pale violet	center invtd (u)	—	—
POL47	C13a	(1946)	5z grnsh blk	without control number	4.00	.40
POL48	J3a		15h rose red	invtd ovpt (vc)	150.00	—
POL49	J10a		10k ultra (r)	blk ovpt (vc)	NA	—
POL50	J12a	(1919)	50h on 42h choc	dbl surch (vc)	—	NA

Poland, Polska, see the millions of vc´s
You´re not going to see much else from this country
Poland vc Polska, it gets to be a bore
Poland vc Polska, the eyes soon get sore. —The Bard

POR11

POR13

POR23A

POR20A

POR27

POR28

PONTA DELGADA has produced no errors

PORTUGAL

POR1	79a	(1892)	5r gray blk	dbl surch (vc)	NA	
POR2	80a		10r green	invtd ovpt (vc)	—	—
POR3	80b			dbl ovpt (vc)	NA	
POR4	82a	(1892-93)	10r green (r)	invtd ovpt (vc)	165.00	100.00
POR5	83a		20r rose	invtd ovpt (vc)	NA	200.00
POR6	89a		(10r green (r)	"1938,"	NA	160.00
POR7	89b			"1863,"	175.00	175.00
POR8	89c			"1838,"	NA	160.00
POR9	90a		20r rose	invtd ovpt (vc)	110.00	65.00
POR10	90b			"1938,"	NA	175.00
POR11	92a		25r lilac rose	invtd ovpt	NA	165.00
POR12	185a	(1911)	2-1/2r blue green	invtd ovpt (vc)	10.00	6.00
POR13	186a		15r on 5r red	invtd surch (vc)	10.00	6.00
POR14	188a		50r dark blue	invtd ovpt (vc)	—	—
POR15	191a		100r bister brn	invtd ovpt (vc)	25.00	25.00
POR16	193a		5r black	dbl ovpt, one invtd	16.00	16.00
POR17	198a		500r on 100r car, pink	invtd surch (vc)	60.00	60.00
POR18	199a		2-1/2r blue grn	dbl ovpt (vc)	—	—
POR19	200a		15r on 5r red	invtd surch (vc)	12.50	12.50
POR20	202a		50r dk blue	invtd surch (vc)	—	—
POR21	203a		75r violet brn	invtd ovpt (vc)	—	—
POR22	204a		80r on 150r bis	invtd surch (vc)	—	—
POR23	205a		100r bist brn	invtd ovpt (vc)	75.00	75.00
POR24	341a	(1924)	3e dk bl, bl	value double	60.00	
POR25	341b			value omitted	—	—
POR26	350a	(1925)	6c brown vio	"6," & "C" omitted	—	—
POR27	455a	(1928-29)	10c on 1/4c dk olive	invtd surch (vc)	5.00	—
POR28	495a	(1929)	1.60e brt blue	dbl ovpt (vc)	—	—
POR29	536a	(1931)	40c orange	value omitted	120.00	120.00
POR20	539a		4.50e choc & lt grn	value omitted	NA	
POR21	841a	(1958)	1.50e bis, blk, bl & dk bis brn	dark bister brown omitted	—	—
POR22	885a	(1962)	20c gray, bis, yel & blk	dbl impression of gray frame lettering	—	—
POR23	909a	(1963)	20c lt blue & ultra	gold inscriptions omitted	55.00	
POR24	911a	(1963)	2.80e green & slate	gold inscription omitted	65.00	—
POR25	J1a	(1898)	5r black value	"Continente" omitted	10.00	5.00
POR26	IS3a		rose & black	invtd ovpt (vc)	150.00	150.00

POR29

POR30

POR31

PRG19

PRI83

PRI85

Azores has produced no errors

Portuguese Congo

PCO1	42a	(1902)	130r on 5r yellow	invtd surch (vc)		27.50	27.50
PCO2	44a		130r on 100r brn, yel	invtd surch (vc)		40.00	35.00
PCO3	48a		115r on 2-1/2r brn	invtd surch (vc)		25.00	25.00
PCO4	56a	(1911)	10r lt green	"REPUBLICA" invtd		17.50	17.50
PCO5	57a		15r gray green	"REPUBLICA" invtd		17.50	17.50
PCO6	58a		25r on 200r red vio pnksh	"REPBLICA" invtd		17.50	17.50
PCO7	58b			"CONGO" dbl		17.50	17.50
PCO8	60a		2-1/2r gray	invtd ovpt (vc)		15.00	11.00
PCO9	65a		25r car rose	invtd ovpt (vc)		17.50	13.00
PCO10	89a		10c on 100r bis brn	invtd surch (vc)		22.50	22.50
PCO11	95a		5c on 8a dk blue	dbl surch (vc)		22.50	22.50

Portuguese Guinea

PRG1	4a	(1881)	40r blue	cliche of Mozambique in Cape Verde plate		NA	
PRG2	12a	(1885)	20r rose	dbl ovpt (vc)		—	—
PRG3	14a		25r violet	dbl ovpt (vc)		—	—
PRG4	15a		40r blue	cliche of Mozambique in Cape Verde plate		NA	
PRG5	16a		40r yellow	as 15a		27.50	25.00
PRG6	16d			dbl ovpt (vc)		—	—
PRG7	18a		50r blue	dbl ovpt (vc)		—	—
PRG8	19a		100r lilac	invtd ovpt (vc)		—	—
PRG9	81a	(1902)	115r on 5r yel	invtd surch (vc)		40.00	45.00
PRG10	95a	(1911)	2-1/2r gray	invtd ovpt (vc)		17.50	17.50
PRG11	100a		25r carmine	dbl ovpt (vc)		14.00	14.00
PRG12	111a	(1913)	75r lilac	invtd ovpt (vc)		—	—
PRG13	112a		100r bl	bl invtd ovpt (vc)		—	—
PRG14	113a		200r red lil	pnksh invtd ovpt (vc)		—	—
PRG15	114a		15r brown	"REPUBLICA" double		—	—
PRG16	114b			"REPUBLICA" invtd		27.50	27.50
PRG17	115a		75r rose	"REPUBLICA" invtd			
PRG18	122a		10c on 16a bis brn	invtd surch (vc)		27.50	27.50
PRG19	189b	(1915)	115r on 2-1/2r brn	invtd ovpt (vc)		20.00	20.00

Portuguese India

PRI1	11a	(1872)	20r vermillion	"20," omitted		—	NA
PRI2	16a		600r red violet	"600," double		NA	
PRI3	20a		40r blue	"40,"double		NA	—
PRI4	20b			tete beche pair		NA	
PRI5	21a		100r green	"100," dbl Na		—	
PRI6	24a		10r black	"1,l" invtd		150.00	125.00

PRI86

PRI87

PRI88

PRI89

PRI90

PRI91

PRI7	24b			"10," double	NA	—
PRI8	25a		20r vermillion	"20," dbl	NA	—
PRI9	25b			"20," invtd	—	—
PRI10	26a		300r dp violet	"300," double	NA	—
PRI11	27a		600r dp violet	"600," double	NA	—
PRI12	27b			"600," invtd	NA	—
PRI13	28a		900r dp violet	"900," double	NA	—
PRI14	28b			"900," triple	NA	
PRI15	30a	(1874)	20r vermillion	"20," double	—	NA
PRI16	32a	(1875)	15re rose	"15," invtd	NA	—
PRI17	32b			"15,"double	—	—
PRI18	33a		20r vermillion	"O," missing	NA	—
PRI19	33b			"20," sideways	NA	—
PRI20	33c			"20," double	—	—
PRI21	35a	(18876)	20r vermillion	"20," double	—	—
PRI22	36a		10r black	dbl impression	—	—
PRI23	36b			"10," double	NA	—
PRI24			15r rose	"15," omitted	NA	—
PRI25	42a		300r violet	"300," omitted	—	—
PRI26	47a	(1877)	10r black	"10," omitted	—	—
PRI27	50a		40r blue	"100," omitted	—	—
PRI28	51a		100r green	"100," omitted	—	—
PRI29	74a	(1881)	1-1/2r on 20r	invtd surch(vc)	—	—
PRI30	78a		5r on 15r	dbl surch (vc)	—	—
PRI31	78b			invtd surch (vc)	—	—
PRI32	79a		5r on 20r	dbl surch (vc)	—	—
PRI33	79b			invtd surch (vc)	—	—
PRI34	80a		5r on 20r	dbl surch (vc)	—	—
PRI35	80b			invtd surch (vc)	—	—
PRI36	81a		5r on 20r	dbl surch (vc)	—	—
PRI37	81b			invtd surch (vc)	—	—
PRI38	86a		5r on 10r	dbl surch (vc)	—	—
PRI39	87a		5r on 10r	invtd surch (vc)	—	—
PRI40	88a		5r on 10r	invtd surch (vc)	—	—
PRI41	90a		5r on 10r	invtd surch (vc)	—	—
PRI42	90b			dbl surch (vc)	—	—
PRI43	113a	(1881-82)	1-1/2r on 5r blk	additional surch "4-1/2," in blue	75.00	60.00
PRI44	114a		1-1/2r on 10r grn	additional surch "6,"	100.00	80.00
PRI45	115a		1-1/2r on 20r bis	invtd surch (vc)	—	—
PRI46	115b			dbl surch (vc)	—	—
PRI47	115c			pair, one without surch	—	—
PRI48	119a		4-1/2r on 20r bis	invtd surch (vc)	—	—
PRI49	131a		1t on 10r grn	with additional surch "6,"	—	—
PRI50	140a		2t on 25r slate	small "T"	50.00	35.00
PRI51	144a		2t on 50r grn	invtd surch (vc)	—	—
PRI52	149a		4t on 10r grn	invtd surch (vc)	—	—
PRI53	150a		4t on 50r grn	with additional surch "2,"	150.00	95.00
PRI54	162a	(1882-83)	1-1/2r black	"1/2" for "1-1/2"	—	—
PRI55	169b	(1883)	1-1/2r black	"1-1/2," double	NA	
PRI56	170a		4-1/2r olive grn	"4-1/2," omitted	NA	
PRI57	171b		6r green	"6," omitted	NA	
PRI58	172a		1-1/2r black	"1-1/2," omitted	NA	
PRI59	173a		6r green	"6," omitted	NA	
PRI60	223a	(1900)	1-1/2r on 2t blue	invtd surch (vc)	—	—
PRI61	225a	(1902)	2r on 4-1/2r bis	invtd surch (vc)	20.00	20.00
PRI62	225b			dbl surch (vc)	—	—
PRI63	234a		3r on 4-1/2r yel	invtd surch (vc)	21.00	21.00
PRI64	239a	(1902)	6r brown	invtd ovpt (vc)	—	—
PRI65	244a	(1911)	1r gray	invtd ovpt (vc)	10.00	10.00
PRI66	245a		1-1/2r slate	dbl ovpt (vc)	10.00	10.00
PRI67	246a		2r orange	dbl ovpt (vc)	—	—
PRI68	246b			invtd ovpt (vc)	10.00	10.00

PRI69	260a	(1911)	1r on 2r orange	without diagonal perf	4.00	3.50
PRI70	260b			cut diagonally instead of perf	3.25	3.00
PRI71	291a	(1913)	4-1/2r red	dbl ovpt (vc)	—	—
PRI72	292a		6r red violet	dbl ovpt (vc)	—	—
PRI73	317a		1r on 2t blue	"REPUBLICA" invtd	—	—
PRI74	318a		2r on 4-1/2r bis	"REPUBLICA" invtd	—	—
PRI75	319a		2-1/2r on 6r grn	"REPUBLICA" invtd	17.00	17.00
PRI76	323a		5t on 8t org	red ovpt	10.00	7.50
PRI77	325		2r on 8t vio	invtd surch (vc)	—	—
PRI78	331a		5t on 4t bl (r)	"REPUBLICA" invtd	—	—
PRI79	331b			"REPUBLICA" double	—	—
PRI80	390a	(1915)	1-1/2r on 4-1/2r grn	"REPUBLICA" omitted	42.50	42.50
PRI81	390b			"REPUBLICA" invtd	—	—
PRI82	391a		1-1/2r on 9r gray lil	"REPUBLICA" omitted	—	—

PORTUGUESE COLONIES THAT ISSUED STAMPS UNDER PORTUGUESE DOMAIN AT VARIOUS TIMES:

The Azores, Madiera and Portuguese Africa produced no errors

Portuguese Congo produced, surprise of all
Only vc's short, fat, skinny, and tall.
The Guinea vc's shocked no one at all
But its cliches gave errorists a real ball.
India surprised everyone with vc's and the number game
Among its errors were "20 omitted"
"600 double" "200 double" and "900 the same." —The Bard

PUERTO RICO

PUE1	4a	(1874)	25c ultramarine	dbl ovpt (vc)	140.00	—
PUE2	4b			invtd ovpt (vc)	140.00	—
PUE3	5a		25c ultra	invtd ovpt (vc)	55.00	35.00
PUE4	6a		50c green	invtd ovpt (vc)	150.00	75.00
PUE5	65a	(1882-86)	3c yellow	cliche of 8c in plate of 3c	110.00	—
PUE6	66a	(1884)	3c yellow brn	cliche of 8c in plate of 3c	22.50	—
PUE7	72a		20c gray lilac	20c olive brown (error)	100.00	—
PUE7A	155					

See Photo in Color Section

PUE8	210a	(1899)	1c yellow green	ovpt at 25 degree angle	7.50	2.25
PUE9	211a		2c car, type III	ovpt at 25 degree angle	5.50	2.25
PUE10	213a		8c violet brown	ovpt at 25 degree angle	32.50	18.50
PUE11	213c			"PORTO RIC"	125.00	110.00
PUE12	216b	(1900)	2c carmine	invtd ovpt (vc)	—	NA
PUE13	J1	(1899)	1c deep claret	ovpt at 25 degree angle	22.50	7.50
PUE14	J2a		2c deep claret	ovpt at 25 degree angle	15.00	7.00
PUE15	J3a		10c deep claret	ovpt at 25 degree angle	180.00	85.00

Some vc's here but others at play
Perhaps most important was the cliche
Other errors can be found here
O'erprints at 25 degrees and color errors too.
We really have a mixed bag true. —The Bard

QATAR has produced no errors

QUELIMANE

QUE1	7a	(1913)	10c on 16a bis brn	invtd surch (vc)	22.50	—

Quelimane or the Lion's Mane
Whichever should it be
Quelimane stands for vc's
As few as they may be. —The Bard

R

RAS AL KHAIMAH has produced no errors

RHODESIA I

RHD1	40a	(1896)	1p on 3p	"P" of "PENNY" invtd	NA	—
RHD2	41a		1p on 4sh	"P" of "PENNY" invtd	NA	—
RHD3	41b			single bar in surch	NA	—
RHD4	41c			"y" of "PENNY" invtd	NA	—
RHD5	42a		3p on 5s yellow	"T" of "THREE" invtd	NA	—
RHD6	42b			"Rkk" of "THREE" invtd	NA	—
RHD7	46a	(1896)	4p deep blue	"COMPANY" omitted	NA	—
RHD8	86a	(1909)	3p claret	dbl ovpt (vc)	—	—
RHD9	99a		gray violet	pair , one without ovpt	NA	—
RHD10	107a	(1910)	5p ol grn & brn	5p olive yel & brn (error)	NA	115.00
RHD11	139a		1/2p on 1p	invtd surch (vc)	NA	—

RHODESIA II

RHO1	214a	(1966)	9p ol grn, yel & brn	dbl ovpt (vc)	125.00	—
RHO2	214b			invtd ovpt (vc)	—	—
RHO3	215a		1sh ocher & brt grn	dbl ovpt (vc)	150.00	—
RHO4	218a		2shop ultra & red	red omitted	—	—
RHO5	225a	(1966)	3p lt blue & choc	Queen's head omitted	—	—

RHODESIA AND NYASALAND

RNY1	159b	(1959-63)	1p blk & rose red	rose red center omitted	NA	—
RNY2	162b		3p blue & blackk	black omitted	—	—
RNY3	172a		3p orange & sl grn	orange omitted	—	—

RIO DE ORO

RDO1	30a	(1907)	3p blue green	cliche of 4p in plate of 3p		
RDO2	34a		10c on 50c dk green	"10." omitted	125.00	70.00
RDO3	40a	(1908)	15c on 75c org brn	green surch	37.50	14.00
RDO4	60a	(1910)	10c on 5p	dull bl red surch	47.50	27.50

RIO MUNI has produced no errors

RHD8

RHD9

RHD10

ROM47

ROM14

ROM29

RUS67

ROMANIA

ROM1	19b	(1864)	3pa yellow	pair, one sideways	70.00	—
ROM2	20b		6pa deep rose	pair, one sideways	27.50	—
ROM3	21b		30pa deep blue	pair, one sideways	10.00	—
ROM4	61b	(1876-79)	5b bister, yellowish	printed on both sides	—	75.00
ROM5	62d	(1879)	10b, bl yellowish	cliche of 5b in plate of 10b	—	—
ROM6	65a		30b org red, yellowish		—	NA
ROM7	69b		10b rose, yellowish	cliche of 5b in plate of 10b	100.00	NA
ROM8	75a	(1885-89)	1-1/2b black	printed on both sides	—	—
ROM9	101b	(1891)	1-1/2b lilac rose	printed on both sides	—	65.00
ROM10	102b		3b lilac	printed on both sides (u)	—	—
ROM11	102c			impressions of 5b on back	100.00	75.00
ROM12	104a		10b pale red	printed on both sides (u)	140.00	110.00
ROM13	171a	(1903)	2l dull red	2l orange (error)	57.50	40.00
ROM14	204a	(1906)	1.50l red lili & blk brn	center invtd (u)	—	—
ROM15	205a		2.50l yellow & brn	center invtd (u)	—	—
ROM16	241a	(1918)	5b yellow green	invtd ovpt (vc)	9.00	5.00
ROM17	241b			dbl ovpt (vc)	9.00	—
ROM18	242a		10b rose	invtd ovpt (vc)	9.00	5.00
ROM19	242b			dbl ovpt (vc)	9.00	—
ROM20	245a		1b black (r)	invtd ovpt (vc)	6.00	—
ROM21	245b			dbl ovpt (vc)	9.00	2.00
ROM22	246a		5b yel grn (bk)	dbl ovpt (vc)	9.00	2.00
ROM23	246b			invtd ovpt (vc)	6.00	1.75
ROM24	247a		10b rose (bk)	invtd ovpt (vc)	6.00	1.75
ROM25	247b			dbl ovpt (vc)	9.00	2.50
ROM26	283a	(1922)	5b black	engraver's name omitted (u)	12.00	1.40
ROM27	298a	(1926)	6l dk olive	6l bright blue (error)(u)	70.00	70.00
ROM28	301b		10 l brt blue	10 l brown carmine (error) (u)	70.00	70.00
ROM29	863a	(1952)	35b on 4l yel brn (bk)	red surch	15.00	8.00
ROM30	1081a	(1956)	1.75 l emerald & red brn	center invtd (u)	200.00	200.00
ROM31	1107a		55b "1949-1956,"	"1951-1956," (error)		
ROM32	3869a	(1993-94)	1060 l Romania in one color	Romania in 4 colors	10.00	10.00
ROM33	J50a	(1918)	5b yellow green	invtd ovpt (vc)	4.25	4.25
ROM34	J51a		10b rose	invtd ovpt (vc)	2.50	2.50
ROM35	RA7a	(1918)	5b gray blk (r)	dbl ovpt (vc)	3.00	—
ROM36	RA7c			black ovpt	4.50	—
ROM37	RA8a		10b brn (bk)	dbl ovpt (vc)	4.50	
ROM38	RA8b			dbl ovpt , one invtd	4.50	
ROM39	RA8c			invtd ovpt	4.50	—
ROM40	RA16a	(1931)	50b prussian	blue dbl impression	15.00	—
ROM41	RA33a	(1947)	1l on 2l + 2l pink	invtd surch (vc)	—	—
ROM42	RAJ7a	(1918)	5b gray blk)r)	invtd ovpt (vc)	—	—
ROM43	RAJ8a		10b brn (bk)	invtd ovpt (vc)	—	—
ROM44	RAJ9a		10b brn (bl)	vertical ovpt (vc)	15.00	15.00
ROM45	3N7a	(1917-18)	40b on 30pf org & blk, buff	"40," omitted	50.00	67.50
ROM46	3NRa3A	(1917-18)	5b gray blk (r)	black overprint	5.00	5.00

ROUAD, ILE

ROU1	6a	(1916)	3c red orange	dbl ovpt (vc)	75.00	75.00

RUANDA-URUNDI

RUA1	66a	(1942)	75c on 90c car & brn	invtd surch (vc)	8.00	8.00
RUA2	67a		2.50fr on 10fr rose red	invtd surch (vc)	6.50	6.50

RUSSIA

RUS1	19d	(1866-70)	1k black & yellow	groundwork invtd	NA	
RUS2	20d	(1970)	3k black & dp green	V's in groundwork (error)		
RUS3	23a		10k brown & blue	center invtd (u)	—	NA
RUS4	26b	(1875-79)	2k black & red	groundwork invtd	—	NA

RUS5	27d	(1979)	7k gray & rose	center invtd (u)	—	NA
RUS6	27e			center omitted (u)	—	NA
RUS7	28c		8k gray & rose	"C" instead of "B" in "Bocem"	200.00	70.00
RUS8	29a		10k brown & blue	center invtd	—	NA
RUS9	30a		20k blue & orange	cross-shaped "T" in bottom word	100.00	27.50
RUS10	30b			center invtd	—	NA
RUS11	31b	(1883-88)	1k orange groundwork	invtd	NA	
RUS12	32d		2k dark green	groundwork invtd	—	NA
RUS13	33b		3k carmine	groundwork invtd	—	NA
RUS14	34a		5k red violet	groundwork invtd	—	NA
RUS15	35b		7k blue	groundwork invtd	NA	
RUS16	36b		14k blue & rose	center invtd (u)	NA	
RUS17	36c		diagonal half surcharge	"7" in red, one cover ('84)	—	NA
RUS16	41a	(1889)	4k rose	groundwork invtd	—	NA
RUS17	45b		1r lt brn, brn & org	center omitted (u)	NA	
RUS18	47b	(1889-92)	2k green	groundwork invtd	NA	
RUS19	49a		5k red violet	groundwork invtd	NA	
RUS20	50b		7k dark blue	groundwork invtd	—	NA
RUS21	51a		14k blue & rose	center invtd (u)	NA	
RUS22	54a		7r black & yellow	dbl impression of black	—	NA
RUS23	55b	(1902-05)	1k orange	groundwork invtd	NA	
RUS24	55c			groundwork omitted	200.00	200.00
RUS25	56b		2k yellow green	groundwork omitted	NA	
RUS26	56c			groundwork inverted	NA	
RUS27	56d			groundwork double	NA	
RUS28	57a		3k rose red	groundwork omitted	NA	175.00
RUS29	57b			dbl impression	200.00	165.00
RUS30	57e			groundwork inverted	NA	
RUS31	57Cf		4k rose red ('04)	dbl impression (u)	200.00	200.00
RUS32	57Cg			groundwork invtd	NA	
RUS33	58b		5k red violet	groundwork invtd	NA	
RUS34	58d			groundwork omitted	NA	165.00
RUS35	59a		7k dark blue	groundwork omitted	NA	
RUS36	60a		10k dark blue ('04)	groundwork invtd	12.50	5.00
RUS37	60b			groundwork omitted	165.00	35.00
RUS38	60c			groundwork double	165.00	35.00
RUS39	61a		14k blue & rose	center invtd (u)	NA	
RUS40	61b			center omitted (u)	NA	
RUS41	62a		15k brown vio & blue ('05)	center omitted	NA	
RUS42	62b			center invtd (u)	NA	
RUS43	64a		25k dull grn & lil	center invtd (u)	NA	
RUS44	64b			center omitted	NA	
RUS45	65a		35k dak vio & grn	center invtd	—	—
RUS46	65b			center omitted (u)	NA	—
RUS47	68d		1r lt brown, brn & orange	center invtd (u)	NA	
RUS48	68e			center omitted (u)	NA	150.00
RUS49	69a		3.50 black & gray	center invtd	NA	
RUS50	70a		7r black & yel	center invtd (u)	NA	
RUS51	73c	(1909-12)	1k dull orange yellow	dbl impression (u)	85.00	85.00
RUS52	74b		2k dull green	dbl impression (u)	25.00	25.00
RUS53	77b		5k claret	dbl impressions (u)	22.50	22.50
RUS54	81c		15k red brown & dp blue	center omitted (u)	115.00	85.00
RUS55	81d			center dbl (u)	50.00	50.00
RUS56	82b		20k dull bl & dk car	groundwork omitted	20.00	13.00
RUS57	82c			center dbl (u)	30.00	30.00
RUS58	82d			center & value omitted (u)	85.00	85.00
RUS59	83b		25k dull grn & dk vio	center omitted (u)	115.00	115.00
RUS60	83c			center double	25.00	25.00
RUS61	84c		35k red brn & grn	center dbl (u)	25.00	25.00

RUS62	85b		50k red brn & grn	groundwork omitted (u)	20.00	20.00
RUS63	85c			center dbl (u)	32.50	32.50
RUS64	85d			center & value omitted	115.00	115.00
RUS65	86b		70k brn & red org	center dbl (u)	40.00	40.00
RUS66	86c			center omitted (u)	115.00	115.00
RUS67	87c		1r pale brown, dk brn & org	groundwork invtd	20.00	20.00
RUS68	87e			center invtd	25.00	25.00
RUS69	87f			center dbl (u)	16.00	16.00
RUS70	90b	(1913)	3k rose red	dbl impression (u)	NA	—
RUS71	92b		7k brown	dbl impression (u)	NA	
RUS72	108c		5r ind, grn & lt blue	center dbl (u)	40.00	—
RUS73	109c		10r car kajem yek & gray	10r car, yel & gray blue (error)	NA	—
RUS74	109d			groundwork invtd	NA	
RUS75	109e			center double	50.00	50.00
RUS76	117a	(1917)	10k on 7k lt blue	invtd surch (vc)	50.00	50.00
RUS77	117b			dbl surch (vc)	60.00	—
RUS78	118a		20k on 14k bl & rose	invtd surch (vc)	50.00	50.00
RUS79	125a		15k red brn & dp blue	center omitted (u)	55.00	—
RUS80	126a		15k red brn & dp blue	groundwork omitted	20.00	20.00
RUS81	129a		50k brn vio & grn	groundwork omitted	18.00	18.00
RUS82	130a		70k brn & orange	center omitted	115.00	—
RUS83	131a		1r pale brn brn & red org	center invtd (u)	20.00	20.00
RUS84	131b			center omitted	20.00	20.00
RUS85	131c			center double	20.00	20.00
RUS86	131d			groundwork double	14.00	14.00
RUS87	131e			groundwork invtd	20.00	20.00
RUS88	131f			groundwork omitted	22.50	22.50
RUS89	131g			frame double	16.00	16.00
RUS90	133b		5r dk blue, grn & pale blue	groundwork invtd	NA	—
RUS91	134a		7r dk green & pink	center invtd (u)	—	—
RUS92	138i	(1917)	7r dark green & pink	center omitted (u)	22.50	—
RUS93	138j			center invtd (u)	22.50	—
RUS94	138k			center dbl (u)	22.50	—
RUS95	140b		2 on 2k yel green	surch omitted imperf	45.00	45.00
RUS96	181b	(1921)	20r blue	dbl impression (u)	35.00	—
RUS97	183d		250r dull violet	dbl impression (u)	35.00	—
RUS98	191a	(1922)	5000r on 1r orange	invtd surch (vc)	75.00	22.50
RUS99	191b			dbl surch, red & black	75.00	22.50
RUS100	191c			pair, one without surch	125.00	—
RUS101	192a		5000r on 2r lt brown	invtd surch (vc)	65.00	15.00
RUS102	192b			dbl surch (vc)	70.00	—
RUS103	193a		5000r on 5r ultra	invtd surch (vc)	75.00	30.00
RUS104	193b			dbl surch (vc)	75.00	—
RUS105	194b		5000r on 20r blue	pair, one without surch	100.00	—
RUS106	195a		10,000r on 40r, type I	invtd surch	65.00	15.00
RUS107	195c			"1.0000," instead of "10.000,"	125.00	—
RUS108	195d			dbl surch (vc)	85.00	—
RUS109	196a		5000r on 1r orange	invtd surch (vc)	75.00	15.00
RUS110	197a		5000r on 2r lt brown	invtd surch (vc)	75.00	30.00
RUS111	199a		5000r on 20r blue	invtd surch (vc)	75.00	35.00
RUS112	200a		10,000r on 40r type I (r)	invtd surch (vc)	65.00	18.00
RUS113	200b			dbl surch (vc)	65.00	18.00
RUS114	200c			with periods after Russian letters	125.00	35.00
RUS115	201c	(1922)	7500r on 250r (bk)	blue black surch	.15	.15
RUS116	205a		7500r blue, buff	dbl impression (u)	60.00	—
RUS117	210a		100,000 on 250r	invtd surch (vc)	60.00	60.00

RUS118	210d			invtd surch on pelure paper (vc)	70.00	70.00
RUS119	216a	(1922-23)	5r on 20k	invtd surch (vc)	22.50	22.50
RUS120	216b			dbl surch (vc)	35.00	35.00
RUS121	217a		20r on 15k	invtd surch (vc)	45.00	—
RUS122	218a		20r on 70k	invtd surch (vc)	15.00	17.00
RUS123	218b			dbl surch (vc)	20.00	20.00
RUS124	219a		30r on 50k	invtd surch (vc)	25.00	25.00
RUS125	219c			groundwork omitted	30.00	30.00
RUS126	219d			dbl surch (vc)	16.00	16.00
RUS127	220a		40r on 15k	invtd surch (vc)	20.00	20.00
RUS128	220b			dbl surch (vc)	25.00	25.00
RUS129	221a		100r on 15k	invtd surch (vc)	22.50	22.50
RUS130	221b			dbl surch (vc)	25.00	25.00
RUS131	222a		200r on 15k	invtd surch (vc)	20.00	20.00
RUS132	222b			dbl surch (vc)	20.00	20.00
RUS133	225a		20r on 70k	invtd surch imperf (vc)	16.00	16.00
RUS134	227a		40r on 15k	invtd surch (vc)	35.00	35.00
RUS135	227b			dbl surch (vc)	27.50	27.50
RUS136	228a		100r on 15k	invtd surch (vc)	50.00	50.00
RUS137	229a		200r on 15k	invtd surch (vc)	50.00	50.00
RUS138	229b			dbl surch (vc)	35.00	35.00
RUS139	237a	(1923)	100r red	cliche of 70r in plate of 100r	30.00	35.00
RUS140	237b			corrected cliche	75.00	100.00
RUS141	240a		5r light blue	dbl impression (u)	50.00	50.00
RUS142	241e		10r gray	dbl impression (u)	75.00	—
RUS143	241Ab		20r brown violet	dbl impression (u)	75.00	—
RUS144	239a		b4r brown		10.00	25.00
RUS145	241df		10r gray	as "d" dbl impression (u)	50.00	
RUS146	349b	(1927)	8k on 7k chocolate	invtd surch (vc)	125.00	105.00
RUS147	350a		8k on 7k choc	invtd surch (vc)	45.00	35.00
RUS148	3915a	(1971)	10k brown & black	(1961) "1964,"	10.00	7.25
RUS149	6261b	(1995)	300r multicolored	min. Sheet of 8, different margin	3.25	2.50
RUS150	B18a		100r+100r on 70k	"100p.+p.100,"	55.00	65.00
RUS151	B38a	(1923)	1r+1r on 10r	invtd surch (vc)	250.00	250.00
RUS152	B39a		1r+1r on 10r	invtd surch (vc)	250.00	250.00
RUS153	B40b		2r + 2r on 250r	invtd surch (vc)	250.00	250.00
RUS154	B40c			dbl surch (vc)	200.00	200.00
RUS155	B41a		4r+4r on 5000r	date spaced "1 923,"	165.00	165.00
RUS156	B41b			invtd surch (vc)	NA	
RUS157	B42a		4r+4r on 5000r	invtd surch (vc)	NA	
RUS158	B42b			date space "1923,"	NA	
RUS159	B42c			as "b" invtd surch (vc)	NA	—
RUS160	B43b	(1924)	3k+10k on 100r	invtd surch (vc)	175.00	125.00
RUS161	B44a		7k+20k on 200r	invtd surch (vc)	175.00	125.00
RUS162	B46a		12k + 40k on 500r	dbl surch (vc)	115.00	115.00
RUS163	B46b			invtd surch (vc)	115.00	115.00
RUS164	C4a	(1923)	5r green	wide "5,"	NA	—
RUS165	C7a	(1924)	10k on 5r green	wide "5,"	NA	
RUS166	C7b			invtd surch (vc)	NA	
RUS167	C8a		15k on 1r red brown	invtd surch (vc)	NA	
RUS168	C9a		20k on 10r car	invtd surch (vc)	NA	
RUS169	C23a	(1931-32)	50k black brown	50k gray blue (error)	200.00	200.00
RUS170	C68a	(1935)	1r on 10k dk brn	invtd surch (vc)	NA	
RUS171	C68b			small cyrillic "f"	NA	
RUS172		(1924-25)	J5a 10k on 35k blue	pair, one without surch	25.00	—
RUS173	J10c	(1924)	1k on 100r orange	invtd surch (vc)	67.50	—
RUS174	L2a	(1863)	(2k) rose & black	backround invtd	150.00	150.00
RUS175	L3c		(4k) blue grn & blk	background invtd	150.00	150.00
RUS176	L3d		half used as 2k on cover	background invtd	NA	
RUS177	L8a	(1875)	2k yel grn & red	numeral in upper right corner resembles an invtd "3,"	27.50	27.50

RUS178	L11a	(1884)	2k black, green, red	green arm omitted (u)	21.00	—
RUS179	L11b			arm invtd (u)	21.00	
RUS180	L11c			arm dbl (u)	27.50	—

RUSSIAN OFFICES ABROAD
OFFICES IN CHINA

RUC1	11a	(1904-08)	10k dk blue (r)	groundwork invtd	NA	
RUC2	27a	(1910-16)	2k green(bl)	dbl ovpt (bk & bl)	—	—
RUC3	52a	(1917)	3c on3k car	invtd surch (vc)	65.00	
RUC4	52b			dbl surch (vc)	150.00	—
RUC5	55a		10c on 10k dk blue	invtd surch (vc)	85.00	85.00
RUC6	55b			dbl surch (vc)	115.00	—
RUC6	56b		14c on 14k dk blue & carmine	invtd surch	100.00	
RUC7	60a		35c on 35k brn vio & green	invtd surch (vc)	27.50	—
RUC8	68a		$5 on 5r ind, grn & lt blue	invtd surch (vc)	NA	—
RUC9	75a	(1920)	4c on 4k car	invtd surch (vc)	130.00	—
RUC10	79a		1c on 1k orange	invtd surch (vc)	45.00	75.00
RUC11	80a		5c on 5k claret	invtd surch (vc)	140.00	—
RUC12	80b			dbl surch (vc)	200.00	—
RUC13	80c			surch "Cent" only	95.00	

OFFICES IN THE TURKISH EMPIRE

RUT1	16a	(1876)	8k on 10k (bk)	invtd surch (vc)	NA	
RUT2	17b		8k on 10k (bl)	invtd surch	NA	—
RUT3	18b	(1879)		invtd surch (vc)	—	—
RUT4	19b		7k on 10k (bl)	invtd surch (vc)	—	—
RUT5	27a	(1900)	4pa on 1k orange (bl)	invtd surch	30.00	30.00
RUT6	28a		4pa on 1k orange (bk)	invtd surch (vc)	30.00	30.00
RUT7	29a		10pa on 2k green	invtd surch (vc)	—	—
RUT8	30a		1pi on 10k dk blue	invtd surch (vc)	—	—
RUT9	31a	(1903-05)	10pa on 2k yel green	invtd surch (vc)	70.00	—
RUT10	32a		20pa on 4k rose red (bl)	invtd surch (vc)	25.00	—
RUT11	33a		1pi on 10k dk blue	groundwork invtd	55.00	17.50
RUT12	41a	(1909)	10pa on 2k green	invtd surch (vc)	7.25	8.50
RUT13	67a		10pi on 1r	"Constanttnople"	14.00	
RUT14	70a		5pa on 1k	"Consnantinople	8.00	—
RUT15	71a		5pa on 1k	invtd ovpt (vc)	11.50	—
RUT16	72a		10pa on 2k	invtd ovpt (vc)	11.50	—
RUT17	73a		20pa on 4k	invtd ovpt (vc)	27.50	—
RUT18	74a		1pi on 10k	dbl ovpt (vc)	32.50	—
RUT19	81a		5pa on 1k	invtd ovpt (vc)	13.00	—
RUT20	81b			"erusalem"	8.25	—
RUT21	82a		10pa on 2k	invtd ovpt (vc)	13.00	—
RUT22	82b			"erusalem"	8.25	—
RUT23	83a		20pa on 4k	invtd ovpt (vc)	13.00	—
RUT24	83b			"erusalem"	8.25	—
RUT25	84a		1pi on 10k	"erusalem"	11.50	—
RUT26	85a		5pi on 50k	"erusalem"	22.50	—
RUT27	86a		7pi on 70k	"erusalem"	22.50	—
RUT28	91a		5pa on 1k	invtd ovpt (vc)	8.75	—
RUT29	92a		10pa on 2k	invtd ovpt (vc)	8.75	—
RUT30	93a		20pa on 4k	invtd ovpt(vc)	10.50	—
RUT31	101b		5pa on 1k	invtd ovpt (vc)	14.00	—
RUT32	102b		10pa on 2k	invtd ovpt (vc)	14.00	—
RUT33	103b		20pa on 4k	invtd ovpt (vc)	15.00	—
RUT34	104b		1pi on 10k	dbl ovpt (vc)	22.50	—
RUT35	106b		7pi on 70k	pair, one without "Mont Athos"	16.00	—
RUT36	104ac		1pi on 10k	as "a" dbl ovpt (vc)	85.00	—
RUT37	131a		5pa on 1k	invtd ovpt (vc)	6.50	—
RUT38	131b			pair, one without ovpt	—	—
RUT39	132a		10pa on 2k	invtd ovpt (vc)	10.00	—

RUT40	133a		20pa on 4k	invtd ovpt (vc)	13.00	—
RUT41	141a	(1909-10) 5pa on 1k		dbl ovpt (vc)	—	—
RUT42	141b			invtd ovpt	—	—
RUT43	142a		10pa on 2k	invtd ovpt (vc)	8.25	—
RUT44	143a		20pa on 4k	invtd ovpt (vc)	10.00	—
RUT45	151a		5pa on 1k	invtd ovpt (vc)	4.50	—
RUT46	152a		10pa on 2k	invtd ovpt (vc)	6.50	—
RUT47	152b			pair, one without "Trebizonde"	—	—
RUT48	153a		20pa on 4k	invtd ovpt (vc)	10.00	—
RUT49	154a		1pi on 10k	pair, one without "Trebizonde"	27.50	—
RUT50	162a	(1910)	10pa on 2k	invtd ovpt (vc)	20.00	—
RUT51	172a		10pa on 2k	pair, one without ovpt	—	—
RUT52	173a		20pa on 4k	invtd ovpt (vc)	10.00	—
RUT53	178a		35pi on 3.50r	center & ovpt invtd	—	—
RUT54	181a		5pa on 1k	invtd ovpt (vc)	10.00	—
RUT55	182a		10pa on 2k	invtd ovpt (vc)	13.00	—
RUT56	183a		20pa on 4k	invtd ovpt (vc)	13.00	—
RUT57	191a		5pa on 1k	invtd ovpt (vc)	6.50	—
RUT58	192a		10pa on 2k	invtd ovpt (vc)	10.00	—
RUT59	193a		20pa on 4k	invtd ovpt (vc)	10.00	—
RUT60	211a		2-1/2 pi on 25k grn & vio	dbl surch (vc)	50.00	50.00
RUT61	231a	(1913)	100pi on 10r	dbl surch (vc)	24.00	40.00
RUT62	238a	(1921)	1000r on 3k	invtd surch (vc)	1.25	1.25
RUT63	239a		1000r on 4k	invtd surch (vc)	1.25	1.25
RUT64	240a		1000r on 5k	invtd surch (vc)	1.25	1.25
RUT65	241a		1000r on 7k	invtd surch (vc)	1.25	1.25
RUT66	242a		1000r on 10k	invtd surch	1.25	1.25
RUT67	246a		5000r on 15k	"PYCCKIN"	3.50	3.50
RUT68	247a		5000r on 20k	"PYCCKIN"	3.50	3.50
RUT69	250a		5000r on 35k	invtd surch (vc)	1.25	1.25
RUT70	250b			value omitted	—	—
RUT71	251a		5000r on 50k	invtd surch (vc)	—	—
RUT72	252a		5000r on 70k	invtd surch (vc)	2.00	2.00
RUT73	259a		20,000r on 3.50r	invtd surch (vc)	6.50	6.50
RUT74	259b			new value omitted	55.00	55.00
RUT75	272a		10,000r on 1r (bl)	invtd surch (vc)	1.00	.65
RUT76	277a		20,000r on 1r (bl)	invtd surch (vc)	1.00	1.00
RUT77	283a		10,000r on 5k grn, buff	invtd surch (vc)	2.75	—
RUT78	284a		10,000r on 10k brn, buff	invtd surch (vc)	2.75	—
RUT79	291a		10,000r on 10pi on 1r	invtd surch (vc)	4.75	4.75
RUT80	291b			pair, one without surch	4.75	4.75
RUT81	292a		20,000r on 10pi on 1r	invtd surch (vc)	4.75	4.75
RUT82	292b			pair, one without surch	4.75	4.75
RUT83	303a		5000r on 5k org	invtd surch (vc)	—	—
RUT84	309a		10,000r on 2r gray l vio & ye	invtd surch (vc)	1.25	1.25
RUT85	315a		20,000r on 2r gray vio & yel (bl)		3.25	3.25
RUT86	322a	(1921)	10,000r on 3k red	invtd surch (vc)	1.25	1.25
RUT87	325a		10,000r on 7k lt bl	invtd surch (vc)	1.25	1.25
RUT88	326a		10,000r on 10k dk bl	invtd surch (vc)	1.25	1.25
RUT89	327a		10,000 on 20k bl & car (br)	invtd surch (vc)	1.25	1.25
RUT90	328a		20,000r on 20k bl & car (br)	invtd surch (vc)	1.25	1.25
RUT91	329a		20,000r on 20k bl & car (bk)	invtd surch (vc)	1.25	1.25
RUT92	332a		20,000r on 50k brn vio & grn	invtd surch (vc)	1.25	1.25
RUT93	333a		10,000r on 1k org	invtd surch (vc)	1.65	—

RWANDA has produced no errors

CHAPTER VII: S-Z

SAAR

SAA1	1b	(1920)	2pf gray	dbl ovpt (vc)	NA	
SAA2	4b		5pf green	dbl ovpt (vc)	NA	
SAA3	6b		10pf carmine	dbl ovpt (vc)	NA	
SAA4	7a		15pf dk violet	dbl ovpt (vc)	NA	
SAA5	8a		20pr blue violet	dbl ovpt (vc)	NA	
SAA6	17b		1m carmine rose	dbl ovpt (vc)	NA	
SAA7- SAA17 all invtd ovpt (vc)						
SAA7	1a		2pf gray		NA	
SAA8	3a		3pf brown		NA	
SAA9	4a		5pf green		NA	
SAA10	5a		7-1/2 pf orange		NA	
SAA11	6a		10pf carmine		NA	
SAA12	9a		25pf Org & blk, yel		NA	
SAA13	11a		35pf red brown		NA	
SAA14	12a		40pf lake & blk		NA	
SAA15	13a		50pf pur & blk, buff		NA	
SAA16	15a		75pf green & blk		165.00	NA
SAA17	17a		I m carmine rose		NA	
SAA18	21a	(1920)	5pf yellow grn	dbl ovpt (vc)	NA	
SAA19	23a		10pf carmine rose	dbl ovpt (vc)	165.00	NA
SAA20	24a		15pf vermillion	dbl ovpt (vc)	175.00	NA
SAA21	26a		20pf blue	dbl ovpt (vc)	160.00	NA
SAA22	31a		50pf red brown	dbl ovpt (vc)	140.00	NA
SAA23	39a		10m yellow green	dbl ovpt (vc)	NA	
SAA24	47a	(1920)	20pf green	dbl ovpt (vc)	—	—
SAA25	48a		30pf org & blk, buff	dbl ovpt (vc)	55.00	—
SAA26	52a		50pf pur & blk, buff	dbl ovpt (vc)	55.00	—
SAA27	54a		75pf green & blk	dbl ovpt (vc)	90.00	—
SAA28	58a		4m black & rose	dbl ovpt (vc)	40.00	—
SAA29 41a-SAA40 56a all invtd overprints						
SAA29	41a		5pf green		12.50	125.00
SAA30	43a		10pf carmine		32.50	
SAA31	44a		10pf orange		10.50	
SAA32	45a		15pf dark violet		21.00	175.00
SAA33	46a		20pf blue violet		21.00	
SAA34	48b		30pf org & blk, buff		—	—
SAA35	50a		40pf lake & blk		—	—
SAA36	52b		50pf pur & blk, buff		—	—
SAA37	53a		60pf red violet		57.50	150.00
SAA38	54b		75pf green & blk		90.00	—
SAA39	55a		1.25m green		72.50	—
SAA40	56a		1.50m yellow brown		72.50	—
SAA41	65a	(1921)	20pf on 75pf grn & blk	invtd surch (vc)	16.00	25.00
SAA42	65b			dbl surch (vc)	42.50	70.00
SAA43	68c	(1921)	5pf ol grn & vio	center invtd (u)	50.00	—
SAA44	80a		3m brown & dk olive	center invtd (u)	85.00	—
SAA45	87b	(1921)	10c on 30pf (bl)	invtd surch (vc)	90.00	NA
SAA46	88b		15c on 40pf (bk)	invtd surch (vc)	90.00	NA
SAA47	91c		30c on 80pf (bk)	invtd surch (vc)	125.00	NA
SAA48	91d			dbl surch (vc)	125.00	NA
SAA49	92a		40c on 1m (bl)	invtd surch (vc)	125.00	NA
SAA50	97b		3fr on 10m (bk	dbl surch (vc)	165.00	NA

ST. CHRISTOPHER

STC1	17a	(1885)	1/2p on half of 1p		NA	110.00
STC2	17d			unsevered pair, one surch invtd	NA	
STC3	18a	(1885-86)	1p on 6p green	invtd surch (vc)		
STC4	19a		4p on 6p green	period after "PENCE"	47.50	60.00

STC5	19b			dbl surch (vc)	NA	
STC6	20a		4p on 6p green	without period after "d"	NA	
STC7	20b			dbl surch (vc)	NA	
STC8	22a	(1888)	1p on 2-1/2p	invtd surch (vc)	NA	

One can flutter around St. Chris like a bee
One will find, however, nothing much like a vc. —The Bard

ST. HELENA

STH1	8a	(1863)	1p on 6p brown red (surch 17mm)	dbl surch (vc)	NA	
STH2	10a		4p on 6p carmine	surch omitted	NA	165.00
STH3	10b			dbl surch (vc)	NA	
STH4	12a	(1864-73)	1p on 6p brn red ('71)	blue black surch	NA	
STH5	13a		2p on 6p yel '73	blue black surch	NA	
STH6	15a		4p on 6p carmine	dbl surch (vc)	NA	
STH7	17a		1sh on 6p dp grn (bar 18mm) '73	blue black surch	NA	14.00
STH8	18b	(1868)	1p on 6p brn red	dbl surch (vc)	NA	
STH9	20a		3p on 6p dk vio	dbl surch (vc)	NA	
STH10	21a		4p on 6p car (words 19mm)	words dbl, 18 & 19 mm	NA	
STH11	22a		4p on 6p car (words 19mm)	words dbl, 18mm & 19mm	NA	
STH12	23a		1sh on 6p yel grn	dbl surch (vc)	NA	
STH13	23b			pair, one without surch	NA	
STH14	33a	(1884-94)	1/2p on 6p grn (words 17mm)	1/2p on 6p emer, blurred print	5.00	5.00
STH15	33b			dbl surch (vc)	NA	
STH16	37a		3p on 6p dp vio '87	3p on 6p red vio	3.50	2.00
STH17	37b			dbl surch (vc)	NA	
STH18	38a		4p on 6p dk brn '90	with thin bar below thick one	—	—
STH19	39a	(1894)	1sh on 6p yel grn	dbl surch (vc)	NA	—
STH20	47a	(1893)	2-1/2p on 6p blue	dbl surch (vc)	NA	
STH21	47b			dbl impression (u)	NA	
STH22	196a	(1967)	2shop blue & multi	carmine omitted	NA	
STH23	MR1a	(1916)	1p+1p scarlet & blk	dbl surch (vc)	NA	

ST. KITTS

STK1	112a	(1983)	5c multicolored	local ovpt	8.25	4.25

No vc or inverted center
No double impression or color omitted
What then do we have
Something rare and bare
A local overprint everywhere. —The Bard

ST. KITTS-NEVIS

STK1	147a	(1963)	2c multicolored	yellow omitted		

One error from Kitts
And it involves omits
Specifically yellow
Round and mellow
Another from the commonwealth. —The Bard

ST. LUCIA

STL1		(1860)	1a rose red	dbl impressions (u)	NA	—
STL2	40b	(1892)	1/2p on 3p lil & grn	dbl surch, die B(vc)	NA	
STL3	40c			invtd surch, die B(vc)	NA	
STL4	40d			triple surch, one on back	NA	
STL5	41a		1/2p on half of 6p lilac & blue	slanting serif	180.00	180.00
STL6	41c			without the bar of "1/2,"	180.00	160.00
STL7	41d			"2" on "1/2," omitted	NA	

STL8	41e			surched sideways	NA	
STL9	41f			dbl surch (vc)	NA	
STL10	42b		1p on 4p brown	dbl surch (vc)	165.00	—
STL11	42c			invtd surch (vc)	NA	
STL12	MR1a	(1916)	1p scarlet	dbl ovpt (vc)	NA	

STE.-MARIE DE MADEGASCAR has produced no errors

ST. PIERRE & MIQUELON

STM1	2a	(1885)	10c on 40c ver, straw	"M" invtd	150.00	125.00
STM2	15a	(1891)	15c on 30c brn, bis	invtd surch (vc)	150.00	110.00
STM3	16a		15c on 35c blk, org	invtd surch (vc)	NA	
STM4	17a		15c on 35c blk, org	invtd surch (vc)	—	—
STM5	18a		15c on 40c red, straw	invtd surch (vc)	140.00	140.00
STM6	19a	(1891)	1c blk, lil bl	invtd ovpt (vc)	15.00	15.00
STM7	20a		1c blk, lil bl (r)	invtd ovpt (vc)	12.00	12.00
STM8	21a		2c brn, buff	invtd ovpt	16.00	16.00
STM9	22a		2c brn, buff (r)	invtd ovpt (vc)	42.50	42.50
STM10	23a		4c claret, lav	invtd ovpt (vc)	18.00	18.00
STM11	24a		4c claret, lav (r)	invtd ovpt (vc)	32.50	32.50
STM12	25a		5c grn, grnsh	dbl surch (vc)	60.00	—
STM13	26a		10c blk, lav	invtd ovpt (vc)	45.00	45.00
STM14	27a		10c blk, lav (r)	invtd ovpt (vc)	32.50	32.50
STM15	33a		40c red, straw	dbl surch (vc)	125.00	
STM16	34a		75c car, rose	invtd ovpt (vc)	125.00	110.00
STM17	35a		1fr brnz grn, straw	invtd ovpt (vc)	100.00	90.00
STM18	39a	(1891-92)	2c on 10c blk, lav	dbl surch (vc)	57.50	—
STM19	43a	(1892)	4c on 25c blk, rose	dbl surch (vc)	57.50	
STM20	121a	(1925)	25c on 15c dull vio & rose	dbl surch (vc)	100.00	
STM21	121b			triple surch (u)	100.00	—
STM22	123a		25c on 5fr brn & ol grn (bl)	triple surch (u)	100.00	—
STM23	183a	(1940)	45c deep green	value omitted	55.00	—
STM24	J46a	(1942)	3fr on 2fr dp vio & blk	"F.N.F.L." omitted	4.00	4.00
STM25	Q1a	(1901)	10c black, lavender	invtd ovpt (vc)	60.00	60.00
STM26	Q3a		10c	dbl ovpt (vc)	—	—
STM27	Q4a	(1925)	20c	dbl ovpt (vc)	85.00	85.00

ST. THOMAS AND PRINCE ISLANDS

STT1	64a	(1902)	400r on 10r yel	dbl surch (vc)	25.00	12.00
STT2	66a		65r on 25r violet	invtd surch (vc)	—	—
STT3	81a		130r on 100r brn, yel	dbl surch (vc)	—	—
STT4	85a		400r on 2-1/2r brown	dbl surch (vc)	—	—
STT5	91a	(1911)	2-1/2r gray	invtd ovpt (vc)	15.00	11.00
STT6	93a		10r lt green	invtd ovpt (vc)	15.00	12.00
STT7	97a		50r brown	invtd ovpt (vc)	15.00	12.00
STT8	99a		100r dk bl, bl	invtd ovpt (vc)	17.50	14.00
STT9	106a	(1912)	2-1/2r violet	dbl ovpt (vc)	16.00	16.00
STT10	106b			dbl ovpt, one invtd	—	—
STT11	108a		10r gray green	dbl ovpt (vc)	14.00	14.00
STT12	116a	(1913)	2-1/2r gray	invtd ovpt (vc)	15.00	15.00
STT13	116b			dbl ovpt (vc)	12.00	12.00
STT14	118a		15r gray green	invtd ovpt (vc)	—	—
STT15	119a		20r gray violet	invtd ovpt (vc)	—	—
STT16	120a		25r carmine	invtd ovpt (vc)	—	—
STT17	120b			dbl ovpt (vc)	—	—
STT18	123a		115r org brn, pink	dbl ovpt (vc)	75.00	60.00
STT19	129a		115r on 50r green	invtd ovpt (vc)	—	—
STT20	130a		115r on 10r blue grn	invtd ovpt (vc)	—	—
STT21	132a		115r pm 25r green	invtd ovpt (vc)	—	—
STT22	133a		115r on 150r car, rose	invtd ovpt (vc)	—	—
STT23	135a		130r on 75r rose	invtd ovpt (vc)	—	—

STT24	141a		2-1/2r gray	invtd ovpt (vc)	9.00	—
STT25	141b			dbl ovpt (vc)	11.00	11.00
STT26	143a		15r gray green	invtd ovpt (vc)	—	—
STT27	144a		20r gray violet	invtd ovpt	—	—
STT28	145a		25r carmine	invtd ovpt (vc)	—	—
STT29	146a		75r red lilac	invtd ovpt (vc)	—	—
STT30	148a		org brn, pink	invtd ovpt (vc)	—	—
STT31	149a		130r brn, straw	invtd ovpt (vc)	—	—
STT32	150a		200r red lil, pinksh	invtd ovpt (vc)	—	—
STT33	160a		115r on 150r car, rose	"REPUBLICA" invtd	—	—
STT34	162a		130r on 75r rose	invtd surch (vc)	—	—
STT35	167a		15r brown	invtd ovpt (vc)	—	—
STT36	168a		50r blue	invtd ovpt (vc)	—	—
STT37	374a	(1962)	50c gray green	"$50 CORRELOS"omitted	—	—
STT38	J28a	(1913)	130c dull blue	invtd ovpt (vc)	40.00	40.00
STT39	J31a		5c yellow green	invtd ovpt (vc)	—	—
STT40	J34a		30r orange	invtd ovpt (vc)	—	—

SAINT VINCENT

STV1	30a	(1880)	1p on half of 6p	unsevered pair	NA	
STV2	31a	(1881)	1/2p on half of 60	yel grn unsevered pair	NA	—
STV3	31b			"I" with straight top	NA	—
STV4	31d			without fraction bar, pair #31, 31c	NA	
STV5	57a	(1890)	2-1/2p on 4p vio brn	without fraction bar	NA	
STV6	59b	(1893)	5p on 6p dp lake	dbl surch (vc)	—	NA
STV7	117a	(1915)	1p on 1sh black, grn	"PENNY" & bar dbl	NA	—
STV8	117b			without period	14.00	—
STV9	117c			"ONE" omitted	NA	—
STV10	117d			"ONE" dbl	NA	—
STV11	MR1a	(1916)	1p carmine type III	dbl ovpt, type III	175.00	200.00
STV12	MR1c			comma after "STAMP", type I	150.00	150.00
STV13	MR1d			dbl ovpt, type I, (vc)	150.00	150.00
STV14	1018					

ST. VINCENT GRENADINES has produced no errors

EL SALVADOR

ELS1	13a	(1879)	1c green	invtd "V" for 2nd "A" in "SALVADOR"	—	—
ELS2	13b			invtd "V" for "A" in REPUBLICA"	4.00	2.00
ELS3	13c			invtd "V" for "A" in "universal"	4.00	2.00
ELS4	14a		2c rose	invtd scroll in upper left corner	8.00	5.00
ELS5	25a	(1889)	13 on 3c brn, type II	dbl surch (vc)	1.50	—

ELS162

ELS162

ELS6	25b			triple surch	3.50	—
ELS7	25c			type 1	.65	—
ELS8	57a	(1891)	1c on 2c yellow grn	invtd surch (vc)	4.00	—
ELS9	70a	(1892)	1c on 5c gray (bk) (down)	surch reading up	1.75	1.10
ELS10	72a		1c on 5c gray (r) (up)	surch reading down	—	—
ELS11	73a		1c on 20c org (bk)	invtd surch (vc)	3.50	2.50
ELS12	73b			"V" or "CENTAVO" invtd	3.50	2.50
ELS13	74a		1c on 25c maroon (y)	invtd surch (vc)	2.50	2.50
ELS14	75a		1c on 25c mar (bl)	dbl surch (bl+bk) (vc)	NA	
ELS15	89a	(1893)	1c on 2c brn red	"CENTNVO"	3.00	3.00
ELS16	104a		1c on 11c vermillion	"Centavo"	20.00	20.00
ELS17	104b			dbl surch (vc)	—	—
ELS18	112a	(1895)	20c yellow & brn	invt ovpt (vc)	2.00	—
ELS19	133a		3c on 30c dp blue	dbl surch (vc)	4.50	—
ELS20	158a	(1896)	15c on 24c violet	dbl surch (vc)	—	—
ELS21	158b			invtd surch (vc)	8.50	—
ELS22	189a	(1899)	5c blue grn (bk)	italic 3rd "r" in "Terroritorial"	12.50	12.50
ELS23	189b			dbl ovpt (bk +y)	37.50	37.50
ELS24	226a	(1900)	1c on 10c gray blue	invtd surch (vc)	7.50	6.50
ELS25	228a		2c on 112c vio	"eentavo"	—	—
ELS26	228b			invtd surch (vc)	—	—
ELS27	228c			"centavos"	30.00	—
ELS28	228d			as "c" dbl surch	—	—
ELS29	228e			vertical surch	—	—
ELS30	229a		2c on 13c brn lake	"eentavo"	3.25	2.75
ELS31	229b			invtd surch (vc)	5.00	5.00
ELS32	229c			"1900," omitted	—	—
ELS33	230a		2c on 20c dp blue	invtd surch (vc)	3.25	3.25
ELS34	231a		3c on 12c vio	"eentavo"	—	—
ELS35	231b			invtd surch (vc)	—	—
ELS36	231c			dbl surch (vc)	—	—
ELS37	232a		3c on 50c org	invtd surch (vc)	10.00	10.00
ELS38	234a		5c on 24c ultra	"eentavo"	—	—
ELS39	234b			"centavos"	11.00	—
ELS40	235a		5c on 26c bis brn	invtd surch (vc)	35.00	35.00
ELS41	236a		5c on 1p yel	invtd surch (vc)	15.00	15.00
ELS42	237a		2c on 12c vio	invtd surch (vc)	2.50	2.50
ELS43	237b			"eentavo"	8.00	—
ELS44	237c			"centavos" (plural)	75.00	—
ELS45	237d			"1900," omitted	—	—
ELS46	238a		3c on 12c vio	"eentavo"	35.00	35.00
ELS47	239a		5c on 26c bis brn	invtd surch (vc)	—	—
ELS48	241a		5c on 12c vio	surch reading downward	—	—
ELS49	242a	(1900)	1c on 13c dp rose	invtd surch (vc)	.75	.75
ELS50	242b			"eentavo"	.75	.75
ELS51	242c			"ecntavo"	1.25	.75
ELS52	242d			"1 ceentavo 1,"	4.00	3.00
ELS53	242e			dbl surch (vc)	—	—
ELS54	243a		2c on 12c dk grn	invtd surch (vc)	2.50	2.50
ELS55	244a		2c on 13c dp rose	"eentavo"	1.25	1.25
ELS56	244b			"ecntavo"	1.40	1.40
ELS57	244c			invtd surch (vc)	—	—
ELS58	245a		3c on 12c dk grn	invtd surch (vc)	2.00	1.50
ELS59	245b			"eentavo"	4.00	4.00
ELS60	245c			dbl surch (vc)	2.00	—
ELS61	246a		1c on 2c gray grn	"eentavo"	.90	.65
ELS62	246b			invtd surch (vc)	4.00	3.00
ELS63	247a		1c on 13c dp rose	"eentavo"	4.00	—
ELS64	247b			"1centavo 1,"	—	—
ELS65	248a		2c on 12c dk grn	"eentavo,"	4.00	—
ELS66	248b			invtd surch (vc)	1.25	—

ELS67	248c		dbl surch (vc)	2.00	—
ELS68	249a	2c on 13c dp rose	"eentavo"	—	—
ELS69	249b		dbl surch (vc)	75.00	75.00
ELS70	250a	3c on 12c dk grn	invtd surch (vc)	1.50	1.25
ELS71	250b		"eentavo"	2.50	2.25
ELS72	250c		date doouble	4.00	—
ELS73	251a	5c on 24c lt bl	"eentavo"	4.00	4.00
ELS74	252a	5c on 26c car rose	invtd surch (vc)	4.00	2.50
ELS75	252b		"eentavo"	1.75	1.50
ELS76	294a	(1905-06) 3c gray blk	without shield	—	—
ELS77	299Bc	2c rose	"1905," vert	.80	—
ELS78	306a	2c rose (ovpt vert)	ovpt horiz	—	—
ELS79	311a	2c rose	without shield	4.00	3.00
ELS80	312a	1c on 2c car	dbl surch (vc)	3.00	3.00
ELS81	312Bc	5c on 12c slate	dbl surch (vc)	—	—
ELS82	312Bd		blk surch	3.50	3.50
ELS83	312Be		as "d" dbl surch	—	—
ELS84	319a	5c on 12c slate	blue surch	2.25	1.75
ELS85	324a	1c on 13c red brn	dbl surch (vc)	4.00	3.00
ELS86	324b		right "1," & dot omitted	—	—
ELS87	324c		both numerals omitted	—	—
ELS88	326a	(1905) 1c green	invtd ovpt (vc)	—	—
ELS89	327a	2c rose	vertical ovpt	6.00	5.00
ELS90	329a	(1906) 2c on 26c brn org	"2," & dot double	7.50	7.50
ELS91	330a	3c on 26c brn org	"3," & dot double	—	—
ELS92	331a	3c on 26c brn org	disks & numerals omitted	—	—
ELS93	331b		"3." & disks double	—	—
ELS94	331c		"1906,"omitted	—	—
ELS95	334a	26c brn org	"1906," in blue	—	—
ELS96	335a	10c dp bl (shield in violet)	ovpt type "p"	—	—
ELS97	349a	(1907) 1c green & blk	shield in red	3.50	—
ELS98	350a	2c red & blk	shield in red	3.50	—
ELS99	352b	1c on 5c ultra & blk	invtd surch (vc)	—	—
ELS100	353c		dbl surch (vc)	—	—
ELS101	352Db	1c on 5c ultra & blk	invtd surch (vc)	—	—
ELS102	359a	(1907) 6c ver & blk	shield in red	3.75	—
ELS103	367a	(1908) 1c on 2c red & blk	dbl surch (vc)	1.00	1.00
ELS104	367b		invtd surch (vc)	.50	.50
ELS105	367c		dbl surch, one invtd	.50	.50
ELS106	367d		red surch	—	—
ELS107	374a	(1909) 1c green & blk	invtd ovpt (vc)	10.00	—
ELS108	375a	1c green & blk	invtd ovpt (vc)	—	—
ELS109	376a	2c on 13c sep& blk	invtd surch (vc)	—	—
ELS110	441a	(1917) 2c red	dbl bar	—	—
ELS111	442a	5c ultramarine	dbl bar	—	—
ELS112	443a	6c pale blue	dbl bar	—	—
ELS113	442a	5c ultramarine	dbl bar	—	—
ELS114	443a	6c pale blue	dbl bar	—	—
ELS115	444a	12c brown	dbl bar	—	—
ELS116	444b		"CORRIENTE" invtd	—	—
ELS117	445a	1c gray green	"CORRIENTE" invtd	—	—
ELS118	445b		dbl bar	—	—
ELS119	445c		"CORRIENTE" omitted	—	—
ELS120	446a	2c red	dbl bar	—	—
ELS121	447a	5c ultra	dbl bar, both in black	—	—
ELS122	448a	10c yellow	dbl bar	—	—
ELS123	448b		"OFICIAL" & bar omitted	—	—
ELS124	449a	50c violet	dbl bar	—	—
ELS125	450a	5c deep blue	"CORRIENTE" dbl	—	—
ELS126	451a	1c on 6c gray vio	"CORRIERTE"	—	—
ELS127	451b		"CORRIENRE"	—	—
ELS128	451c		"CORRIENTE" dbl	—	—

ELS129	452a	(1918)	1c on 6c gray vio	dbl surch (vc)	—	—
ELS130	452b			invtd surch (vc)	—	—
ELS131	453a		1c on 6c gray vio	"Centado"	2.25	1.50
ELS132	453b			dbl surch (vc)	2.50	1.75
ELS133	453c			invtd surch (vc)	—	—
ELS134	454a		1c on 6c gray vio	dbl surch (vc)		
ELS135	454b			invtd surch (vc)	5.00	5.00
ELS136	455a		1c on 6c gray vio (r)	dbl surch (vc)	—	—
ELS137	455b			invtd surch (vc)	5.00	5.00
ELS138	457a	(1919)	1c on 17c orange	invtd surch (vc)	.75	.75
ELS139	457b			dbl surch (vc)	.75	.75
ELS140	458a	(1920-21)	1c on 12c violet	dbl surch (vc)	1.00	1.00
ELS141	462a		1c on 12c violet	dbl surch (vc)	—	—
ELS142	468a	(1921)	1c on 1c ol grn	dbl surch (vc)	.75	
ELS143	469a		1c on 5c yellow	invtd surch (vc)	—	
ELS144	469b			dbl surch (vc)	—	
ELS145	470a		1c on 10c blue	dbl surch (vc)	.50	
ELS146	471a		1c on 25c green	dbl surch (vc) ·	—	
ELS147	472a		1c on 50c olive	dbl surch (vc)	—	
ELS148	473a		1c on 1p gray blk	dbl surch (vc)	—	
ELS149	487a	(1924)	1c on 25c ol grn (r)	numeral at right invtd	—	
ELS150	487b			dbl surch (vc)	—	—
ELS151	493a		2c on 5c orange	top ornament omitted	2.00	2.00
ELS152	494a		5c on 60c violet	"1781," for "1874"	10.00	8.75
ELS153	494b			"1934," for "1924,"	10.00	8.75
ELS154	500a	(1924-25)	10c orange	"ATLANT CO,"	5.25	5.25
ELS155	510a	(1928)	3c on 10c orange	"ATLANT CO"	12.50	12.50
ELS156	511a		1c on 5c olive black	bar instead of top left "1,"	.38	.25
ELS157	512a	(1929)	1c dull violet	center invtd (u)	12.50	12.50
ELS158	513a		3c bister brn	center invtd (u)	37.50	37.50
ELS159	525a	(1932)	10c orange	"ATLANT CO"	7.50	6.25
ELS160	530a	(1934)	2c on 5c grnsh blk	dbl surch (vc)	—	
ELS161	531a		3c on 10c org (bk)	"ATLANT CO"	4.00	4.00
ELS162	532a		2c on 50c	dbl surch (vc)	3.00	—
ELS163	C3a	(1929)	15c on 10c orange	"ATLANT CO"	14.00	14.00
ELS164	C4a		25c on 35c scar & grn	bars invtd	7.50	7.50
ELS165	C8a	(1930)	15c on 10c orange	"ATLANT CO"	17.50	—
ELS166	C8b			dbl surch (vc)	10.00	—
ELS167	C8c			as "a" dbl surch (vc)	75.00	—
ELS168	C8d			pair, one without surch (vc)	175.00	—
ELS169	C10a		50c on 1 col grn & vio	without bars over "UN COLON"	2.50	—
ELS170	C10b			as "a" without block over "l,"	2.50	—
ELS171	C15a		15c deep red	"15,"dbl	82.50	—
ELS172	C52a	(1937)	15c dk olive bister	dbl ovpt (vc)	25.00	—
ELS173	C126a	(1949)	10c dk green	yellow omitted (u)	20.00	—
ELS174	O2a	(1896)	2c dk brown	dbl ovpt (vc)	—	—
ELS175	O15a		3c yellow brn	invtd ovpt (vc)	1.00	—
ELS176	O17a		10c brown	invtd ovpt (vc)	1.25	—
ELS177	O20a		20c car rose	invtd ovpt (vc)	—	—
ELS178	O25a		1c emerald	dbl ovpt (vc)	—	—
ELS179	O29a		10c brown	invtd oovpt (vc)	—	—
ELS180	O32a		20c car rose	invtd ovpt (vc)	—	—
ELS181	O87a	(1897)	24c yellow	invtd ovpt	—	—
ELS182	O209a	(1900)	2c orange	invtd ovpt (vc)	—	—
ELS183	O223a		1c lt green	invtd ovpt (vc)	—	—
ELS184	O224a		2c rose	invtd ovpt (vc)	—	1.75
ELS185	O225a		3c gray black	ovpt vertical	—	—
ELS186	O227a		10c blue	invtd ovpt (vc)	—	—
ELS187	O231a		26c yellow brn	invtd ovpt (vc)	—	—
ELS188	O232a		50c dull rose	invtd ovpt (vc)	—	—
ELS189	O234A		2c ROSE	"FRANQUEO OFICIAL" invtd	—	—
ELS190	O255a	(1905)	3c on 5c dk bl	dbl surch (vc)	—	—

EL SALVADOR

ELS191	O261a	(1906)	3c gray black	ovpt "1906," in blk	—	—
ELS192	O323a	(1915)	1c gray green	"1915," dbl	—	—
ELS193	O323b			"OFICIAL," invtd	—	—
ELS194	O326a		10c yellow	date omitted	—	—
ELS195	O343a	(1921)	2c black	invtd ovpt (vc)	—	—
ELS196	O351a	(1925)	10c orange (r)	"ATLANT CO,"	7.50	6.25
ELS197	O356a		10c orange	"ATLANT CO"	12.50	11.50
ELS198	O361a	(1932)	10c orange	"ATLANT CO"	14.00	12.50
ELS199	RA1a	(1931)	1c on 50c org brn	dbl surch (vc)	2.00	2.00
ELS200	RA4a		2c on 50c org brn	without period in "0.02,"	1.25	—

SAMOA

SAM1	26a	(1898-1900)	2-1/2p on 1sh rose (bk)	dbl surch (vc)	NA	—
SAM2	28a		2-1/2p on 1p bl grn (r)	invtd surch (vc)	—	NA
SAM3	101a	(1914)	1/2p on 3pf brown	dbl surch (vc)	NA	
SAM4	101b			fraction bar omitted	50.00	30.00
SAM5	101c			comma after "I"	NA	
SAM6	102a		1/2p on 5pf green	dbl surch (vc)	NA	
SAM7	102b			fraction bar omitted	125.00	55.00
SAM8	102d			comma after "I"	NA	
SAM9	103a		1p on 10pf car	dbl surch (vc)	NA	
SAM10	104a		2-1/2p on 20pf ultra	fraction bar omitted	65.00	37.50
SAM11	104b			invtd surch (vc)	NA	
SAM12	104c			dbl surch (vc)	NA	
SAM13	104d			commas after "I"	NA	
SAM14	105a		3p on 25pf org & blk, yel	dbl surch (vc)	NA	
SAM15	105b			comma afteer "I"	NA	
SAM16	108a		6p on 50pf pur & blk, salmon	invtd "9," for "6,"	165.00	110.00
SAM17	108b			dbl surch (vc)	NA	
SAM18	110a		1sh on 1m car ("1Shillings")	"1Shilling,"	NA	
SAM19	112a		3sh on 3m blk vio	dbl surch (vc)	NA	

**Samoa is a beautiful land
With less than beautiful errors
Of course there is the fabled vc
For all to come and see
But the rest is hoi polloi
A little here, a little there, a little everywhere. —The Bard**

SAN MARINO

SAN1	25a	(1892)	5c on 10c blue	invtd surch (vc)	32.50	6.25
SAN2	25c		on ultramarine,	invtd surch	NA	
SAN3	26a		5c on 30c brown	invtd surch (vc)	NA	32.50
SAN4	26b			dbl surch, one invtd	NA	85.00
SAN5	26c			dbl invtd surch	NA	85.00
SAN6	27a		10c on 20c ver	invtd surch (vc)	22.50	4.00
SAN7	27b			dbl surch, one invtd	20.00	7.00
SAN8	27c			dbl surch (vc)	20.00	7.00
SAN9	77a	(1905)	15c on 20c brown org	large 5 in 1905 on level with 9	30.00	19.00
SAN10	C54a	(1947)	100l sepia	dbl ovpt (vc)	22.50	
SAN11	C54b			invtd ovpt (vc)	65.00	—
SAN12	E5a	(1927)	1.25l on 60c on 25c	invtd surch (vc)	57.50	—
SAN13	E5b			vert pair, imperf between	NA	
SAN14	E5c			dbl surch (vc)	NA	—
SAN15	J2a	(1897-1920)	10c bl grn & dk brn	numerals invtd	100.00	100.00
SAN16	J4a		50c bl grn& dk brn	numerals invtd	100.00	100.00
SAN17	J19a		5c blue & brn	numerals invtd	42.50	42.50
SAN18	J20a		10c blue 7 brn	numerals invtd	42.50	42.50
SAN19	J26a		50c blue & brn	numerals invtd	42.50	42.50

SARAWAK

SAR1	22a	(1889-91)	22a 2c on 8c	dbl surch (vc)	NA	—
SAR2	22b			pair, one without surch (vc)	NA	—
SAR3	22c			invtd surch (vc)	NA	—
SAR4	23a		5c on 12c ('91)	dbl surch (vc)	NA	
SAR5	23b			pair, one without surch (vc)	—	—
SAR6	23c			no period after "C"	18.00	21.00
SAR7	23d			without "C"	NA	—
SAR8	23e			dbl surch, one vert	NA	—
SAR9	24a		5c on 12c ('91)	no period after "C"	45.00	105.00
SAR10	24b			dbl surch (vc)	NA	—
SAR11	24c			"C' omitted	NA	
SAR12	25b	(1892)	1c on 3c brown, yel	without bar		
SAR13	25c			period after "THREE"	13.00	18.00
SAR14	25d			dbl surch (vc)	NA	—
SAR15	26a		1c on 3c lilac & blue	no period after "cent"	100.00	100.00
SAR16	27b		1c on 3c lilac & blue	dbl surch (vc)	NA	
SAR17	32a	(1899)	2c on 3c brown, yel	period after "THREE"	50.00	—
SAR18	33a		2c on 12c red, rose	invtd surch (vc)	NA	
SAR19	34a		4c on 6c green, grn (r)	invtd surch (vc)	—	—
SAR20	77a	(1923)	1c on 10c ultra	"cnet"	NA	
SAR21	77b			bars 3/4 mm apart	45.00	—
SAR22	78a		2c on 12c violet	bars 3/4 mm apart	45.00	—

Quack, quack for Sarawak
A land of mix-em-upper
You have your vc's of course
You have oxen, cats and even the horse
A land of mixed errors and demi-terrors
Makes it hard to categorize. —The Bard

SASENO

SAS1	8a	(1923)	1l brown & green	dbl ovpt (vc)	70.00	—

SAUDI ARABIA

SAU1	L15a	(1921)	1/8pi orange	invtd ovpt (vc)	100.00	—
SAU2	L15b			dbl ovpt (vc)	200.00	—
SAU3	L15c			roulette 20	NA	
SAU4	L15d			as "C" invtd ovpt	—	NA
SAU5	L16a		pi green	invtd ovpt (vc)	100.00	
SAU6	L16b			dbl ovpt (vc)	200.00	—
SAU7	L16c			roulette 20	NA	—
SAU8	L16d		as "c"	invtd ovpt (vc)	—	—
SAU9	L17a		1/2pi red	invtd ovpt (vc)	150.00	85.00
SAU10	L17b			roulette 20	NA	—
SAU11	L18a		1pi blue (r)	brown ovpt	27.50	20.00
SAU12	L18b			black ovpt	35.00	30.00
SAU13	L18c			as "b" invtd ovpt	NA	—
SAU14	L18d			roulette 20	NA	—
SAU15	L24a	(1922)	1pa lilac brown	invtd ovpt (vc)	150.00	—
SAU16	L24b			dbl ovpt (vc)	100.00	—
SAU17	L24c			dbl ovpt (vc) one invtd	200.00	—
SAU18	L25a		1/8pi orange	invtd ovpt (vc)	100.00	—
SAU19	L25b			dbl ovpt, one invtd (vc)	200.00	—
SAU20	L26a		1/4pi green	invrtd ovpt (vc)	100.00	—
SAU21	L26b			dbl ovpt, one invtd	200.00	—
SAU22	L27a		1/2pi red	invtd ovpt (vc)	100.00	—
SAU23	L27b			dbl ovpt, one invtd (vc)	200.00	—
SAU24	L28a		1pi blue	dbl ovpt (vc)	90.00	—
SAU25	L28b			invtd ovpt (vc)	150.00	—
SAU26	L29a		2pi magenta	dbl ovpt (vc)	150.00	—
SAU27	L31a		1pi on 1pa lilac brn	invtd surch (vc)	100.00	—
SAU28	L31b			dbl surch (vc)	90.00	—

SAU29	L31c			dbl surch (vc) one invtd, ovpt invtd	—	—
SAU30	L40a	(1923)	1/4pi on 1/8 pi org brn	dbl surch (vc)	—	—
SAU31	L40b			dbl invtd surch	—	—
SAU32	L40c			dbl surch, one invtd	—	—
SAU33	L41a		10pi on 5pi ol grn	dbl surch, one invtd	—	—
SAU34	L41b			invtd surch (vc)	—	—
SAU35	L50a	(1924)	10pi vio &dk brn	center invtd (u)	60.00	60.00
SAU36	L50b			center omitted (u)	75.00	—
SAU37	L51a	(1925)	1/8pi orange	invtd ovpt (vc)	100.00	—
SAU38	L51b			ovpt on face & back	200.00	—
SAU39	L52a		1/4pi green	invtd ovpt (vc)	65.00	—
SAU40	L52b			dbl ovpt	60.00	—
SAU41	L52c			dbl ovpt, one invtd	150.00	—
SAU42	L53a		1/2pi red	invtd ovpt (vc)	165.00	—
SAU43	L54a		1pi blue	invtd ovpt (vc)	150.00	—
SAU44	L54b			dbl ovpt one invtd	140.00	—
SAU45	L55a		1pa lilac brown	invtd ovpt (vc)	75.00	—
SAU46	L55b			dbl ovpt (vc)	65.00	—
SAU47	L56a		1/8pi orange	invtd ovpt (vc)	90.00	—
SAU48	L57a		1/4 pi green	pair, one without ovpt (vc)	NA	—
SAU49	L57b			invtd ovpt (vc)	50.00	—
SAU50	L57c			dbl ovpt, one invtd	NA	—
SAU51	L58a		1/2pi red	invtd ovpt (vc)	150.00	—
SAU51	L59a		1pi blue	invtd ovpt (vc)	110.00	—
SAU52	L60a		2pi magenta	invtd ovpt (vc)	150.00	—
SAU53	L62a		1/4pi green	invtd ovpt (vc)	110.00	—
SAU54	L63a		1/4pi green	invtd ovpt (vc)	90.00	—
SAU55	L63b			ovpt on face & back	90.00	—
SAU56	L64a		1/2pi red,	invtd ovpt upright ovpt	150.00	—
SAU57	L65a		1/4pi green	invtd ovpt (vc)	75.00	—
SAU58	L65b			vertical ovpt	NA	—
SAU59	L66a		1/2pi red	invtd ovpt	100.00	—
SAU60	L69a		1/8pi orange	invtd ovpt (vc)	—	—
SAU61	L70a		1/4pi green	invtd ovpt (vc)	—	—
SAU62	L71a		1/2pi red	invtd ovpt (vc)	NA	—
SAU63	L73a		2pi magenta	invtd ovpt (vc)	NA	—
SAU64	L75a		1pi on 1pa	invtd ovpt (vc)	NA	—
SAU65	L82a	(1925)	1/8pi red brown	invtd ovpt (vc)	50.00	—
SAU66	L83a		1/2pi red	dbl ovpt (vc)	75.00	—
SAU67	L83b			invtd ovpt (vc)	50.00	50.00
SAU68	L83c			dbl ovpt, one invtd (vc)	75.00	—
SAU69	L83d			ovpt reading up	—	—
SAU70	L84a		1pi dark blue	invtd ovpt (vc)	NA	—
SAU71	L85a		1-1/2pi violet	invtd ovpt (vc)	50.00	50.00
SAU72	L86a		2pi orange	dbl ovpt, one invtd	75.00	—
SAU73	L86b			invtd ovpt (vc)	50.00	50.00
SAU74	L86c			dbl ovpt (vc)	75.00	—
SAU75	L87a		3pi olive brown	invtd ovpt (vc)	50.00	—
SAU76	L87b			dbl ovpt , one invtd	75.00	—
SAU77	L87c			ovpt reading up	175.00	—
SAU78	L87d			dbl ovpt, both invtd	100.00	—
SAU79	L88a		3pi dull red	invtd ovpt (vc)	50.00	—
SAU80	L88b			dbl ovpt, one invtd	75.00	—
SAU81	L89a		5pi olive green	invtd ovpt	50.00	—
SAU82	L90a		1/8pi red brown	invtd ovpt (vc)	150.00	—
SAU83	L91a		1/2pi red	invtd ovpt	NA	—
SAU84	L92a		1pi dark blue	invtd ovpt (vc)	NA	—
SAU85	L93a		1-1/2pi violet	invtd ovpt (vc)	75.00	—
SAU86	L94a		2pi orange	invtd ovpt (vc)	50.00	—
SAU87	L95a		3pi olive brown	invtd ovpt (vc)	75.00	75.00
SAU88	L96a		3pi dull red	invtd ovpt (vc)	75.00	75.00

SAU89	L97a		5pi olive green	invtd ovpt	50.00	—
SAU90	L99b		1/4pi yellow green	invtd ovpt (vc)	50.00	—
SAU91	L100a		1/2pi red	invtd ovpt (vc)	50.00	—
SAU92	L101		1pi dark blue	invtd ovpt (vc)	50.00	—
SAU93	L102		1-1/2pi violet	invtd ovpt (vc)	50.00	—
SAU94	L103		2pi orange	invtd ovpt (vc)	50.00	—
SAU95	L104			ovpt reaading up	175.00	—
SAU96	L106a		5pi olive green	invtd ovpt (vc)	50.00	—
SAU97	L106b			ovpt reading up	—	—
SAU98	L107a		10pi vio & dk brn	invtd ovpt (vc)	50.00	—
SAU99	L107b			center invtd (vc)	100.00	—
SAU100	L107c			as "b" invtd ovpt	150.00	—
SAU101	L116a		1/8pi red brown	dbl ovpt, one invtd	NA	—
SAU102	L120a		2pi orange	invtd ovpt (vc)	NA	—
SAU103	L121a		3pi olive brown	invtd ovpt (vc)	NA	—
SAU104	122a		5pi olive green	invtd ovpt (vc)	NA	—
SAU105	L123a		1/8pi red brown	invtd ovpt	NA	—
SAU106	L125a		1-1/2pi violet	invtd ovpt (vc)	NA	—
SAU107	L127a		3pi olive brown	invtd ovpt (vc)	NA	—
SAU108	L128a		5pi olive green	invtd ovpt	NA	—
SAU109	L135a	(1925)	1/4pi on 1/4pi on 1/8pi red brn		—	—
SAU110	L136c		1/4pi on 1/4pi on 1pi 1/2pi red		60.00	60.00
SAU111	L138a		1pi on 1pi on 2pi orange 1/2pi on 1/2pi on 2pi orange		—	—
SAU112	L138b		10pi on 1pi on 2pi orange		100.00	—
SAU113	L138c		1/4pi on 1pi on 2pi orange		50.00	—
SAU114	L138d		1pi on 1/4pi on 2pi orange		100.00	—
SAU115	L140b		1pi on 1pi on 3pi dl red 1/4pi on 1pi on 3pi dl red		—	—
SAU116	L141b		10pi on 10pi on 5pi ol grn 1pi on 10pi on 5pi		—	—
SAU117	L142a		1/8pi on 1/2pi red	invtd surch (vc)	40.00	—
SAU118	L143a		1/4pi on 1/2pi red	invtd surch (vc)	40.00	—
SAU119	L144a		1pi on 1/2pi red	invtd surch (vc)	25.00	—
SAU120	L145a		1pi on 1-1/2 pi violet	invtd surch (vc)	35.00	—
SAU121	L146a		1pi on 2pi orange	"10pi"	85.00	—
SAU122	L147a		1pi on 3pi olive brn	"10pi"	75.00	—
SAU123	L148a		10pi on 5pi olive green	invtd surch (vc)	65.00	—
SAU124	L149a		1/8pi on 1/2pi red	invtd surch (vc)	65.00	—
SAU125	L150a		1/8pi on 1/2pi red	invtd surch	50.00	—
SAU126	L151a		1pi on 1/2pi red	invtd surch (vc)	50.00	—
SAU127	L151b			dbl surch (vc)	—	—
SAU128	L152a		1pi on 1-1/2pi violet	invtd surch (vc)	65.00	—
SAU129	L153a		1pi on 2pi orange	"10pi"	70.00	—
SAU130	L153b			invtd surch (vc)	65.00	—
SAU131	L154a		1pi on 3pi olive brn	"10pi"	85.00	—
SAU132	L154b			invtd surch (vc)	70.00	—
SAU133	L155a		10pi on 5pi olive green	invtd surch (vc)	60.00	—
SAU134	L156a		1pi on 1-1/2pi violet	invtd surch (vc)	80.00	—
SAU135	L157a		1pi on 2pi orange	"10pi"	80.00	—
SAU136	L157b			invtd surch (vc)	80.00	—
SAU137	L158a		1pi on 3pi olive brown	"10pi"	100.00	—
SAU138	L158b			invtd surch (vc)	80.00	—
SAU139	L159a		10pi on 5pi olive green	invtd surch (vc)	80.00	—
SAU140	L16a		10pi red & green	center invtd (u)	75.00	—
SAU141	L186a		10pi red & green	dbl impression of center	100.00	—

SAU142	56a	(1925-26)	1-1/2pi violet	violet ovpt	NA	
SAU143	727a	(1977)	20h dk brn & brt green	incorrect date	25.00	—
SAU144	728a		80h bl blk & brt green	incorrect date	25.00	—
SAU145	740a		50h rose & orange	50h dull org & org (error)	75.00	7.50
SAU146	LJ4a		20pa red	dbl ovpt, one at left	150.00	—
SAU147	LJ4b			ovpt at left	32.50	22.50
SAU148	LJ6a		1pi bl	ovpt at left ovpt at right	30.00	35.00
SAU149	LJ7a		2pi magenta	dbl ovpt, one at left	70.00	—
SAU150	LJ7b			ovpt at left	30.00	—
SAU151	LJ8a	(1922)	20pa red	ovpt at left	40.00	—
SAU152	LJ9a		1pi blue	ovpt at left	50.00	—
SAU153	LJ10a		2pi magenta	ovpt at left	35.00	—
SAU154	LJ22a	(1925)	20pa red (bl)	invtd ovpt (vc)	NA	
SAU155	LJ4a		1pi blue (r)	invtd ovpt	35.00	35.00
SAU156	LJ25a		2pi magenta (bl)	invtd ovpt (vc)	40.00	50.00
SAU157	LJ25b			dbl ovpt (vc)	NA	—
SAU158	O36a	(1965-70)	16p black	"19" instead of "16,"	NA	

Saudi vc stamps around the town
Vc, vc makes a golden crown
But inverted centers too, and centers omitted
Centers too with impression double
Blows up like one big bubble. —The Bard

SCHLESWIG

SCH1	O7a	(1920)	25pf orange	invtd ovpt	NA	—

SENEGAL

SEN1	1a	(1887)	5c on 20c red, grn	dbl surch (vc)	—	—
SEN2	57a	(1906)	1c slate	"SENEGAL" omitted	80.00	80.00
SEN3	61a		10c car (bl)	"SENEGAL" omitted	NA	
SEN4	132a	(1927)	90c on 75c brn red & cer	dbl surch (vc)	80.00	80.00
SEN5	140a	(1931)	90c red orange	"SENEGAL" dbl	70.00	—

SENEGAMBIA & NIGER has produced no errors

SERBIA

SER1	58a	(1901)	15p on 1d red brn, bl	invtd surch (vc)	100.00	110.00
SER2	68a	(1903-04)	1p red lil & blk (bl)	invtd ovpt (vc)	10.00	—
SER3	70a			gray & blk (bl) dbl ovpt	8.75	—
SER4	73a		25p bl & blk (bk)	dbl ovpt (vc)	10.00	—
SER5	115a	(1914)	15p slate blk	15p red (error)	—	—
SER6	K5a	(1895)	50p rose	cliche of 5p in plate of 50p	75.00	95.00

SEYCHELLES has produced no errors

SHARJAH (TRUCIAL STATES)

SHA1	M52T	(1964)	Apr.7., Airmail; 10r multicolored complete set	T47x-52x red ovpt	100.00
SHA2	M160E	(1965)	160G: Exist	violet ovpt "3 bars"	

SHANGHAI

SHA1	2b	(1865-66)	4ca yellow	dbl impression (u)	—	—
SHA2	15a		16ca vermillion	"1," of "16," omitted	—	—
SHA3	25a		16ca vermillion	"1." of "16." omitted	—	—
SHA4	46a	(1866)	1ca brown	"CANDS"	45.00	50.00
SHA5	113a	(1888)	60 cash rose	third character at left lacks dot at top	6.25	7.00
SHA6	121a	(1889)	100 cash on 20c l on 100c ye	without the surch "100,"	NA	
SHA7	121b			blue & red surch	—	—
SHA8	151c	(1893)	1c on half of 2c	dbl surch, one in green	—	NA

SHA9	151d		dbl surch, one in black	NA	
SHA10	161a	1c brown & blk	dbl ovpt (vc)	25.00	25.00
SHA11	162a	2c vermillion & blk	invtd ovpt (vc)	110.00	—
SHA12	163a	5c blue & blk	invtd ovpt (vc)	110.00	—

With vc's relatively low in number
Other errors resting in slumber
We find a hoi poloi of errors
Some are monstrous hopeless terrors
Others are timid gentle errors
BUT ONE a valued double impression
Makes every errorists selection. —The Bard

SHARJAH & DEPENDENCIES has produced no errors

SIBERIA

SIB1	1a	(1919)	35k on dk dull green	invtd surch (vc)	27.50	—
SIB2	2a		50k on 3k carmine	invtd surch (vc)	35.00	—
SIB3	3a		0k on 1k dl org yel	invtd surch (vc)	27.50	—
SIB4	4a		1r on 4k carmine	dbl surch, one invtd	45.00	—
SIB5	4b			invtd surch (vc)	50.00	—
SIB6	5a		3r on 7k blue	dbl surch (vc)	22.50	—
SIB7	5b			invtd surch (vc)	20.00	—
SIB8	6a		5r on 14k dk bl & car	dbl surch (vc)	22.50	—
SIB9	6b			invtd surch (vc)	22.50	—
SIB10	8a		50k on 3k red, imperf	invtd surch	100.00	—
SIB11	9a		70k on 1k orange	invtd surch (vc)	25.00	—
SIB12	60a		on 20k dl bl & dk bl & car	15k on 20k on 14k dk bl & car (error)	—	—
SIB12	78a	(1922)	2k gray green	invtd ovpt (vc)	125.00	—
SIB13	97a		35k red brn & green	invtd ovpt (vc)	80.00	—
SIB14	100a		1k orange	invtd ovpt (vc)	65.00	85.00
SIB15	112a		5k claret	invtd ovpt (vc)	100.00	—

Siberia has produced 14vc's, one color error.

SIERRA LEONE

SIE1	32a	(1893)	1/2p on 1-1/2p violet	"PFNNY"	NA	
SIE2	33a		1/2p on 1-1/2p violet	"PFNNY"	65.00	65.00
SIE3	33b			invtd surch (vc)	110.00	110.00
SIE4	33c			same as "a" invtd	NA	
SIE5	33d			dbl surch (vc)	NA	

SINGAPORE

SIN1	54a	(1962)	4c red orange & blk	black omitted (u)	110.00	—
SIN2	55a		5c gray & red orange	red org omitted (u)	110.00	—
SIN3	57a		10c dk gray & red orange	red org omitted (u)	85.00	—
SIN4	58a		20c org & blue	org omitted (u)	125.00	—
SIN5	59a		25c orange & blk	blk omitted (u)	100.00	—
SIN6	65a		30c tan & olive green	tan omitted (u)	50.00	—
SIN7	76a	(1966)	15c blue & black	orange (eye) omitted (u)	12.50	—

SLOVAKIA has produced no errors

SLOVENIA has produced no errors

SOLOMON ISLANDS

SOL1	156b		8c on 9p multi	"8," invtd	13.00	13.00

Every game has a call
And one of these is 8-ball
8-ball up and 8-ball down
Inverted eight ball Solomon. —The Bard

SOMALIA

SOM1	98a	(1927)	50c deep orange	dbl ovpt (vc)	40.00	—
SOM2	100a	(1928-30)	7-1/2c lt brown	dbl ovpt (vc)	150.00	—
SOM3	124a	(1923)	2b buff & black	num & ovpt invtd	62.50	—
SOM4	132a	(1926)	10C	num & ovpt invtd	20.00	—
SOM5	133a	(1926)	20C	num & ovpt invtd	110.00	—
SOM6	134a	(1926)	30C	num & ovpt invtd	20.00	—
SOM7	135a	(1926)	40C	num & ovpt invtd	20.00	—
SOM8	136a	(1926)	50C	num & ovpt invtd	20.00	—
SOM9	137a	(1926)	60C	num & ovpt invtd	20.00	—
SOM10	Q1a	(1917-19)	5c brown	dbl ovpt (vc)	150.00	—
SOM11	Q4a	(1917-19)	25c red	dbl ovpt (vc)	NA	—

As we would expect from any land
Vc's flourish from any band
But numerals and overprints
From Somalia take rarer stints. —The Bard

SOMALI COAST

SOC1	1a	(1894)	5c grn & red, grnsh	without bar	NA	NA
SOC2	2a	(1894)	25c on 2c brn & bl, buff	"25" omitted	NA	NA
SOC3	2b			"DJIBOUTI" omitted	NA	NA
SOC4	2c	(1894)	25c on 2c brn & bl, buff	"DJIBOUTI" invtd	NA	NA
SOC5	3a	(1894)	50c on 1c blk & red, bl	"5" instead of "50"	NA	NA
SOC6	3b			"o" instead of "50"	NA	NA
SOC7	3c			"DJIBOUTI" omitted	NA	NA
SOC8	23a	(1899)	40c on 4c brn & bl	dbl surch (vc)	NA	NA
SOC9	24a	(1902)	0.05c on 75c	invtd surch (vc)	NA	NA
SOC10	25a	(1902)	0.10c on 1fr	invtd surch (vc)	NA	NA
SOC11	27a	(1902)	0.75 on 5fr	invtd surch (vc)	NA	NA
SOC12	28a		5c on 40c	dbl surch (vc)	85.00	85.00
SOC13	29a		10c on 50c	invtd surch (vc)	NA	NA
SOC14	30a		5c on 30c bis & yel grn	invtd surch (vc)	190.00	190.00
SOC15	30b			dbl surch (vc)	175.00	140.00
SOC16	30c			triple surch (u)	—	—
SOC17	32a		10c on 10fr org & red vio	dbl surch (vc)	175.00	165.00
SOC18	32b			triple surch, one invtd (u)	NA	NA
SOC19	33a		10c on 2fr dl vio & org	"DJIBOUTI" invtd	200.00	165.00
SOC20	33b			large "O" in "10"	90.00	65.00

SOC32

SOC33

SOC34

SOC35

SOC36

SOC37

SOC38

SPA22A

SPA22A

SOC21	33c			dbl surch (vc)	NA	NA
SOC22	33Fg		10c on 50fr red vio & grn	"01" instead of "10"	150.00	125.00
SOC23	33Fh			"CENTIMES" invtd	NA	NA
SOC24	33Fi			dbl surch (vc)	NA	NA
SOC25	47a	(1902)	2fr yel grn & car	without names of designer & engraver at bottom	100.00	100.00
SOC26	62a	(1903)	2fr yel grn & blk	without names of designer & engraver at bottom	27.50	27.50
SOC27	119a	(1922)	10c on 5c (G)	dbl surch (vc)	55.00	55.00
SOC28	208a	(1943)	70c lt vio (R)	invtd ovpt (vc)	90.00	90.00
SOC29	242a	(1945)	70c on 5c (C)	invtd surch (vc)	65.00	—
SOC30	244a	(1945)	2.40fr on 25c	invtd surch (vc)	60.00	—
SOC31	246a	(1945)	4.50fr on 25C	invtd surch (vc)	60.00	—

SOMALILAND PROTECTORATE

SOP1	3a	(1903)	2a violet	dbl ovpt (vc)	NA	—
SOP2	8a	(1903)	12a brown, red	invtd ovpt (vc)	—	NA
SOP3	18a	(1903)	3r green & brn	invtd ovpt (vc)	NA	—

SOUTH AFRICA

SOF1	2a	(1913-24)	1/2p green	dbl impression (u)	NA	—
SOF2	23d	(1926)	1/2p dk grn & blk, pair	center omitted (u)	NA	—
SOF3	23e			booklet pane of 6 (u)	50.00	—
SOF4	24e	(1926)	1p car & blk, pair	center omitted (u)	NA	—
SOF5	34c	(1930-45)	1p car & blk	pair center omitted (u)	NA	—
SOF6	34d			frame omitted (u)	NA	—
SOF7	35c	(1930-45)	1p rose & blk, pair ('32)	center omitted (u)	NA	—
SOF8	36c	(1930-45)	2p vio & gray, pair ('31)	frame omitted (u)	NA	—
SOF9	39c	(1930-45)	3p ultra & bl, pair ('33)	center omitted (u)	NA	—
SOF10	48g	(1933-54)	1p car & gray, pair ('34)	as "e," single, Afrikaans (u)	1.40	1.00
SOF11	48h			center omitted, pair (u)	NA	—
SOF12	51d	(1933-54)	1-1/2 p dk grn & gold, 27x21-1/2mm, pair ('36)	center omitted, pair (u)	NA	—
SOF13	52c	(1933-54)	1 -1/2 p sl grn & ocher, 22x18mm, pair ('41)	center omitted, pair (u)	NA	—
SOF14	219a	(1959)	3p brt blue & dk blue	dark blue omitted (u)	NA	—
SOF15	261a	(1961)	7-1/2 emerald & brn	brown omitted (u)	—	—
SOF16	263a	(1961)	12-1/2 c dk grn, red & yel	yellow omitted (u)	—	—
SOF17	286a	(1963)	12-1/2 C dk bl gray & red	red cross omitted (u)	NA	—
SOF18	287a	(1963)	2-1/2 c dk brown & lt grn	light green omitted (u)	NA	—
SOF19	305a	(1964)	12 -1/2 c ultra & gold	gold omitted (u)	NA	—
SOF20	07c	(1929)	1/2 p grn & blk, pair	period after "OFFISIEEL" on English stamp	3.25	3.25
SOF21	07e			period after "OFFISIEEL" on Afrikaans stamp	3.25	3.25
SOF22	09c	(1929)	6p org & grn, pair	period after "OFFISIEEL" on English stamp	8.00	10.00
SOF23	09e			period after "OFFISIEEL" on Afrikaans stamp	8.00	10.00
SOF24	010c	(1931)	1sh dp bl & bis brn, pair	period after "OFFICIAL" on Afrikaans stamp	50.00	50.00
SOF25	011c	(1930-47)	2shop brn & bl grn, pair	period after "OFFICIAL" on Afrikaans stamp	72.50	72.50
SOF26	012c	(1930-47)	1/2p bl grn & blk (#33), pair ('31)	period after "OFFISIEEL" on English stamp	4.50	5.00
SOF27	012e			period after "OFFISIEEL" on Afrikaans stamp	4.50	5.00
SOF28	014c	(1930-47)	1p car & blk, pair (#34)	period after "OFFISIEEL" on English stamp	4.25	4.75
SOF29	014e			period after "OFFISIEEL" on Afrikaans stamp	4.25	5.75

SOF30	015c	(1930-47) 1p rose & blk, pair (#35) ('33)	dbl ovpt, pair (u)	NA	NA
SOF31	018c	(1930-47) 6p org & grn, pair (#42)	period after "OFFISIEEL" on English stamp	11.00	11.00
SOF32	018e		period after "OFFISIEEL" on Afrikaans stamp	11.00	11.00
SOF33	020c	(1930-47) 2sh6p red brn & grn, pair (#44) ('33)	spaced 21mm, pair	50.00	80.00
SOF34	020d		as "c" single, English	4.50	8.00
SOF35	020e		as "c," single, Afrikaans	4.50	8.00

There is an official stamp that is extremely rare
It is commonly called a double overprint pair.
The other issue errors with beauteous concession
Are almost every man's obsession
But centrality is at each man's heart
And center omitted a goodly part
Colors may be omitted too
Yellow, brown and dark blue. —The Bard

Bophuthatswana has produced no errors
Ciskei has produced no errors
Transkei has produced no errors
Venda has produced no errors

SOUTHERN NIGERIA has produced no errors

SOUTHERN RHODESIA

SOR1	96a	(1964)	1p Cape buffalo	purple omitted (u)	NA	—
SOR2	102a	(1964)	1sh Emeralds	green omitted (u)	NA	—

SOUTH GEORGIA has produced no errors

SOUTH KASAI has produced no errors

SOUTH RUSSIA

SRU1	1a	(1918)	25k on 1k dl org yel	invtd surch (vc)	20.00	40.00
SRU2	2a	(1918)	25k on 2k dl grn	invtd surch (vc)	16.00	35.00
SRU3	3a	(1918)	25k on 3k car	dbl surch (vc)	30.00	55.00
SRU4	4a	(1918)	25k on 4k car	invtd surch (vc)	16.00	35.00
SRU5	6a	(1918)	25k on 1k orange	invtd surch (vc)	16.00	40.00
SRU6	20a	(1918-20)	25k on 1k dl org yel	invtd surch (vc)	20.00	27.50
SRU7	20b			dbl surch, one inverted	16.00	27.50
SRU8	21a	(1918-20)	50k on 2k dl grn	invtd surch (vc)	16.00	27.50
SRU9	21b			dbl surch (vc)	10.50	13.00
SRU10	21c			dbl surch invtd	10.50	13.00
SRU11	23a	(1918-20)	1r on 3k car	invtd surch (vc)	11.50	16.00
SRU12	23b			dbl surch (vc)	5.25	10.00
SRU13	23c			pair, one without surch	5.25	10.00
SRU14	24a	(1918-20)	1r on 3k car	invtd surch (vc)	8.00	13.00
SRU15	24b			dbl surch (vc)	8.00	13.00
SRU16	24c			pair, one without surch	11.50	13.00
SRU17	25b	(1918-20)	3r on 4k rose	invtd surch (vc)	27.50	50.00
SRU18	25c			dbl surch (vc)	30.00	52.50
SRU19	25d			dbl surch invtd	30.00	52.50
SRU20	26b	(1918-20)	10r on 4k rose	invtd surch (vc)	32.50	50.00
SRU21	27a	(1918-20)	10r on 15k red brn & dp bl	surch on face & back	13.00	13.00
SRU22	27b			dbl surch, one invtd	30.00	60.00
SRU23	28a	(1981-20)	25r on 3k car	invtd surch (vc)	4.50	10.00
SRU24	29a	(1918-20)	25r on 7k bl	invtd surch (vc)	50.00	52.50
SRU25	30a	(1918-20)	25r on 14k bl & car	invtd surch (vc)	52.50	70.00
SRU26	31a	(1918-20)	25r on 25k dl grn & dk vio	invtd surch (vc)	52.50	70.00
SRU27	36a	(1918-20)	50k on 2k gray grn	invtd surch (vc)	20.00	22.50
SRU28	36b			dbl surch (vc)	20.00	22.50

SRU29			pair, one without surch	20.00	27.50
SRU30	38a	(1918-20) 1r on 3k red	invtd surch (vc)	13.00	16.00
SRU31	38b		dbl surch (vc)	7.25	11.50
SRU32	38c		pair, one without surch	4.00	8.00
SRU33	39a	(1918-20) 1r on 3k red	dbl surch (vc)	7.25	16.00
SRU34	39b		pair, one without surch	7.25	16.00
SRU35	39c		as "a" invtd	21.00	40.00
SRU36	41a	(1918-20) 25r on 3k red	invtd surch (vc)	42.50	—
SRU37	46a	(1919) 70k on 1k orange	invtd surch (vc)	10.50	14.00
SRU38	46b		dbl surch, one invtd	20.00	20.00
SRU39	47a	(1919) 10r on 1k red, buff	invtd surch (vc)	70.00	—
SRU40	48a	(1919) 10r on 5k grn, buff	dbl surch (vc)	NA	—
SRU41	51a	(1919) 35k on 1k orange	comma instead of period in surch	.85	—
SRU42	53a	(1920) 5r on 5k dk claret	invtd surch (vc)	35.00	—
SRU43	53b		dbl surch (vc)	42.50	—
SRU44	54a	(1920) 5r on 20k dl bl & dk car	invtd surch (vc)	15.00	—
SRU45	54b		dbl surch (vc)	35.00	—
SRU46	54c		"5" omitted	14.00	—
SRU47	55a	(1920) 5r on 5k claret	dbl surch (vc)	15.00	—
SRU48	57a	(1920) 5r on 35k lt bl	dbl surch (vc)	75.00	—
SRU49	58a	(1920) 100r on 1k dl org yel	"10" in place of "100"	50.00	—
SRU50	58b		invtd surch (vc)	22.50	—
SRU51	58c		dbl surch (vc)	50.00	—

SOUTH-WEST AFRICA

SWA1	2b	(1923) 1p red, pair	invtd ovpt, pair	NA	—
SWA2	2c		as "b" single, English	140.00	—
SWA3	2d		as "b" single, Dutch	140.00	—
SWA4	2f		dbl ovpt, pair (vc)	—	—
SWA5	2g		as "f" single, English	NA	—
SWA6	2h		as "f" single, Dutch	NA	—
SWA7	3b	(1923) 2p dull vio, pair	invtd ovpt, pair	NA	—
SWA8	3c		as "b" single, English	110.00	—
SWA9	3d		as "b" single, Dutch	110.00	—
SWA10	8b	(1923) 1sh3p violet, pair	invtd ovprt, pair	NA	—
SWA11	13c	(1923) 5sh blue & cl, pair	As #13 without period after "Afrika"	NA	—
SWA12	14c	(1923) 10sh ol grn & bl, pair	as #14 without period after "Afrika"	NA	NA
SWA13	15c	(1923) 1 red & green, pair	as #15 without period after "Afrika"	NA	—
SWA14	18c	(1923-24) 2p dull vio, pair	dbl ovpt, pair	NA	—
SWA15	18d		as "c" single, English	90.00	—
SWA16	18e		as "c" single, Dutch	90.00	—
SWA17	85c	(1926) 1/2p dk green & blk, pair	ovpt "q" on English stamp	.35	1.00
SWA18	85d		ovpt "p" on Afrikaans stamp	.35	1.00
SWA19	85e		pair "c" + "d"	4.50	7.50
SWA20	85f		as "e" without period after "Africa"	200.00	—
SWA21	86c	(1926) 1p car & blk, pair	ovpt "q" on English stamp	.20	1.00
SWA22	86d		ovpt "p" on Afrikaans stamp	.20	1.00
SWA23	86e		pair "c" + "d"	2.50	8.00
SWA24	86f		as "e" without period after "Africa"	NA	—
SWA25	87c	(1926) 6p org & grn, pair	ovpt "q" on English stamp	2.00	5.00
SWA26	87d		ovpt "p" on Afrikaans stamp	2.00	5.00
SWA27	87e		pair "c" + "d"	20.00	40.00
SWA28	87f		as "e" without period after "Africa"	200.00	—
SWA29	94a	(1927) 1sh3p violet	without period after "A"	110.00	—
SWA30	95a	(1927) 1 lt red & gray grn	without period after "A"	NA	NA

SWA31	96c	(1927)	1/2p green & blk, pair	as #96 without period after "A" on one stamp	75.00	—
SWA32	97c	(1927)	1p car & blk, pair	as #97 without period after "A" on one stamp	75.00	75.00
SWA33	97d			ovpt at top pair ('30)	3.25	12.50
SWA34	97e			as "d" single, English	.35	1.75
SWA35	97f			as "d" single, Afrikaans	.35	1.75
SWA36	98c	(1927)	6p org & grn, pair	as #98 without period after "A" on one stamp	125.00	—
SWA37	99c	(1927-28)	2p vio brn & gray, pair	as #99 without period after "A" on one stamp	100.00	100.00
SWA38	99d			dbl ovpt, one invtd	NA	NA
SWA39	100c	(1927-28)	3p red & blk, pair	as #100 without period after "A" on one stamp	125.00	125.00
SWA40	101c	(1928)	4p brn, pair	as #101 without period after "A" on one stamp	85.00	125.00
SWA41	102c	(1927-28)	1sh dp bl & bis brn, pair	as #102 without period after "A" on one stamp	NA	—
SWA42	103c	(1927-28)	2sh6p brn & bl grn, pair	as #103 without period after "A" on one stamp	175.00	NA
SWA43	104c	(1927-28)	5sh dp grn & blk, pair	as #104 without period after "A" on one stamp	NA	—
SWA44	105c	(1927-28)	10sh ol brn & bl, pair	as #105 without period after "A" on one stamp	NA	—
SWA45	144b	(1942-45)	1/2p dp grn, horiz strip of 3	single, Afrikaans	.15	.15
SWA46	144c		1/2p dp bl grn, horiz, strip of 3		31.50	2.25
SWA47	144d			as "c" single, English	.15	.15
SWA48	144e			as "c" single, Afrikaans	.15	.15
SWA49	145b	(1942-45)	1p brt car, horiz strip of 3	single, Afrikaans	.15	.15
SWA50	153c	(1945)	1p rose pink & choc, pair	invtd ovpt, pair	NA	NA
SWA51	153d			as "c" single, English	42.50	—
SWA52	153e			as "c" single, Afrikaans	42.50	—
SWA53	312c	(1968)	strip of 3	A68 3c single, German	.52	.30
SWA54	313c	(1968)	strip of 3	A68 15c single, German	3.00	2.50
SWA55	C1a	(1930)	4p blue green	without period after "A"	80.00	110.00
SWA56	C2a	(1930)	1sh orange	without period after "A"	NA	NA
SWA57	C3a	(1930)	4p blue green	dbl ovpt (vc)	150.00	—

SPAIN

SPA1	9a	(1851)	5r rose	5r red brown (error) (u)	NA	NA
SPA2	10a	(1851)	6r blue	cliche of 2r in plate of 6r (u)	NA	NA
SPA3	38b	(1855)	1r green blue	cliche of 2r in plate of 1r (u)	NA	NA
SPA4	69a	(1865)	12c blue & rose	frame invtd (u)	NA	NA
SPA5	76a	(1865)	12c blue & rose	frame invtd (u)	NA	NA

SPA23B

SPA47A

SPA56

AFFORDABLE FOREIGN ERRORS

SPA6	96a	(1867-68)	25m blue & rose	frame invtd (u)	—	NA
SPA7	120b	(1868-69)	25m blue & rose	frame invtd (u)	NA	—
SPA8	117e	(1868-69)	20c lilac		60.00	45.00
SPA9	120e	(1868-69)	25m blue & rose		75.00	45.00
SPA10	122e	(1868-69)	50m bister brown		55.00	27.50
SPA11	123e	(1868-69)	50m violet		55.00	27.50
SPA12	124e	(1868-69)	100m brown		125.00	60.00
SPA13	125e	(1868-69)	200m green		90.00	35.00
SPA14	126e	(1868-69)	12c orange		75.00	45.00
SPA15	205a	(1874)	25c red brown	25c lilac (error) (u)	NA	NA
SPA16	205b			imperf pair (u)	—	100.00
SPA17	279b	(1900-05)	25c blue	25c green (error) (u)	NA	—
SPA18	283b	(1900-05)	50c slate blue	50c blue green (error) (u)	NA	NA
SPA19	331a	(1922-26)	2c olive green	2c deep orange (error) (u)	85.00	175.00
SPA20	338b	(1922-26)	25c carmine (1)	25c lilac rose (error) (u)	70.00	150.00
SPA21	599a	(1938)	45c car rose	printed on both sides (u)	10.00	10.00
SPA22	637a	(1937)	1p blue & orange	center invtd (u)	NA	NA
SPA23	B6a	(1926)	20c dull violet	20c violet brown (error) (u)	NA	—
SPA24	B21a	(1927)	5c vio brn (R)	dbl ovpt (vc)	35.00	—
SPA25	B47a		15c (Br)	dbl ovpt (vc)	27.50	—
SPA26	B48a		20c (Bl)	brown ovpt (error) (vc)	60.00	—
SPA27	B50b		30c (R)	dbl ovpt (vc)	27.50	—
SPA28	B52b		40c (Br)	dbl ovpt (Bl + Br) (vc)	85.00	—
SPA29	B53a		4p (Bl)	invtd ovpt (vc)	150.00	—
SPA30	B55a		5c (R)	invtd ovpt (vc)	27.50	—
SPA31	B56a		10c (R)	invtd ovpt (vc)	27.50	—
SPA32	B58a		50c (Bl)	dbl ovpt, one invtd	65.00	—
SPA33	B59a		1p (R)	invtd ovpt (vc)	85.00	—
SPA34	B60a		75c on 5c (R)	invtd surch (vc)	27.50	—
SPA35	B61a		75c on 10c (R)	invtd surch (vc)	27.50	—
SPA36	B62a		75c on 25c (Bl)	dbl surch (vc)	50.00	—
SPA37	B137a	(1950)	50c + 10c	"Caudillo" 14 3/4mm wide	90.00	80.00
SPA38	B138a	(1950)	1p + 10c	"Caudillo" 14 3/4mm wide	85.00	70.00
SPA39	C1b	(1920)	5c green (R)	dbl ovpt (vc)	30.00	30.00
SPA40	C1c			invtd ovpt (vc)	75.00	75.00
SPA41	C1d			dbl ovpt, one invtd	30.00	25.00
SPA42	C1e			triple ovpt	30.00	25.00
SPA43	C2b	(1920)	10c car (Bk)	dbl ovpt (vc)	30.00	30.00
SPA44	C2			dbl ovpt, one invtd	30.00	25.00
SPA45	C3a	(1920)	25c dp blue (R)	invtd ovpt (vc)	75.00	75.00
SPA46	C3b			dbl ovpt (vc)	30.00	30.00
SPA47	C97b	(1938)	5p on 1p multi	invtd surch (vc)	NA	NA
SPA48	C97e			dbl surch (vc)	NA	NA
SPA49	CB6d	(1938)	45c + 2p + 5p	souv sheet, surch invtd (vc)	NA	NA
SPA50	CE1a	(1930)	20c bl blk & lt brn (Bk)	blue ovpt	11.00	11.00
SPA51	CE1b			ovpt omitted	20.00	20.00
SPA52	MR6a	(1876)	10c blue	cliche of 5c in plate of 10c (u)	40.00	—
SPA53	7LC1a	(1936)	25c gray grn & blk (R)	blue ovpt	22.50	22.50
SPA54	7LE3a	(1936)	20c (10c + 10c) emer	ovpt invtd (vc)	10.00	—
SPA55	C5					

See Photo in Color Section

SPANISH GUINEA

SPG1	8Fa	(1903)	10c on 2p cl (Bk)	blue surch	NA	65.00
SPG2	78a	(1908-09)	05C on 10c orange	red surch	6.00	2.75
SPG3	98a	(1909)	10c on 50c bl grn	red or violet surch	75.00	55.00
SPG4	157a	(1918)	25c on 10p bl grn	"52" for "25"	NA	NA
SPG5	206a	(1924)	1p dk vio & blk	center invtd (u)	NA	125.00

The Spanish Guinea has a strange appetite
No vc's nor any marks of bite
But one does find colors of surcharge uninvited
And a rare inverted center often cited. —The Bard

SPANISH MOROCCO

SPM1	68a	(1920)	10c on half of 20c	"10/crs" surch added	80.00	20.00
SPM2	71a	(1920)	10c on 25p dk grn	invtd surch (vc)	10.00	9.00
SPM3	C32b	(1953)	50c on 75c ultra (I)	vert gutter pair, types I & II	2.50	—
SPM4	CB1a	(1936)	25c + 2p on 25c	bars at right omitted	30.00	30.00
SPM5	CB1b			blue surch	21.00	10.50

Philatelists of Morocco have erred
But major ones have generally been spared
A blue surcharge or a missing bar
Won't take error hunters far.
To have to search for a lone vc
Means that Morocco is a "clear air" country. —The Bard

SPANISH SAHARA (Spanish Western Sahara, Rio De Oro)

RDO1	30a	(1907)	3p blue green	cliche of 4p in plate of 3p		
RDO2	34a		10c on 50c dk green	"10" omitted	125.00	70.00
RDO3	40a	(1908)	15c on 75c org brn	green surch	37.50	14.00
RDO4	60a	(1910)	10c on 5p dull bl	red surch	47.50	27.50
RDO5	M34x	(1907)	10c on 50c slate blue green	invtd ovpt	95.00	65.00
RDO6	M35x		10c on 75c violet	invtd ovpt	95.00	65.00
RDO7	M36x	(1908)	2c on 2p lt yellow brown (V)		80.00	55.00
RDO8	M39x		15c on 25c black green (R)	invtd ovpt	75.00	25.00
RDO9	M40x		15c on 75c dp orange brn (V)	green ovpt	75.00	32.50
RDO10	M40x1			invtd ovpt	30.00	30.00
RDO11	M40x2			dbl ovpt, one in green	40.00	40.00
RDO12	M41x		15c on 1p brown orange (V)		50.00	12.00
RDO13	M41x1			red ovpt	60.00	25.00
RDO14	M41x2			ovpt invtd	40.00	30.00
RDO15	M41x3			as x, ovpt invtd	75.00	50.00
RDO16	M41x4			dbl ovpt, red & green	90.00	60.00
RDO17	M41x5			pair, one no ovpt	30.00	22.50
RDO18		(1908)	42t Revenue stamp handstamped locally in red; 5c on 50c light slate green	no control number on back	70.00	35.00
RDO19	M42x			violet ovpt	165.00	82.50
RDO20	M56x1	(1910)	10c on 5p prussian blue	dbl ovpt, one in red	45.00	45.00
RDO21	M56x2			invtd ovpt	22.50	22.50
RDO22	M56x3			as x, invtd ovpt	45.00	45.00
RDO23	M57x		10c on 10p venetian red	green ovpt	150.00	75.00
RDO24	M57x1			violet ovpt	150.00	75.00
RDO25	M57x2			invtd ovpt	25.00	25.00
RDO26	M57x3			dbl ovpt	30.00	30.00
RDO27	M57x4			dbl ovpt, one green	45.00	45.00
RDO28	M57x5			dbl ovpt, green & violet	75.00	75.00
RDO29	M58x		15c on 3p slate purple	invtd ovpt	22.50	22.50
RDO30	M59x		15c on 4p dull turq blue	invtd ovpt	22.50	22.50
RDO31	M59x1			dbl ovpt	30.00	30.00
RDO32	M59x2		10c on 4p		60.00	45.00
RDO33	M62x	(1911)	10c on 2p slate purple	invtd ovpt	—	—
RDO34	M62x1			dbl ovpt	—	—
RDO35	M93x	(1917)	1c dull carmine rose	invtd ovpt	12.50	5.00
RDO36	M94x		2c light dull purple	invtd ovpt	12.50	5.00
RDO37	M95x		5c emerald green	invtd ovpt	8.00	4.00
RDO38	M96x		10c red orange	invtd ovpt	10.00	5.00
RDO39	M97x		15c light brown orange	invtd ovpt	10.00	5.00
RDO40	M93-105		with dbl ovpt, in dk blue	9//7 for 1917; pairs, one without ovpt	set 30.00	

SPANISH WEST AFRICA has produced no errors

SRI LANKA has produced no errors

STELLALAND has produced no errors

STRAITS SETTLEMENTS

STS1	7a	(1867)	12c on 4a grn (R)	dbl surch (vc)	NA	—
STS2	20a	(1879)	5c on 8c yellow	no period after "CENTS"	NA	NA
STS3	21a	(1879)	7c on 32c pale red	no period after "CENTS"	NA	NA
STS4	58a	(1883-84)	2c on 8c orange	dbl surch (vc)	NA	NA
STS5	59a	(1883-84)	2c on 32c pale red	dbl surch (vc)		
STS6	60a	(1883-84)	2c on 5c ultra ('84)	pair, one without surch	—	—
STS7	60b			dbl surch (vc)	—	—
STS8	61b	(1883)	2c on 4c rose	"s" of "Cents" invtd	NA	NA
STS9	62a	(1883)	2c on 12c blue	"s" of "Cents" invtd	NA	NA
STS10	70a	(1885-87)	3c on 5c ultra	dbl surch (vc)	NA	
STS11	72a	(1885-87)	2c on 5c ultra ('87)	dbl surch (vc)	NA	NA
STS12	72b			"c" omitted	—	NA
STA13	74a	(1885-94)	3c on 32c rose ('94)	without surch	NA	—
STS14	75a	(1891)	10c on 24c green	narrow "0" in "10"	25.00	30.00
STS15	78a	(1892)	1c on 4c bister brn	dbl surch (vc)	NA	
STS16	79a	(1892)	1c on 6c violet	dbl surch, one invtd	NA	—
STS17	91a	(1899)	4c on 8c ultra	dbl surch (vc)	NA	NA
STS18	92a	(1899)	4c on 5c rose	without surch	NA	—
STS19	137a	(1907)	4c on 12c yel & blk	no period after "CENTS"	110.00	110.00
STS20	138a	(1907)	4c on 16c org brn & grn (Bk)	with additional name in red	NA	NA
STS21	139a	(1907)	4c on 18c bis & blk	no period after "CENTS"	100.00	100.00
STS22	139b			"FOUR CENTS" & bar dbl	NA	
STS23	141a	(1907)	10c sl bl & brn	no period after "Settlements"	125.00	—
STS24	266a	(1945-48)	25c rose red & vio	dbl ovpt (vc)	—	—
STS25	B1a	(1917)	3c + 2c scarlet	no period after "C"	55.00	—
STS26	B2a	(1917)	4c + 2c gray violet	no period after "C"	77.50	—
STS27	N20a	(1942)	2c brown orange	invtd ovpt (vc)	7.00	5.00
STS28	N20b			dbl ovpt, one invtd	25.00	—
STS29	N22a	(1942)	8c gray	invtd ovpt (vc)	19.00	—
STS30	N24a	(1942)	2c brown orange	invtd ovpt (vc)	NA	NA
STS31	N25a	(1942)	8c gray	invtd ovpt (vc)	NA	NA
STS32	N26a	(1943)	8c gray (Bk)	invtd ovpt (vc)	30.00	—

The Straits are not as crooked
If we understand their wares
Essentially we run from vc's
To numerous typographical errors
By typos we mean narrow "o"s to inverted "s"s
And any related thing.
Often very picayune
For the twice-crowned error king. —The Bard

SUDAN*

SUD1	1a	(1897)	1m brown	invtd ovpt (vc)	NA	—
SUD2	4a	(1897)	5m carmine rose	invtd ovpt (vc)	NA	—
SUD3	7a	(1897)	5p gray	dbl ovpt (vc)	—	—
SUD4	84a	(1948)	10m black & car	center invtd (u)	—	—
SUD5	C17a	(1935)	15m on 10m	dbl surch (vc)	NA	NA
SUD6	C17b			Arabic characters omitted	NA	—
SUD7	C18a	(1935)	2-1/2 on 3m	"1/2" 2-1/4mm high instead of 3mm	8.25	8.25
SUD8	C18b			second Arabic character of surch omitted	140.00	140.00
SUD9	C19a	(1935)	2-1/2p on 5m	"1/2" 2-1/4mm high instead of 3mm	8.00	8.00

SUD10	C19b			second Arabic character of surch omitted	80.00	80.00
SUD11	C19c			invtd surch (vc)	NA	NA
SUD12	C19d			as "b" invtd	NA	—
SUD13	C21c	(1935)	7-1/2p on 4-1/2 p	"7 1/4" instead of "7-1/2"	—	—
SUD14	MO1a	(1905)	1m rose & brown	"OFFICIAL"	—	NA
SUD15	MO3a	(1905)	1m car rose & brn	"OFFICIAL"	32.50	15.00
SUD16	MO3b			invtd ovpt (vc)	70.00	60.00
SUD17	MO3c			horizontal ovpt	NA	—
SUD18	MO4a	(1905)	1m car rose & brn	invtd ovpt (vc)	NA	NA
SUD19	MO5a	(1906-11)	1m car rose & brn	"Army" & "Service" 14mm apart (vc)	NA	200.00
SUD20	MO5b			invtd ovpt (vc)	NA	NA
SUD21	MO5c			pair, one without ovpt	—	NA
SUD22	MO5d			dbl ovpt (vc)	—	NA
SUD23	MO5e			"Service" omitted (vc)	—	NA
SUD24	MO6a	(1906-11)	2m brown & green	pair, one without ovpt (vc)	NA	—
SUD25	MO6b			"Armu" omitted (vc)	NA	—
SUD26	MO7a	(1906-11)	3m green & violet	invtd ovpt (vc)	NA	—
SUD27	MO8a	(1906-11)	5m blk & rose red	invtd ovpt (vc)	—	200.00
SUD28	MO8b			dbl ovpt (vc)	NA	NA
SUD29	MO8c			dbl ovpt, one invtd (vc)	NA	NA
SUD30	MO9a	(1906-11)	1p yel brn & ultra	"Army" omitted (vc)	NA	NA
SUD34	O3a	(1903-12)	1m car rose & brn ('04)	dbl ovpt (vc)	—	—
SUD35	O4a	(1903-12)	3m grn & vio ('04)	dbl ovpt (vc)	—	—
SUD36	O51a	(1951)	2p lt bl & dk bl	invtd ovpt (vc)	NA	—
SUD37	O59a	(1951)	20p blk & bl grn	invtd ovpt (vc)	—	NA

*The Official stamps are excluded from this evaluation

With fewer than four vc's
We usually "smile and say cheese"
But when the very commons
Are joined by the very rares
We have a Sudanian situation
"Inverted Center!" Everyone cares. —The Bard

SURINAM

SUR1	22a	(1892)	2-1/2c black & org	first & fifth vertical words have fancy "F"	25.00	14.00
SUR2	22c			As "a" imperf	26.00	—
SUR3	23c	(1892)	2-1/2c on 50c	dbl surch (vc)	NA	NA
SUR4	35a	(1898)	10c on 30c red brn	dbl surch (vc)	NA	—
SUR5	183a	(1945)	7-1/2c on 10c	dbl surch (vc)	175.00	190.00
SUR6	C8a	(1931)	10c red (Bk)	dbl ovpt (vc)	NA	—
SUR7	C11a	(1931)	40c orange (Bk)	dbl ovpt (vc)	NA	—
SUR8	C23a 22	(1945)	1/2c on 60c	invtd surch (vc)	NA	NA

SWAZILAND

SWA1	1a	(1889)	1/2p gray	invtd ovpt (vc)	NA	NA
SWA2	1b			"Swazielan"	NA	NA
SWA2	1c			As "b" invtd ovpt	—	NA
SWA3	2a	(1889)	1p rose	invtd ovpt (vc)	NA	NA
SWA4	3a	(1889)	2p olive bister	invtd ovpt (vc)	NA	NA
SWA5	3b			"Swazielan"	NA	NA
SWA6	5a	(1889)	1sh green	invtd ovpt (vc)	NA	NA
SWA7	7a	(1889)	5sh slate	invtd ovpt (vc)	NA	NA
SWA8	7b			"Swazielan"	NA	—
SWA9	7c			As "b" invtd ovpt	—	—
SWA10	9a	(1892)	1/2p gray	invtd ovpt (vc)	—	—
SWA11	9b			dbl ovpt (vc)	NA	NA
SWA12	67a	(1961)	1/2c on-1/2p	invtd surch (vc)	NA	—

SWA13	68a	(1961)	1c on 1p	"1c" at center	27.50	—
SWA14	68b			dbl surch (vc)	NA	—
SWA15	75a	(1961)	10c on 1sh	dbl surch (vc)	NA	—

Something borrowed something blue
Something something really new?
The answer to the last must be
Not much more than a good vc.
A spelling error of the country's name
No real sin although perhaps a shame
Here's to "Swaziland"! —The Bard

SWEDEN

SWE1	1a	(1855)	3s blue green	3s orange (error) (u)	—	—
SWE2	13a	(1862-69)	3o bister brown	printed on both sides (u)	—	NA
SWE3	23b	(1872-77)	20o vermillion	dbl impression, dull yel	NA	30.00
				& ver ('76) (u)		
SWE4	33a	(1877-79)	20o vermillion	"TRETIO" instead of	NA	NA
				"TJUGO" ('79)		
SWE5	40a	(1886-91)	2o orange ('91)	period before "FRIMARKE"	10.00	20.00
SWE6	100a	(1918)	12o on 25o	invtd surch (vc)	NA	NA
SWE7	C1a	(1920)	10o on 3o brn	invtd surch (vc)	NA	NA
SWE8	C2a	(1920)	20o on 2o org	invtd surch (vc)	NA	NA
SWE9	C3a	(1920)	50o on 4o vio	invtd surch (vc)	NA	NA
SWE10	J15a	(1877-86)	6o yellow	printed on both sides (u)	NA	—
SWE11	O26a	(1889)	10o on 12o blue	invtd surch (vc)	NA	NA

SWITZERLAND

SWI1	43c	(1862-63)	5c dark brown	dbl embossing, one invtd	NA	NA
SWI2	43d			dbl impression on lower left "5"	—	NA
SWI3	44a	(1862-63)	10c blue	dbl embossing, one invtd	—	NA
SWI4	55b	(1867-78)	25c blue green	dbl embossing, one invtd	—	NA
SWI5	60a	(1881)	2c bister	dbl embossing, one invtd	NA	—
SWI6	61a	(1881)	5c brown	dbl embossing, one invtd	26.00	NA
SWI7	61b			dbl impression of lower left "5"	—	NA
SWI8	67b	(1881)	50c deep violet	dbl embossing, one invtd	NA	NA
SWI9	122a	(1907)	40c gray	Helvetia without diadem	NA	NA
SWI10	136a	(1907-25)	40c red vio & yel ('08)	designer's name in full on	10.00	20.00
				the rock ('08)		
SWI11	193b	(1921)	2-1/2 on 3c (Bl)	nvtd surch (vc)	NA	NA
SWI12	193c			dbl surch (vc)	NA	NA
SWI13	194a	(1921)	5c on 2c (R)	dbl surch (vc)	NA	NA
SWI14	195b	(1921)	5c on 7-1/2c (R)	dbl surch (vc)	NA	NA
SWI15	196a	(1921)	10c on 13c (R)	dbl surch (vc)	NA	NA
SWI16	197b	(1921)	20c on 15c (Bk)	dbl surch (vc)	NA	NA
SWI17	198b	(1921)	20c on 15c (Bl)	dbl surch (vc)	NA	NA
SWI18	B90a	(1938)	10C + 10C brt vio & yel	grilled gum	20.00	75.00
SWI19	C20a	(1935-38)	10c on 15c	invtd surch (vc)	NA	NA
SWI20	C25a	(1935-38)	40c on 90c ('36) (R)	vermillion surch	77.50	NA
SWI21	2032b	(1935-36)	1.20 fr brn rose	invtd ovpt (vc)	—	NA
			& red, rose ('36)			

Switzerland is like going to the dentist without flossing
It has several errors of double embossing
This is the first such error we've seen
Will we generate more from the error machine? —The Bard

SYRIA

SYR1	11a	(1919)	1m on 1c gray	invtd surch (vc)	10.00	10.00
SYR2	12a	(1919)	2m on 2c violet brn	invtd surch (vc)	10.00	10.00
SYR3	14a	(1919)	4m on 15c pale red	invtd surch (vc)	10.00	10.00
SYR4	16a	(1919)	1p on 25c blue	invtd ovpt (vc)	10.00	10.00
SYR5	19a	(1919)	8p on 2fr gray vio & yel	"T.E.O." dbl	35.00	35.00

SYR6	21a	(1920)	1m on 1c gray	invtd surch (vc)	27.50	27.50
SYR7	21b			dbl surch (vc)	—	—
SYR8	22a	(1920)	2m on 2c vio brn	dbl surch (vc)	—	—
SYR9	23a	(1920)	3m on 5c green	dbl surch (vc)	—	—
SYR10	28a	(1920)	5m on 10c red	invtd surch (vc)	—	—
SYR11	53a	(1920)	100p on 5fr dk bl & buff (Bk)	"PIASRTES"	NA	NA
SYR12	56a	(1920-23)	25c on 1c dk gray	50c on 1c dk gray (error) (u)	1.25	1.25
SYR13	58a	(1920-23)	25c on 5c orange ('22)	"CENTIEMES" omitted	13.00	13.00
SYR14	82a	(1921)	25c on 1/10p lt brn	"25 Centiemes" omitted	—	—
SYR15	84a	(1921)	1p on 3/10p yel	"2/10" for "3/10"	7.50	7.50
SYR16	93a	(1921-22)	2.50p on 50c bis brn & lav ('22)	2p on 50c bister brown & lavender (error)	35.00	27.50
SYR17	106a	(1923)	50c on 10c green	25c on 10c green (error)	110.00	—
SYR18	116a	(1923)	2p on 40c red & pale bl	invtd surch (vc)	12.50	—
SYR19	116b			dbl surch (vc)	15.00	—
SYR20	116c			"Liabn"	—	—
SYR21	117a	(1923)	3p on 60c vio & ultra	"Liabn"	—	—
SYR22	118a	(1923)	5p on 1fr cl & ol grn	"Liabn"	—	—
SYR23	119a	(1923)	10p on 2fr org & pale bl	"Liabn"	—	—
SYR24	120a	(1923)	25p on 5fr dk bl & buff	invtd surch (vc)	—	—
SRY25	121a	(1924)	10c on 2c vio brn	dbl surch (vc)	—	—
SYR26	122a	(1924)	25c on 5c orange	"25" omitted	3.00	—
SYR27	125a	(1924)	1p on 20c red brn	"1 PIASTRES"	4.50	—
SYR28	143a	(1924-25)	10c on 2c vio	brn dbl surch (vc)	10.00	—
SYR29	143b			invtd surch (vc)	12.50	—
SYR30	144a	(1924-25)	25c on 5c orange	dbl surch (vc)	10.00	—
SYR31	145a	(1924-25)	50c on 10c green	dbl surch (vc)	10.00	—
SYR32	145b			invtd surch (vc)	12.50	—
SYR33	146a	(1924-25)	75c on 15c gray grn	dbl surch (vc)	10.00	—
SYR34	146b			invtd surch (vc)	12.50	—
SYR35	147a	(1924-25)	1p on 20c red brn	invtd surch (vc)	12.50	—
SYR36	148a	(1924-25)	1.25p on 25c blue	invtd surch (vc)	12.50	—
SYR37	149a	(1924-25)	1.50p on 30c red	dbl surch (vc)	10.00	—
SYR38	152a	(1924-25)	2p on 40c red & pale bl	Arabic "Piastre" in singular	.20	.20
SYR39	187a	(1926-30)	2p on 1p25 dp grn (R) ('28)	dbl surch (vc)	—	—
SYR40	188a	(1926-30)	3.50p on 75c org brn	dbl surch (vc)	5.00	5.00
SYR41	195a	(1926-30)	7.50p on 2p50 pck bl (R) ('28)	dbl surch (vc)	6.50	—
SYR42	196a	(1926-30)	12p on 1p25 dp grn	surch on face & back	37.50	37.50
SYR43	C8a	(1921)	5p on 1fr	invtd ovpt (vc)	200.00	165.00
SYR44	C9a	(1921)	10p on 2fr	dbl ovpt (vc)	NA	NA
SYR45	C10a	(1922)	2p on 40c	invtd ovpt (vc)	—	—
SYR46	C14b	(1923)	2p on 40c	invtd surch (vc)	—	—
SYR47	C17b	(1923)	10p on 2fr	dbl ovpt (vc)	—	—
SYR48	C18a	(1924)	2p on 40c	dbl ovpt (vc)	—	—
SYR49	C19a	(1924)	3p on 60c	invtd ovpt (vc)	35.00	—
SYR50	C20a	(1924)	5p on 1fr	dbl ovpt (vc)	—	—
SYR51	C22a	(1924)	2p on 40c	invtd ovpt (vc)	20.00	—
SYR52	C23a	(1924)	3p on 60c	invtd ovpt (vc)	20.00	—
SYR53	C23b			dbl ovpt (vc)	12.50	—
SYR54	C25a	(1924)	10p on 2fr	invtd ovpt (vc)	20.00	—
SYR55	C30a	(1926)	2p dark brown	invtd ovpt (vc)	20.00	—
SYR56	C31a	(1926)	3p orange brown	invtd ovpt (vc)	20.00	—
SYR57	C32a	(1926)	5p violet	invtd ovpt (vc)	20.00	—
SYR58	C32b			dbl ovpt (vc)	—	—
SYR59	C33a	(1926)	10p violet brown	invtd ovpt (vc)	20.00	—
SYR60	C33b			dbl ovpt (vc)	—	—
SYR61	C34a	(1929)	50c yellow green (R)	invtd ovpt (vc)	30.00	—
SYR62	C34b			ovpt on face & back	—	—

SYR63	C34c			dbl ovpt (vc)	30.00	—
SYR64	C34d			dbl ovpt, one invtd	45.00	—
SYR65	C34e			pair, one without ovpt	—	—
SYR66	C35a	(1929)	1p magenta (Bk)	reversed ovpt	—	—
SYR67	C35b			red ovpt	—	—
SYR68	C36a	(1929)	25p ultra (R)	invtd ovpt (vc)	60.00	—
SYR69	C36b			pair, one without ovpt	—	—
SYR70	C37a	(1929)	15p on 25p ultra	invtd ovpt (vc)	—	—
SYR71	C41a	(1929)	3p orange brn (Bl)	invtd ovpt (vc)	—	—
SYR72	C45a	(1930)	2p on 1.25p dp grn	invtd surch (vc)	—	—
SYR73	C45b			dbl surch (vc)	45.00	—
SYR74	J6a	(1920)	2p on 20c ol grn (R)	"PIASTRE"	NA	NA
SYR75	J7a	(1920)	D23p on 30c red	"PIASTRE"	—	—
SYR76	J8a	(1920)	4p on 50c brn vio	3p in setting of 4p	NA	NA
SYR77	J9a	(1921-22)	50c on 10c brown	"75" instead of "50"	40.00	—
SYR78	J9b			"CENTI MES" instead of "CENTIEMES"	5.50	—
SYR79	J16a	(1922)	D42p on 5m rose	"AX" of "TAXE" invtd	140.00	140.00
SYR80	86b	(1919-20)	5m rose	invtd ovpt (vc)	100.00	75.00
SYR81	88a	(1919-20)	2/10pi yel grn	2/10pi yellow (error)	6.25	4.00
SYR82	C48a	(1961)	50p brt lil & blk	black omitd	—	—

T

TAZHIKISTAN has produced no errors

TAHITI

TAH1	17a	(1893)	1c blk, lil bl	invtd ovpt (vc)	NA	—
TAH2	18a	(1893)	2c brn, buff	invtd ovpt (vc)	NA	—
TAH3	19a	(1893)	4c claret, lav	invtd ovpt (vc)	NA	—
TAH4	20a	(1893)	5c grn, grnsh	invtd ovpt (vc)	NA	NA
TAH5	21a	(1893)	10c black, lav	invtd ovpt (vc)	NA	NA
TAH6	22a	(1893)	15c blue	invtd ovpt (vc)	100.00	100.00
TAH7	23a	(1893)	20c red, grn	invtd ovpt (vc)	100.00	100.00
TAH8	25a	(1893)	25c black, rose	invtd ovpt (vc)	100.00	100.00
TAH9	26a	(1893)	35c violet, org	invtd ovpt (vc)	NA	—
TAH10	27a	(1893)	75c carmine, rose	invtd ovpt (vc)	100.00	100.00
TAH11	27b			dbl ovpt (vc)	200.00	200.00
TAH12	28a	(1893)	1fr brnz grn, straw	invtd ovpt (vc)	100.00	100.00
TAH13	29a	(1903)	10c on 15c bl (BK)	dbl surch (vc)	25.00	25.00
TAH14	29b			invtd surch (vc)	25.00	25.00
TAH15	30a	(1903)	10c on 25c blk, rose (C)	dbl surch (vc)	25.00	25.00
TAH16	30b			invtd surch (vc)	25.00	25.00
TAH17	31a	(1903)	10c on 40c red, straw (Bk)	dbl surch (vc)	25.00	25.00
TAH18	31b			invtd surch (vc)	25.00	25.00
TAH19	B1a	(1915)	15c blue	invtd ovpt (vc)	NA	NA
TAH20	B2a	(1915)	15c gray	invtd ovpt (vc)	165.00	165.00

SYR73A

THR1

THR2A

TAH21	47b	(1961)	15c sepia & blue	blue omitted (u)	200.00	—
TAH22	55a	(1961)	10sh blk, blue & rose	Rose (diamond) omitted (u)	75.00	—
TAH23	O4a	(1959)	20c orange & blk	dbl ovpt (vc)	—	NA

Water, water all around
And not a drop to drink
Water, water water all around
And vc's the only error link
No centers inverted or other pie
Its simply vc's do or die. —The Bard

TANGANYIKA

TAN1	31a	(1932)	3k on 70k (Bl)	invtd surch (vc)	140.00	—

TANNU TUVA

TAN1	31a	(1932)	3k on 70k (Bl)	invtd surch (vc)	140.00	—

One vc to see no more to say
On this bright Mongolian day. —The Bard

TANZANIA has produced no errors

TETE

TET1	19a	(1913)	1c on 1a red vio	invtd ovpt (vc)	37.50	37.50

THAILAND

THA1	7c	(1885)	1t on 1sol blue	"1" invtd	NA	NA
THA2	20a	(1889-90)	1a on 2a	"1" omitted	NA	NA
THA3	20c			1st Siamese character invtd	—	—
THA4	20d			1st Siamese character omitted	NA	NA
THA5	21a	(1889-90)	1a on 3a ('90)	invtd "1"	150.00	150.00
THA6	28a	(1891)	2a on 3a grn & bl	dbl surch (vc)	NA	NA
THA7	28b			"2" omitted	NA	
THA8	35c	(1892)	4a on 24a lil & bl	invtd "s"	40.00	40.00
THA9	36a	(1892)	4a on 24a lik & bl	invtd "s"	40.00	40.00
THA10	39a	(1894)	1a on 64a lil & org brn	invtd "s"	40.00	40.00
THA11	39b			invtd surch (vc)	NA	NA
THA12	39d			italic "s"	50.00	50.00
THA13	39e			italic "1"	50.00	50.00
THA14	40a	(1894)	1a on 64a lil & org brn	invtd capital "S" added to the surch	175.00	200.00
THA15	41a	(1894)	2a on 64a	invtd "s"	40.00	40.00
THA16	41b			dbl surch (vc)	100.00	100.00
THA17	46a	(1894)	2a on 64a	"Att.s"	40.00	40.00
THA18	47a	(1894)	1a on 64a	surch on face & back	150.00	—
THA19	47b			surch on back invtd	200.00	—
THA20	47c			dbl surch (vc)	NA	—
THA21	47d			invtd surch (vc)	NA	—
THA22	47e			Siamese surch omitted	NA	—
THA23	48a	(1894)	2a on 64a	"ATtt"	35.00	30.00
THA24	48b			invtd surch (vc)	NA	NA
THA25	48c			surch on face & back	NA	NA
THA26	48d			surch on back invtd	NA	NA
THA27	48e			dbl surch (vc)	NA	NA
THA28	48f			dbl surch, one invtd	NA	NA
THA29	48g			invtd "s"	40.00	40.00
THA30	49a	(1895)	10a on 24a lil & bl	invtd "s"	40.00	25.00
THA31	49b			surch on face & back	175.00	175.00
THA32	49c			surch on back invtd	175.00	175.00
THA33	50a	(1896)	4a on 12a lil & car	invtd "s"	50.00	50.00
THA34	50b			surch on face & back	175.00	175.00
THA35	50c			dbl surch on back	175.00	175.00
THA36	54a	(1898-99)	3a on 12a	dbl surch (vc)	NA	NA
THA37	55a	(1898-99)	4a on 12a	dbl surch (vc)	NA	NA
THA38	62a	(1898-99)	4a on 12a	dbl surch (vc)	175.00	175.00

THA39	62b			no period after "Atts."	30.00	30.00
THA40	66a	(1894-99)	1a on 12a	invtd "1"	150.00	150.00
THA41	66b			invtd 1st "t"	150.00	150.00
THA42	68a	(1894-99)	2a on 64a	"1 Atts."	NA	NA
THA43	90a	(1905)	1a on 14a	no period after "Att"	35.00	35.00
THA44	91a	(1905)	2a on 28a	dbl surch (vc)	110.00	110.00
THA45	109a	(1907)	1a on 24a lil & bl	dbl surch (vc)	125.00	125.00
THA46	111a	(1908)	2a on 24a lil & bl	invtd surch (vc)	NA	NA
THA47	112a	(1908)	9a on 10a ultra	invtd surch (vc)	NA	NA
THA48	113a	(1908)	1a	Siamese date "137" instead of "127"	NA	NA
THA49	113b			pair, one without ovpt	—	—
THA50	130a	(1909)	2s on 2a #94	"2" omitted	100.00	—
THA51	157b	(1914-15)	2s on 14s (R) ('15)	dbl surch (vc)	70.00	45.00
THA52	158b	(1914-15)	5s on 6s (Bl)	dbl surch (vc)	70.00	70.00
THA53	159a	(1914-15)	10s on 12s (R)	dbl surch (vc)	75.00	60.00
THA54	161a	(1915)	2s on 1a org & grn	pair, one without surch	62.50	62.50
THA55	176a	(1918)	2s orange brown	dbl ovpt (vc)	50.00	—
THA56	178a	(1918)	5s rose red	dbl ovpt (vc)	50.00	—
THA57	239a	(1940)	3s dp yellow grn	Cliche of 5s in plate of 3s (u)	NA	NA
THA58	B9a	(1918)	5b dp vio & blk	dbl ovpt (vc)	NA	NA
THA59	B16a	(1920)	5s on 6s (+ 20s)	ovpt invtd (vc)	—	—
THA60	B19a	(1920)	3s (+ 2s) green	pair, one without ovpt	—	—

Nothing exciting about the Thais
When it comes to errors they cover their eyes
When they open them they see some vc's
And also some nitty nit-pieces.
A nit-piece in case you didn't know
Is something that's too small to show
A number, a fraction or even a toe. —The Bard

THRACE

THR1	N20a	(1920)	5s green	invtd ovpt (vc)	10.00	—
THR2	N21a	(1920)	10s rose	invtd ovpt (vc)	10.00	—
THR3	N26a	(1920)	1 1 green	invtd ovpt (vc)	8.00	—
THR4	N31a	(1920)	15 1 dull blue	invtd ovpt (vc)	10.00	10.00
THR5	N31b			dbl ovpt, one invtd	12.00	12.00
THR6	N47a	(1920)	2 1 rose	invtd ovpt (vc)	—	—
THR7	N54a	(1920)	10d deep blue	dbl ovpt (vc)	—	—
THR8	N55a	(1920)	1 1 green	pair, one without ovpt	5.00	—
THR9	N57a	(1920)	3 1 vermillion	dbl ovpt (vc)	3.00	—
THR10	N58a	(1920)	5 1 green	pair, one without ovpt	3.00	—
THR11	N59a	(1920)	10 1 rose	dbl ovpt (vc)	4.00	—
THR12	N60a	(1920)	20 1 slate	invtd ovpt (vc)	5.00	—

Is Thrace a disgrace
Or simply a hiding place
For all the errors it has?
The number wouldn't be that small
But when their names we call
Vc's would be all
Nothing else short or tall. —The Bard

TIBET

TIB1	4a	(1912-50)	2/3t carmine	"POTSAGE"	125.00	140.00
TIB2	4hi	(1920)	2/3t carmine	"POTSAGE"	200.00	NA

TIMOR

TIM1	1a	(1885)	5r black (C)	dbl ovpt (vc)	22.50	22.50
TIM2	1b			triple ovpt	—	—
TIM3	2a	(1885)	10r green	ovpt on Mozambique stamp	20.00	12.50
TIM4	2b			ovptd on Portuguese India stamp	190.00	140.00
TIM5	3a	(1885)	20r rose	dbl ovpt (vc)	5.50	4.00

TIMOR

TIM6	5a	(1885)	40r yellow	dbl ovpt (vc)	—	—
TIM7	5b			invtd ovpt (vc)	16.00	16.00
TIM8	8a	(1885)	100r lilac	dbl ovpt (vc)	—	—
TIM9	35a	(1895)	2a on 10r green	dbl surch (vc)	—	—
TIM10	92a	(1894)	5a on 5r yellow	invtd surch (vc)	30.00	30.00
TIM11	103a	(1893)	6a on 2-1/2r brn	invtd surch (vc)	27.50	27.50
TIM12	106a	(1911)	1/2a gray	invtd ovprt (vc)	11.00	11.00
TIM13	132a	(1913)	15a on 10r red vio (G)	invtd ovpt (vc)	27.50	27.50
TIM14	133a	(1913)	15a on 300r bl, sal (R)	"REUBPLICA"	19.00	19.00
TIM15	133b			"REPBLICAU"	19.00	19.00
TIM16	138a	(1913)	13a violet	invtd ovpt (vc)	27.50	27.50
TIM17	245Jm	(1947)	20a blue	invtd ovpt (vc)	70.00	70.00
TIM18	302a	(1961)	10c pale green	value & legend invtd	72.50	72.50
See Photo in Color Section						
TIM19	J12a	(1911)	2a slate	invtd ovpt (vc)	—	—
TIM20	J24a	(1913)	6a deep orange	invtd surch (vc)	—	—
TIM21	P1a	(1892)	2-1/2r on 20r brt rose	"TIMOR" invtd	—	—
TIM22	P2a	(1892)	2-1/2r on 40r chocolate	"TIMOR" invtd	—	—
TIM23	P2c			as "a" perf. 13-1/2	—	—
TIM24	P3a	(1892)	2-1/2r on 80r gray	"TIMOR" invtd	—	—

TOBAGO

TOB1	13a	(1883)	2-1/2p on 6p bister brn	dbl surch (vc)	NA	NA
TOB2	25a	(1886-92)	1/2p on 2-1/2p ultra	invtd surch (vc)	—	—
TOB3	25b			pair, one without surch	NA	—
TOB4	26b	(1886-92)	1/2p on 4p gray	dbl surch (vc)	NA	—
TOB5	27a	(1886-92)	1/2p on 6p bis brn	invtd surch (vc)	NA	—
TOB6	27c			dbl surch (vc)	NA	—
TOB7	28b	(1886-92)	1/2p on 6p brn org	dbl surch (vc)	—	NA
TOB8	30a	(1886-92)	2-1/2p on 4p gray	dbl surch (vc)	NA	NA

Vc stands for very common
And mm. a distance small
In the great great land of Tobago
The Error King finds them all.
Spaces between "1/2," and "PENNY"s
Must neither be too "short" nor "tall"
Or the error ref is sure to make a call. —The Bard

TOGO

TOG1	33a	(1914)	1/2p on 3pf brown	thin "y" in "penny"	NA	NA
TOG2	34a	(1914)	1p on 5pf green	thin "y" in "penny"	NA	NA
TOG3	37a	(1914)	10pf carmine	invtd ovpt	NA	NA
TOG4	45a	(1914)	2m blue	invtd ovpt	—	—
TOG5	45b			"Occupation" dbl	—	—
TOG6	46a	(1914)	1/2p on 3pf brown	thin "y" in "penny"	55.00	45.00
TOG7	46b			"TOG"	NA	NA
TOG8	47a	(1914)	1p on 5pf green	thin "y" in "penny"	15.00	15.00
TOG9	47b			"TOG"	125.00	100.00
TOG10	48a	(1914)	3pf brown	"Occupation" omitted	—	—
TOG11	51a	(1914)	20pf ultra	"TOG"	NA	NA
TOG12	52a	(1914)	25pf org & blk, yel	"TOG"	NA	—
TOG13	66a	(1915)	1/2p green	dbl ovpt (vc)	NA	NA
TOG14	67a	(1915)	1p scarlet	dbl ovpt (vc)	NA	NA
TOG15	67b			invtd ovpt (vc)	125.00	150.00
TOG16	67c			as "b" "Togo" omitted	—	—
TOG17	72a	(1915)	1sh black, grn	dbl ovpt (vc)	NA	—
TOG18	81a	(1916)	1p scarlet	invtd ovpt (vc)	—	—
TOG19	154a	(1914)	10c on 5pf green	dbl surch (vc)	NA	NA
TOG20	158a	(1914)	20pf ultra	3-1/2mm between "TOGO' & "Occupation"	—	NA
TOG21	166a	(1915)	10pf carmine	invtd ovpt (vc)	—	NA
TOG22	178a	(1916-17)	4c black & brn	dbl ovpt (vc)	NA	NA
TOG23	193a	(1921)	1c gray & yel grn	ovpt omitted (vc)	110.00	—

TOG24	196a	(1921)	5c dull red & blk	ovpt omitted	NA	—
TOG25	213a	(1922-25)	60c on 75c vio. pnksh	"60" omitted	125.00	125.00
TOG26	214a	(1922-25)	65c on 45c red brn & ol	"TOGO" omitted	100.00	—
TOG27	421a	(1962)	100fr on 50c green	carmine surch	.75	.50

The fall of man came early
In the land of the Togolese
No interest was there found in nickel and dime vc's
Thousands here and thousands there to the newly crowned
Error King
Money is and was the only precious thing
But since the '20s it all has stopped
No more erroring
So go way back and find a juicy bit
Just remember that the error machine has quit. —The Bard

TOKELAU has produced no errors

TONGA

TON1	8a	(1891)	1p car rose (I)	ovptd with 3 start (I)	NA	—
TON2	8b			ovptd with 4 start (I)	NA	—
TON3	8c			ovptd with 5 start (I)	NA	—
TON4	15a	(1893)	1/2p on 1p ultra (C)	surch omitted	—	—
TON5	18a	(1893)	2-1/2p on blue grn	dbl surch (vc)	—	NA
TON6	21a	(1894)	1/2p on 4p red brn (Bl)	"SURCHARCE"	7.00	17.00
TON7	21b			pair, one without surch	—	—
TON8	21c			"HALF PENNY" omitted	—	—
TON9	22a	(1894)	1/2p on 1sh brown (Bk)	dbl surch (vc)	NA	—
TON10	22b			"SURCHARCE"	10.00	—
TON11	22c			as "b," dbl surch (vc)	NA	—
TON12	23a	(1894)	2-1/2p on 8p violet (Bk)	no period after "SURCHARGE"	30.00	45.00
TON13	24a	(1894)	2-1/2p on 1sh blue grn (Bk)	no period after "SURCHARGE"	110.00	—
TON14	27b	(1895)	2-1/2p on 2p lt blue	without period	NA	NA
TON15	33a	(1895)	1/2p on 2-1/2p red	"SURCHARCE"	70.00	—
TON16	33b			period after "Postage"	80.00	—
TON17	34a	(1895)	1p on 2-1/2p red	period after "Postage"	85.00	—
TON18	35a	(1895)	7-1/2p on 2-1/2p red	period after "Postage"	85.00	—
TON19	36a	(1896)	1/2p on 1-1/2p on 2p	Tongan surch reading upwards	NA	—
TON20	36d			"Haalf"	NA	—
TON21	37a	(1896)	1/2p on 7-1/2p on 2p	"Half penny" invtd	NA	—
TON22	37b			"Half penny" dbl	—	—
TON23	37c			Tongan surch reading upwards	27.50	40.00
TON24	37d			Tongan surch as "c" & dbl	—	—
TON25	37e			"Hafl Penny"	NA	NA
TON26	37f			"Hafl" only	NA	—
TON27	37g			"Hwlf"	—	—
TON28	37h			periods instead of hyphens after words	NA	—
TON29	42a	(1897-1934)	2-1/2p lt blue & blk	"1/2" without fraction bar	60.00	55.00
TON30	47a	(1897-1934)	7-1/2p green & blk	center invtd (u)	NA	—
TON31	53a	(1899)	1p red & black	"1889"instead of "1899"	NA	NA
TON32	53b			Comma omitted after June	—	—
TON33	53c			dbl ovpt (vc)	—	—

Tonga is an island group
Out into the sea....
When asking for an error there
I never say vc
That's because there are so many
Other errors to see
Surcharge, wrong dates
And a center invert too
Don't you think Tonga is the place for you? —The Bard

TRANSCAUCASIAN FEDERATED REPUBLICS

TFR1	4a	(1923)	35k red brn & grn (R)	dbl ovpt (vc)	40.00	40.00

TRANSVAAL

TRA1	28b	(1870)	1p dull rose	printed on both sides (u)	—	—
TRA2	50a	(1877)	3p lilac	ovptd on back (u)	NA	—
TRA3	50b			dbl ovpt, red & black	NA	—
TRA4	53a	(1877)	6p blue	6p deep blue (vc)	—	NA
TRA5	54b	(1877)	1sh yellow grn	invta ovpt (vc)	—	NA
TRA6	59a	(1877)	1p red	invtd ovpt (vc)	NA	NA
TRA7	60b	(1877)	1p red	invtd ovpt (vc)	—	—
TRA8	60c			dbl ovpt (vc)	—	—
TRA9	61a	(1877)	1p red	dbl ovpt (vc)	—	NA
TRA10	62b	(1877)	3p lilac	invtd ovpt (vc)	NA	—
TRA11	63d	(1877)	6p dull blue	invtd ovpt (vc)	NA	NA
TRA12	63e			dbl ovpt (vc)	NA	—
TRA13	64b	(1877)	6p blue, rose	invtd ovpt (vc)	45.00	20.00
TRA14	64c			ovpt omitted	NA	—
TRA15	65b	(1877)	1sh yellow grn	invtd ovpt (vc)	NA	NA
TRA16	68a	(1877)	6p dull blue	invtd ovpt (vc)	NA	NA
TRA17	69a	(1877)	6p blue, rose	invtd ovpt (vc)	NA	70.00
TRA18	69d			ovpt omitted	—	—
TRA19	70a	(1877)	1sh yellow grn	invtd ovpt (vc)	NA	NA
TRA20	71a	(1877-79)	1p red, blue	"Transvral" (u)	NA	NA
TRA21	71b			invtd ovpt (vc)	NA	NA
TRA22	71c			dbl ovpt (vc)	NA	—
TRA23	71d			ovpt omitted	—	—
TRA24	72a	(1877-79)	1p red, org ('78)	printed on both sides (u)	—	—
TRA25	72b			pin perf. (u)	—	—
TRA26	73a	(1877-79)	3p lilac, buff	invtd ovpt (vc)	—	NA
TRA27	74a	(1877-79)	3p lilac, grn ('79)	invtd ovpt (vc)	—	NA
TRA28	74b			dbl ovpt (vc)	—	—
TRA29	75b	(1877-79)	6p blue, grn	invtd ovpt (vc)	—	NA
TRA30	76b	(1877-79)	6p blue, bl ('78)	ovpt omitted	—	NA
TRA31	76c			invtd ovpt (vc)	—	NA
TRA32	76e			dbl ovpt (vc)	—	NA
TRA33	77a	(1877-79)	1p red, blue	"Transvral" (u)	—	NA
TRA34	77b			invtd ovpt (vc)	—	—
TRA35	77c			dbl ovpt (vc)	—	—
TRA36	79a	(1877-79)	3p lilac, buff	invtd ovpt (vc)	—	NA
TRA37	80a	(1877-79)	3p lilac, grn	invtd ovpt (vc)	—	—
TRA38	81a	(1877-79)	6p blue, green	invtd ovpt (vc)	—	NA
TRA39	81b			ovpt omitted	—	NA
TRA40	82a	(1877-79)	6p blue, bl ('78)	invtd ovpt (vc)	NA	NA
TRA41	82b			ovpt omitted	NA	NA
TRA42	82f			dbl ovpt (vc)	—	—
TRA43	85a	(1877-79)	3p lilac, grn ('79)	invtd ovpt (vc)	—	NA
TRA44	85b			ovpt omitted	—	NA
TRA45	85c			printed on both sides (u)	—	—
TRA46	86b	(1877-79)	6p blue, bl ('78)	invtd ovpt (vc)	—	NA
TRA47	89a	(1877-79)	3p lilac, grn ('79)	invtd ovpt (vc)	—	—
TRA48	89b			ovpt omitted	—	—
TRA49	90b	(1877-79)	6p blue, bl ('78)	invtd ovpt (vc)	NA	NA
TRA50	91b	(1879)	1p red, orange	small capital "T"	200.00	165.00
TRA51	92a	(1879)	3p lilac, green	small capital "T" (u)	NA	165.00
TRA52	93a	(1879)	3p lilac, blue	small capital "T" (u)	165.00	75.00
TRA53	94b	(1879)	1p red, yellow	small capital "T" (u)	NA	NA
TRA54	95a	(1879)	3p lilac, green	small capital "T" (u)	—	—
TRA55	96a	(1879)	3p lilac, blue	small capital "T" (u)	—	NA
TRA56	111a	(1879)	1p on 6p slate (Bk)	pair, one without surch	—	—
TRA57	136a	(1885)	1/2p on 3p red	surch reading down	3.00	5.00
TRA58	137a	(1885)	1/2p on 1sh green	surch reading down	7.00	15.00

TRA59	140a	(1885)	1/2p on 3p vio (Bk)	"PRNNY"	50.00	—
TRA60	140b			2nd "N" of "PENNY" invtd	125.00	
TRA61	141a	(1887)	2p on 3p violet	dbl surch (vc)	—	150.00
TRA62	142a	(1887)	2p on 3p violet	dbl surch (vc)	—	NA
TRA63	143a	(1893)	1/2p on 2p olive bis	invtd surch (vc)	2.25	2.25
TRA64	143b			bars 14mm apart	1.30	1.30
TRA65	143c			As "b," invtd	6.50	6.50
TRA66	144a	(1893)	1/2p on 2p olive bis	invtd surch (vc)	4.25	4.25
TRA67	144b			bars 14mm apart	1.30	1.30
TRA68	144c			As "b," invtd	13.00	11.00
TRA69	145a	(1893)	1p on 6p blue	invtd surch (vc)	1.30	1.30
TRA70	145b			dbl surch (vc)	50.00	50.00
TRA71	145c			pair, one without surch	175.00	—
TRA72	145d			Bars 14mm apart	.55	.55
TRA73	145e			as "d," invtd	5.50	5.50
TRA74	145f			as "d," dbl	—	90.00
TRA75	146a	(1893)	2-1/2p on 1sh green	invtd surch (vc)	5.00	6.00
TRA76	146b			fraction line misplaced "2/12"	27.50	27.50
TRA77	146c			as "b," invtd	NA	NA
TRA78	146d			bars 14mm apart	1.50	1.50
TRA79	146e			as "d," invtd	7.25	10.00
TRA80	147a	(1893)	2-1/2p on 1sh green	invtd surch (vc)	6.50	6.50
TRA81	147b			bars 14mm apart	5.00	5.00
TRA82	147c			as "b," invtd	32.50	20.00
TRA83	147d			dbl surch (vc)	60.00	75.00
TRA84	162a	(1895)	1/2p on 1sh green (R)	invtd surch (vc)	5.25	5.25
TRA85	162b			"Pennij" instead of "Penny"	60.00	60.00
TRA86	162c			dbl surch (vc)	60.00	60.00
TRA87	163a	(1895)	1p on 2-1/2p pur (G)	invtd surch (vc)	20.00	20.00
TRA88	163b			surch sideways	—	—
TRA89	163c			surch on back	—	—
TRA90	163d			space between "I" & "d"	1.30	1.30
TRA91	175a	(1901)	1/2p black, green	initials omitted	125.00	—
TRA92	175b			initials in black	45.00	—
TRA93	176a	(1901)	1/2p black	green initials omitted	125.00	—
TRA94	176b			initials in black	45.00	—
TRA95	177a	(1901)	1/2p black, green	initials omitted	125.00	—
TRA96	177b			initials in black	45.00	—
TRA97	202a	(1900)	1/2p green	"V.I.R."	NA	—
TRA98	204a	(1900)	2p brown & grn	"V.I.R."	NA	—
TRA99	207a	(1900)	4p olive & grn	"V.I.R."	NA	—
TRA100	248a	(1900)	1p rose & grn	ovpt "E" omitted	65.00	—

Does this nation mean "across" the "valley"?
If so, errors are up its alley.
Even pennys, half pennys and VRI's
Dozens of vc's fill your eyes.
Some stamps are also printed on their back
For them there's not enough money in my sack. —The Bard

TRINIDAD

TRI1	67b	(1882)	1p on 6p green (R)	black surch	—	NA
TRI2	78a	(1896-1904)	1p blk, red, type II	value omitted	NA	—
TRI3	09a	(1909-10)	1p carmine	dbl ovpt (vc)	—	NA
TRI4	09b			invtd ovpt (vc)	—	165.00
TRI5	09c			vertical ovpt	50.00	—

TRINIDAD AND TOBAGO

TAT1	B3a	(1916)	1p scarlet	date omitted	—	—
TAT2	MR1a	(1917)	1p scarlet	invtd ovpt (vc)	200.00	150.00
TAT3	MR2a	(1917)	1/2p green	ovptd on face & back	NA	—
TAT4	MR2b			pair, one without ovpt	NA	—

TAT5	MR3a	(1917)	1p scarlet	pair, one without ovpt	NA	—
TAT6	MR3b			dbl ovpt (vc)	125.00	—
TAT7	MR10a	(1917)	1p scarlet	invtd ovpt (vc)	100.00	100.00
TAT8	MR11a	(1917)	1p scarlet	dbl ovpt (vc)	200.00	150.00
TAT9	MR11b			invtd ovpt (vc)	100.00	100.00
TAT10	MR13a	(1918)	1p scarlet	dbl ovpt (vc)	120.00	120.00
TAT11	O3a	(1916)	1/2p green	dbl ovpt (vc)	22.50	—

TRIPOLITANIA

TRI1	26a	(1927)	50c deep orange	dbl ovpt (vc)	50.00	—

TRISTAN DA CUNHA

TDC1	58a	(1963)	3p dkbl, rose & grnsh bl	dbl ovpt (vc)	—	—

TUNISIA

TUN1	63a	(1917)	15c on 10c red	"15c" omitted	13.00	—
TUN2	63b			dbl surch (vc)	40.00	—
TUN3	70a	(1923-25)	10c on 5c grn, grnsh (R)	dbl surch (vc)	40.00	—
TUN4	143b	(1937)	65c on 50c (R)	dbl surch (vc)	55.00	50.00
TUN5	144a	(1937)	1.75fr on 1.50fr (R)	dbl surch (vc)	50.00	50.00
TUN6	C1a	(1919)	30c on 35c ol grn & brn	invtd surch (vc)	90.00	90.00
TUN7	C1b			dbl surch (vc)	90.00	90.00
TUN8	C1c			dbl invtd surch (vc)	100.00	100.00
TUN9	C1d			dbl surch, one invtd (vc)	90.00	90.00

TURKEY

TUR1	1b	(1863)	20pa blk, yellow	without band	65.00	—
TUR2	1c			green band	—	—
TUR3	2c	(1863)	1pi blk, dl vio	without band	70.00	—
TUR4	2d			design reversed	—	175.00
TUR5	2e			1pi blk, yel (error)	190.00	125.00
TUR6	4c	(1863)	2pi blk, grnsh bl	without band	85.00	—
TUR7	5b	(1863)	5pi blk, rose	without band	140.00	—
TUR8	5c			green band	150.00	—
TUR9	5d			red band	150.00	—
TUR10	6b	(1863)	20pa blk, yellow	design reversed	NA	NA
TUR11	6c			without band	125.00	125.00
TUR12	6d			paper colored through	110.00	110.00
TUR13	7b	(1863)	1pi blk, gray	design reversed	—	—
TUR14	7c			without band	—	—
TUR15	7d			paper colored through	165.00	165.00
TUR16	8c	(1865)	10pa deep green	"1" instead of "10" in each corner	NA	NA
TUR17	9a	(1865)	20pa yellow	star without rays	3.50	7.00
TUR18	10a	(1865)	1pi lilac	star without rays	8.50	6.00
TUR19	12d	(1865)	5pi carmine	invtd surch (vc)	—	NA
TUR20	16b	(1867)	1pi lilac	imperf with surch of 5pi	15.00	—
TUR21	20a	(1869)	10pa dull violet	printed on both sides	—	—
TUR22	20c			invtd surch (vc)	—	90.00
TUR23	20d			dbl surch (vc)	—	—
TUR24	20e			10pa yellow (error)	—	NA
TUR25	21a	(1869)	20pa pale green	printed on both sides	90.00	90.00
TUR26	22c	(1869)	1pi yellow	invtd surch (vc)	80.00	80.00
TUR27	22d			dbl surch (vc)	—	—
TUR28	22e			surcharged on both sides	—	—
TUR29	22f			printed on both sides	—	—
TUR30	23c	(1869)	2pi orange red	printed on both sides	—	130.00
TUR31	24d			invtd surch (vc)	70.00	70.00
TUR32	24e			surcharged on both sides	—	140.00
TUR33	29a	(1870-71)	20pa on gray green	printed on both sides	—	—
TUR34	30a	(1870-71)	1pi yellow	invtd surch (vc)	100.00	80.00
TUR35	30b			without surch	—	—
TUR36	31b	(1870-71)	2pi red	printed on both sides	—	32.50

TUR37	31c			surcharged on both sides	—	—
TUR38	33a	(1870-71)	5pi slate	printed on both sides	—	—
TUR39	33b			surcharged on both sides	—	32.50
TUR40	35a	(1873)	10pa dark lilac	invtd surch (vc)	—	90.00
TUR41	37a	(1873)	2pi vermillion	surcharged on both sides	22.50	22.50
TUR42	39b	(1874-75)	20pa yellow green	invtd surch (vc)	30.00	13.00
TUR43	39c			dbl surch (vc)	—	—
TUR44	41a	(1874-75)	10pa red violet	invtd surch (vc)	45.00	60.00
TUR45	42a	(1876)	10pa red lilac	invtd surch (vc)	70.00	—
TUR46	43b	(1876)	20pa pale green	invtd surch (vc)	70.00	—
TUR47	57b	(1876)	5pi red & blue	cliche of 25pi in plate of 5pi	NA	NA
TUR48	64a	(1881-82)	20pa gray	invtd surch (vc)	13.50	—
TUR49	65a	(1881-82)	2pi pale salmon	invtd surch (vc)	22.50	—
TUR50	71c	(1884-86)	5pi red brn & pale brn	5pi ocher & pale ocher (error)	12.00	12.00
TUR51	96a	(1892098)	20pa violet brn ('98)	20pa dark pink	7.50	.15
TUR52	99a	(1892-98)	5pi dull violet	Turkish numeral in upper right corner reads "50" instead of "5"	12.50	12.50
TUR53	100a	(1897)	5pa on 10pa gray grn	"Cniq" instead of "Cinq"	10.00	10.00
TUR54	277a	(1914)	1pi on 1-1/2pi car & blk	"1330" omitted	2.50	1.50
TUR55	277b			dbl surch (vc)		
TUR56	277c			triple surch (u)	5.00	5.00
TUR57	286a	(1915)	10pi on 100pi	invtd surch (vc)	75.00	75.00
TUR58	288a	(1892)	10pa gray green	invtd ovpt (vc)	7.50	7.50
TUR59	289a	(1892)	2pi brown orange	invtd ovpt (vc)	7.50	7.50
TUR60	290a	(1892)	5pi dull violet	on no. 99a	16.50	16.50
TUR61	291a	(1897)	5pa on 10pa gray grn	invtd ovpt (vc)	5.00	5.00
TUR62	291b			on no.100a	10.00	10.00
TUR63	299a	(1901)	20pa carmine	invtd ovpt (vc)	7.50	7.50
TUR64	300a	(1901)	1pi blue	invtd ovpt (vc)	5.00	5.00
TUR65	301a	(1901)	2pi orange	invtd ovpt (vc)	7.50	7.50
TUR66	301b			dbl ovpt (R & Bk)	5.00	5.00
TUR67	305a	(1905)	10pa dull green	invtd ovpt (vc)	5.00	5.00
TUR68	306a	(1905)	20pa carmine	invtd ovprt (vc)	5.00	5.00
TUR69	307a	(1905)	1pi brt blue	invtd ovpt (vc)	5.00	5.00
TUR70	308a	(1905)	2pi slate	invtd ovpt (vc)	10.00	10.00
TUR71	310a	(1905)	5pi brown	invtd ovpt (vc)	10.00	10.00
TUR72	314a	(1906)	2pi slate	invtd ovpt (vc)	5.00	5.00
TUR73	316a	(1908)	25pi dark green	invtd ovpt (vc)	16.50	16.50
TUR74	317a	(1909)	5pa ocher	invtd ovpt (vc)	10.00	10.00
TUR75	317b			dbl ovpt (vc)	10.00	10.00
TUR76	318a	(1909)	20pa carmine rose	invtd ovpt (vc)	5.00	5.00
TUR77	319a	(1909)	1pi ultra	invtd ovpt (vc)	5.00	5.00
TUR78	320a	(1909)	2pi blue black	invtd ovpt (vc)	5.00	5.00
TUR79	322a	(1909)	5pi dark violet	invtd ovpt (vc)	6.50	6.50
TUR80	325a	(1909)	20pa carmine rose	invtd ovpt (vc)	5.00	5.00
TUR81	328a	(1913)	5pa ocher	invtd ovpt (vc)	7.50	7.50
TUR82	329a	(1913)	10pa blue green	invtd ovpt (vc)	10.00	10.00
TUR83	330a	(1913)	20pa carmine rose	invtd ovpt (vc)	7.50	7.50
TUR84	331a	(1913)	1pi ultra	invtd ovpt (vc)	5.00	5.00
TUR85	332a	(1913)	2pi indigo	invtd ovpt (vc)	5.00	5.00
TUR86	334a	(1913)	10pi dull red	invtd ovprt (vc)	10.00	10.00
TUR87	339a	(1913)	2pi indigo	invtd ovpt (vc)	10.00	10.00
TUR88	340a	(1916)	5pa purple	5pa purple, #P43	80.00	80.00
TUR89	341a	(1916)	10pa green	dbl ovpt (vc)	6.50	6.50
TUR90	355Aa	(1916)	20pa violet brown	invtd ovpt (vc)	10.00	10.00
TUR91	361a	(1901)	5pa bister	dbl ovpt (vc)	7.50	7.50
TUR92	364a	(1901)	1pi violet blue	invtd ovpt (vc)	7.50	7.50
TUR93	371a	(1901)	20pa carmine	invtd ovpt (vc)	7.50	7.50
TUR94	372a	(1901)	1pi blue	invtd ovpt (vc)	7.50	7.50
TUR95	379a	(1905)	20pa carmine	invtd ovpt (vc)	10.00	5.00
TUR96	380a	(1905)	1pi brt blue	invtd ovpt (vc)	10.00	5.00
TUR97	419a	(1916)	60pa on 1pi on 1-1/2pi	"1330" omitted	10.00	10.00

TUR98	446a	(1865)	20pa yellow (R)	star without rays (R)	35.00	35.00
TUR99	447a	(1865)	1pi pearl gray (R)	star without rays (R)	35.00	35.00
TUR100	472a	(1886)	5pa blk & pale gray (R)	invtd ovpt (vc)	20.00	20.00
TUR101	473a	(1886)	2pi orange & bl (Bk)	invtd ovpt (vc)	20.00	20.00
TUR102	479a	(1901)	5pa bister (R)	invtd ovpt (vc)	20.00	20.00
TUR103	480a	(1901)	20pa magenta (Bk)	invtd ovpt (vc)	25.00	25.00
TUR104	481a	(1901)	1pi violet blue (R)	invtd ovpt (vc)	20.00	20.00
TUR105	488a	(1901)	20pa carmine (Bk)	invtd ovpt (vc)	20.00	20.00
TUR106	490a	(1901)	2pi orange (Bk)	invtd ovpt (vc)	20.00	20.00
TUR107	494a	(1905)	5pa ocher (R)	invtd ovprt (vc)	20.00	20.00
TUR108	496a	(1905)	20pa carmine (Bk)	dbl ovpt, one invtd	20.00	20.00
TUR109	496b			invtd ovpt (vc)	20.00	20.00
TUR110	497a	(1905)	1pi blue (R)	invtd ovpt (vc)	20.00	20.00
TUR111	499a	(1905)	2-1/2pi red violet (Bk)	invtd orpt (vc)	20.00	20.00
TUR112	504a		10pa dull green (R)	invtd ovpt (vc)	20.00	20.00
TUR113	505a		20pa carmine (Bk)	dbl ovpt, one invtd (vc)	20.00	20.00
TUR114	505b			invtd ovpt (vc)	20.00	20.00
TUR115	506a		1pi brt blue (Bk)	invtd ovpt (vc)	20.00	20.00
TUR116	507a		1pi brt blue (R)	invtd ovpt (vc)	20.00	20.00
TUR117	518a	(1908-09)	5pa ocher (R)	dbl ovpt (vc)	20.00	20.00
TUR118	518b			dbl ovpt, one invtd	20.00	20.00
TUR119	520a	(1908-09)	20pa carmine rose (Bk)	dbl ovpt (vc)	20.00	20.00
TUR120	536a	(1913)	10pa blue green (Bk)	invtd ovpt (vc)	20.00	20.00
TUR121	537a	(1913)	1pi ultra (Bk)	invtd ovpt (vc)	20.00	20.00
TUR122	539a	(1913)	10pa green (R)	invtd ovpt (vc)	20.00	20.00
TUR123	540a	(1913)	40pa blue (R)	invtd ovpt (vc)	20.00	20.00
TUR124	541a		60pa on 1pi on 1-1/2pi (Bk)	"1330" omitted	25.00	25.00
TUR125	548a	(1918)	5pi on 2pa Prus blue	invtd surch (vc)	10.00	10.00
TUR126	548Ab	(1918)	2pa on 5pa on 1pi red	dbl surch (vc)	10.00	10.00
TUR127	548Ac			invtd surch (vc)	10.00	10.00
TUR128	548Ad			dbl surch invtd	10.00	10.00
TUR129	548Ae			dbl surch, one invtd	10.00	10.00
TUR130	567a	(1919)	5pa on 2pa ol grn	invtd surch (vc)	10.00	10.00
TUR131	569a	(1919)	10pa green	invtd ovpt (vc)	25.00	25.00
TUR132	570a	(1919)	20pa deep rose	invtd ovpt (vc)	12.00	12.00
TUR133	586a	(1919)	25pi slate blue	invtd ovpt (vc)	—	100.00
TUR134	600a	(1921-22)	30pa on 10pa red vio	dbl surch (vc)	37.50	37.50
TUR135	601a	(1921-22)	60pa on 10pa green	dbl surch (vc)	22.50	22.50
TUR136	602a	(1921-22)	4-1/2pi on 1pi red	invtd surch (vc)	20.00	20.00
TUR137	604a	(1921-22)	7-1/2pi on 3pi bl (R) ('22)	dbl surch (vc)	30.00	30.00
TUR138	607a	(1923-25)	1pi deep violet	slanting numeral in lower left corner	.50	.25
TUR139	673a	(1929)	20pa on 1g brt rose	invtd surch (vc)	3.50	3.50
TUR140	674a	(1929)	2-1/2k on 5g lilac gray	invtd surch (vc)	7.50	7.50
TUR141	1596a	(1963)	10k black, yel & rose	rose omitted	—	—
TUR142	1718a	(1966)	50k lt bl, vio bl & blk	black (inscriptions & imprint) omitted	65.00	—
TUR143	B7a	(1909)	10pa blue green	invtd ovpt (vc)	22.50	22.50
TUR144	B7b			dbl ovpt, one invtd	30.00	30.00
TUR145	B11b	(1909)	10pa, blue green	dbl ovpt, one invtd	5.00	5.00
TUR146	B14a	(1913)	10pa blue green	invtd ovpt (vc)	22.50	22.50
TUR147	B15a	(1913)	1pi ultra	dbl ovpt (vc)	5.00	5.00
TUR148	B16a	(1913)	10pa blue green	invtd ovpt (vc)	27.50	27.50
TUR149	B34a	(1913)	1pi ultra	invtd ovpt (vc)	5.00	5.00
TUR150	B42a	(1893-99)	10pa carmine	invtd ovpt (vc)	6.75	6.75
TUR151	B43a	(1893-99)	20pa ultra	invtd ovpt (vc)	6.75	6.75
TUR152	B44a	(1893-99)	1pi violet & blk	invtd ovpt (vc)	6.75	6.75
TUR153	B45a	(1893-99)	5pi yel brn & blk	invtd ovpt (vc)	11.00	11.00
TUR154	B120a	(1967)	100K + 10k multi	dark blue ("Europa") omitted	—	—
TUR155	J1b	(1863)	20pa blk, red brn	without band	35.00	—
TUR156	J1c			red band	90.00	40.00

TUR157	J2b	(1863)	1pi blk, red brn	without band		35.00	—
TUR158	J4b	(1863)	5pi blk, red brn	without band		100.00	—
TUR159	J4c			red band		150.00	—
TUR160	J12a	(1867)	1pi bister brn	with surch of 5pi		13.50	—
TUR161	J16a	(1869)	20pa bister brn	without surch		—	—
TUR162	J17a	(1869)	1pi bister brn	without surch		—	—
TUR163	J19b	(1869)	5pi bister brn	without border		—	—
TUR164	J19c			printed on both sides		14.00	—
TUR165	J21a	(1869)	20pa bister brn	invtd surch (vc)		—	—
TUR166	J21b			without surch		—	—
TUR167	J22a	(1869)	1pi bister brn	without surch		—	—
TUR168	J23b	(1869)	2pi bister brn	invtd surch (vc)		—	—
TUR169	J24b	(1869)	5pi bister brn	without surch		—	—
TUR170	J31c	(1871)	20pa bister brn	printed on both sides		40.00	40.00
TUR171	J32c	(1871)	1pi bister brn	invtd surch (vc)		50.00	35.00
TUR172	J32d			printed on both sides		—	—
TUR173	J34c	(1871)	5pi bister brn	printed on both sides		—	—
TUR174	J35a	(1871)	25pi bister brn	invtd surch (vc)		—	—
TUR175	J40a	(1892)	1pi black	printed on both sides		—	—
TUR176	J85a		40pa on 10pa on 40pa (Bk)	"40pa" dbl		—	—
TUR177	O23Af	(1953-54)	0.25k dk red (G Bk)	('53) black ovpt		4.00	4.00
TUR178	O23Ag			violet ovprt ('53)		4.00	4.00
TUR179	O31ac	(1955)	10k on 15k violet	"10" without serif		.15	.15
TUR180	P29a	(1892)	5pi pale violet	on no. 99a		NA	—
TUR181	P31b	(1893-98)	20pa vio brn ('98)	20pa pink		15.00	8.00
TUR182	P34b	(1893-98)	5pi pale violet	on no. 99a		135.00	65.00
TUR183	P36a	(1897)	5pa on 10pa gray grn	"Cniq" instead of "Cinq"		7.50	7.50
TUR184	P37a	(1901)	5pa bister	invtd ovpt (vc)		—	—
TUR185	P45a	(1901)	20pa carmine	ovptd on back		—	—
TUR186	P47a	(1901)	2pi orange	invtd ovpt (vc)		—	—
TUR187	P121a	(1893-98)	10pa gray green	invtd ovpt (vc)		10.00	10.00
TUR188	P122a	(1893-98)	2pi yellow brn	invtd ovpt (vc)		10.00	10.00
TUR189	P127a	(1905)	5pa ocher	invtd ovpt (vc)		7.50	7.50
TUR190	P140a	(1901)	20pa magenta	invtd ovpt (vc)		10.00	10.00
TUR191	P155a	(1901)	5pa bister (Bk)	invtd ovpt (vc)		20.00	20.00
TUR192	P159a	(1901)	5pa purple (Bk)	invtd ovpt (vc)		20.00	20.00
TUR193	P159b			dbl ovpt (vc)		20.00	20.00
TUR194	P159c			dbl ovpt, one invtd		25.00	25.00
TUR195	P165a	(1905)	5pa ocher (R)	invtd ovpt (vc)		10.00	10.00
TUR196	P166a	(1905)	5pa ocher (Bk)	invtd ovpt (vc)		10.00	10.00
TUR197	P168a	(1905)	20pa carmine (Bk)	dbl ovpt (vc)		15.00	15.00
TUR198	P169a	(1905)	1pi blue (R)	invtd ovpt (vc)		25.00	25.00
TUR199	RA13a	(1932)	3k on 1k	3 "kruus"		2.50	2.50

Turkey, Turkey in the straw
Turkey Turkey goes hee-haw
What do all these strange words mean
In light of our error machine
They mean that one can simply find
Turkish errors of every kind.
Printed on one side, printed on two
Common inverts and surcharges too.
They're not all cheap nor old or new.
However Turkey is a land for you. —The Bard

TURKEY IN ASIA

TIA1	5a	(1913)	3pi on 2pa red lilac	on no. 1		20.00	20.00
TIA2	6a	(1913)	3pi on 4pa dk brown	on no. 2		20.00	20.00
TIA3	7a	(1913)	3pi on 4pa dk brn (R)	on no. 2		10.50	10.50
TIA4	8a	(1913)	3pi on 6pa dk blue	on no. 3		32.50	32.50
TIA5	9a	(1913)	3pi on 6pa dk bl (R)	on no. 3		40.00	40.00
TIA6	29a		10pa slate	handstamped ovpt		15.00	15.00

TIA7	29b			dbl ovpt (vc)	—	—
TIA8	30b		1pi green	handstamped ovpt	—	—
TIA9	31a		5pi ultra	"1337" invtd	90.00	82.50
TIA10	31c			handstamped ovpt	30.00	30.00
TIA11	33a		10pa green	handstamped ovpt		
TIA12	34a			ultra handstamped ovpt	22.50	22.50
TIA13	35a		5pi red	invtd ovpt (vc)	—	—
TIA14	35c			half used as 2-1/2pi on cover	—	—
TIA15	35d			handstamped ovpt	—	—
TIA16	36a		50pi ocher	handstamped ovpt	—	—
TIA17	37a		10a green (R) black	ovpt invtd	100.00	100.00
TIA18	39a		5pi rose (Bk)	"1337" invtd	140.00	140.00
TIA19	40a		2pi blue black	handstamped ovpt	—	—
TIA20	41a		5pi green	handstamped ovpt	—	—
TIA21	42a		1pi ultra	handstamped ovpt	NA	NA
TIA22	43a		5pi deep green	handstamped ovpt	NA	NA
TIA23	45a		20pa black	data 4-1/2mm high	15.00	10.00
TIA24	45b			"337" for "1337"	25.00	25.00
TIA25	46a		10pa green	ovpt 21mm long	—	—
TIA26	46b			"131" for "1337"		
TIA27	47a		1pi ultra	"13" for "1337"	25.00	25.00
TIA28	47b			"131" for "1337"	25.00	25.00
TIA29	47c			invtd ovpt	32.50	32.50
TIA30	47d			handstamped ovpt		
TIA31	48a		5pi red	invtd ovpt (vc)	67.50	60.00
TIA32	48b			"131" for "1337"	60.00	60.00
TIA33	48c			handstamped ovpt		
TIA34	49b		10pa pink	date "1237"	1.75	1.00
TIA35	49d			invtd ovpt (vc)		
TIA36	50a		1pi yellow	ovpt 18mm long	3.50	.80
TIA37	50b			date "1332"	5.50	—
TIA38	50c			date "1317"		
TIA39	50d			invtd ovpt (vc)	9.50	9.50
TIA40	51a		2pi yellow grn	date "1237"	5.50	—
TIA41	51b			date "1317"		
TIA42	51d			invtd ovpt (vc)	17.50	3.25
TIA43	52b		5pi red	invtd ovpt (vc)	12.50	7.50
TIA44	52c			dbl ovpt (vc)	15.00	12.50
TIA45	52d			date "1332"	20.00	—
TIA46	52f			ovpt 18mm long	9.00	6.75
TIA47	55a	(1921)	2pi on 1pi	invtd surch (vc)	—	—
TIA48	58a	(1921)	1pi grn & brn red	dbl ovpt (vc)	—	—
TIA49	58b			handstamped ovpt	—	—
TIA50	59a	(1921)	1pa orange	date "1327"	1.10	1.10
TIA51	65a	(1921)	10pa green	invtd ovpt (vc)	16.50	16.50
TIA52	66a	(1921)	25pi car, straw	dbl ovpt (vc)	—	—
TIA53	66b			invtd ovpt (vc)	37.50	37.50
TIA54	71a	(1919)	35pi on 1pi bl (Bk)	invtd surch (vc)	10.00	10.00
TIA55	76a	(1921)	20pa red	invtd ovpt (vc)	—	—
TIA56	77a	(1921)	1pi dark blue	invtd ovpt (vc)	70.00	70.00
TIA57	103a	(1921)	3pi rose	Arabic "13" in right corner	6.50	3.50
TIA58	103b			thin grayish paper	14.00	1.40

TURKISH REPUBLIC OF NORTHERN CYPRUS has produced no errors

TURKMENISTAN has produced no errors

TURKS AND CAICOS ISLANDS

TCI1	148a	(1966)	8p brown	gold impression dbl	200.00	—
TCI2	MR1a	(1917)	1p carmine	dbl ovpt (vc)	150.00	—
TCI3	MR1b			"TAX" omitted	—	—
TCI4	MR1c			pair, one without ovpt	—	—
TCI5	MR2a	(1917)	3p violet, yel	dbl ovpt (vc)	90.00	—

TCl6	MR3a	(1917)	1p carmine	invtd ovpt (vc)	25.00	—
TCl7	MR3b			dbl ovpt (vc)	37.50	16.00
TCl8	MR3c			pair, one without ovpt	200.00	—
TCl9	MR4a	(1917)	3p violet, yel	dbl ovpt (vc)	17.50	—
TCl10	MR4b			dbl ovpt, one invtd	37.50	—
TCl11	MR5a	(1918-19)	1p car (V)	('19) dbl ovpt (vc)	14.00	—
TCl12	MR5b			"WAR" omitted	100.00	—
TCl13	MR6a	(1918-19)	3p violet, yel (R)	dbl ovpt (vc)	75.00	—
TCl14	MR10a		1p carmine	dbl ovpt (vc)	100.00	100.00
TCl15	MR12a		1p carmine	dbl ovpt (vc)	100.00	—

A gold impression double
Spells much error trouble
But's the only one at T + C
Most of the rest are our old friends vc
But here's the one getting the ax
Instead of goldie are stamps for war tax. —The Bard

CAICOS has produced no errors

TURKS ISLANDS

TUI1	8a	(1881)	1/2p on 1sh slate bl	dbl surch (vc)	NA	—
TUI2	8Bc	(1881)	1/2p on 1sh slate bl	without fraction bar	—	—
TUI3	9a	(1881)	1/2p on 1p dull red	dbl surch (vc)	—	—
TUI4	11a	(1881)	1/2p on 1p dull red	dbl surch (vc)	NA	—
TUI5	12a	(1881)	1/2p on 1p dull red	without fraction bar	NA	—
TUI6	12b			dbl surch (vc)	—	—
TUI7	14a	(1881)	1/2p on 1sh violet	dbl surch (vc)	NA	—
TUI8	15a	(1881)	1/2p on 1sh violet	without fraction bar	NA	—
TUI9	18b	(1881)	2-1/2p on 6p gray blk	dbl surch (vc)	NA	—
TUI10	27a	(1881)	2-1/2p on 1sh slate bl	without fraction bar	NA	—
TUI11	31a	(1881)	2-1/2p on 1sh violet	dbl surch of "1/2" (u)	NA	—
TUI12	32b	(1881)	2-1/2p on 1sh violet	dbl surch of "1/2" (u)	NA	—
TUI13	36a	(1881)	4p on 1p dull red	invtd surch (vc)	NA	—
TUI14	37a	(1881)	4p on 1p dull red	invtd surch (vc)	—	—
TUI15	55a	(1889)	1p on 2-1/2p red brown	dbl surch (vc)	—	—

TUVALU has produced no errors

U

UBANGI-SHARI

UBS1	1a	(1915-22)	1c olgray & brn	dbl ovpt (vc)	125.00	—
UBS2	23a	(1922)	1c violet & grn	ovpt omitted	125.00	—
UBS3	25a	(1922)	4c ol brn & brn	ovpt omitted	150.00	—
UBS4	38a	(1922)	1fr grn & dl bl (R)	ovpt omitted	—	—
UBS5	41a	(1924-33)	1c vio & grn (Bl)	"OUBANGUI CHARI" omitted	80.00	—
UBS6	42a	(1924-33)	2c grn & sal (Bl)	"OUBANGUI CHARI" omitted	80.00	—
UBS7	42b			dbl ovpt (vc)	85.00	—
UBS8	43a	(1924-33)	4c ol brn & brn (Bl)	dbl ovpt (Bl + Bk) (vc)	110.00	—
UBS9	43b			"OUBANGUI CHARI" omitted	110.00	—
UBS10	44a	(1924-33)	5c ind & rose	"OUBANGUI CHARI" omitted	85.00	—
UBS11	52a	(1924-33)	30c cho & red ('25)	"OUBANBUI CHARI" omitted	100.00	—
UBS12	54a	(1924-33)	35c vio & grn (Bl)	"OUBANBUI CHARI" omitted	—	—
See Photo in Color Section						
UBS13	62a	(1924-33)	75c dp bl & lt bl ('25) (R)	"OUBANGUI CHARI" omitted	90.00	—
UBS14	71a	(1924-33)	2fr grn & red	"OUBANGUI CHARI" omitted	NA	NA
UBS15	74a	(1925-26)	65c on 1fr vio & ol	"65" omitted	75.00	—
UBS16	75a		85c on 1fr vio & ol	"AFRIQUE EQUATORIALE FRANCAISE" omitted	80.00	—
UBS17	75b			dbl surch (vc)	90.00	—
UBS18	76a	(1926)	1.25fr on 1fr dk bl & ultra (R)	"1125" omitted	100.00	100.00

UBS19	B1a	(1916)	10c + 5c car & blue	invtd surch (vc)	65.00	65.00
UBS20	B1b			dbl surch (vc)	65.00	65.00
UBS21	B1c			dbl surch, one invtd	90.00	90.00
UBS22	B1d			vertical surch	65.00	65.00
UBS23	B1e			no period under "C"	7.50	7.50

UGANDA

UGA1	54a	(1896)	1a black (thin "1")	small "O" in "POSTAGE"	NA	—
UGA2	55a	(1896)	2a black	small "O" in "POSTAGE"	150.00	175.00
UGA3	56a	(1896)	3a black	small "O" in "POSTAGE"	NA	—
UGA4	57a	(1896)	4a black	small "O" in "POSTAGE"	175.00	—
UGA5	58a	(1896)	8a black	small "O" in "POSTAGE"	NA	—
UGA6	59a	(1896)	1r black	small "O" in "POSTAGE"	NA	—
UGA7	61a	(1896)	1a black (thin "1")	small "O" in "POSTAGE"	200.00	200.00
UGA8	62a	(1896)	1a black (thick "1")	small "O" in "POSTAGE"	40.00	40.00
UGA9	63a	(1896)	2a black	small "O" in "POSTAGE"	40.00	45.00
UGA10	64a	(1896)	3a black	small "O" in "POSTAGE"	45.00	50.00
UGA11	65a	(1896)	4a black	small "O" in "POSTAGE"	45.00	50.00
UGA12	66a	(1896)	8a black	small "O" in "POSTAGE"	85.00	85.00
UGA13	67a	(1896)	1r black	small "O" in "POSTAGE"	150.00	175.00
UGA14	68a	(1896)	5r black	small "O" in "POSTAGE"	NA	NA
UGA15	77a	(1902)	1/2a yellow green	invtd ovpt (vc)	NA	—
UGA16	77b			dbl ovpt (vc)	NA	—
UGA17	78a	(1902)	2-1/2a dark blue	dbl ovpt (vc)	NA	—

UKRAINE

UKR1	73a	(1919)	70k on 50sh red	surch invtd (vc)	45.00	—

UNITED ARAB EMIRATES has produced no errors

UPPER SENEGAL AND NIGER has produced no errors

UPPER SILESIA has produced no errors

URUGUAY

URU1	24b	(1866)	5c on 12c blue	invtd surch (vc)	45.00	—
URU2	24c			dbl surch (vc)	25.00	—
URU3	24d			pair, one without surch	—	—
URU4	24e			triple surch (u)	55.00	—
URU5	25c	(1866)	10c on 8c brt grn	dbl surch (vc)	35.00	—
URU6	26c	(1866)	15c on 10c ocher	dbl surch (vc)	30.00	—
URU7	27b	(1866)	20c on 6c rose	invtd surch (vc)	65.00	—
URU8	27c			dbl surch (vc)	35.00	—
URU9	27d			pair, one without surch	—	—
URU10	28a	(1866)	20c on 6c brick red	dbl surch (vc)	—	—
URU11	30c	(1866)	5c blue	numeral with white flag	20.00	8.50
URU12	30d			"ENTECIMOS"	20.00	9.00
URU13	30e			"CENTECIMO"	20.00	9.00
URU14	30f			"CENTECIMOS" with small "S"	18.00	8.50
URU15	31b	(1866)	10c yellow green	"1" of "CENTECIMOS" omitted	27.50	11.00
URU16	31c			"CENIECIMOS"	27.50	11.00
URU17	31d			"CENTRCIMOS"	27.50	11.00
URU18	35b	(1866-67)	5c blue	numeral with white flag	11.00	8.00

URU35

URU42

URU77A

URU77B

AFFORDABLE FOREIGN ERRORS

URU19	35c		"ENTECIMOS"	12.50	3.25
URU20	35d		"CENTECIMO"	12.50	3.25
URU21	35e		"CENTECIMOS" with small "S"	12.50	1.90
URU22	36c	(1866-67) 10c green	"I" of "CENTECIMOS" omitted	15.00	3.25
URU23	36d		"CENTRCIMOS"		
URU24	52a	(1883) 5c green	dbl ovpt (vc)	15.00	15.00
URU25	52b		ovpt reading down	4.50	4.50
URU26	52c		"Provisorio" omitted	7.00	7.00
URU27	52d		"1883" omitted	4.50	4.50
URU28	53a	(1884) 1c on 10c ver	small figure "1"	3.50	3.50
URU29	53b		invtd surch (vc)	3.50	3.50
URU30	53c		dbl surch (vc)	8.00	5.00
URU31	54a	(1884) 2c rose	dbl ovpt (vc)	14.00	—
URU32	73a	(1889) 5c violet	invtd ovpt (vc)	5.00	3.00
URU33	73b		invtd "A" for "V" in "Provisorio"	3.00	—
URU34	84a	(1889-1901) 10c blue grn	printed on both sides (u)	20.00	—
URU35	98a	(1891-92) 1c green ('92)	invtd ovpt (vc)	4.25	3.75
URU36	98b		dbl ovpt (vc)	5.50	5.00
URU37	98c		dbl ovpt, one invtd	3.00	2.50
URU38	98d		"Previsorio"	2.75	2.50
URU39	99a	(1891-92) 1c green ('92)	"1391"	2.50	1.75
URU40	99b		dbl ovpt (vc)	2.50	1.75
URU41	99c		invtd ovpt (vc)	2.50	1.75
URU42	99c		dbl ovpt, one invtd	5.00	3.00
URU43	100a	(1892) 1c on 20c org (Bk)	invtd surch)vc)	3.00	3.00
URU44	101a	(1892) 5c on 7cq bis brn (R)	invtd surch (vc)	1.00	1.00
URU45	101c		dbl surch	3.00	3.00
URU46	101d		vertical surch (vc)	10.00	—
URU47	101e		"PREVISORIO"	2.00	2.00
URU48	101f		"Cinco" omitted	4.50	—
URU49	109a	(1895-99) 1c slate b ('97)	printed on both sides (u)	14.00	—
URU50	120a	(1895-99) 25c red brn & blk	center invtd (u)	—	NA
URU51	133a	(1897) 1c brn vio & blk	invtd ovpt (vc)	3.50	3.00
URU52	134a	(1897) 5c pale blue & blk	invtd ovpt (vc)	6.00	4.50
URU53	135a	(1897) 10c lake & blk	invtd ovpt (vc)	8.50	7.50
URU54	135b		dbl ovpt (vc)	7.50	—
URU55	138a	(1897) 1c slate bl (R)	invtd ovpt (vc)	3.00	3.00
URU56	139a	(1897) 2c claret (Bl)	invtd ovpt (vc)	2.50	2.50
URU57	140a	(1897) 5c green (Bl)	invtd ovpt (vc)	5.00	5.00
URU58	140b		dbl ovpt (vc)	—	—
URU59	141a	(1897) 10c red (Bl)	invtd ovpt (vc)	10.00	10.00
URU60	142a	(1898) 1/2c on 1c bl (Bk)	invtd surch (vc)	3.00	3.00
URU61	143a	(1898) 1/2c on 1c bis (Bl)	invtd surch (vc)	3.00	—
URU62	143b		dbl surch (vc)	2.50	—
URU63	146a	(1898) 1/2c on 5c pale bl & blk (R)	dbl surch (vc)	6.25	—
URU64	152a	(1900) 5c on 10c lake & blk	black bar covering "1897" omitted	15.00	—
URU65	179a	(1909) 8c on 10c dull vio	"Contesimos"	2.00	1.10
URU66	184a	(1910) 5m on 1c yel grn	invtd surch (vc)	4.50	3.75
URU67	185a	(1910) 5c on 50c dull red	invtd surch (vc)	4.50	4.50
URU68	186a	(1910) 5c on 50c rose	dbl surch (vc)	20.00	—
URU69	186b		invtd surch (vc)	10.00	8.75
URU70	198a	(1911) 5c on 7c grn org (Bl)	invtd surch (vc)	6.00	—
URU71	211a	(1913) 2c brown orange	invtd ovpt (vc)	5.00	4.50
URU72	525a	(1943) 2c on 2c dl vio brn (V)	invtd surch (vc)	12.50	12.50
URU73	546a	(1946-51) 5m orange ('49)	invtd ovpt (vc)	—	—
URU74	627a	(1957-58) 10c on 7c	surch invtd (vc)	17.00	17.00
URU75	714a	(1965) 20c gold, emer & blk	gold omitted (u)	—	—
URU76	715a	(1965) 40c gold, redsh brn & blk	gold omitted (u)	—	—

URU77	C2a	(1921-22)	25c bister brn (R)	invtd ovpt (vc)	65.00	65.00
URU78	C61b	(1934)	17c ver, gray & vio	gray omitted	100.00	—
URU79	C61c			dbl ovpt (vc)	100.00	—
URU80	C116a	(1945-46)	14c on 50c (V)	('46) invtd surch (vc)	37.50	—
URU81	C117a	(1945-46)	23c on 1.38p	invtd surch (vc)	75.00	—
URU82	C118a	(1945-46)	23c on 50c	invtd surch (vc)	75.00	—
URU83	C119a	(1945-46)	1p on 1.38p (Bl)	invtd surch (vc)	75.00	—
URU84	C121a	(1946-49)	8c car rose	invtd ovpt (vc)	—	—
URU85	C122a	(1946-49)	50c brown	dbl ovpt (vc)	25.00	—
URU86	E1a	(1921)	2c fawn	dbl ovpt (vc)	3.25	—
URU87	J6a	(1904)	1c on 10c dk bl	invtd surch (vc)	6.00	6.00
URU88	O10a	(1884)	1c on 10c ver	small "1" (No. 53a)	5.00	—
URU89	O61a	(1891)	5c violet	"1391"	9.00	—
URU90	O78a	(1895-1900)	1p yel brn & bl ('97)	invtd ovpt	—	—
URU91	O91a	(1901)	1p deep green	invtd ovpt (vc)	9.00	7.00
URU92	O96a	(1905)	20c gray green	invtd ovpt (vc)	—	—
URU93	O102a	(1907)	20c gray green	invtd ovpt (vc)	4.00	—
URU94	O110a	(1910)	50c rose	invtd ovpt (vc)	15.00	10.00
URU95	O125a	(1919)	2c red & black	invtd ovpt (vc)	3.50	—
URU96	O127a	(1919)	8c gray bl & lt brn	invtd ovpt (vc)	3.50	—
URU97	O131a	(1919)	1p dull red & bl	dbl ovpt (vc)	12.50	—
URU98	P1a	(1922)	3c on 4c orange	invtd surch (vc)	6.00	6.00
URU99	P1b			dbl surch (vc)	2.50	2.50
URU100	P5a	(1926)	3c gray green	dbl ovpt (vc)	1.00	1.00
URU101	P6a	(1926)	9c on 10c turq bl	dbl surch (vc)	1.00	1.00

Uruguay is the place to play...
If you have an error collection.
Variety is rampant and most
Prices reasonable for your selection.
Now there are exceptions
Such as inverted centers
But printed both sides can easily join the collection. —The Bard

UZBEKISTAN has produced no errors

V

VANAUTU has produced no errors

VATICAN CITY

VAT1	36a	(1934)	1.30 1 on 1.25 1	small figures "30" in "1.30"	NA	NA
VAT2	37a	(1934)	2.05 1 on 2 1	no comma btwn 2 & 0	NA	35.00
VAT3	38a	(1934)	2.55 1 on 2.50	1 no comma btwn 2 & 5	165.00	165.00
VAT4	40a	(1934)	3.70 1 on 10 1	no comma btwn 3 & 7	NA	NA
VAT5	65a	(1939)	30c indigo & yellow	pair, one without ovpt	NA	—
VAT6	82a	(1942)	1.25l saphire & vio bl	name & value panel omitted	—	—
VAT7	88a	(1944)	80c claret & rose vio	dbl impression of center	NA	—
VAT8	100a	(1945)	3 1 dk carmine	Jesus image omitted	100.00	100.00
VAT9	103b	(1946)	25c on 30c (I)	invtd surch (II) (vc)	NA	NA
VAT10	105a	(1946)	1.50l on 1 1 (Bl)	dbl surch (vc)	175.00	—
VAT11	154a	(1952)	12 1 on 13 1 dull grn	pair, one without surch	NA	NA
VAT12	397a	(1964)	10 1 multicolored	yellow omitted	—	—
VAT13	J1a	(1931)	5c dk brown & pink	dbl frame	—	—
VAT14	J2a	(1931)	10c dk grn & lt grn	frame omitted	NA	—
VAT15	Q10a	(1931)	2 1 olive brown	invtd ovpt (vc)	NA	NA
VAT16	Q11a	(1931)	2.50 1 red orange	dbl ovpt (vc)	NA	—
VAT17	Q11b			invtd ovpt (vc)	NA	—
VAT18	Q13a	(1931)	10 1 olive black	dbl ovpt (vc)	NA	—

VENEZUELA

VEN1	23e	(1871-76)	2c yellow	frame invtd	NA	NA
VEN2	41a	(1871-76)	2c green	invtd ovpt (vc)	40.00	50.00
VEN3	42a	(1871-76)	1/2r rose	invtd ovpt (vc)	30.00	4.00
VEN4	43a	(1871-76)	1r vermillion	invtd ovpt (vc)	35.00	9.00
VEN5	44a	(1871-76)	2r yellow	invtd ovpt (vc)	110.00	50.00
VEN6	45a	(1875)	1/2r rose	invtd ovpt (vc)	125.00	25.00
VEN7	45b			dbl ovpt (vc)	165.00	90.00
VEN8	46a	(1875)	1r vermillion	invtd ovpt (vc)	200.00	80.00
VEN9	47b	(1876-77)	1/2r rose	invtd ovpt (vc)	65.00	7.00
VEN10	47c			both lines of ovpt read "Contrasena"	75.00	17.50
VEN11	47d			both lines of ovpt read "Estampillas de correo"	75.00	17.50
VEN12	47e			dbl ovpt (vc)	125.00	35.00
VEN13	48a	(1876-77)	1r vermillion ('77)	invtd ovpt (vc)	85.00	24.00
VEN14	50b	(1879)	5c yellow	dbl ovpt (vc)	20.00	10.00
VEN15	58b	(1880)	5c yellow	printed on both sides (u)	150.00	85.00
VEN16	60b	(1880)	25c yellow	printed on both sides (u)	110.00	52.50
VEN17	60c			impression on 5c black (u)	175.00	90.00
VEN18	61c	(1880)	50c yellow	printed on both sides (u)	150.00	90.00
VEN19	68a	(1880)	5c blue	printed on both sides (u)	NA	140.00
VEN20	69b	(1880)	10c rose	dbl impression (u)	90.00	75.00
VEN21	72b	(1880)	50c brown	printed on both sides (u)	NA	140.00
VEN22	76a	(1882)	25c yellow brown	printed onboth sides (u)	50.00	27.50
VEN23	108a	(1893)	5c blue (R)	invtd ovpt (vc)	3.25	3.25
VEN24	108b			dbl ovpt (vc)	16.00	16.00
VEN25	109a	(1893)	10c red brn (Bk)	invtd ovpt (vc)	4.00	4.00
VEN26	109b			dbl ovpt (vc)	16.00	16.00
VEN27	110a	(1893)	25c yel brn (R)	invtd ovpt (vc)	5.25	5.25
VEN28	110b			dbl ovpt (vc)	16.00	16.00
VEN29	111a	(1893)	50c green (R)	invtd ovpt (vc)	5.25	5.20
VEN30	111b			dbl ovpt (vc)	27.50	27.50
VEN31	112a	(1893)	1b pur (R)	invtd ovpt (vc)	10.00	10.00
VEN32	114a	(1893)	5c bl grn (R)	invtd ovpt (vc)	3.25	3.25
VEN33	114b			dbl ovpt (vc)	5.25	5.25
VEN34	115a	(1893)	10c brn (R)	invtd ovpt (vc)	3.25	3.25
VEN35	116a	(1893)	25c org (R)	invtd ovpt (vc)	3.25	3.25
VEN36	117a	(1893)	25c org (Bk)	invtd ovpt (vc)	8.25	5.00
VEN37	118a	(1893)	50c blue (R)	invtd ovpt (vc)	3.25	3.25
VEN38	119a	(1893)	1b ver (Bk)	invtd ovpt (vc)	4.00	4.00
VEN39	120a	(1893)	3b dl vio (R)	dbl ovpt (vc)	8.25	8.25
VEN40	121a	(1893)	10b dk brn (R)	dbl ovpt (vc)	10.00	10.00
VEN41	121b			invtd ovpt (vc)	20.00	20.00
VEN42	122a	(1893)	20b plum (Bk)	dbl ovpt (vc)	10.00	20.00
VEN43	122b			invtd ovpt (vc)	—	—
VEN44	150a	(1900)	5c dk grn	invtd ovpt (vc)	4.00	4.00
VEN45	151a	(1900)	10c red	invtd ovpt (vc)	5.25	5.25
VEN46	151b			dbl ovpt (vc)	10.50	10.50
VEN47	152a	(1900)	25c blue	invtd ovpt (vc)	10.50	10.50
VEN48	153a	(1900)	50c gray blk	invtd ovpt (vc)	9.25	9.25

VEN81A

VEN99A

VENEZUELA

VEN49	154a	(1900)	1b yel grn	dbl ovpt (vc)	13.00	13.00
VEN50	154b			invtd ovpt (vc)	9.25	9.25
VEN51	155a	(1900)	2b orange	invtd ovpt (vc)	27.50	27.50
VEN52	155b			dbl ovpt (vc)	32.50	32.50
VEN53	160a	(1900)	1b slate	without ovpt	NA	—
VEN54	230a	(1904)	5c on 50c green	"Vele"	18.00	18.00
VEN55	230b			surch reading up	.75	.35
VEN56	230c			dbl surch (vc)	18.00	18.00
VEN57	287a	(1926)	5c on 1b ol grn	dbl surch (vc)	8.00	8.00
VEN58	287c			invtd surch (vc)	8.00	8.00
VEN59	288a	(1926)	25c on 5c dk brn (R)	invtd surch (vc)	8.00	8.00
VEN60	288b			dbl surch (vc)	8.00	8.00
VEN61	307a	(1933)	7-1/2c on 10c grn	dbl surch (vc)	2.50	2.50
VEN62	307b			invtd surch (vc)	3.25	3.25
VEN63	309a	(1933)	22-1/2c on 25c (#277)	dbl surch (vc)	10.00	10.00
VEN64	310a	(1933)	37-1/2c on 40c dp bl	dbl surch (vc)	11.50	11.50
VEN65	310b			invtd surch (vc)	8.25	8.25
VEN66	318a	(1937)	25c on 40c indigo	dbl surch (vc)	16.00	16.00
VEN67	310a			dbl surch (vc)	16.00	16.00
VEN68	318b			invtd surch (vc)	13.00	13.00
VEN69	318c			triple surch (u)	32.50	32.50
VEN70	319a	(1937)	25c on 40c indigo	dbl surch (vc)	NA	NA
VEN71	322a	(1937)	10c dk slate grn	invtd ovpt (vc)	13.00	13.00
VEN72	323a	(1937)	25c cerise	invtd ovpt (vc)	16.00	16.00
VEN73	345a	(1938)	40c on 5b lt brn	invtd surch (vc)	21.00	21.00
VEN74	375a	(1941)	20c on 25c lt blue	invtd surch (vc)	10.00	10.00
VEN75	376a	(1941)	5c deep violet	dbl ovpt (vc)	10.00	8.25
VEN76	377a	(1941)	10c dk slate grn	dbl ovpt (vc)	13.00	13.00
VEN77	387a	(1943)	20c on 25c dk blue	invtd ovpt (vc)	25.00	25.00
VEN78	396a	(1947)	15c on 1b dk vio brn	invtd surch (vc)	6.00	5.00
VEN79	401a	(1947)	5c on 30c black	invtd surch (vc)	5.00	5.00
VEN80	402a	(1947)	5c on 37-1/2c dk bl	invtd surch (vc)	5.00	5.00
VEN81	451a	(1951)	10c on 37-1/2c brn	invtd surch (vc)	16.00	16.00
VEN82	C66a	(1937)	10c org red	invtd ovpt (vc)	13.00	10.00
VEN83	C69a	(1937)	70c red	invtd ovpt (vc)	13.00	11.50
VEN84	C69b			dbl ovpt (vc)	20.00	16.00
VEN85	C70a	(1937)	1b dk gray	invtd ovpt (vc)	16.00	13.00
VEN86	C70b			dbl ovpt (vc)	13.00	—
VEN87	C71a	(1937)	1.20b pck grn	invtd ovpt (vc)	65.00	—
VEN88	C73a	(1937)	1.95b lt ultra	invtd ovpt (vc)	50.00	30.00
VEN89	C74a	(1937)	2b chocolate	invtd ovpt (vc)	100.00	90.00
VEN90	C74b			dbl ovpt (vc)	82.50	82.50
VEN91	C75a	(1937)	2.50b gray bl	dbl ovpt (vc)	70.00	—
VEN92	C75b			invtd ovpt (vc)	105.00	82.50
VEN93	C78a	(1937)	20b gray	dbl ovpt (vc)	145.00	145.00
VEN94	C114a	(1938)	5c on 1.80b	invtd surch (vc)	14.00	7.50
VEN95	C115a	(1938)	10c on 2.50b	invtd surch (vc)	12.00	7.50
VEN96	C189a	(1944)	5c dull vio brn	"AEREO" dbl	—	8.25
VEN97	C196a	(1944)	1.20b yellow grn	"AEREO" invtd	15.00	13.00
VEN98	C198a	(1944)	30c on 1.40b	dbl surch (vc)	32.50	32.50
VEN99	C198b			invtd surch (vc)	13.00	13.00
VEN100	C223a	(1947)	10c on 22-1/2c dp car	invtd surch (vc)	4.00	4.00
VEN101	C225a	(1947)	20c on 50c blue	invtd surch (vc)	5.00	5.00
VEN102	C226a	(1947)	70c on 1b dk vio brn	invtd surch (vc)	4.00	4.00
VEN103	C227a			20b on 20b org red	surch omitted	85.00	25.00
VEN104	C238a	(1947)	10c on 20c blue	invtd surch (vc)	5.00	5.00
VEN105	O27a	(1912)	50c pur & blk	center dbl	19.00	—

VIETNAM

VIN1	1L14a	(1945-46)	25c dk bl (planting rice, #165A, R)	top line 20mm wide	90.00	—
				top line 18mm wide		

VIRGIN ISLANDS

VIR1	2a	(1866)	6p rose	large "V" in "VIRGIN"	NA	NA
VIR2	2c			as "a" white paper	NA	NA
VIR3	7b	(1867-70) 1sh rose & blk		dbl lined frame	190.00	NA
VIR4	7c			as "b," bluish paper	200.00	NA
VIR5	8a	(1867-70) 1sh rose & blk		white paper (u)	42.50	55.00
VIR6	8b			bluish paper	NA	NA
VIR7	8c			central figure omitted	NA	—
VIR8	18a	(1888)	4p on 1sh dp rose & blk. toned paper	dbl surch (vc)	NA	—
VIR9	18b			invtd surch (vc)	NA	—
VIR10	21a	(1899)	1/2p yellow grn	"PFNNY"	80.00	120.00
VIR11	21b			"F" without cross bar	80.00	120.00
VIR12	24a	(1899)	4p chocolate	"PENCF"	NA	NA
VIR14	O14					

W

WALLIS AND FUTUNA ISLANDS

WFA1	1a	(1920-28) 1c black, green	dbl ovpt (vc)	60.00	—
WFA2	25a	(1920-28) 1fr blue, yel grn	triple ovpt (vc)	85.00	—
WFA3	39a	(1924-27) 1.50fr on 1fr dp bl, bl ('27)	dbl surch (vc)	140.00	—
WFA4	39b		surch omitted (vc)	140.00	—
WFA5	40a	(1924-27) 3fr on 5fr red vio ('27)	surch omitted (vc)	125.00	—
WFA6	40b		dbl surch (vc)	150.00	—
WFA7	43a	(1930-40) 1c brn vio & indigo	dbl ovpt (vc)	80.00	—
WFA8	53a	(1930-40) 35c Prus grn & dk grn ('38)	without ovpt (vc)	110.00	—
WFI9	J4a	(1920) 20c blk, yel (R)	dbl ovpt (vc)	75.00	—
WFI10	J7a	(1920) 60c olive, azure	dbl ovpt (vc)	75.00	—

WEST IRIAN has produced no errors

WESTERN UKRAINE

WEU1	80a	(1919)	5hr on 2k rose, straw	invtd surch (vc)	NA	—

Y

YEMEN

YEM1	64a	(1949)	4b on 1b purple	handstamp type "b"	2.00	2.00
YEM2	65a	(1949)	4b on 2b ultra	handstamp type "b"	4.00	3.50
YEM3	65b			handstamp 13 x 15mm	—	—
YEM4	67a	(1953)	4b on 2b org & yel grn	handstamp type "c"	—	—
YEM5	C48a	(1975)	120f on 18b multi	ovptd in red (vc)	—	—

Yemen is an uncommon country
With uncommon philately
Ten soldiers marching, nine maids a milking
No vc-ing, no inverted center, no omitted colors
No partridge in a pear tree: just four
Handstamps and an overprint in an elm tree. —The Bard

People's Republic of Southern Yemen has produced no errors

YUGOSLAVIA

YUG1	1L21a	(1918)	3h on 2h ultra	dbl surch (vc)	14.00	—
YUG2	1L22a	(1918)	5h on 6h violet	dbl surch (vc)	14.00	—
YUG3	1LB1a	(1918)	10h greenish bl	ovptd as no. 1Lb2	27.50	37.50

YUG4	1LB2a	(1918)	15h red brown	ovptd as no. 1LB1	27.50	37.50
YUG5	1LB3a	(1916)	5h green	ovptd as no. 1LB1	NA	NA
YUG6	1LE1a	(1918)	2h vermillion	invtd ovpt (vc)	32.50	—
YUG7	1LE1b			ovptd as no. 1LE2	30.00	35.00
YUG8	1LE2a	(1918)	5h deep green	invtd ovpt (vc)	18.00	—
YUG9	1LE2b			ovptd as no. 1LE1	30.00	35.00
YUG10	2L5a	(1918)	15f violet	invtd ovpt (vc)	125.00	—
YUG11	2LJ2a	(1918)	1f green & red	invtd ovpt (vc)	22.50	22.50
YUG12	3L27a	(1919-20)	20f dark brown	serrate x straight roul	.55	.15
YUG13	3L28a	(1919-20)	30f car rose	serrate x straight roul	.60	.18
YUG14	3LJ12a	(1920)	1k Prussian blue	1k dark blue	5.00	4.50
YUG15	3LJ13a	(1920)	5k Prussian blue	5k dark blue	8.00	6.75
YUG16	3LJ14a	(1920)	10k Prussian blue	10k dark blue	14.00	15.00
YUG17	3LJ30a	(1920)	1d on 30f dp rose	serratex straight roulette	7.00	4.50
YUG18	3LJ31a	(1920)	3d on 30f dp rose	serrate x straight roulette	8.00	5.50
YUG19	3LJ32a	(1920)	8d on 30f dp rose	serrate x straight roulette	90.00	7.50
YUG20	18a	(1922-24)	3d on 15p (G)	blue surch	1.65	.15
YUG21	19a	(1922-24)	8d on 15p (G)	dbl surch (vc)	32.50	30.00
YUG22	19b		9d on 15p (error)		100.00	—
YUG23	53a	(1928)	1d scarlet	surch "0.50" invtd	—	—
YUG24	1765a	(1985-86)	2d on 5p (DB)	on #1482a	—	—
YUG25	1766a	(1985-86)	3d on 35p (DB)	on #1485a	—	—
YUG26	1767b	(1985-86)	4d on 5.60d (B)	on #1490	—	—
YUG27	1767Ac	(1985-86)	5d on 8d (B)	on #1491a	—	—
YUG28	1768a	(1985-86)	8d on 6d	on #1713	—	—
YUG29	1769a	(1985-86)	20d on 26d	on #1717	—	—
YUG30	1770a	(1985-86)	50d on 16/50d (B)	on #1603c	—	—
YUG31	B16a	(1926)	30d + 1d orange	dbl surch (vc)	—	—
YUG32	J9a	(1921-22)	10d violet brown	cliche of 10p in sheet of 10d (u)	75.00	100.00
YUG33	J22a	(1928)	10d on 50d green	invtd surch (vc)	30.00	18.00
YUG34	NC10a	(1941)	50d sl bl & gray bl	invtd ovpt (vc)	200.00	NA

Trieste has produced no errors

Z

ZAIRE has produced no errors

ZAMBEZI

ZAM1	56a	(1911)	10r light green	invtd ovpt (vc)	12.50	12.50
ZAM2	93a	(1915)	50r blue	"Republica" invtd (vc)	—	—

ZAMBIA has produced no errors

ZANZIBAR

ZAN1	13a	(1895-96)	1r car rose & grn	vertical ovpt	NA	—
ZAN2	14a	(1895-96)	2r brn & rose	"Zanziba"	NA	NA
ZAN3	14b			invtd "r"	NA	NA
ZAN4	14c			pair, one without ovpt	—	—
ZAN5	17e	(1873-76)	6a bister	dbl ovpt (vc)	—	—
ZAN6	97a	(1904)	2-1/2a on 8a	"Hlaf"	—	NA
ZAN7	98a	(1904)	2-1/2a on 8a	"Hlaf"	—	NA
ZAN8	304a	(1964)	2.50sh multi	green omitted (u)	60.00	—

ZIMBABWE has produced no errors

ZULULAND

ZUL1	12a	(1888-94)	1/2p green, no period	period after "Zululand"	60.00	60.00
ZUL2	12b			as "a," dbl ovpt	NA	NA
ZUL3	12c			as "a," invtd ovpt	NA	—
ZUL4	12d			as "a," pair, one without ovpt	NA	NA
ZUL5	12e			as no. 12, dbl ovpt	NA	NA

CHAPTER VIII: EPILOGUE

The Theory of Foreign Errors

When it comes to foreign errors, the name of the game is overprints. We have inundated this book with (vc) very common errors, and pointed out triple and quadruple overprints, which are very rare. We have seen the founder of the postage stamp (Rowland Hill) duly imprinted (inverted) on Liberian stamps and upside-down airplanes on stamps from Ecuador, Czechoslovakia and Syria.

But why? Why are non-overprints less susceptible to error? The reason is these stamps are produced by one or more primary or basic printing processes—they are engraved, lithographed, set with photogravure, etc. (We exclude crude handstamped or typed.) These types of processes usually involve careful craftsmanship.

But then add an overprint. Often done hastily, these usually contain a larger percentage of errors than the parent adhesive.

But why the haste? Often overprints are produced during unstable periods of time, such as war, revolution, or economic upheaval. The overprinted Belgian stamps shown in this volume are an example of a currency reform problem. This may be true whether the stamp is "affordable" or not. We have used the term "affordable" to conceptualize a multifaceted relationship between seller and buyer, having provided the most realistic price we know for almost all affordable errors in this volume. In doing so, we avoided the Herculean task of developing any mathematical, logical or other model of any foreign error pricing. Will Diana's premature death enhance the value of the Montserrat error? Will Elvis Presley's extreme popularity as a topical subject affect the price of his twenty-one Central African errors? We just do not know.

There are a number of foreign errors types that don't involve overprints, and the U.S. overprint is virtually non-existent. Color omission is commonplace among U.S. errors and in Datz's classic, eight topics in his table of contents are devoted to this subject.[1] At the other extreme, some countries have no problems with color omission while others are in the middle. An interesting phenomenon that we are unable to explain is that British Commonwealth nations generally have more omissions, other than Great Britain, than other nations. As of 1998, Great Britain had approximately 68 color omissions. Australia and Malta were also among the high commonwealth color omission nations.

In Chapter 1 we pointed out that certain stamps are manufactured (or suspiciously so) for collectors. Although we have no more than suspicion, it does seem that many stamps of Guinea, Haiti, and Liberia are suspect. Certain popular stamps seem notoriously suspect, for one—the ever-popular inverted center. Liberia also turned out such anomalies as inverted flags. With approximately 43 in existence in 1998, this country can probably be considered the "King" of inverted centers. The United States has not produced a significant number of these.[2] Collectors should also be aware of the remarkable difference between stamps that are imperforate-oriented and non-such-oriented countries.[3]

The timing of an error is also a factor that must be taken into consideration. In literally dozens of countries no errors will be found after 1965 or 1970. Why?

Probably because printing technology had improved by that time. On the other hand, some of Abjan's stamps have been strangely designed, which is made possible only because of modern printing technology.

Finally, we have the "cliche" error. A cliche of Mozambique in a Cape Verde plate exists, for example, in the pair with #13. (See the illustration in the text under Cape Verde). Two final points concerning cliches are the following. First, cliches are affordable—the example given above would cost about $50 either used or unused. Second, in our search for errors to photograph for this volume, we could find only two cliches—they are quite uncommon.

NOTES:

1. Stephen Datz, 1998 Catalogue of Errors on U.S. Postage Stamps (Iola, WI: Krause Publications) 1997, p.(unnumbered).
2. Datz, pp. 148-150
3. See Chapter 1 of this volume.